On the Swamp

RYAN E. EMANUEL

On the Swamp
Fighting for Indigenous Environmental Justice

The University of North Carolina Press *Chapel Hill*

© 2024 The University of North Carolina Press
All rights reserved
Set in Arno Pro by Westchester Publishing Services
Manufactured in the United States of America

Library of Congress Cataloging-in-Publication Data

Names: Emanuel, Ryan E., author.
Title: On the swamp : fighting for Indigenous environmental justice / Ryan Emanuel.
Description: Chapel Hill : The University of North Carolina Press, 2024. |
    Includes bibliographical references and index.
Identifiers: LCCN 2023047030 | ISBN 9781469678313 (cloth ; alk. paper) |
    ISBN 9781469678320 (pbk. ; alk. paper) | ISBN 9781469678337 (epub) |
    ISBN 9798890887160 (pdf)
Subjects: LCSH: Traditional ecological knowledge—North Carolina. | Environmental
    policy—Social aspects—North Carolina. | Lumbee Indians—Land tenure—North
    Carolina—Robeson County. | Tuscarora Indians—Land tenure—North Carolina. |
    Swamp ecology—Political aspects—North Carolina. | Indians of North America—
    Political activity—North Carolina. | Indians of North America—Civil rights—
    North Carolina. | BISAC: SOCIAL SCIENCE / Ethnic Studies / American / Native American
    Studies | POLITICAL SCIENCE / Public Policy / Environmental Policy
Classification: LCC GE185.N8 E63 2024 | DDC 333.7089/970756—dc23/eng/20231103
    LC record available at https://lccn.loc.gov/2023047030

Cover photo and river outline by author.

For my grandmother, Martha Dimery Odom

There is more than one way to own a thing. Some of the most precious things we all own were not bought and paid for with money.

—Ruth Revels

Contents

Graph, Illustrations, Maps, and Table

Preface

Indigenous peoples have lived on the Coastal Plain of what is now North Carolina for millennia. This is especially true of the place now called Robeson County—one thousand square miles of swamps and sandy fields tucked into the southwestern corner of North Carolina's portion of the Coastal Plain. Today, Robeson County is the epicenter of history and culture for the Lumbee, the Indigenous people to whom I belong. If a Lumbee worldview exists, it radiates from Robeson.

Robeson County's deep archaeological record includes a fourteen-thousand-year-old Clovis projectile point, displayed in the Museum of the Southeastern American Indian at the University of North Carolina at Pembroke. The museum also exhibits a one-thousand-year-old dugout canoe, extracted from the sandy bed of the Lumbee River. Together, the two items remind visitors that Indigenous people have not only walked but also paddled this place for millennia.[1]

Written records left behind by settlers and colonial officials capture only a tiny fraction of human history in the Coastal Plain. Indigenous oral traditions extend somewhat farther back, but the time span of human habitation on the Coastal Plain is still mind-bogglingly difficult to imagine. Here is a thought experiment to help.[2]

Imagine a time span that begins six thousand years ago and extends until the present.[3] Six thousand years ago, pottery and farming—technologies that marked the Early Woodland period—had not yet spread across the Coastal Plain, but people had lived here for thousands of years by that point. Now imagine those six thousand years compressed into a twelve-month calendar year.

For the first eleven months of the imaginary year—from New Year's Day until sometime in early December—the Coastal Plain belonged entirely to Indigenous peoples. Diverse languages and cultures flourished and evolved. Groups of people traded with one another, built and broke kinship ties, waged war, and made peace. People introduced information and technology from faraway places. Towns and villages sprang up near rivers and on the shores of freshwater lakes and brackish estuaries. People refined fishing, foraging, and hunting practices, and they used fire to create and maintain large park-like

landscapes full of wildlife, food, and medicine. Through hundreds of generations, Indigenous peoples passed along an ever-evolving body of knowledge
about themselves and the world they occupied.

In contrast, settlers are extreme latecomers to the Coastal Plain. European
sailors appeared offshore around December 10 of the imaginary year. On
December 11, Elizabethans attempted to colonize Roanoke, a low-lying patch
of salt marsh and scrubby forest surrounded by a shallow estuary. Their failed
attempts occurred between 6:00 a.m. and 6:10 a.m. On the morning of
December 15, Europeans built a permanent town in the Coastal Plain of what
is now North Carolina. At 12:45 that afternoon, colonial militias killed and
enslaved nearly one thousand Indigenous people during a war of conquest in
eastern North Carolina. A few days later, the American Revolution lasted
most of December 20. As I write this, it is just before midnight on New Year's
Eve. The United States has existed for eleven days.

Settler history takes up only a tiny fraction of this imaginary year. The rest
of the calendar belongs entirely to Indigenous peoples—an expanse of time
that tribal nations sometimes call *time immemorial*. It is unfathomably longer
than the histories that settlers write for themselves. For Indigenous peoples,
time immemorial is forever.

Students in North Carolina learn mostly about the brief sliver of time
after the arrival of European settlers. Some of those students grow up to become policymakers, corporate leaders, and other influential figures who
know virtually nothing about North Carolina's history beyond this brief
glimpse of the past. Their myopia leaves them blind to the knowledge systems and values that accumulated in Indigenous communities over centuries
and millennia—and that still exist today in tribal communities throughout
the state.

Hopefully this thought experiment reveals the extremely limited perspective of people who believe that history begins in December of my imaginary
year. The situation is frustrating for Indigenous peoples, because those who
have the least experience caring for our home have the loudest voices and
make nearly all of the important decisions. The situation also poses an existential threat to Indigenous peoples because it promotes mythologies that erase
us from the place we come from. One example of this erasure appears in a description of North Carolina's founding embedded in the 1857 commencement
speech at Wake Forest College. The speech was delivered by the school's co-
principal, C. S. Ellis, and it paints a romantic but utterly false image of the state
rising from untouched wilderness: "Founded on virgin soil, with no crum-
bling towers and moss-covered ruins, no remnants of another civilization to

cause old, worn out theories and prejudices to check her progress, with the most correct notions of liberty and human rights, she has sprung into an existence alike wonderful and great."[4]

The erasure of Indigenous peoples persists to this day. Native people are generally absent from policy discussions on a wide range of topics, including energy, food, and the environment. We do not have seats at the proverbial tables where decisions are made about the future of land and water on the Coastal Plain—our ancestral home. Decision-makers do not consult us before they issue permits for harmful and polluting infrastructure, or when they implement policies that transform our homelands in myriad other ways.

When Indigenous peoples assert ourselves, we are talked over, ignored, or subjected to healthy doses of 'splaining by people who grew up believing that Indigenous people never lived here, or if they once lived here, they either left or assimilated long ago.[5] And even when people realize that we are still here, they deem our knowledge systems and values irrelevant or unscientific. If we oppose ongoing colonial exploitation of our homelands, they say it is because we are backward people who do not understand regulatory frameworks or economic markets—not because we have lived here long enough to foresee the harm that comes from prioritizing short-term profit over long-term care of people and place.

Our erasure is aided by the trauma we have experienced during the metaphorical month of December. Settlers brought disease, war, and an insatiable desire to exploit land and water for profit. They seized our territories and fractured our societies, triggering events that drove many of our languages into extinction and permanently reshaped our cultures.

In the chaos of colonialism, Indigenous peoples not only lost lands and languages, but we also lost some of the knowledge acquired by our ancestors and passed down from time immemorial. We do not know the full extent of what was lost, but we celebrate—and build on—the fraction that survives today. Ancestral knowledge lives on in our values around kinship and place-based communities. It lives on in our desire to protect our homelands for generations yet to come.

Lumbee homelands are mosaics of forested swamps and sandy fields that all drain toward the Lumbee River—a rich, tea-colored stream that meanders among cypress trunks and sand banks. Our Indigenous neighbors on the Coastal Plain call similar landscapes *home*. No matter how we define our homelands, Indigenous peoples recognize that survival as distinct people depends on maintaining our connections to the places we call *home*.

Unfortunately, many of these places are already threatened by pollution, unsustainable development, and climate change. And so tribal nations are left to save what we can, while we can. We take on this work even as we are talked over, ignored, and erased by settlers—latecomers with disproportionate power and influence. The situation is not fair, but it was not designed to be. This work aims to even the field.

A Note on Terminology

Throughout this book, I use the specific names of Indigenous groups wherever possible. Some names used by present-day tribal nations in North Carolina are geographic names (often the names of rivers) and may not have been the names that our ancestors used to refer to themselves before colonization. To avoid confusion in these cases, I use terms such as *Lumbee ancestors* to denote ancestors of present-day tribal peoples. I promise to be as clear as I can.

For stylistic reasons, I use multiple terms to refer to the original peoples of the place now known as North Carolina. These terms include *Indigenous (people/s)*, *Native (people/s)*, *Native Americans*, and *American Indians*. For what it's worth, there is no consensus, scholarly or otherwise, that any particular term is preferred by Indigenous peoples in North Carolina, within any particular region of the United States, or within the United States as a whole. There is not even consensus on whether or not a consensus exists. Some folks will insist otherwise. However, if you are a non-Indigenous reader seeking guidance on appropriate terminology, my advice is to always read the room and defer to any Indigenous people present. And if you are in a room where discussions about Indigenous peoples are happening, but no Indigenous people are present, ask yourself: Why is that?

Lastly, some of the historical documents quoted in this book use outdated and possibly offensive terms for Native peoples. If seeing these terms on the page or hearing them read aloud makes you uncomfortable, then you're headed in the right direction.

On the Swamp

Introduction
On the Swamp, February 2017

February is winter's last breath in Robeson County—a crazy quilt of crop fields, forests, and swamps on the southwestern edge of North Carolina's Coastal Plain. A few miles west of Robeson County lies the Fall Line, a natural boundary that divides the gently sloping Coastal Plain from the rolling Piedmont farther west. The Fall Line is a subtle landform and hard to point out on the ground, but once you cross it, you know. Red clay soils and stony riverbeds vanish. Replacing them are flat, sandy uplands dissected by dark streams of smooth-flowing water.

Some two hundred miles west of the Fall Line, beyond the western edge of the Piedmont, ancient mountains rise to green cloud-strafed summits. East of the Fall Line—not quite two hours by car—the Atlantic Ocean breaks on barrier island beaches, narrow ribbons of sand linked by sharp elbows that jut toward the warm and salty Gulf Stream.

Back in Robeson County, a short distance east of the Fall Line, I am parked by the side of NC Highway 710. The two-lane road cuts through farmland and links rural communities scattered across a county that is about two-thirds as large as the state of Rhode Island. I am Lumbee, and Robeson County is the heart of our homeland. Lumbee people are Indigenous to the Southeast; we are first peoples of the Fall Line. Our ancestors lived, for millennia, on both the Piedmont and Coastal Plain sides. Centuries ago, they sought refuge from colonial violence and oppression here, below the Fall Line, amid vast forested wetlands and slow-moving streams. My parents raised me in Charlotte, two hours away from Robeson County, but like many Lumbees reared outside our homeland, I learned that no matter where I live, Robeson is home.

Today I am home, in Robeson County, standing next to my car on a hard-packed dirt driveway that runs three hundred yards from the highway to a distant house. The driveway bisects a fallow field. Long, straight rows of stubble run parallel to the dirt track and exaggerate the flatness of the landscape. Despite the cold, a few green shoots already poke through the gray and tan soil.

At the far end of the driveway, white siding on the house gleams in the afternoon light. Beyond, Bear Swamp bristles with naked sweet gum and bald cypress trunks. An occasional pine tree adds a shock of green to an otherwise colorless canopy. Clumps of mistletoe hang, shadowy, from several limbs. Below the trees and far out of my sight, water pools and trickles through Bear Swamp on its way to the Lumbee River, some ten miles downstream.[1]

Back on the driveway, I can see my breath. Cold wind bites my exposed hands and face. The wind carries a hint of wood smoke, a reminder that even now, people live close to the land. In rural Robeson County, people still cut firewood, harvest greens, preserve food, and continue the seasonal rhythms of life practiced by their parents, grandparents, and on and on since time immemorial.

The house, the driveway, the field, and the swamp are part of Prospect, a community in Robeson County made up almost entirely of Indigenous people. Most of them, like me, are Lumbee. The name *Lumbee* is a cultural and political designation for the knit-together remnants of Native American peoples who retreated into vast networks of swamps and interstitial uplands to survive early and violent waves of European colonization.[2] Some of the earliest colonizers were Elizabethans, who in the sixteenth century paraded across barrier islands, ruffled collars and all. They reconnoitered the estuaries and coastal rivers, searching for treasure and strategic outposts in North America. They returned to England with vital intelligence about the land and its people, and they left behind virulent infections that brought unprecedented sickness and death to our ancestors' world.

Those who survived faced new European incursions in the seventeenth and eighteenth centuries. Disease, warfare, and the ceaseless flow of settlers upended Indigenous societies on both sides of the Fall Line. A colonial slave trade emerged, and it fueled a horrific epidemic of kidnappings and disappearances. In 1711, the entire Coastal Plain of what is now North Carolina erupted into war between a desperate alliance of Native peoples and colonial forces sent to eradicate them. The Coastal Plain burned. The conflict reached a grisly zenith in 1713 near the banks of Contentnea Creek, where hundreds of Tuscarora people and their Indigenous allies were brutally slaughtered on the orders of a South Carolina militia leader. Hundreds more were carried off into slavery—some to plantations in the Caribbean—never to see their homelands again.

Against steep odds, Native people survived the conflagration. Some fled hundreds of miles north to seek refuge with distant kin, and others accepted confinement on reservations—tiny fragments of land within their former territories. Still others retreated into the remotest parts of their homelands. East of the Fall Line, people retreated to tracts of sandy ground surrounded by ancient bald cypress swamps and gnarled, scrubby peatlands. They were places that settlers either knew nothing about or believed to be impenetrable, festering, worthless wastelands. Roads were few and far between. To outsiders, the waterways were unnavigable mazes of dark currents that meandered tortuously and doubled back on themselves. Channels were clogged with fallen trees or simply diffused into endless swamps. In places like these, survivors of a ravaged Fall Line rebuilt their lives as best they could.

One such enclave emerged along twenty or so miles of the Lumbee River, several miles beyond the upstream limit of settlers' boats and rafts. Colonial maps and surveys betray settlers' unfamiliarity with this section of the river and its many backwaters; these documents give confusing and conflicting accounts of a river that settlers called *Drowning Creek*. Drowning Creek remained poorly represented on their maps even as other river networks gained impressive accuracy and precision. Until the early 1800s, many of these maps simply hinted at endless swampland above the limit of colonial navigation on the river. Some maps showed nothing at all. A few maps include what appear to be the Lumbee River's headwaters, but they flow into the wrong basin—a sign that surveyors probably never traveled the entire river from mouth to headwaters. Even though the enclave was surrounded by white settlers, it was apparently not a place they visited often, or at all.[3] Similarly, settlers knew very little about the Indigenous peoples who occupied these colonial backwaters. James Merrell, a historian of contact-era tribal nations in the Southeast, described the Native peoples of this region as "among the most poorly documented peoples in American history."[4]

Yet along this stretch of the Lumbee River, Native people held fast on sandy plains nestled amid the river's long fingers of swampy tributaries. They fished and hunted along the river and its swamps, and they raised crops and livestock on the uplands. Here, they forged kinship networks and alliances that grew into a constellation of interrelated communities. One of the oldest communities, Long Swamp, would eventually become Prospect.[5]

Today, about one thousand people live in the core of Prospect—an area of about three square miles (map 1.1). It is one of the largest non-reservation communities of Native Americans in the eastern United States. Prospect is not an incorporated town, but it has a distinct identity as a community. Road signs on thoroughfares leading into Prospect welcome visitors to "the cradle of Indian prosperity."

Robeson County holds a dozen or so Native American communities that are not quite as large as Prospect, but they still have unique identities, often anchored around a historic church or school (or both). The county also has

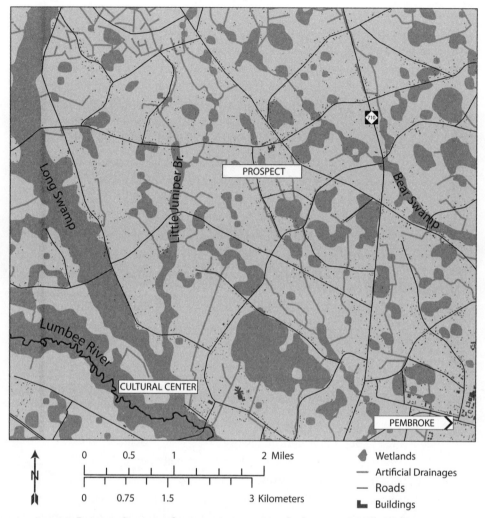

MAP I.1 Prospect. Signposts show prominent present-day locations. Map by author.

several towns with sizable Native American populations. Overall, a plurality of the county's residents—more than fifty thousand people—are Native Americans. Most are Lumbee, but one thousand or so people reject Lumbee political identity altogether and instead identify as Tuscarora. Specifically, these individuals identify as the descendants of Tuscarora people who survived the 1713 massacre and subsequent confinement to reservations in northeastern North Carolina, some two hundred miles away from the Lumbee River. They separated from the main body of Tuscarora people, who migrated from North Carolina to New York during the eighteenth century, joined the

Haudenosaunee confederacy, and were later recognized as tribal nations in both the United States and Canada. Presently, Tuscarora political bodies in the United States and Canada do not hold formal ties with Robeson County Tuscaroras or claim them as part of their nation.[6]

Robeson County Tuscaroras are blood relatives to Lumbees, and they live side by side with Lumbees throughout the county. The distinction between Lumbee and Tuscarora is nuanced, and there are cultural and political situations in which the difference matters deeply to people. But for the most part, the distinctions do not factor into daily life in Prospect.

Whether they identify as Lumbee or Tuscarora, Native Americans in Prospect value land in ways that are not reflected in Robeson County's real estate market, the worst-performing in the state according to recent data from a national realty group.[7] What real estate data do not reveal is that people in Prospect consider land to be tied, inextricably, to history and culture. In the twentieth century, many Lumbee families first gained legal title to land they had farmed for generations, and they have held it close ever since. Properties are passed down from generation to generation. Siblings build homes on family land within earshot of their parents, and they leave room for future generations to do the same. Neatly arrayed gardens, blueberry bushes, and grapevines surround houses. Clusters of outbuildings—sheds, garages, and barns—delineate the edges of a family's property. To many Lumbee families, these multigenerational settlements are simply called the *homeplace*.

Dozens of homeplaces radiate from the center of Prospect—usually described as the area surrounding Prospect Elementary School and Prospect United Methodist Church. According to the United Methodists, the church boasts the largest Native American congregation in the United States. Behind sprawling church facilities, rows of gravestones—hundreds in all—mark the boundaries of a large cemetery. A ditch bank separates the cemetery from crop fields beyond. Other small burial plots are scattered throughout Prospect. Eastern red cedar, fragrant and sacred, grows between graves and around the edges of cemeteries. The trees grow slowly, but after a century, some are large enough to shade nearby graves with scraggly green boughs.

Before the widespread adoption of Christianity, our ancestors interred the remains of their loved ones in earthen mounds. Out on the Coastal Plain, burial mounds were only one or two feet high. The mounds were filled with tight bundles, each containing a person's bones and other sacred objects. The largest held the remains of hundreds of people. But no more. Most burial mounds on the Coastal Plain were looted, mined for fill dirt, or simply plowed level more than a century ago. A few were excavated by anthropologists who documented their work with clinical precision and then discarded the human remains. The desecration was complete and irreversible.[8]

Today, Prospect is indistinguishable, in some ways, from hundreds of other small farming communities in the region. In a few months, rows of corn, soy, cotton, and other crops will blanket now-barren fields, just as they will across the Coastal Plain. Livestock will graze in pastures along NC 710 as they will along roads throughout eastern North Carolina. Kitchen gardens will sprout greens and other fresh produce. And while I enjoy collards, field peas, and sweet corn as much as the next Lumbee, I am also a water scientist, and I notice what lies in between the fields and pastures and homeplaces of Prospect—water.

Prospect, like the rest of Robeson County, is a watery world. An intricate web of waterways—a hybrid network of natural streams and artificial channels—extends through much of the county. Ditches delineate crop fields and separate homeplaces from one another. The ditches feed into larger canals—some as deep as ten feet—that carry water toward any number of swamps, or directly to the Lumbee River itself. The waterways are stitches in the crazy quilt that dissect Prospect into a maze of land and water. And everywhere, water flows slowly toward the Lumbee River.

On the east side of Prospect, the land drains into Bear Swamp, a dark rivulet beneath a ribbon of dense forest. Bear Swamp snakes through Robeson County for twelve miles before joining the Lumbee River just upstream of Lumberton, the county seat. The west side of Prospect drains toward Long Swamp, the community's old namesake. Decades ago, the confluence of Long Swamp and the Lumbee River was a watery thicket of shrubs and trees. In 1961, the lower reaches of Long Swamp were dammed and flooded to form a small recreational lake. Long Swamp now empties into the lake and spills into the Lumbee River near a place called *Red Banks*. In the 1930s, Red Banks was the site of a New Deal resettlement project for Lumbee people. Today, the lake and the property that surrounds it make up a cultural center operated by the Lumbee Tribal government.

A third and much smaller stream, Little Juniper Branch, drains the center of Prospect. Like Long Swamp, Little Juniper Branch also empties into the cultural center's lake. Perhaps it is fitting that the lake, which has been a source of beauty and refreshment to Lumbee people for many decades, is filled almost entirely with water that drained through the soils of Prospect.

Long Swamp, Bear Swamp, and Little Juniper Branch are a few of the waterways that shape the contours of Robeson County. Most of the county's waterways flow from northwest to southeast. The effect is so pronounced that satellite images show the swamps as long and nearly parallel fingers of green that give the entire landscape a woodgrain-like appearance. The waterways track the gradient—the line of steepest descent—of the Coastal Plain as it dips gently from the Fall Line toward the Atlantic Ocean. Within each swamp flows one or more channels in which water pools, trickles, and occasionally rushes toward the Lumbee River.

Visitors to Robeson County are often surprised by the dark color of water that flows through the swamps and in the main stem of the Lumbee River. The water appears opaque and nearly black from a distance, but up close, it is the color of richly steeped tea. The dark color is not a sign of pollution; it is the natural color of streams in this part of the world. It derives from organic compounds that leach from the surrounding soils, which are ladened with decaying plant matter. As water seeps through these soils en route to the river, it steeps in organic matter and takes on the characteristic hue. Scientists classify the Lumbee River as a "blackwater" stream, and Lumbee people often call themselves *People of the Dark Water*.

Swamps funnel dark water downstream, each adding to the Lumbee River's cumulative flow. Most of these streams are lined by bald cypress, sweet gum, tupelo, and other flood-tolerant trees. A few are flanked by open marshes, thick with river cane. Together, the swamps and the river make up a vascular system—a network that gathers and transports water, sediment, and waste downstream. Moving from upstream to downstream, the river and its floodplain grow larger to accommodate flow from each successive tributary. Beneath it all, groundwater seeps, capillary-like, from one pore to another, through soils and sediments, until it emerges into the channel and joins the downstream flow.

Swamps and other wetlands cover about one quarter of Robeson County's one thousand square miles. They are so prevalent that it is hard to find anywhere in the county that is more than a few hundred yards away from water. Even where canals and ditches have drained wetlands to make room for crop fields and neighborhoods, water is not far off. Lumbee communities everywhere in Robeson County share names with adjacent swamps and are reminders of water's ubiquity: Burnt Swamp, Back Swamp, Deep Branch, and Saddletree Swamp, to name a few.

Our communities are not actually situated inside swamps; they sit adjacent to them. For Lumbee ancestors, swamps were places to fish, forage, and hunt. They held medicinal plants, timber, and other raw materials. Occasionally they were hideouts or escape routes. But generally, the high ground was for living. Footpaths led into the swamps from farms, churches, and schools and down through the swamps to the riverbank. Few of these paths still exist; bridges and boat ramps are more typical ways to reach the river nowadays.

Centuries ago, the main stem of the Lumbee River was the only transportation artery through the region. Dugout canoes and other small watercraft were the only boats capable of navigating the tortuous channel. Today, people navigate the river in small motorboats, canoes, and kayaks. Others swim or fish from the banks. The river's reputation as an outdoor recreation destination grew after the National Park Service declared it a National Wild and Scenic River in the 1990s. It is the only blackwater stream in North Carolina with that designation.

The Lumbee River is not always kind to people. Hurricanes and tropical storms can overload the region with rain. The most severe storms can bring a foot or more of rainfall in a single day. Tributaries swell with runoff and disgorge into the river. The river expands in response, reclaiming the land. Subsiding floods reveal scarred and resculpted landscapes—a reminder that water allows land to exist in Robeson County.

Here, the boundaries between land and water are fickle and subject to change. For Lumbees, floods mark the duality of water; it is a creator and sustainer of life, but it also immerses, divides, and kills. I have come to understand water from the standpoint of a hydrologist—preoccupied with the measure of water as a substance—and from the standpoint of a Lumbee—respectful of water as place. I do not think that I have any special insight on the balance between these perspectives, but I do see both of them, at once, and all the time.

Water flows, at measurable rates, through our communities. Rivers accumulate and integrate physical, chemical, and biological processes happening all around. But rivers also accumulate and integrate the stories that define us as people. This is especially true for Indigenous peoples, who have established close cultural ties to specific waterways over the course of centuries or millennia. In the case of Lumbee people, the remoteness and inaccessibility of our river and its adjacent swamps allowed our ancestors to survive and grow into the tribal nation that exists today. We are not so different from many other eastern Indigenous peoples who retreated and coalesced with others to survive the traumas of first contact and to emerge as the tribal nations that exist today.[9]

For Lumbee people, the river is a central character in the story of our survival. Our story is indelibly marked by settler colonialism—a type of colonialism that not only extracts wealth from a place but also seeks to replace Indigenous people with settlers. Despite the settler colonial project in North

Carolina, Lumbee people have managed to preserve and strengthen their relationships to place. Our ancestors passed on an affinity and respect for the Lumbee River and for other watery places in Robeson County. Whether it is a slow trickle of water through Bear Swamp or a violent post-hurricane flood, water defines the Lumbee world. If Lumbee people survive into the future as a distinct people, I am convinced that our river and the surrounding landscapes that drain into it must remain at the center.

BACK ON THE SIDE of NC 710, the crazy quilt that is Prospect spreads in all directions. The treetops above Bear Swamp block out an arc of the horizon. The wood smoke smell still lingers. Prospect feels almost insulated from the outside world. Almost. In my peripheral vision, sunlight glints from coiled razor wire atop a chain-link fence. A second coil snakes around the fence's base. The barbed loops flash in the cold light. The bristling wire encircles a gravel-lined yard studded with pipe elbows, valves, and metal enclosures.

I turn to face the fenced-in compound; it is a compressor station that pressurizes the network of transmission pipelines that runs through eastern North Carolina. Those pipelines converge here, in Prospect. The pipelines and the compressor station are operated by a subsidiary of Duke Energy, the state's largest energy company. The pipeline network supplies electric power plants, cities, and factories throughout the eastern part of the state.

Large transmission pipelines radiate east, west, and north from the compound. The pipes themselves are buried a few feet belowground, but their trajectories are clearly visible from the surface in the form of easements that shoot, arrow-like, through nearby fields and forests. The easements slice across the natural grain of the wetland-strewn landscape. I can see the clearcut gash left by the nearest easement where it carves through Bear Swamp. In satellite images, they are unnaturally straight lines, discolored by perpetually flooded soils or stunted crops. Easements limit the rights of property owners on their own land, and they give companies perpetual access to the strips of land to the pipe buried beneath. In Prospect, easements whittle away at homeplaces and remind people that their land has been sacrificed for the convenience and profit of far-away corporations and their shareholders.

The transmission pipelines operate at high pressures—hundreds of pounds of gas per square inch. Inside the compound, two gas-fired compressors— massive engines—run ceaselessly to keep the lines pressurized and to keep the gas flowing through hundreds of miles of pipe. The compressors have been here for decades. Their giant engines are protected from the elements by a garage-sized metal building encircled by a garden of pipes, valves, sensors, and manifolds. Two large and rusty exhaust stacks jut from one end of the building. Each stack emits an invisible plume of exhaust into the cold afternoon air. Besides carbon dioxide, the exhaust is laden with carbon monoxide, nitrogen oxides, sulfur dioxide, and particulate matter.[10] I cannot see the plumes of exhaust or the engines themselves, but the shed emits an incessant hum, a sure sign that the compressors are running. Immediately beyond the exhaust stacks is a copse of dead cedar trees. Frail gray branches rattle in the February wind, or perhaps they quiver from an invisible plume of gas.

With few exceptions, people in Prospect do not have access to natural gas. Most of the gas that flows underfoot travels to one of Duke Energy's gas-fired power plants. The company began to move away from coal a few years ago, and rightly so, given the litany of problems that come with mining and burning coal. But instead of pivoting from fossil fuels altogether, the company began to substitute natural gas for coal in its portfolio of electricity generation. The fleet of gas-fired power plants is single-handedly responsible for the drastic increase in natural gas consumption in North Carolina during the past several years.[11] The infrastructure in Prospect seems to have grown along with the company's appetite.

Across NC 710, a newly constructed compound signals the latest expansion (figure 1.1). The compound straddles an easement that leads off to the northwest, back toward the Fall Line. The new construction is why I visited Prospect today. I am here with two friends, one of whom grew up on this land. The compressor station was carved out of her family's homeplace. The two of them want my opinion on the expanding industrial compounds and what they could mean for people in Prospect. I speculate that the construction may somehow be connected to one of the new pipeline projects supposedly headed this way, but it is hard to say for sure. I say that I will look into it.

I will look into it, but I already know where to start. I teach about state and federal permitting requirements for activities that damage and destroy streams and wetlands. Oil and gas pipelines transform the water bodies that they cross, and developers cannot build them without prior authorization, usually from the US Army Corps of Engineers. The Corps uses a streamlined (some say fast-tracked) authorization for oil and gas pipelines called *Nationwide Permit 12*. I am certain that any new pipelines in Prospect will need this permit to cross Bear Swamp or other wetlands nearby. I will look for a permit application online. If it exists, it should contain information about the size and purpose of any new gas pipelines headed this way.

Nationwide Permit 12 is also at the heart of a legal battle by the Standing Rock and Cheyenne River Sioux Tribes against the US Army Corps of

FIGURE I.1 Natural gas compound in Prospect, 2017. Photo by author.

Engineers over the Dakota Access Pipeline. Last summer, controversy over the project spurred a historic gathering of Indigenous people—Water Protectors—on the prairie near the pipeline's Missouri River crossing. The Water Protectors' encampments and their peaceful demonstrations grew larger throughout the summer and fall of 2016. I remember a few months back when Lumbee tribal leaders sent emissaries and a resolution of support to Standing Rock.[12]

The Water Protector movement brought international attention to injustices stemming from the Dakota Access Pipeline and from similar projects on Native lands. The movement also revealed the connection between fossil fuel development and violence against Indigenous peoples; for months, private security guards and law enforcement officers have brutalized Water Protectors in an effort to uphold the company's contested rights. Just a few days before my trip to Prospect, militarized law enforcement officers cleared out one of the last encampments of Water Protectors. My mind drifts back to a jittery video of the eviction, live streamed onto Facebook from a snow-covered rise above the river.

While I am lost in thought, my friends have already walked across NC 710 for a closer look at the new compound. Like the older compressor station, it is delineated by a chain-link fence lined with razor wire. But the new compound is much larger, and it is surrounded by high-wattage flood lights and surveillance cameras. No company people are inside; everything appears to be remote-controlled.

The bristling metal reminds me of a colonial fort, a barricade to protect settlers on their way through Indian Country. I imagine the company does not see it this way. The security deterrents around the complex suggest that Prospect may occupy a strategically important node in the company's massive infrastructure network, but nothing more. I suspect that corporate leaders and decision-makers are blind to the settler colonial optics of their outpost.

Back on my side of NC 710, the rusty exhaust stacks, glinting razor wire, and arrow-straight easements remind me that Lumbees—like other first contact peoples—have endured centuries of settler colonialism. Violence, oppression, and extraction have left indelible marks on our people and homelands, but we are still here. We thrive by some metrics. The Lumbee Tribe is the largest of any tribe in the eastern United States. Lumbees are well-represented in a number of professions. But our homelands are unwell, and the earthen scars that radiate from these compounds only tell part of the story.

Fossil fuel development, deforestation, wetland drainage, factory farming, and other unsustainable practices are transforming Robeson County and other places throughout the Coastal Plain. The stench of industrial livestock waste hangs in the air. Rivers flow with nutrients and pathogens. Pipeline easements carve up the landscape. Climate change hangs over it all, threatening the Coastal Plain with intense floods, droughts, and heat waves. The transformation feels sacrificial and permanent. It alters the way that people relate to the world around them.

For Lumbee people and our Indigenous neighbors, the stakes couldn't be higher. Our collective identities are intimately tied to the Coastal Plain, and our collective fates are bound to its future. Lumbees, after all, are People of the Dark Water. To damage or destroy the dark waters and surrounding landscapes of Robeson County is to erase a critical part of our identity as Indigenous people.

At the same time that we face erasure through the transformation of our homelands, Indigenous peoples are also left out of important decisions about the Coastal Plain. Food, energy, and environmental policies have evolved without the participation of tribal nations. Corporations propose harmful and polluting projects, and regulators routinely authorize them, without first consulting Native people.

The situation seems especially dire in Robeson County, which seems to be full of infrastructure that would never find a home elsewhere.[13] Still,

Robeson County is home. I take another look at the treetops above Bear Swamp before dashing across NC 710 to catch up with my friends. It is only a short sprint over the blacktop, but I still breathe hard on the other side. Cold air fills my lungs, and it is still tinged with wood smoke from an unseen homeplace.

I SET OUT TO WRITE a book that examined how Indigenous peoples preserve, steward, and express sovereignty over their homelands at a time when those places are threatened with degradation and destruction. When I began this project, Water Protectors were still assembled near Standing Rock. Throughout 2016, images and reports from North Dakota prompted me to think more critically about the policies and governance structures that affect the ability of Indigenous peoples to participate in decisions that shape the future of their homelands.

The Dakota Access Pipeline narrative contrasted sharply with Executive Order 12898, the backbone of current environmental justice policy in the United States. The executive order calls for the fair treatment and meaningful involvement of all people in environmental decisions and policies, and it charges federal agencies with "identifying and addressing, as appropriate, disproportionately high and adverse human health or environmental effects of its programs, policies, and activities on minority populations and low-income populations in the United States."[14]

President Clinton issued Executive Order 12898 in 1994, after more than a decade of grassroots leadership and advocacy that sought to end the buildup of toxic landfills, power plants, and other harmful and polluting facilities in low-wealth and racially minoritized communities.[15] The executive order and its associated policies set the stage for truth-telling and redress, but they have not prevented ongoing harm to people who have long shouldered oversized shares of harmful burdens created by extractive and unsustainable practices.[16] Fossil fuel pipelines, hazardous waste sites, and polluting infrastructure still plague vulnerable communities. Marginalized groups continue to face barriers to meaningful participation in environmental governance. Tribal nations are ignored, and their perspectives are devalued in environmental policies and permitting decisions.

As I watched and read reports from Standing Rock, I also pondered the United States' commitment to Indigenous rights, specifically the federal government's nominal support for the United Nations Declaration on the Rights of Indigenous Peoples (UNDRIP). The declaration supports Indigenous self-determination and affirms the right of Indigenous groups to freely give (or withhold) their informed consent for activities that affect their present-day or ancestral territories. The right to consent is a major step beyond the current US legal and political paradigm of tribal consultation.[17]

But just as environmental justice policies have not stopped disproportionate harm to poor or minority communities in the United States, the federal government's support of UNDRIP has not stopped the widespread disregard for Indigenous values and perspectives at the sharp end of environmental governance—the point where decisions are made.

STANDING ROCK IS NOT PROSPECT, and a natural gas compressor station is not a crude oil pipeline. Still, the two situations highlight points of connection between environmental justice and Indigenous rights. Even though a gulf of legal and political differences separates the two cases, they both highlight the limited regard for Indigenous peoples' interests and concerns—particularly in comparison to the interests of large corporations. Both cases also highlight the face of colonialism in the twenty-first century, which is inextricably linked to the extraction and consumption fossil fuels, and to the accompanying environmental degradation and climate change.[18]

As I thought critically about these issues, I realized that very little has been written about Indigenous environmental struggles in North Carolina—past or present—even though North Carolina has one of the largest Native American populations in the United States. And despite eastern North Carolina's storied setting as a birthplace of the modern environmental justice movement, Indigenous environmental issues are not particularly well-known outside of the communities where these struggles take place. This book aims to share some of these stories and their broader meanings with the wider world.

Chapter 1 sets the stage by recounting my early experiences with the controversial practice of land acknowledgments on university campuses. The story becomes a call to reimagine the practice of land acknowledgments, unconstrained by academic formality, as a way to convey the complex histories of Indigenous peoples and their lands. The chapter provides background on the deep and complicated histories that Indigenous peoples share with their homelands on the Coastal Plain of what is now North Carolina. It is a precursor to understanding how and why climate change, extractivism, pollution, and natural disasters threaten our communities and our ties to home.

Chapter 2 uses the story of an iconic Lumbee building to relate critical information about historic and present-day policies and practices that either empower or erase Indigenous peoples from decision-making processes. The chapter introduces key concepts around environmental justice and Indigenous rights that reemerge in later chapters.

Chapter 3 tells about the Lumbee River and how it has shaped the history and culture and Lumbee people. It sheds light on some of the ways that outsiders have misunderstood the river and have manipulated it for their own purposes—sometimes at the expense of Lumbees and their neighbors.

Chapter 4 is the story of the former Atlantic Coast Pipeline, a project that threatened tribal territories for several years before it was scrapped in 2020. The threat of yet another major fossil fuel pipeline in Indian Country motivated Coastal Plain tribes to flex their muscles of inherent sovereignty in new ways. The chapter covers fossil fuel infrastructure and related energy policies—and the high stakes of these policies for Indigenous peoples in North Carolina and elsewhere. This work occupied much of my time during the past few years, and it altered my thinking about environmental justice and Indigenous rights more than any of the other stories in this book.

Chapter 5 describes the radical transformation of the Coastal Plain by swine and poultry industries. In a mere four decades—the blink of an eye for Indigenous peoples—heavily industrialized food production systems altered Native homelands and introduced unprecedented levels of pollution and environmental degradation. The chapter goes beyond simply demonstrating that the negative impacts of these facilities fall disproportionately on people of color; it reveals the disruptive nature of these industries on Indigenous communities and our connections to the places we come from.

Chapter 6 uses the stories of Hurricanes Matthew and Florence—and the accompanying regional floods—to examine ways that climate change is already altering the Coastal Plain and the Indigenous communities that have called it home since time immemorial. These stories help explain some of the ways that climate change exacerbates existing issues of inequity and brings entirely new threats to humans and nonhumans alike.

Chapter 7 is a glimpse of what I view to be a hopeful and redemptive future. It tells about the Great Coharie River Initiative, a multiyear effort by the Coharie Tribe to restore their namesake waterway on the Coastal Plain. The chapter is a case study in overcoming adversity and renewing cultural connections to water.

Chapter 8 offers lessons and recommendations aimed at various groups—tribal governments, individual Native people, and non-Native governments and corporations. The chapter summarizes what I view to be critical next steps for anyone who wants to see Indigenous people preserve, steward, and exert sovereignty over their homelands. Although the work is centered in present-day North Carolina, the lessons and recommendations have broader relevance beyond these colonial borders.

National Academy of Education member and Lumbee Bryan Brayboy writes that "the concepts of culture, knowledge, and power take on new meaning when examined through an Indigenous lens."[19] I took Brayboy at his word and decided to adopt such a lens in hopes that these issues might take on new meaning for readers. To be clear, this book is one Indigenous lens—there is no singular Indigenous perspective. More specifically, the book is my lens. I am a Lumbee scientist, educator, and advocate for Native peoples. Most of my day-to-day work focuses on my own community's homelands in eastern North Carolina, and these are the stories that I am best qualified to tell.

Brayboy also notes that stories are crucial to the development of theory, particularly for Native peoples, because stories are "roadmaps for our communities and reminders of our individual responsibilities to the survival of our communities."[20] I agree, and the book's structure as a collection of stories reflects my desire to help guide and remind Native people about what matters. The stories also hold lessons for non-Native people, who all too often make decisions about tribal nations and our homelands without involving us or even contemplating the cost to future generations of Indigenous or non-Indigenous people.

Many but not all of the stories are grim. The good news is that colonialism is powerful but incomplete. Against the odds, Lumbees and our Indigenous neighbors continue to thrive in the Coastal Plain. We are forever changed by colonialism, but like the water that pools and trickles through Bear Swamp and other backwaters of the Coastal Plain, we flow on.

CHAPTER ONE

Whose Land?
Reimagining Land Acknowledgment

Several years ago, a colleague from the Pacific Northwest contacted me during a visit to North Carolina. She was preparing to give an invited lecture at a nearby university and reached out for help assembling a detailed and appropriate statement to acknowledge the Indigenous peoples on whose lands the neighboring university sat. I was happy to oblige. At the time, I knew it was common in the northwestern United States to open academic seminars and lectures with these kinds of statements, but it was not widely practiced in other parts of the country—especially not in North Carolina. Even though North Carolina had, at that time, the largest American Indian population of any state east of the Mississippi River, it was rare to hear even the names of our tribes spoken on campuses except among Native students themselves or in a handful of specialized courses.

I knew that my colleague worked closely with tribal nations in the Pacific Northwest and that she would want to extend a measure of gratitude and respect to tribal nations here in North Carolina during her visit. I thought it would be a positive experience for students and faculty in the audience to hear someone speak the names of our tribal nations and acknowledge our continued presence in our ancestral homelands. Yes, I was happy to oblige.

I was familiar with the university where my colleague planned to speak, and I knew which tribes claimed the campus within their ancestral territories. My people, the Lumbee, did not consider it part of our lands, but it was located in the traditional territories of Indigenous communities that I knew well. I had friends, colleagues, and students who belonged to these communities. We socialized, collaborated, and volunteered together. Earlier that year, several of us had even created a continuing education course on Indigenous peoples for public school teachers in North Carolina. As an individual Lumbee person, I had no authority to speak on behalf of any of these Indigenous groups, but it was a simple and appropriate task for me to share information that was factual, culturally relevant, and sensitive to the political contours of what it means to acknowledge Indigenous territory in the twenty-first century.

I was especially happy to oblige my colleague because I knew that she would use the information in ways that were both respectful and instructive.

The statement she had planned is now widely recognized as a "land acknowledgment" in the United States and Canada, and these statements are much more common today than they were when this story took place. At the time of my colleague's visit, land acknowledgments were so uncommon in our region that I had never heard or read such a statement anywhere in North Carolina. The closest thing I could recall was a statement that I had made back in 2010, during my first year as an assistant professor at North Carolina State University. At a welcome breakfast for new faculty, university administrators asked us to introduce ourselves and tell where we came from. I gave my name and departmental affiliation before boldly (or foolishly) welcoming my fellow faculty members to North Carolina on behalf of the tribal nations who had always been here. Years later, when it came time to assist my colleague from the Pacific Northwest, I thought about that welcome event for new faculty, but I did not use it as a model for the language I shared with her. She and I occupied completely different relationships to the information; I was an insider, and she was a visitor.

Land acknowledgments vary in format, but people today generally recognize them as brief oral or written declarations that identify specific Indigenous peoples—past and present—who claim ties to a specific place, usually the place where the declaration is made. Well-researched and respectful land acknowledgments instruct, and they also invite meaningful reflection and action. Universities, museums, governments, and other institutions sometimes use land acknowledgments to affirm existing relationships with Indigenous peoples. Or they use aspirational language to remind themselves of how these relationships ought to be.

Too often, however, land acknowledgments are throwaway statements. They are fill-in-the-blank exercises that amount to nothing more than looking up the name of a specific group and announcing that these people were the original inhabitants of the land where an office, lecture hall, or conference center is located today. Thankfully, this is not what my colleague intended. Her objective was to give due respect to past and present Indigenous communities in the place that we sometimes call the Research Triangle of North Carolina.

As land acknowledgments—and especially institutional land acknowledgments—become commonplace, Indigenous and non-Indigenous people have pointed to an overwhelming lack of action to back up the statements. Critics predict that land acknowledgments will become yet another rote exercise in the rhythm of professional and academic lives.[1] Beneath the eloquence—they warn—statements lack not only action but also measures of accountability and reciprocity needed to address historical injustices and build relationships with present-day Indigenous peoples.[2] Other critics call on institutions to move beyond acknowledging Indigenous lands and to return what was taken—a movement known as "Land Back."[3] Their critiques revolve around the idea that words alone are cheap and easy to come by. Words matter, but so do actions when it comes to setting things aright.

I agree with these critiques. In recent years, land acknowledgments have become cheap and easy. Today, anyone with internet access can find information about Indigenous territorial claims (i.e., who lived or lives where) in the present-day United States. Web-based tools display maps that purport to show historic and present-day tribal boundaries. They can even deliver the name of a local tribe via text message based on one's postal code. Unfortunately, there is presently no way to verify the accuracy of this information or to know whether Indigenous people are even involved in the collection, verification, and dissemination of information about territorial claims.

More than fifty years ago, Lakota scholar Vine Deloria Jr. lamented the proliferation of what he called "easy knowledge about Indians." In his groundbreaking book *Custer Died for Your Sins*, Deloria explained that settlers have always been quick to explain who Native Americans are, where we came from, and even—unnervingly—what it is like to be us.[4] Deloria's words ring true today when it comes to the accessibility of resources for crafting land acknowledgments. Maps and more are at our fingertips. Unfortunately, this "easy knowledge" does little to promote reciprocity, accountability, or redress for the expropriation of Indigenous territory. Instead, it reinforces the idea that land acknowledgments are simply fill-in-the-blank exercises in which the only tricky part is correctly pronouncing the name of a tribe that one has discovered through a web-based tool.[5]

At the heart of criticism over land acknowledgments is a need to reckon with the exploitative histories of governments, universities, and other institutions that are now clamoring to adopt their own official statements. In the United States, especially harsh critiques have been reserved for land grant universities, which were initially funded through the Congressionally authorized sale of expropriated Indigenous territory. Whether the territory was ceded by treaty or acquired in some other way, the terms were rarely fair toward Indigenous people. Coercion and deceit abounded. By no means are land grant institutions the sole beneficiaries of Indigenous exploitation, but the federally sanctioned sale left a massive paper trail that made it possible to document—down to the acre and dollar—how institutions throughout the United States benefited from the sale of ill-gotten Indigenous lands.[6]

Even when land acknowledgments mention the exploitation and dispossession of Indigenous peoples, and even when they remember that descendants of those peoples still live nearby, the statements rarely call for more than a moment of somber reflection before moving on to other business. Whatever the intentions behind land acknowledgments, I am intrigued that otherwise well-educated listeners (especially university audiences) require continuous reminders that they occupy stolen land. Settler colonialism not only erases, it feeds on its own forgetfulness.

There is more to say about land acknowledgments, but it will have to wait. For now, I propose a thought experiment. What might it look like to acknowledge Indigenous connections to place in a way that is unchained from the comfortable format of a land acknowledgment—a brief recitation at the opening of a conference or lecture, a paragraph on a university website, or a plaque displayed somewhere on campus? One answer is that it looks like an extended opportunity for non-Natives to sit down and learn something about us. It is an opportunity to sit and learn about the complexities of our lands and waters, our ancestors, and our relationships to the places that shape our collective identities as Indigenous peoples. It is an opportunity to examine— with a critical eye—the very sources of information that survive to assist in telling our stories. Whatever the case, it is not a brief recitation. The reimagining of a land acknowledgment is a story that takes a while to tell.

A reimagined land acknowledgment tells about the painful severing and reshaping of relationships between Indigenous peoples and the places they come from, because telling and remembering are important first steps in the journey of transformation and healing of colonized people and lands.[7] Here, in the Coastal Plain, any account must include our survival in the wake of war, disease, and the erasing power of settler colonialism.

Many parts of the story in eastern North Carolina are difficult to tell. Here, histories are dominated by records and narratives put down by colonial explorers and settlers. By their accounts, Native peoples faded from existence after the first decade or two of the eighteenth century. Our "sudden" reappearance in settler narratives is accompanied by surprise or disbelief. I think the reason is because our existence complicates the comfortable narrative that Indigenous peoples all died, left the region, or abandoned our collective identities and assimilated into settler society.

But comfortable narratives are not always true. Historian Francis Jennings warned that "the blank places in the histories do not represent a paucity of events."[8] My own work on historical maps of the Coastal Plain shows that the homelands of Lumbee ancestors (in what would become Robeson County) were literally "blank places" on maps until the late eighteenth or early nineteenth century—a relatively late date for an area that is not very far from the literal beachheads of colonial expansion from the Atlantic Coast.[9]

To imagine that these spaces were empty before the arrival of white settlers plays directly into the misconception that North Carolina (and the United States as a whole) was carved from pristine wilderness and given freely to settlers by vanishing Natives. Historian Roxanne Dunbar-Ortiz called this misconception the "founding myth" of the United States.[10] The alternative, as Deloria wrote in *Custer Died for Your Sins*, is to discard the "(m)ythical generalities of what built this country and made it great."[11]

Deloria also demanded that these myths give way to "contractual obligations due to the Indian people."[12] He counted, among these obligations, a moral duty for the United States to recognize Native peoples in the eastern United States—including Native peoples in the Coastal Plain of North Carolina—who lacked treaties and were unrecognized by the federal government.[13]

More than half a century after Deloria issued these demands, most of these Native peoples are still unrecognized by the federal government. As a direct result, tribes in eastern North Carolina remain massively underresourced and underprepared to face the tremendous environmental and societal challenges heaped on their communities, lands, and waters. To acknowledge the fullness and complexity of their connections to place is no substitute for the redress that Native peoples deserve, but an honest and instructive account of our stories is an important first step toward fulfilling the moral duties described by Deloria.[14]

The rest of this chapter is a window into the complex connections to place held by Lumbee people and our Indigenous neighbors. It is partly a re-imagined land acknowledgment in the sense that I invite readers to pull up a seat, listen, and take in a few important ideas about Indigenous peoples of the Coastal Plain.[15] As you listen, absorb some sense of our long tenure here in our homelands. Appreciate our history of stewarding the land and water. Recognize that our ancestors experienced traumas that shattered their societies and that we—their descendants—are still learning what it means to forge ahead without forgetting where we came from. Acknowledge the power of colonial myths and narratives in shaping your own perceptions of Indigenous peoples here and elsewhere.

This chapter also contains necessary background information for many readers, specifically because the colonial project has been so successful in

North Carolina. Stereotypes, misconceptions, and ignorance have led to a situation that many of my Indigenous friends will find familiar; we must regularly give introductory lectures on our histories and cultures before even cursory conversations with outsiders about the present-day issues that face our communities. In other words, Indigenous people cannot assume that the general public knows enough about us to engage in meaningful dialogue about politics, education, the environment, or a host of other topics, and many of us keep some form of this lecture ready to give at a moment's notice. Most versions boil down to a simple assertion: we are still here.

By the end of this chapter, I hope that readers will see in a new light some of the perfunctory phrases embedded in popular land acknowledgments. One that I hear regularly is, "these are the ancestral lands of. . . ." The phrase carries both truth and trauma that can slip past uneducated ears. Indigenous homelands on the Coastal Plain are places of deep connection and remembrance, but they are also places where horrific colonial experiences befell our ancestors. The trauma of those experiences still flows through our communities today. The pain of racial oppression and cultural loss combines with the radical transformation of our homelands, and it haunts us from generation to generation.[16]

I know the look and feel of these traumatic experiences. I belong to a people who are still afflicted by legacies of oppression. We cannot talk about our connections to place unless we grapple with the long-term impacts of settler colonialism on the Coastal Plain, the 25,000-square-mile swath of present-day North Carolina that stretches from the base of the Piedmont to the barrier islands that jut into the Atlantic Ocean.[17] Not all Lumbee ancestors lived on the Coastal Plain; some of our ancestors moved here from across the Fall Line. But Lumbees consider the Coastal Plain to be our home today. The connections that Lumbee people and our Indigenous neighbors hold to our ancestral landscapes and waterways on the Coastal Plain are strong, but they are also colored by the trauma of generations. My intent is not to give an oversized platform to violence and oppression, but rather to set the stage for other stories that explain present-day environmental issues faced by Lumbee people and our Indigenous neighbors. It is not possible to understand these issues without a basic grasp of what Lumbee people and our Indigenous neighbors have experienced in the long centuries since settlers first arrived.

This chapter is not the "easy knowledge" that Deloria criticized, but it is also not a thorough telling of our histories. Instead, consider it a partial antidote to the trend of cheap and easy land acknowledgments that reduce Indigenous peoples' long and complex relationships to place to a brief recitation.

If it helps, consider this chapter a reimagined land acknowledgment for eastern North Carolina. Or maybe simply take a seat and listen.

THE FALL LINE—the ancient landform that divides the Coastal Plain from the Piedmont—traces a path from present-day New Jersey to Georgia and then bends in a great arc toward the Mississippi Delta. Simply put, the Fall Line is an extremely old high-water mark, the last remnant of an ancient shoreline where ocean waves, sea breezes, and storms beat against primordial beaches some three million years ago.[18] Back then, coastal winds piled sand into towering dunes in a few places along the ancient shoreline. Relicts of these dunes are still visible today in a region called the *Sandhills*[19]—a bulge of rolling, sandy terrain that lies on the Fall Line to the northwest of Robeson County.[20]

Through millennia, Earth's climate cooled. Glaciers and polar ice caps, emaciated by global warming, re-formed. As the frozen masses expanded, oceans contracted in response, and sea level fell globally. In the place that would become the Coastal Plain, the ancient ocean slowly receded eastward, exposing a vast wedge of sediments—sand, silt, and clay. Rivers that drained the Piedmont and Appalachian Mountains lengthened eastward to reach the ocean. Rapids and, occasionally, waterfalls formed where rivers reached the rocky edge of the Piedmont and tumbled across the Fall Line.

Rain and melting snow pulsed through the Coastal Plain and filled the nascent soil with fresh water. Trees rooted and forests spread. Soils grew rich in nutrients and organic matter from decaying flora and fauna. Excess water leaked downward through layers of sediment and created vast freshwater aquifers from the accumulated volume of billions of tiny interconnected voids.

Everywhere, flowing water sculpted the Coastal Plain. Rivers carved channels into the ancient seafloor and exposed high bluffs of strata and fossilized remains of earlier marine life. Some rivers, including the Neuse and Roanoke, drained landscapes west of the Fall Line. Those places had clay-rich soils and rocky outcrops. Rivers there usually ran crystal clear but turned reddish-brown during floods. They carried loads of sand, silt, and clay across the Fall Line and into the Coastal Plain.

Other rivers drained lands that were located completely east of the Fall Line. Sometimes they nibbled into places like the Sandhills. These rivers flowed dark with organic matter derived from Coastal Plain soils. Whether they rose east or west of the Fall Line, rivers flowed to the beat of seasonal droughts and floods. They carried sand, silt, clay, and organic matter eastward, toward the ocean. Overflowing rivers doused floodplains with fresh supplies of nutrient-laden silt. Swamps thick with bald cypress and black gum filled the floodplains and lined the riverbanks. Below the riverbanks, a few bald cypress trees clung tightly to streambeds and withstood currents long enough to grow into heavily buttressed sentinels. In some places, fires burned regularly, and river cane sprouted to create giant marshes, or canebrakes.[21] Streams flowed with sustenance. The rivers were alive, and they brought life to the Coastal Plain.

Broad, sandy plains separated swamps from one another. In places, the plains constricted and became small necks of high ground separating vast wetlands. Where uplands were large enough, wildfires, sparked by lightning, created a vast savanna of longleaf pine and wiregrass. This ecosystem would eventually cover ninety million acres in eastern North America, much of which straddled the Fall Line. Longleaf pine trees withstood smoldering, low-intensity fires with the aid of thick bark and needle-shrouded buds. The largest trees grew more than one hundred feet high and were more than two feet in diameter. Wiregrass survived fires by storing most of its growth below ground, away from flames that consumed maple, sweet gum, and other would-be competitors. Fires consumed much of the forest floor, but pines and grasses survived. Other survivors reemerged as well. Wildflowers, herbs, blueberries, and huckleberries all resprouted on the fire-swept sand. Exceptionally rare plants, including the insect-eating Venus flytrap and pitcher plant, grew in a small swath of the savanna between present-day Robeson County and the Atlantic Ocean.

As the ancient ocean retreated eastward, thousands of shallow, oblong depressions formed throughout the Coastal Plain, ranging in diameter from a few hundred yards to a few miles.[22] The depressions filled with rain and groundwater, and they became shallow lakes. Bald cypress trees grew along the lakes' sandy rims and some ventured into open water. In time, most of the lakes dried up or filled with peat and became densely vegetated wetlands. Some held tall stands of bald cypress and black gum, and others hosted a scrubby mix of pond pines, vines, and evergreen shrubs. From a birds-eye view, the depressions look like massive thumbprints pressed into the surrounding terrain. Whether they remained lakes or became wetlands, the features were dubbed Carolina Bays by geologists who studied early aerial photographs of the region.[23]

Shrubby wetland plants that overtook Carolina Bays also grew on the interstitial ridges between Coastal Plain streams. Unlike the sharp backbones of mountains west of the Fall Line, Coastal Plain ridges were subtle arcs in a predominantly flat landscape. The wetlands that formed on these arcs were named *pocosins* in at least one of the Algonquian dialects spoken on the

Coastal Plain at the time of European contact.[24] As pocosins aged, partially decayed plant matter formed layer upon layer of spongy peat. The wetlands, atop thick peat formations, sat several feet higher than the surrounding stream valleys. The sponge-like soils absorbed rains that fell across the Coastal Plain. In dry weather, pocosin soils released water, slowly, into rivulets that converged into larger streams and kept them flowing year-round.

During severe droughts, pocosins dried out and became flammable. Lightning set desiccated plants and, sometimes, soil aflame. Dry herbs and shrubs burned in a matter of hours or days. However, peat soils—once alight—smoldered for weeks or months until wet weather returned to refill the spongy pores with water, extinguishing the flames. Rare large fires could consume so much soil that they lowered the ground elevation by a few feet.[25] More frequent, less severe fires left peat intact but cleared the underbrush. The heat from their flames prompted cones from pond pines to relax and release tightly held seeds. The next generation of life sprouted quickly in freshly burned soil.

Nearer the coast, pocosins and longleaf savannas gave way to maritime forests. Live oak, yaupon, and wax myrtle grew in sandy soils that held in reserve small amounts of rainfall for thirsty roots. The forests sprawled across barrier islands and along sections of the mainland adjacent to grass-covered dunes and tidal marshes.

Between the mainland and the barrier islands lay an expansive estuary. It formed when brackish water slowly began to fill ancient river valleys nearly twenty thousand years ago—around the end of the last Ice Age—as glaciers melted and sea levels rose. Eventually, a shallow estuary grew to encompass more than three thousand square miles of open water between the mainland and narrow sand bars that grew into barrier islands. The drowned and sediment-choked valleys of the Roanoke, Chowan, Pamlico, and Neuse Rivers formed lobes of brackish water that mingled in a giant estuary ringed by marsh grass and bald cypress forest.[26]

The Coastal Plain may have lacked the dramatic topography of the Piedmont and Appalachian Mountains to the west, but it did not lack in richness or diversity of life. East of the Fall Line, the watery world of wetlands—floodplain forests, marshes, pocosins, lakes, and estuaries—coexisted with fire-swept savannas in one of the most biodiverse regions of the world.[27] White-tailed deer, black bears, and turkeys inhabited wetlands and uplands. Bison grazed the savannas.[28] Ducks, geese, and other water birds covered the Carolina Bays and marshes. Water birds shared rivers with fish, otters, turtles, and alligators. Sturgeon migrated annually up Coastal Plain rivers from the Atlantic Ocean to their spawning grounds near the Fall Line. Estuaries held expansive shellfish beds and nurtured young saltwater fish, shrimp, and crabs. Still today, the Coastal Plain is a hotspot for biodiversity; it holds more than six thousand native plant species, more than four hundred native fish, and hundreds of native mammals, reptiles, and amphibians.[29]

Indigenous people came to the Coastal Plain well over ten thousand years ago. When European colonists arrived millennia later, the Coastal Plain was a robust network of Native communities that interacted regularly among themselves and with distant peoples from various parts of the continent.[30] Lumbee, Coharie, Waccamaw Siouan, Meherrin, Sappony, Haliwa-Saponi, Occaneechi, Nottoway, Pee Dee, Tuscarora, and other Native peoples all descend from Indigenous groups who lived throughout this region—on both sides of the Fall Line—at the time of colonization. Most shared the Eastern Woodland culture, but their languages were diverse.[31] In the Coastal Plain alone, languages spanned three major families—Iroquoian, Algonquian, and Siouan. Some languages and dialects were mutually unintelligible.[32] Within these complex societies, groups of people made and dissolved political alliances, traded with one another, fought wars, established kinship, and interacted in countless other ways (map 1.1).

On the eastern edge of the Coastal Plain, Algonquian-speaking communities built towns along the relatively calm, estuarine coastlines of the mainland and barrier islands—a watery world. Their dialects—Roanoke, Secotan, Pamlico, and several others—are no longer spoken, but colonial records note that at least one of these groups called their homeland *Ossomocomuck*—the place where we live.[33] Their immediate neighbors to the west were Tuscarora, Nottoway, Meherrin, and other Iroquoian-speaking peoples whose towns lined the lower and middle reaches of the Chowan, Roanoke, Tar, and Neuse Rivers and their tributaries. These rivers flowed into the vast brackish waters of Ossomocomuck. Farther southwest, Siouan-speaking peoples—Waccamaw, Cheraw, Pee Dee, and others—lived along the Cape Fear and Pee Dee Rivers and their tributaries. These may have been the southeasternmost communities in a large swath of Siouan-speaking peoples that extended across the upper reaches of several river basins that stretched northwest, into the Piedmont and Appalachian Mountains.[34]

Whether they lived along coastlines or rivers, all were people of water. Their lives and livelihoods depended on the ability to observe and predict the seasonal rhythms of rivers, which were vital transportation arteries and sources of devastating floods. Farming and foraging required a clear understanding of the seasonality of rainfall and dry spells. Hunting and fishing required knowledge of hydrological processes and about the life cycles and

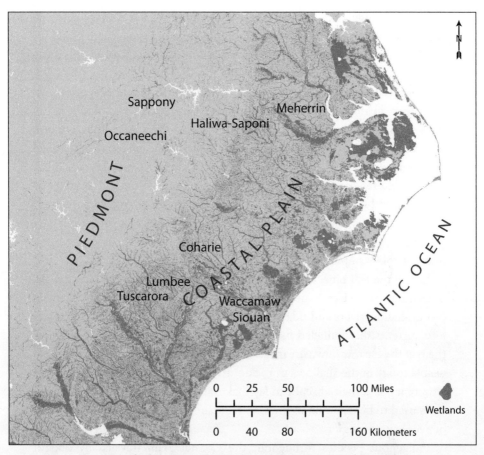

MAP 1.1 Locations of tribal communities in present-day eastern North Carolina.
Map by author.

migration patterns of fish and other aquatic life. Seasonal spawning runs of
sturgeon and shad allowed Native peoples of the Coastal Plain to stock up on
food supplies for themselves and to trade with peoples who lived beyond the
Fall Line.

Life in the Coastal Plain required careful attention to other aspects of nature too. Thunderstorms brought lightning and wildfires in the summer, and
tropical storms brought violent winds and floods in the fall. Indigenous
peoples of the Coastal Plain had a deep understanding of how these disturbances shaped the landscapes around them. They situated towns away from
flood-prone areas and adopted fire as a tool to manage vast areas of the
Coastal Plain. In particular, Indigenous people used controlled burns to
maintain and even expand the longleaf pine ecosystem as habitat for deer,

turkey, and other game. Indigenous people carefully timed burns to coincide with favorable weather; overly dry conditions or unfavorable winds could expand low-intensity fires into major conflagrations that could jump across rivers and streams used as natural fire breaks.[35]

Indigenous farmers also used fire to clear land for agriculture, taking advantage of nutrient-rich soils in floodplains adjacent to rivers.[36] Throughout the region, farmers cultivated the Three Sisters—the staple crops of corn, beans, and squash.[37] They raised pumpkins, sunflowers, and tobacco, and they gathered wild berries, leaves, and medicinal plants for salves, teas, and poultices.[38] Near the coast, people gathered yaupon leaves. Dried and roasted, the leaves could be steeped to make a caffeinated tea much like yerba mate.[39] Farther out, along the coastline, people gathered shellfish, including quahog, the large Atlantic clam whose purple and cream-colored shells were crafted into valuable wampum.[40]

East of the Fall Line, where streambeds had few stones or cobbles, Indigenous fishers wove river cane into V-shaped weirs, which they used to harvest fish in shallow rivers and tidal creeks. Arms of the weirs extended upstream into currents that funneled fish toward fishers who waited to trap or spear them at the narrow downstream end. Farther inland, stone fish traps are still visible today in the shallows of rockier rivers and streams. Cane weirs were temporary, and their absence today makes it easy to forget that these structures used to be common in the Coastal Plain and helped to feed thousands of people in the region.

Indigenous peoples throughout the Coastal Plain traveled by dugout canoe, a heavy-duty boat fashioned from a single log of bald cypress or pine. Carvers burned and scraped logs into sleeker shapes with slightly pointed ends and long, flattened hulls that tracked in a straight line and remained stable on flat or slow-moving water.[41] The boats were much heavier and bulkier than the bark canoes used by people living around the Great Lakes, but weight mattered less on the Coastal Plain. Here, portages were rare and canoes rarely left the water. There are no rapids below the Fall Line, and navigational hazards are limited to downed trees, beaver dams, and extreme low flows during droughts.

For thousands of years, dugout canoes ferried people and goods across rivers, lakes, and estuaries. Canoes were an indispensable part of trade, war, and social life on the Coastal Plain. If circumstances required, a rudimentary dugout could be fashioned in a few hours. These boats did not approach the size and seaworthiness of ocean-going canoes paddled by Indigenous people in the Pacific Northwest, but they were functional, durable, and perfectly suited for travel on relatively flat waters of the Coastal Plain. From time to time, dug-out canoes emerge, well-preserved, from anoxic sediments beneath lakes and rivers throughout the Southeast. Some are as long as thirty feet.[42] Many are displayed in museums around the region, and a few have even been repatriated to tribal nations, including the Coharie Tribe in eastern North Carolina.

Native peoples may have traveled extensively, but they maintained strong ties to their ancestral soil. Some built earthen mounds to bury the dead. These were not massive ceremonial mounds of Mississippian people that are found farther south and west (although there is evidence that Mississippian peoples lived nearby in the Piedmont).[43] Burial mounds in the Coastal Plain were small by comparison; most stood a few feet high and were twenty or thirty feet in diameter. Though modest in size, the mounds could hold the remains of hundreds of people.[44] Some remains were interred with small personal items, carved effigies, or wampum necklaces.

Burial mounds were not only sacred places, but they were also fragile places. In death, the physical remains of Native peoples on the Coastal Plain quickly returned back into the ancient sediments that had given life to countless generations before them. Abundant rainfall, warm soils, and chronically high water tables sped up the process of decay, and human remains interred under these conditions were exceptionally fragile. During the nineteenth and twentieth centuries, an epidemic of looting and scholarly research destroyed human remains buried in mounds throughout the Coastal Plain. Other mounds—and the delicate remains that they held—were simply plowed under to make way for cotton, corn, and tobacco crops.

Despite widespread destruction of archaeological evidence, researchers estimate that Robeson County—now the epicenter of Lumbee culture and politics—has been occupied continuously by Indigenous peoples for several thousand years.[45] Researchers have identified dozens of archaeological sites scattered across Robeson County. Some of these sites appear to be the remains of seasonal camps or permanent towns near the sandy rims of Carolina Bays. Millennia ago, these were lakefront fishing communities. For Lumbees and our Indigenous neighbors in eastern North Carolina, these archaeological sites are tangible reminders that we have lived in a close relationship with water on the Coastal Plain since time immemorial.

LUMBEE ANCESTORS ADOPTED English as a common language some three hundred years ago, more than a century after first contact with Europeans. Colonial documents reveal that Indigenous peoples of the Coastal Plain were proficient if not fluent in English even before they began to gather in isolated backwaters of our present-day tribal territories. Many of these ancestors were internally displaced peoples who sought refuge from war, disease, and enslavement during the early 1700s. They spoke various Algonquian, Iroquoian, and Siouan languages, including dialects that have been dormant for generations. Elements of their languages survive in the names of rivers and other watery places throughout the region: Roanoke, Chowan, Pamlico, Neuse, Contentnea, Pee Dee, Hatteras, Waccamaw, Mattamuskeet, and Meherrin are a few of the more prominent Indigenous place-names that survive.

When I travel to these places, I speak their names out loud. The past few centuries have been tough on these lands and waters, and in my imagination, they take comfort in hearing their proper names spoken with a sense of familiarity. Colonized places give us a flipped sense of what is familiar and what is exotic, and it can be hard to remember that *Bath, New Bern,* and *Raleigh* are foreign names in these lands.

The Europeans who renamed most of the Coastal Plain came here as early as the mid-sixteenth century. Spanish military expeditions wound through central and western North Carolina. Spanish soldiers briefly occupied a string of forts west of the Fall Line. English explorers arrived on the coast in the 1580s and attempted to hold a small coastal area more than two hundred miles away from present-day Robeson County. The English colony, situated on Roanoke Island, ultimately failed and became a widely mythologized story. For many Native peoples in the region, these Spanish and English encounters were the beginning of a centuries-long entanglement with Euro-American powers that shattered precolonial societies and left surviving communities reeling.

Roanoke, an island situated in the shallow estuary between North Carolina's mainland and barrier islands, was the epicenter of several encounters and conflicts between English and Indigenous peoples during the 1580s. In the Euro-American telling—which has received more than enough attention to recount in detail here—Roanoke was a tragedy of compounding errors. That narrative reaches a climax when the governor left Roanoke and traveled back across the Atlantic to fetch supplies for his struggling colonists. War between England and Spain delayed his resupply voyage for years, and the governor returned to an abandoned settlement. A one-word message indicates that at least some colonists have moved elsewhere, but bad weather drove the governor out to sea before he could investigate.

The English attempt to colonize Roanoke involved three separate incursions into the Coastal Plain. During the first two expeditions, English military officers, naturalists, and artists recorded detailed observations for promotional materials intended to recruit settlers and investors for ventures in the "New Found Land of Virginia."[46] Records from these expeditions, especially the detailed watercolors of sixteenth-century Algonquian life by John White (the unlucky governor of the final expedition) evoke complicated emotions from present-day Native peoples of the region. On one hand, the diaries and paintings are priceless snapshots of everyday life in Ossomocomuck. They are rich in historical and anthropological details. White's watercolors, in combination with the notes of natural philosopher Thomas Hariot, reveal the political meanings of tattoos, shed light on Indigenous religious practices, and illustrate foodways during a sliver of time at the moment of English contact. Hariot assembled this material in collaboration with two Indigenous men, Manteo and Wanchese, who traveled back to Elizabethan London as informants and research subjects.

Although records from the Roanoke expeditions focus on a small portion of the 25,000-square-mile Coastal Plain, the materials produced by White and Hariot resonate with tribal nations throughout the Southeast. White's watercolors, and contemporaneous woodcut prints derived from them, have both sentimental value and research significance to Indigenous peoples who hope to renew cultural practices shown in his art, including practices that have been curtailed by language loss and suppressed by centuries of oppression.

Materials from the Roanoke expeditions may be priceless resources for historical and cultural studies, but stories about the colonization of Roanoke are often told in ways that hurt Indigenous peoples. For example, the National Park Service, which now manages the portion of Roanoke Island where Elizabethans are believed to have built their settlement, has—for decades—hosted *The Lost Colony*, an outdoor drama filled with harmful imagery and stereotypes of Native people. For the vast majority of its eight-decade run, non-Native actors have portrayed Algonquian-speaking people of Ossomocomuck. They cavort and gesticulate clownishly as they pantomime Native ceremonies and social gatherings. Stage notes from the original 1937 script by Pulitzer Prize-winning dramatist Paul Green describe one of these characters as a "wild priest or medicine man" and include detailed—and entirely fabricated— choreographies of Native religious ceremonies.[47] What ought to be Algonquian dialogue is gibberish. Actors wear stage makeup to grossly exaggerate body paint and tattoos shown in White's sixteenth-century watercolors. Although the script has evolved through the years, non-Native actors have long donned "redface"—darkening their skin with brown makeup and wearing black wigs to achieve a stereotypical Native appearance.[48]

In 2021, producers announced that they had hired an Indigenous choreographer and would consult with present-day tribes on the representation of Native peoples in the outdoor drama. Beginning that year, the play hired Native actors—including several Lumbees—to fill roles of Native characters. Even though the production no longer relies on characters in "redface," the play's central plotline continues to romanticize the traumatic and deadly invasion of Native communities on the Coastal Plain. In a more realistic telling, the Elizabethans who attempted to colonize Roanoke razed Native villages and stoked political discord among the people of Ossomocomuck. Colonists kidnapped Indigenous people and held them as hostages, and they spread deadly infections in towns that welcomed and hosted them.[49]

Not only does the play gloss over atrocities against Native people, but from start to finish it venerates the vanished colonists as intrepid martyrs. Historian Michael Oberg points out that storytellers, historians, and others frequently discuss the Roanoke expedition in ways that advance colonial narratives and erase Indigenous histories.[50] He calls attention to the nationalistic opening lines of the play: "Friends, we are gathered here this evening to honor the spiritual birthplace of our nation and to memorialize those heroic men and women who made it so ... Here these pioneers of a new order, of a new form of government, lived and struggled, suffered and died."[51]

To be clear, the opening lines refer specifically to colonists as those who "struggled, suffered and died." The play honors English lives, not the lives of the original peoples of the Coastal Plain—people whose societies were upended by the events memorialized in the drama. Until the play comes to grips with the trauma inflicted on Indigenous peoples by these early colonial encounters, the insertion of Native actors, choreographers, and consultants into the production will do little to counteract the miseducation of thousands of tourists and others who visit Ossomocomuck and who watch the play every year.

Almost twelve decades after the failed Roanoke expedition, Englishman John Lawson wandered several hundred miles through the interior of the colonial Carolinas, including parts of the Coastal Plain. A few years later, Lawson published a travel diary of his journey, which took place in 1701 but also included observations that he collected over the next few years working as a colonial surveyor along the Pamlico Sound, the large and brackish water body situated between the mainland and barrier islands of present-day North Carolina.

For centuries, historians and chroniclers of the Colonial South have venerated Lawson as an intrepid explorer and naturalist. I understand the appeal.

Lawson's work is one of the few written, first-hand accounts of the Carolina interior that survives today. It includes detailed observations about people and the environment. I get all of that. But at the same time, I see in Lawson the same ignorance and entitlement that survives today in the treatment of Indigenous peoples by extractive corporations and paternalistic government agencies. If I am left to describe my ancestors' world using Lawson's writing, I will at least do it on my own terms.

Part of me regrets that Lawson's travelogue is one of the few written accounts of my ancestors' world at the turn of the eighteenth century. Another part of me is grateful that it exists. It opens a small window into the complex societies of Native peoples in the Coastal Plain and Piedmont. It hints at the seasonal rhythms of agriculture, hunting, fishing, and trade. Lawson sheds a modicum of light on the importance of dugout canoes for travel below the Fall Line. He documents fire as a tool for managing landscapes and wildlife. Whether I like it or not, Lawson's observations provide useful background knowledge about our ancestors' world.

Lawson wrote about spring runs of herring and sturgeon, explaining how Native people used nets and poles to capture hundreds of migrating fish each day as they attempted to pass the rapids at the Fall Line.[52] They smoked fish near the riverbanks and traded the preserved meat far and wide. These are practices that have disappeared almost entirely from all Native communities on the east coast due to overfishing and dam construction along many of the region's rivers. Today, Atlantic sturgeon are an endangered species, pushed close to extinction because their eggs were highly prized as caviar in the nineteenth century.[53]

In recent years, I have become friends with people from a few of the Coast Salish tribal nations in the Pacific Northwest, and I have learned much about the importance of salmon and in their cultures. In the state of Washington, prior generations of Native people fought for—and won—legal rights to manage their ancestral salmon fisheries.[54] If our ancestral connections to sturgeon in the East resembled—even remotely—the connections to salmon held by Native peoples in the Northwest, then the loss of our ancestral fisheries was an irreplaceable cultural tragedy. Lawson's brief descriptions of this sturgeon-rich world conjure up an alternate reality of Indigenous life on the Coastal Plain.

Lawson also documented other aspects of day-to-day life in Tuscarora, Coree, Bear River, and other Native communities. He wrote about daily rituals of bathing and sharing meals in the villages that hosted him.[55] He observed recordkeeping practices, including potentially widespread use of bundled and inscribed river cane or cordgrass to keep track of historical events. Lawson once noted, "To prove the times more exactly, he produces the Records of the Country, which are a Parcel of Reeds, of different Lengths, with several distinct Marks, known to none but themselves; by which they seem to guess, very exactly, at Accidents that happen'd many Years ago; nay two or three Ages or more."[56]

He was also privy to religious ceremonies and was a guest in the homes of community leaders, but he writes about many of these experiences with irritation and impatience. One particular entry describes a burial ceremony for a Tuscarora man who was killed by lightning. According to Lawson, an elder spoke during the ceremony about lightning and its role in the Tuscarora cosmos. The elder recited a story about a man who acquired supernatural immunity to lightning by capturing it and shaping it into a bird.

Lawson described the elder's story as "the most ridiculous absurd Parcel of Lyes," and he did not hesitate to interrupt the ceremony to share his opinion with a nearby Tuscarora man. To Lawson's surprise, the man, who spoke English, did not share his cynicism. The Tuscarora man contradicted Lawson, explaining that the elder "did never tell Lyes," and moreover, the man knew for himself that the supernatural story was true.[57]

Lawson dropped the subject with the Tuscarora man, but he stayed long enough to hear a second story about a monstrous rattlesnake that inhabited a tributary of the Neuse River. Lawson glossed over what must have been a fascinating story about a creature that devoured "whole Canoes full of Indians" and was ultimately slain by a bald eagle. Lawson justified the cursory treatment by writing that he only meant to give readers a basic sense of "what strange ridiculous Stories these Wretches are inclinable to believe."[58]

I am sure the two stories conveyed some deeper meaning to the Indigenous people in attendance that day. Centuries later, I read Lawson's account and desperately want more. I am especially intrigued by the lightning story because it resonates with many Lumbee people (myself included), who were raised with great reverence for thunderstorms. Even in Charlotte, the large city where I lived as a child, I remember my family turning out the lights and drawing the curtains during thunderstorms. We were not hiding; we did it out of reverence for the supernatural power behind the storm. Similarly, Lumbee people respect rivers as places of unharnessed power. Water enabled life, but it also harbored danger. Elders warned Lumbee children from my generation about venomous snakes, strange currents, and other aquatic hazards in the river. In my opinion, Lawson shortchanged his readers on the best parts of these stories.

While I am grateful for the details embedded in Lawson's work—lacking as they are in some areas—I also know that he came here to reconnoiter the landscape for settler exploitation. He offered advice on how to subjugate Native people and control their lands. Many of Lawson's observations are infused with commentary on how the English might exploit the land and enslave Indigenous people. He imagined radically transformed landscapes, modeled after Europe. One entry noted, "This Valley afforded as large Timber as any I ever met withal, especially of Chesnut-Oaks, which render it an excellent Country for raising great Herds of Swine. Indeed, were it cultivated, we might have good hopes of as pleasant and fertile a Valley, as any our English in America can afford."[59]

The reference to swine eerily foreshadows the extractive practice of industrial livestock production that roared into North Carolina's Coastal Plain during the past few decades. His language also channels that of a present-day public relations specialist; he presages twenty-first-century corporate advertising campaigns that promise economic prosperity through radical transformation of Indigenous homelands.

Lastly, parts of Lawson's travelogue make him out to be an insensitive, ham-fisted, tourist—even by eighteenth-century standards. He was not well-traveled; the diary was a record of his first trip to North America and possibly his first trip away from the British Isles. One particular diary entry epitomizes his sense of entitlement, and it alludes to the grace and hospitality of the Native people who served as guides, chaperones, and hosts.

During his initial travels, Lawson recorded his own breaking and entry into the unoccupied cabin of Scipio, a Sewee man who guided Lawson on an earlier leg of the journey. Lawson shared a detailed inventory of Scipio's pantry—peas, beans, oil, corn, nuts, and peaches prepared several ways—before helping himself to the man's provisions. Because the weather was bad outside, Lawson decided to build a fire inside Scipio's cabin to cook some of the pilfered food. He lost control of the fire and nearly burned Scipio's cabin to the ground.

Lawson abandoned Scipio's smoldering homeplace the next morning. The next diary entry rationalized that it was common practice for whites to enter unoccupied Native homes, taking whatever they wanted and leaving "some small Gratuity of Tobacco, Paint, Beads. &c."[60] It is unclear whether Lawson left any "gratuity" for Scipio besides an empty pantry and a partially burned cabin.

Thankfully, Lawson's diary is not the only written account that documents Native life on the Coastal Plain at the turn of the eighteenth century. Another surviving account—one of my personal favorites—paints a much more colorful and confrontational picture of interactions between settlers and Native people.

In 1704, about three years after Lawson set fire to Scipio's cabin, a group of Native men described in colonial records as Bear River Indians entered the unoccupied dwelling of a newcomer to the Coastal Plain, a man named William Powell. Powell was an English settler whose cabin sat near the mouth of the Neuse River. The exact location is unknown, but the cabin was almost certainly located within the Bear River Indians' territory.

The account comes from Powell himself, in the form of a written complaint that he filed with a local magistrate in the fledgling colonial government. According to Powell, he came home one day to find the Bear River men in his home, helping themselves to Powell's belongings. Powell ordered the men to leave. If they did not, Powell threatened, he would file a complaint.

The leader of the Bear River men, whose name was Souther, responded to the threat by walloping Powell with his bow. Souther—conversant, if not fluent, in English—called Powell a "sonn [*sic*]of a bitch" while beating him. Souther then threatened to burn down Powell's house and crops. A few days later, Powell filed a written complaint, which recounted the entire episode. At the end of the document, Powell relayed a personal message from Souther to the magistrate when the former learned of Powell's plan to lodge a complaint: "I told him I would tell your honor . . . he said you might kiss his arse."[61]

I have shared the story of Souther and Powell several times with other Native people from North Carolina. We joke about Souther's obstinance and how the trait persists in our own communities. The story has sparked serious discussions as well—conversations about the growing tensions between Indigenous peoples and settlers, about the rapid adoption of English by our ancestors, and about ideas of private property contained in this story and in the earlier account of Lawson and Scipio's cabin. On one or two occasions, we have discussed Souther's disregard for the magistrate's authority, which is unsurprising given that the colonial government was recently established and exceptionally weak at the time. More than once, someone has noted that the "speak to your manager" attitude—exposed in recent years via cell phone videos and social media—has actually been around for a very long time.[62]

Lawson returned to London and published his travelogue in 1709. By the time he left North Carolina, he had been named Surveyor-General of the colony and stood to profit considerably from portraying Native lands and people as ripe for exploitation. The colony could be divvied up among new

settlers, and Native peoples—at least those who survived disease and enslavement on English plantations—could serve as trading partners and as buffers
against attack from colonial enemies.[63]

Literary scholar J. V. Ridgely called Lawson's travelogue "as much promotional treatise as history."[64] I agree, but I also think that Lawson's writings—
and many of his actions—foreshadowed the later schemes of loggers, canal
builders, pork companies, pipeline developers, and others who have viewed
the Coastal Plain as ripe for exploitation. All of these schemes are variations
on a colonial project that began before Lawson's time and continues to inflict
trauma on Indigenous peoples to this day.[65]

Still, I read Lawson despite his extractive and exploitative perspective. I
sift through his biases listening for echoes of my ancestors' voices and hoping
to catch the occasional unsullied glimpse of their world. Lawson's insensitiv-
ity and incredulity make this work difficult, but some insights filter through.
In this respect, Lawson's work is both necessary and traumatizing. We have
lost many of the details of our oral traditions. We have lost our "parcels of
reeds." We are often left grasping for scraps of information from Lawson's diary and from other colonial works. We are not utterly dependent on these
resources, but they occupy a disproportionate share of the historical resources available from the early eighteenth century—a time before devastating war, loss, and upheaval.

In some ways, our situation reminds me of the experience of Penobscot
Carol Dana, who mastered her ancestral language while working as an assistant to a white linguist who conducted research with the Penobscot Nation.
Recently, a journalist shared Dana's perspective in the *New Yorker*: "When I
asked Dana whether she ever felt resentful or embarrassed that she had
learned her own language from a white man, she laughed. 'Oh, yes, all of that,'
she said. 'But it didn't quite feel like I was learning it from him.'"[66] Similarly,
our ancestors reach out to us through the pages of Lawson's travelogue. We
do not learn about our ancestors from Lawson. We learn about them in spite
of him.

A FAR MORE SOMBER JOURNEY happened shortly after Lawson published
his travel diary in London. In 1710, a group of Tuscarora people made a much
more deliberate and desperate trek north, four hundred miles up the Fall
Line from eastern North Carolina to Pennsylvania. The group comprised
emissaries from Tuscarora towns in the Coastal Plain. After trekking to Pennsylvania, the group met with colonial officials and representatives of the
Haudenosaunee Confederacy, kindred people to the Tuscarora. The groups

gathered in June 1710 at the confluence of the Conestoga and Susquehanna Rivers, about seventy miles west of the colonial capital in Philadelphia. There, the group delivered eight specific pleas from several allied Tuscarora towns back in eastern North Carolina.[67]

By 1710, Indigenous territories in eastern North Carolina had swollen with colonists. Settlers left the estuarine shoreline and moved inland, appropriating Native farmland and hunting territories.[68] The Tuscarora representatives shared especially dire concerns about kidnapping and enslavement. Fueled by the demand for labor on colonial plantations in North America and in the Caribbean, Indigenous slave traders regularly raided Native communities in eastern North Carolina.[69] By 1710, kidnapping raids were so pervasive that they dominated the list of concerns brought by the Tuscarora emissaries on behalf of their communities.

The emissaries carried eight wampum belts from North Carolina to Pennsylvania.[70] Each belt represented a separate plea for help. The belts, assembled from white and purple shell beads, held beaded patterns that symbolized each plea. The belts themselves are lost, but their messages were transcribed by colonial officials. According to their report, one of the wampum belts represented concerns that elders could not walk in the woods, gather firewood, or draw water without fear of being attacked and killed at the slightest noise. Another belt cited the ever-present fear that Tuscarora children would be captured and enslaved. Together, the report sketches out the collective fears of a people who were no longer safe in their own lands. The Pennsylvania officials summarized this trauma in their explanation of the seventh belt, which had been sent "in order to intreat a Cessation from murdering & taking them, that by the allowance thereof, they may not be affraid [sic] of a mouse, or any other thing that Russles the Leaves."[71]

The messages contained in the wampum belts reveal a deeply traumatized people. The Tuscarora communities whom the emissaries represented were so worn down by kidnapping, killing, and colonial discord that they were willing to uproot from their ancestral homeland and seek refuge with their kin in the Northeast. The colonial officials reported that the Tuscarora emissaries asked both the Pennsylvania and Haudenosaunee representatives to "take them by the hand & lead them, & then they will lift up their heads in the woods without danger or fear."[72]

It is no small thing for Native people to leave their homeland. In the nineteenth century, the forced removals of Indigenous peoples from their ancestral homelands have spawned countless stories of unspeakable loss. Communities today are still processing the collective trauma inflicted by the atrocities of removal and the profound loss of home. That these Tuscarora communities even contemplated fleeing their homeland on the Coastal Plain hints at the desperation they faced.

While the emissaries pleaded their case in Pennsylvania, Tuscarora and other Native peoples back in North Carolina continued to face threats of murder and kidnapping.[73] Around the same time, Lawson returned to North Carolina from London with several hundred Swiss settlers, led by Christoph von Graffenreid. The new settlers planned to occupy lands along the Neuse River, but colonial records do not indicate whether Lawson or anyone else had actually negotiated arrangements with Tuscarora and other Native peoples. In any case, the influx of hundreds of newcomers would have placed further stress on managed game-lands, freshwater supplies, and other resources that had been—until recently—shared exclusively among Native peoples in the region. The unannounced arrival of the new settlers must have heightened tensions in Native communities that were already worn down by disease, kidnapping, and murder and fear for their continued survival.

Under these conditions, it is no surprise that in fall 1711, Lawson and von Graffenreid were apprehended by Native people while the pair were scouting for potential settlement sites in Tuscarora territory. Leaders from Tuscarora, Coree, Neusiok, and other groups traveled to a Tuscarora town where they put Lawson on trial. No one present ever gave an account of the proceedings to colonial authorities. Von Graffenreid, whom they later released, was not privy to the trial. Lawson's contemporaries and later historians went to great lengths to supply gory details based solely on speculation and rumor. But the only historical certainty is that John Lawson—travel writer and promoter of colonial exploitation—was executed by the people whose lands and waters he worked to appropriate.[74]

Perhaps the coalition of Native people decided to hold Lawson accountable for his role in the steady flow of unwanted settlers into their lands, or maybe he was put to death for some other offense. Regardless, they tried and executed Lawson according to their own standards of justice.[75] The trial took place in Tuscarora territory, where Lawson was—in the most charitable terms—a guest who was subject to Indigenous authority. After executing Lawson, the allied Native peoples of the region launched a series of raids on colonial settlements around the Pamlico and Neuse Rivers.[76]

The raids terrified North Carolina's colonial government, which called on both South Carolina and Virginia for help, adding that the first colony to send military aid could enslave any Native captives taken during the liberation of North Carolina.[77] South Carolina colonial officials eventually sent two separate militias north from Charleston. In 1712 and 1713, the militias, which comprised both Native and non-Native fighters, invaded the homelands of Tuscarora and other Native peoples in eastern North Carolina.

The militias, led by South Carolina colonists John Barnwell and James Moore, pillaged Native towns and farms as they moved across the Coastal Plain. They laid siege to defensive earthworks built by Tuscarora people and their allies. Moore's assault was exceptionally brutal. His militia slaughtered hundreds of Tuscarora people and their allies at Nooheroka, a massive earth and wood fortification along Contentnea Creek, a tributary of the Neuse River. As many as one thousand Indigenous men, women, and children had barricaded themselves inside the fortification.

After breaching the outer defenses at Nooheroka, Moore ordered his fighters to set the inner defenses on fire. They did, burning alive hundreds of Indigenous people who had barricaded themselves inside. Hundreds more escaped, only to be captured by Moore's fighters. Most of these were taken back to Charleston and sold into slavery. Colonial records are ambiguous and do not give clear estimates of the numbers of Native people killed and enslaved during the two military campaigns, but historians consider it among the most violent colonial conflicts in the Southeast.[78]

Native societies in this part of the Coastal Plain were virtually shattered in the aftermath of what anthropologist Anthony Wallace describes as "the killing fields of North Carolina."[79] Even before the war, a century of disease, warfare, and a seemingly endless stream of land-hungry settlers had left Native survivors fragmented, orphaned, and elder-less. Survivors of Nooheroka and those who evaded capture or death were reeling. Some of these survivors, along with the residents of several Tuscarora towns that had avoided the conflict, were ordered to reservations on the outer Coastal Plain under the terms of an exploitative agreement with the colonial government of North Carolina.[80] Other Native people moved farther into the interior during and immediately after the war.[81] Over the next few decades, many of the Tuscarora survivors and their descendants migrated north, becoming the sixth nation of the Haudenosaunee confederacy.

In 2013, to commemorate the three-hundredth anniversary of the war, Tuscarora people from the Northeast and Native people from North Carolina attended the dedication of a memorial to the massacre at Fort Nooheroka. The memorial is situated on a small wedge of land between two country roads a short distance from Snow Hill, a tiny community in Greene County. A metal sculpture evokes the entryway to a Haudenosaunee longhouse. Shell beads, tobacco, and other offerings have accumulated steadily near the sculpture's base over the past several years. Across one road lies the site of the fort itself, now a crop field that backs up to the heavily wooded floodplain along Contentnea Creek. Although it is a rural place, both roads can experience heavy traffic, and the memorial is not always quiet. But it is still a place of peace and reverence for Native people who come here to remember what happened to them and for others who come here to learn.

People—scholars and the general public—generally refer to the 1711–13 conflagration as the Tuscarora War, even though the conflict engulfed virtually all Indigenous peoples in North Carolina's Coastal Plain. Certainly, Tuscaroras made up the largest fraction of Native people in the region, but Coree, Bear River, Neusiok, Machapunga and other groups were involved in defending their homelands as well. The defenders spoke different languages and experienced cultural differences, but they were unified for a time by their opposition to colonial expansion in the Coastal Plain. In the aftermath of the war, some of the survivors remained unified by the shared trauma of the cataclysmic loss of friends, families, and homelands.

Collective trauma affects the survivors of war, genocide, and pandemics, and psychologists note that catastrophes cut deep into the bonds of society. Shared traumas can also shatter a group's sense of identity. Generations of descendants are sometimes left to forge and reforge social structures as they work to make sense of it all.[82] Indigenous survivors of the Tuscarora War—those who were not captured and enslaved—faced at least three different fates. Some accepted confinement on reservations, first near Lake Mattamuskeet and later along the lower Roanoke River on a tract that became known as Indian Woods. Others left the region and sought refuge among their Haudenosaunee kin in the Northeast. In time, they were joined by many of the reservation-dwellers from Indian Woods. Still other survivors dispersed deep into the Coastal Plain—distant swamps and backwaters that today are situated in Robeson County—and into other places that were poorly surveyed, poorly mapped, and generally avoided by settlers for the next several decades.

Tuscarora people made up many of the survivors, but among them were also Corees, Neusioks, and members of smaller Indigenous communities who had allied with the Tuscarora or who were otherwise swept up in the regional conflict. Survivors clung together amid vast riverine swamps, Carolina Bays and other wetlands. They found refuge in these remote places and in the new communities that they forged.

PALEOECOLOGISTS, SCIENTISTS WHO STUDY ecosystems in the distant past, use the term *refugia* to describe particular places where individual species or whole ecosystems can survive large-scale glaciation events or other unfavorable climate conditions.[83] Refugia are small pockets of land within much larger regions. They maintain the right balance of temperature, precipitation, and other environmental conditions that allow certain ecosystems to survive. Meanwhile, the world beyond becomes too hot, too cold, too wet, or too dry. North Carolina has its own examples of ecological refugia.

Millennia ago, during the last ice age, what is now North Carolina lay some ways south of the massive glaciers that covered parts of North America. Even though it was not covered by glaciers, the climate of North Carolina was cooler and wetter than it is today. Much of the region was covered by dense forests of conifers—mainly spruce, fir, and hemlock. The needle-leaf trees withstood heavy snow during the winter, and they thrived on cool, misty conditions in the summer. They were slow-growing trees, but they were hardy and well-adapted to the climate of the era. As Earth warmed and glaciers to the north melted away, North Carolina's climate grew warmer and drier. Slow-growing spruce, fir, and hemlock could no longer outcompete other species that were better adapted to warmer climates. A mix of deciduous trees and pines overtook spruce, fir, and hemlock nearly everywhere in the region. However, forests of spruce and fir retained a toehold on the highest peaks of the southern Appalachian Mountains, which today are located in western North Carolina and eastern Tennessee. Today, the slopes and rounded summits of mountains that rise higher than about 5,500 feet in elevation are draped in similar forests of spruce and fir that once covered a much larger region. Up there, winters are long and harsh. Summers are brief, cool, and misty. From a distance, the mountaintops look like islands of deep, dark green emerging from a sea of lighter-colored deciduous foliage. Outside of the high peaks of the southern Appalachian Mountains, one must travel to Maine or the Canadian Maritime provinces to find similar tracts of spruce and fir forest.

Meanwhile, hemlocks kept their footings in the deep, shady wrinkles of lower mountain slopes—coves shaped by intimate creeks and gorges carved by thundering rivers. Even east of the mountains, hemlocks survived on steep, north-facing slopes. In all of these places, microclimates continued to mimic conditions experienced in the region during the ice age. These isolated pockets are the last vestiges of a forest that once covered much of the Southeast. They are refugia.

People also find refugia. Instead of climate change, eighteenth-century colonial encounters brought disease, warfare, and displacement to Native peoples in what is now eastern North Carolina. Everything changed. Violence destroyed families and homes. It upended towns and social networks. Settlers overtook landscapes and waterways, modifying them for their own uses. Many Native people who pushed back against the colonial tide were met with death, enslavement, and brutality that splintered their communities. Some survivors responded by leaving the Coastal Plain or the Southeast entirely, but others found refugia. Lumbee ancestors found protection through isolation among wedges of high ground among the green forested swamps and blackwater streams in the place that became Robeson County. To settlers, they were unmapped places, interstitial lands. But to us, these places were home—backwaters amid swirling currents of colonialism.

Paleoecology teaches that refugia are not only physical places, but they also represent bottlenecks along a timeline. Large populations of trees, insects, birds, and more shrink down to tiny remnants during times of adversity, but when glaciers retreat and weather warms, populations rebound. If conditions permit, populations spring from their refugia into their former ranges or, perhaps, into new places with favorable soils and climate. Sometimes I imagine that Lumbee ancestors who sought refuge in the remotest parts of their lands were biding their time, waiting to spring forth into a radically transformed world.

The ecological metaphor is overly simplistic, but in some ways Lumbees and other Native people of the Coastal Plain have reemerged from our refugia in recent decades. Our ancestors weathered most of the eighteenth and nineteenth centuries in watery places of the Coastal Plain—our refugia. These places became imbued with immense historical and cultural value. The Lumbee River and its tributary swamps are especially holy shrines to my people, just as the Great Coharie, Waccamaw, Meherrin, and other rivers are to our neighbors. It is no wonder that so many Lumbees still call Robeson County "the Holy Land."[84] We reemerged permanently changed by colonialism, but we remember where we come from; we are the original people of the Coastal Plain.

Our ancestors suffered mightily, but they were not driven out or annihilated, they did not waste away or vanish, and they did not succumb to any other euphemisms that textbooks use to signal our extinction. We are still here, and in many cases, we continue to occupy our ancestral lands. Against the odds, we were not erased in the mythmaking of the United States. To acknowledge us is to understand something deeper about the Coastal Plain, the losses we endured, and our fight to survive as distinct peoples in relationship to places that are transforming rapidly because of pollution, climate change, and decisions that cause the destruction of our fragile and watery world.

It is appropriate, therefore, that a book about Native peoples and their present-day environmental challenges might begin by reimagining the idea of land acknowledgments. After all, no one can grasp the fullness of these struggles without first acknowledging the deep historical and cultural connections between Indigenous peoples and their homelands, including connections that have been altered and reshaped by colonialism.

Topics covered in the chapters of this book—ditching and draining, fossil fuels, industrialized livestock, climate change—are continuations of the colonial project that started centuries ago and persists today. If we acknowledge this continuity at the outset, the topics in this book will look less like a series of tragic events and more like the concerted effort that they represent—an ongoing attempt to complete the colonial project of erasing Indigenous peoples and our connections to the Coastal Plain. Awareness of the links between colonialism and environmental degradation must inform our response to all of these issues.

Indigenous survival in the face of erasure speaks to our resilience, adaptability, and—when necessary—an obstinance that has survived three centuries of oppression. So the next time you read or hear in a land acknowledgment that "these are the ancestral lands of . . ." remember that we never left. If that idea seems uncomfortable, feel free to take it up with the colonial authorities. If you do, please let one of us know. We might ask you to relay a message to the magistrate.

CHAPTER TWO

More Than One Way to Own a Thing
Indigenous Empowerment and Erasure

On March 18, 1973, a building that symbolized Indigenous peoples' endurance and achievement in Robeson County burned to a smoldering shell. The building, Old Main, was the first brick structure at Pembroke State University. It was erected in 1923 on the outskirts of Pembroke, a railroad town in western Robeson County.[1] Old Main's entryway, a portico supported by four white columns, looked out across railroad tracks onto Third Street. Large block letters above the columns spelled out "Pembroke State University" and welcomed visitors into town. The building held a six-hundred-person auditorium and a handful of classrooms—the largest indoor space accessible to Native Americans in Robeson County during the racially segregated decades of the twentieth century. The building was stately, but it was far from opulent. It was originally constructed using $50,000 in state-allocated funds.[2]

The story of Old Main's near-destruction—and its resurrection as a hub for American Indian studies in the Southeast—is important for understanding how Lumbee people think about their relationships to culturally significant places. Whether these places are historic buildings, natural landscapes, or something in between, we are rooted to them by way of gratitude for the sacrifices of our ancestors. We are rooted to these places out of respect for rivers as givers of life—and as takers. We are rooted to culturally significant places through the customs and habits that we inherited from our parents, grandparents, great-grandparents, and so on, from time immemorial.

Lumbee people nurture their relationships with culturally important places by visiting them regularly. Robeson County is dotted with river landings, cemeteries, homeplaces, and waysides that remind us of our generations-long responsibilities to steward land and water. We go to these places on special occasions, sometimes with extended families of elders and young children. Or we may go for no reason at all. We press our feet into the sandy earth, breathe the aroma of longleaf pine and red cedar, and absorb the smooth and radiant warmth of painted cinder blocks and worn wooden beams. And we listen to one another tell and retell the stories of these places.

Places, built and unbuilt, shape our collective identity as Lumbee people. These places include schools, churches, cemeteries, tobacco fields, and swamps, but they also include larger mosaics comprising patchworks of these various parts. Prospect is one of these mosaics, and so are Pembroke, Back Swamp, Union Chapel, Saddletree, and dozens of other settlements in and around Robeson County where most Lumbees still live today. These places are rich with stories, and storytelling is a powerful part of Lumbee culture. Stories lose some of their power when they become separated from the places they are about. Thankfully, Old Main holds on to many of its stories.[3]

In 1885, Lumbee ancestors collaborated with state legislator Hamilton McMillan on a bill to formally recognize the Native Americans of Robeson County as a tribe by North Carolina. Before that time, Lumbee ancestors had lived as a loose collective of extended families in several settlements interspersed among the swampy tributaries of the Lumbee River upstream of Lumberton.[4] McMillan, who grew up in Robeson County and had a longtime fascination with Lumbee ancestors, proposed *Croatan* as the name by which the state would recognize them.[5]

The statute that recognized Lumbee ancestors as the Croatan Tribe also set aside $500 in annual funds for their education. At that time, Native Americans in Robeson County had endured half a century of racial discrimination, first under North Carolina's discriminatory 1835 constitution and later as Reconstruction gave way to the Jim Crow era. For well over a century, white supremacist governments denied Lumbee ancestors equal access to education. Although Reconstruction brought a brief respite following the Civil War, many of these policies lasted until the early 1970s, when Robeson County schools finally integrated; they were some of the last schools in the United States to do so.[6]

In 1887, Native Americans in Robeson County used their allocation of state funds to launch a teacher training school on the sandy uplands between Bear Swamp and the Lumbee River.[7] Community leaders envisioned training a corps of teachers in a newly raised wooden schoolhouse to serve in Native-run schools throughout Robeson County.[8] The schoolhouse and the teachers it produced would be an antidote to decades of institutionalized racism that had left generations of Native people in Robeson County with no access to public education and few ways to make a living. They named the new institution *Croatan Normal School*.[9]

In 1973, more than eighty years after community members raised the wooden schoolhouse, the institution had changed names several times, expanded its mission substantially, and relocated to a much larger tract near Pembroke. Academic buildings and residence halls sprawled across former farmland and grew, symbiotically, with the Lumbee community. For decades under Jim Crow, Old Main's six-hundred-person auditorium had hosted not only academic lectures but also concerts, funerals, and other social events.[10] By the 1970s, Old Main had become careworn after half a century of heavy use.[11]

Unlike Carlisle, Haskell, and other Native American boarding schools of the late nineteenth century, Pembroke State was not created by the US government as an institution of assimilation.[12] The Carlisle Institute, founded by Richard Henry Pratt, spawned a nationwide collection of boarding schools that stripped language and culture from thousands of Native youth.[13] In contrast, the founders of Pembroke State were leaders within Robeson County's own Native community. They hoped to alleviate poverty and oppression through schooling on their own terms. Their initial vision, to train Native teachers to work within Robeson County, expanded steadily outward and gradually included services to other Native communities in North Carolina. By the early 1940s, Pembroke State College for Indians was the only four-year institution in the United States created by, and for, Native Americans.[14] In 1954, Pembroke became one of the first racially integrated colleges in the South. Despite its shift from an exclusive focus on Native students, Pembroke remained a vital part of the Lumbee community after campus integration.[15] It was still the default destination for college-bound Lumbees, and Old Main continued to serve an important role as a gathering space.

In 1971, campus administrators announced plans to incorporate the newly renamed Pembroke State University into North Carolina's reorganized statewide university system. The absorption of Pembroke State into the statewide system left Lumbee people without a collective say in campus affairs, although individual Lumbees continued to occupy high-profile positions in the administration. In particular, English Jones, a prominent Lumbee educator, served as university president during the transition. Following news of Pembroke State's absorption into the statewide system, Jones announced plans to demolish Old Main and to replace it with a new and improved performing arts center.[16] Anticipating that work would begin immediately, Jones condemned the aging building and ordered its utilities shut off and entrances padlocked.[17]

The plan to demolish Old Main drew vocal opposition from the Native community. A Lumbee-led grassroots movement floated an alternative: preserve the building as a museum to commemorate the university's founding as a Native American institution. President Jones and other administrators dismissed the plan, insisting that the Native community had no say in the fate of Old Main and citing state ownership of the building. Jones, in particular, insisted that Old Main was no different than any other property on campus.[18]

Jones shrugged off claims that Lumbees had a unique stake in Old Main's future, insisting that "local people have had no more in it than the people of any other county of this state who have been taxpayers and contribute to the general fund of the state."[19]

The grassroots movement intensified as Lumbees feared the building's impending demolition. Letters to the local newspaper, *The Robesonian*, criticized university leaders and renewed calls to preserve the building that had come to symbolize Native perseverance under the discriminatory policies of Jim Crow.[20] One letter-writer was James M. Locklear, a Lumbee from Pembroke who had not attended college. In his letter to *The Robesonian*, Locklear declared that the university "owes its very existence to the blood and sweat of Indian people who were trying to make a better life for their children." He elaborated: "In a generation (1940–1965) we went from a people with no college graduates to the only Indian group in the country with a solid middle class . . . Old Main is a living memorial to all of those 'just plain Indians' who did so much to change conditions here in Lumbee land. This landmark is proof to every young Indian that the cycle of poverty and despair can be broken."[21]

Another Lumbee, Danford Dial, a retired educator from Prospect, launched a petition that articulated specific demands of the growing grassroots movement. The petition called not only for a museum but also for a university program in Indigenous studies to be housed in a fully renovated Old Main. The petition spread rapidly and received more than seven thousand signatures, which Dial claimed to have gathered in a single week.[22] The call to save Old Main received national attention, including support from the National Congress of American Indians (NCAI), a powerful intertribal voice. In 1972, the organization's executive director spoke at a preservation rally in Pembroke. The NCAI also sent a telegram to North Carolina's governor declaring, "Indians everywhere have an interest in the Old Main Building at Pembroke State University."[23]

Eventually, university administrators caved to pressure from the grassroots movement.[24] They found a new location for the new performing arts center, and they backed away from plans to demolish Old Main. President Jones insisted, though, that no state funds were available to renovate the condemned building.[25] Nevertheless, in early 1973, many Lumbees remained optimistic that continued pressure from the community would motivate university administrators to change their minds and seek funding for the building's renovation. In March of that year, Henry Ward Oxendine, the first Lumbee elected to the state legislature, announced that he would lead the efforts himself from

Raleigh.[26] The loosely organized Lumbee movement had built substantial momentum in a short time, and they seemed to be on the cusp of securing the building's future.

Hopes were high for the coming renovation when, shortly before dawn on Sunday, March 18, 1973, a campus security guard spotted a light inside the windows of Old Main's auditorium. On closer inspection, he saw flames. The security guard summoned the local fire department, and an anxious crowd gathered along Third Street in the growing light to watch firefighters quell the blaze. Firefighters doused the building for hours, and by midmorning, the fire in the auditorium seemed to be extinguished. Fire crews withdrew, and most of the bystanders headed off to Sunday church services.[27]

The respite was brief. By noon, the moderate breeze had grown into a strong wind. Pine trees on the grassy quad outside Old Main swayed in gusts that exceeded thirty miles per hour, and buried embers within the auditorium rekindled into open flame.[28] Before long, the building was fully engulfed. This time, nearly every fire department in Robeson County responded. As firefighters sent jets of water arcing over the two-story brick walls and wooden portico, stiff winds threatened to spread the conflagration to adjacent buildings. Efforts soon turned from extinguishing the blaze to containing it to a single structure. A crowd gathered, even larger than before, to watch curtains of smoke and steam billow from Old Main's roof.

When the fire was ultimately extinguished around three o'clock Sunday afternoon, Old Main was gutted. Its brick shell was intact, but most of the woodwork had been consumed by fire or ruined by smoke and water. The roof had collapsed entirely, and sunlight flooded the charred, dripping remains of what had been the auditorium. Flames had consumed much of the portico, and only a few remnants of painted letters had survived the blistering heat. The portico's columns, however, were unburned. The columns still faced Third Street, where a crowd of onlookers-turned-mourners grew as the afternoon wore on.

That evening, the recently inaugurated governor of North Carolina, Jim Holshouser, drove two hours from Raleigh to Pembroke to meet with the stunned community.[29] Holshouser brought with him the director of the State Bureau of Investigation, who promised to follow up on early suspicions of arson. Holshouser and the investigator briefly toured the smoldering ruins with local officials. Afterward, the governor addressed onlookers from the front steps of Old Main. The building's unburned pillars served as a backdrop to Holshouser's brief speech, in which he acknowledged the Native community's loss and pledged state support to find the suspected arsonists.[30] A few days later, the governor met with Native leaders in Raleigh where he also pledged state support for restoring Old Main as a museum and home for an Indigenous studies program.[31]

Although the arsonists were never brought to justice, Holshouser made good on his promise to restore Old Main. Three years later, the governor announced $1.6 million in state funding for the restoration.[32] In 1979, Old Main reopened as a home for the long-anticipated museum and a new academic program in American Indian Studies. In the decades since, the building has become a hub for scholarship and community outreach focused on Lumbees and, increasingly, on other Native peoples of the Southeast. The most recent reboot to the Museum of the Southeastern American Indian added an interactive storytelling area—a testament to the power of story in Lumbee culture.

The story of Old Main holds important lessons about Lumbee people and our relationships to particular places that mark key historical moments and cultural phenomena. Old Main is a quintessential example. The building itself embodied the struggles and sacrifices of Lumbees to educate their children amidst harsh racial segregation. It was, as James Locklear described the building, a "living memorial." The story teaches that Lumbees will go to great lengths to preserve culturally significant places, and they can have bold and progressive visions for how to steward these places. Moreover, Old Main shows that Lumbees can be undeterred by lack of legal ownership when it comes to advocating for their history and culture. So it is with places throughout the Lumbee world—built spaces like Old Main, and unbuilt spaces like the Lumbee River and its flanking swamps.

The story also reveals the precarious position of Lumbees when it comes to the community's collective voice in decisions about historically and culturally significant places. President English Jones correctly observed that the state government held the deed to the property, which meant that legal stewardship of Old Main fell to administrators, trustees, and state officials. Jones and a handful of other Lumbees may have occupied important roles at the university, but they had no obligation to represent Lumbee people as a collective. Simply put, Lumbees lacked a formal, collective voice in decision-making about Old Main; no legal or policy mechanisms mandated the inclusion of Lumbee people in discussions about the building's fate.

Lumbee people, as a collective, may have lacked legal standing in discussions about the fate of Old Main, but they certainly held moral and cultural claims to the building. Ruth Revels, a Lumbee teacher living in Greensboro,

North Carolina, articulated these claims clearly in a January 1972 letter to *The Robesonian*, published soon after President Jones padlocked the doors to Old Main. In her letter, Revels admitted that Jones was probably right about the economic infeasibility of preservation. Nevertheless, she disagreed with his plan. More importantly, Revels disputed Jones' assertion that Lumbee people had no collective stake in Old Main's fate. She wrote, "Regardless of who paid for Old Main, it belongs to the Lumbee Indians and all others who love it and would like to see it preserved. There is more than one way to own a thing. Some of the most precious things we all own were not bought and paid for with money. Old Main belongs to me. I do not want to see it destroyed."[33]

Revels encapsulated the idea that ownership is about more than who holds the deed to a property. Her letter reveals something about Lumbee moral and cultural claims to a building that Lumbee people may not have financed but still owned in their own way. Lumbee ancestors had, after all, imagined and realized a Native-serving institution in the midst of a white supremacist society. As Revels and other Lumbees argued, Old Main—and the university as a whole—would never have existed without the collective efforts of Lumbee ancestors.[34] They supplied not only vision and leadership but also sweat, materials, and political advocacy to sustain the institution for decades prior to its absorption into the statewide university system. Old Main was precious to Lumbees not because they counted its value in dollars, but because the building embodied their ancestors' efforts to ensure that future generations of Native people were educated and equipped to survive in a colonized world.[35]

As the descendants of the first peoples of the Coastal Plain, Lumbees have moral and cultural claims not only to historical buildings but also to natural landscapes, including swamps and streams that have shaped our identities as Indigenous peoples since time immemorial. These claims, however, are largely ignored by current laws and policies that deal with property rights, historic preservation, and more. Just as Lumbee people did not (and still do not) hold the legal title to Old Main, Lumbees also do not hold the title to the vast majority of the patchwork of densely forested wetlands and sandy interstitial uplands that make up their homelands in Robeson County. Nevertheless, the Coastal Plain is—and has always been—our home.

Lumbee people have a long history of organizing to face challenges to families, to communities, and to larger landscapes that we call home. Leaders such as Danford Dial and Ruth Revels emerge periodically to inspire and to speak truth to power. Although these leaders are often effective at advancing many of the shared values and priorities of Lumbee people, they have worked under major disadvantages. One of the disadvantages involves the status of Lumbees under a 1956 federal law, which recognized Lumbee people as Indigenous but barred the tribe from a formal relationship with the United States. The real disadvantages of this bizarre status have emerged in recent decades, as the United States has begun to pay a modicum of attention to the sovereignty of Indigenous peoples.

The remainder of this chapter examines policies around Indigenous rights and environmental justice in the United States today. These policies influence whether and how Lumbees and our Indigenous neighbors engage in discussions about the preservation and stewardship of historically and culturally significant places, whether built or unbuilt. Increasingly, these discussions—which are typically conducted between government agencies and large corporations with little or no tribal participation—have major implications for the fate of the Lumbee River, its tributary swamps, and other parts of our ancestral homelands on the Coastal Plain.

Up to now, Lumbee people and their Indigenous neighbors have had virtually no meaningful involvement in any of the discussions around environmental policies, planning, or permits that impact our lands and waters. Unfortunately, the exclusion of Indigenous peoples from these kinds of discussions is a vicious cycle that feeds cultural loss and weakens sovereignty. But the good news is that Native peoples of the Coastal Plain are beginning to recognize this form of erasure. And the story of Old Main shows that Native voices can be difficult to drown out once they join together.

A VARIETY OF FACTORS CONTRIBUTE to the absence of Lumbee voices from important discussions about the fate of culturally important landscapes and waterways. One key element is the legal framework that currently governs the Lumbee Tribe's relationship with the federal government. To put it more accurately, this legal framework governs the tribe's non-relationship with the federal government. The framework—singularly unique in federal Indian law and policy—creates a situation in which Lumbee values and perspectives rarely show up in federal environmental and cultural studies for infrastructure projects that affect us. Similarly, Lumbee values and perspectives are absent from federal policies that shape the future of our homelands, including policies on energy, agriculture, water, and climate change. Even as the federal government begins to pay a modicum of respect to the rights of Indigenous peoples to determine the fate of culturally important places, Lumbee people are left behind. With that in mind, the Lumbee Tribe's unique status deserves a closer look.

In May 1956, the United States Congress passed a bill to recognize Native Americans living in Robeson County as Lumbee Indians. The next month, President Eisenhower signed the bill into law. Public Law 84–570, often called the *Lumbee Act*, is not lengthy; its four hundred words barely occupy one page in the Federal Register.[36] Despite its brevity, the Lumbee Act still looms large over Lumbee political identity decades after its passage. On one hand, the federal law affirms that Lumbee people are Native Americans. On the other, the Lumbee Act prohibits a formal, government-to-government relationship between the United States and the Lumbee Tribe. Because the Lumbee Act both gives and takes, it is a bizarre half measure of federal recognition. No other tribe in the United States occupies a similar position. Vine Deloria Jr., who spent decades advocating for Congress to amend the law, called it an "anomaly in Federal Indian legislation."[37]

Lumbee ancestors began to seek federal recognition as far back as 1888, soon after they were recognized by North Carolina as Croatan Indians. That year, a group of Native leaders from Robeson County traveled to Washington, DC, to seek recognition as a tribe, mainly for additional education funding. They were sent away empty-handed; the Commissioner of Indian Affairs advised Congress, "I find it quite impractical to render any assistance at this time."[38]

In the decades between the 1880s and 1950s, Lumbee ancestors endured repeated scrutiny by anthropologists and ethnographers commissioned by the federal government. Individual Lumbees were subjected to a parade of genealogical and anthropometric examinations. Deloria recounted the most widely reported of these research campaigns, led by Harvard-based anthropologist, Carl Seltzer:

> When they visited Pembroke, North Carolina, during the 1930s to identify the ancestry of the Lumbee Indians who lived in that vicinity, BIA [Bureau of Indian Affairs] anthropologists used a foolproof method of verifying Indian ancestry. Using a study of the Blackfeet Indians that gave the average measurement of their heads, the BIA anthropologists, after much work measuring Lumbee craniums, announced that twenty-two Lumbees qualified as Indians because their measurements perfectly correlated with the average Blackfeet skull. Recognizing that these people could not possibly be Blackfeet, the BIA pronounced them to be lost "Tuscaroras," and they were formally recognized as Indians. The possible ancestry of the remainder of the Lumbees, including the siblings of the people identified as Indians, remained in doubt. Fortunately, the Blackfeet did not have to satisfy the same morphological criteria.[39]

Deloria's characteristically humorous account highlights the arbitrary nature of Seltzer's methods, but Lumbee Historian Malinda Maynor Lowery describes more fully the invasiveness of the anthropometric examination:

> Each applicant stood on a platform while Seltzer conducted a number of tests. He inspected for freckles, moles, and body hair, and he opened each subject's mouth to see their overbite and the shape of their teeth. He asked subjects to expose the skin on their inner arm, and he noted whether it was "red-brown," "brunet," "light-brown," or a variety of other shades. He measured their earlobes, the tips of their noses, the length from shoulder to hip, and the width of their chests. He felt their hair and noted its form—"straight," "low-wave," "curly," "frizzy," "wooly"—and its texture—"coarse," "medium," "fine." He scratched each one on the breastbone, looking for the color of the mark left behind. Supposedly, a reddish mark indicated mixed blood.[40]

Deloria and Lowery both explain that Seltzer's methods were not only unscientific by today's standards, but they were also irrelevant to the question of Indigenous identity—a characteristic not carried in hair texture or skin color. Nevertheless, Seltzer's work—together with the work of other early twentieth-century anthropologists and ethnographers—answered the federal government's questions about Lumbee identity. According to the 1956 Act, Lumbees were an Indigenous group of mixed ancestry.

When the Lumbee Act passed, it first seemed to be the zenith of a seventy-year struggle by Lumbee people to gain a formal relationship with the United States. But first appearances were deceptive. Prior to final votes in the House and Senate, the bill was modified, at the request of the Bureau of Indian Affairs, to add the following text: "Nothing in this Act shall make such Indians eligible for any services performed by the United States for Indians because of their status as Indians, and none of the statutes of the United States which affect Indians because of their status as Indians shall be applicable to the Lumbee Indians."[41]

The restrictive clause reflected the United States' policy toward Indigenous peoples during the 1950s—termination. During the termination era, the federal government actively sought ways to reduce or even eliminate its formal responsibilities toward tribal nations. In some cases, the federal government severed relationships outright; "terminated" tribes had their reservation lands—including water and mineral rights—broken up and distributed to individual tribal members.[42] In doing so, Congress hoped to force the assimilation of Native peoples into society. Having failed to "kill the Indian" through boarding schools and twentieth-century policy experiments, the federal government looked to termination as a way to divest, once and for all, of its duties toward Indigenous peoples within the United States.

Thus, the decades-long effort by Lumbee people to gain federal status could not have come at a worse time. The United States acknowledged Lumbees as Indigenous people, but it would not enter into a government-to-government relationship with the Lumbee Tribe as a Native nation. The resulting legislation—which forbids a political relationship between Lumbee people and the United States—has produced decades of frustration for Lumbees. Bruce Barton, Lumbee and editor of the *Carolina Indian Voice*, channeled that frustration when he wrote in 1974, "Ever who wrote that evil sentence into the original 1956 Lumbee Bill hated Indians and Shakespeare. It is wretched syntax . . . and logic."[43]

In recent years, the political implications of the Lumbee Act have spilled into the arena of environmental governance. Federal regulators, looking to fulfill the bare minimum legal requirements related to cultural preservation and tribal engagement, have recently cited the 1956 law's termination clause to justify decisions not to consult with the tribal government prior to authorizing harmful and polluting projects in Lumbee communities.[44] It is a frightening precedent, and it also ignores the fact that recognition status does not determine the strength of Indigenous peoples' connections to the places they come from. The precedent also feeds a downward spiral of cultural loss by limiting the tools available for Lumbees to protect their culturally important places. As these places are degraded and destroyed—often through federally sanctioned activities—Lumbee people slowly lose connections to the places that shape and inform their identity as a distinct, sovereign people.

Lumbee leaders have spent decades attempting to persuade Congress to amend the 1956 Lumbee Act by striking the termination-era language and affirming the fully recognized status of the Lumbee Tribe of North Carolina. Such an amendment would place the tribe on equal footing with other federally recognized tribal nations. To be certain, that footing is still shaky when it comes to meaningful protections of places that are culturally and historically important to Native peoples, but it is a start. In any case, the contours of the Lumbee Act—including its limitations and the baggage that accompanies it—define the unique situation of Lumbee people when it comes to the protection and stewardship of Robeson County's environment.

The Lumbee Tribe's unique status with the federal government limits ways in which Lumbee people can advocate, collectively, to protect culturally important places. But the destruction of Lumbee cultural heritage has gone on for much longer than the decades since Congress passed the 1956 Lumbee Act. For centuries, Lumbee homelands on the Coastal Plain have been picked over by looters, plowed under by farmers, and abused or neglected in countless ways. Researchers and other outsiders have long obsessed over Lumbee origins and identity, often to the extent that Lumbee voices are drowned out of important conversations about cultural preservation, environmental protection, and our ability to survive as a distinct people with living connections to our ancestral homelands.

Outsiders are perennially obsessed with Lumbee history and culture. Many Indigenous readers will find this kind of obsession familiar, and they will recognize some of the side effects—targeting by extractive research, cultural appropriation, and myriad other ways that outsiders fetishize our identities. In this respect, the Lumbee experience is not unique. But Lumbees experience a distinct flavor of obsession because of the ways that we defy stereotypes about Native Americans. Lumbees were not forcibly removed from our homelands following the Indian Removal Act of 1830.[45] We did not fit the white supremacist narrative of a black and white racial binary in the Jim Crow South.[46] We speak English, but with an accent that does not meet the preconceptions of people who are expecting Hollywood stereotypes. The obsession goes far beyond healthy curiosity and has created all kinds of mischief.

For more than a century, researchers of all stripes have focused their collective gaze on Lumbee identity. Generations of amateur historians and genealogists have speculated, sometimes wildly, about our origins. A common theme is an almost grail-like quest to divine the mixed racial ancestry of Lumbee people. Lumbees know that we descend from Indigenous peoples who fled war, disease, enslavement, and dispossession during early waves of colonization. We also descend from European Americans and African Americans who found their way into these remote enclaves and became part of Native families and communities. This is not a mystery, and it is not unique among Native peoples in eastern North America. What makes the situation unique is that outsiders have long used Lumbee people to advance their own—often unsubstantiated—hypotheses and conjectures about race, ethnicity, and indigeneity in the South.[47]

Lumbee people sometimes shrug off the obsessive gaze of outsiders, asserting that they do not need researchers or government agents to tell them who they are. I understand this position, but the issue is larger than whether Lumbees feel a personal need for outsiders to validate their Indigenous identity. As a general rule, we do not. The larger issue is that outsider obsessions, which manifest in various ways ranging from extractive research and cultural appropriation to the literal extraction of our ancestors' remains from the earth, hinder the efforts to amend the 1956 Lumbee Act, which currently limits our ability to advocate for environmental protection, cultural preservation, and the stewardship of our homelands.[48]

It is hard to understate the obsession over Lumbee identity and how it has led to cultural loss for our people. The fixation has been around for well over a century. In 1860, twenty-three-year-old Hamilton McMillan—the same man who later advocated for state recognition under the Croatan name—won a prize at the Cumberland County Fair for a "specimen of Bones from an Indian Mound near Rockfish." Rockfish is a community just across the Cumberland County line from Robeson County, not too far from McMillan's home in Red Springs. The burial mound mentioned here is part of a larger complex of cultural sites scattered throughout the Coastal Plain. Unlike the Mississippians, who constructed large ceremonial mounds, often topped with pavilions or other structures, eastern Woodland peoples of the Coastal Plain created relatively small earthen mounds, several meters across and less than a meter high, to inter the remains of their departed relatives. Sometimes the mounds were ossuaries—secondary burial sites—where bones were carefully reinterred alongside valuables, offerings, and sacred objects. Mounds contained the remains of dozens—or in some cases hundreds—of humans. In 1860, the local newspaper described McMillan's desecration of one of these burial sites as casually as it noted the prizewinner for the county's best bushel of sweet potatoes.[49]

McMillian, who is often revered as a champion for Native people, was also a grave robber who exhumed Indigenous ancestral remains, dusted them off, and entered them in a local competition. He was not a trained archaeologist or anthropologist—not that these credentials would have legitimized his actions. Whether he exhumed remains to satisfy his curiosity, to entertain his friends and neighbors, or for some other purpose, it bears repeating that McMillan looted sacred sites and caused irreplaceable harm.

Unfortunately, McMillan's actions were fairly typical of the time. From the mid-nineteenth century through the early twentieth century, an epidemic of grave robbing raged across eastern North Carolina. Newspapers of the era are littered with reports of mound "openings"—a euphemism for exhuming human remains and looting graves. Reports of "openings" are routine enough that they suggest the activity was a casual pastime in eastern North Carolina, especially for white businessmen and landowners. In 1910, the *Wilmington Morning Star* reported that newspaper publisher E. D. Pearsall arrived at a convention in town with a jug of scuppernong wine that he proudly claimed to have extracted from a seventeenth-century burial mound in Pender County, located between Robeson County and Wilmington.[50] He boasted that the drink was a gift for Josephus Daniels, editor of Raleigh's *News & Observer*.[51] The stories of McMillan and Pearsall stand out because of their connections to Lumbee ancestors, but they are two of myriad newspaper reports from the period. Most come from the eastern United States, and nearly all of them celebrate the macabre spectacle of looting Indigenous burials.

Not all grave robbing was amateur. As late as the 1960s, professional anthropologists and archaeologists excavated mounds in eastern North Carolina. The October 1966 issue of *Southern Indian Studies* includes a pair of articles about the excavation of another mound in Cumberland County, where McMillan had displayed human remains at the fair a century before. The first article gives a clinical description of the exhumation process. Human bones were extracted from the mound using hand tools and packed into an array of makeshift containers, including fruit baskets and shoe boxes. The packed boxes were shipped to Washington, DC, for further study at the Smithsonian Institution. The second article in the pair describes the remains as they were received by Smithsonian researchers, who had not participated in the field campaign. The Smithsonian researchers deemed the human remains largely useless for research because of their advanced stage of decomposition—a phenomenon typical of buried objects in the humid climate of the Southeast. After a cursory examination, the lead Smithsonian researcher reported in the journal *Southern Indian Studies* that he decided to keep a small amount of exhumed human remains. He wrote, "Only the calvaria, the cremations, and a few specimens showing pathological changes, anomalies, etc., were saved for future reference; everything else was discarded immediately."[52]

Nowadays, when I travel from Raleigh to Robeson County, I often stop at one of several historic Lumbee cemeteries where my direct ancestors are buried. In the centuries since colonization began, Lumbee people have adopted Christian religious traditions, including common Euro-American burial practices. In the cemeteries, I wander freely among the rows of tombstones. Sand spurs and fire ants notwithstanding, these are some of the most serene and quiet places in Robeson County. Very often, they are places of deep mourning and sadness, and I know what it means to stand among the tombstones with a crowd of mourners. But other times, the cemeteries of Robeson County are places of quiet reflection.

Two feelings usually come to mind in the stillness, where I am surrounded by etched granite, artificial flowers, and the open skies of Robeson County. First, I am grateful to be surrounded by the remains of my ancestors. Some were relatives—grandparents, aunts, uncles, and cousins—whom I knew personally. Others were ancestors from centuries prior who died before I was born. I know them only through stories. I am grounded by a sense of gratitude that comes with physical proximity to the remains of my ancestors. Second, I regret that the oldest Lumbee cemeteries that I can visit barely scratch the surface of our tenure in this place. Burial mounds represent millennia of Indigenous ancestry in the Coastal Plain. More than a century of desecration by treasure hunters, thrill seekers, and researchers has left many of these sacred sites in ruins. Others were simply plowed under or mined for sand. These were the remains of our ancestors—picked over, pored over, and tilled into oblivion. It is no exaggeration when Vivette Jeffries-Logan, a member of the Occaneechi Band of Saponi Nation, opens her public talks in North Carolina by declaring, "I stand on the dust of the bones of my ancestors. I am home."[53]

The systematic destruction of sites that are sacred to Lumbee people and other Indigenous peoples of the Coastal Plain is emotionally traumatic, but it also damages the collective identity of Lumbees and other groups with deep, ancestral connections to colonized places. Historian Tom Arne Midtrød argues that the desecration of sacred sites during the nineteenth and early twentieth centuries was a key method of colonialism because it erased evidence of Indigenous peoples' physical presence in their ancestral lands, and it also promoted Euro-American mythologies about the inevitable replacement of Indigenous peoples by settlers. Midtrød described widespread grave desecration that followed the forced removal of Native American tribes from the eastern United States.[54]

Even though Lumbees and our Indigenous neighbors in the Piedmont and Coastal Plain were not directly affected by the Indian Removal Act of 1830, their identities were heavily impacted by the culture of grave robbing that swept through the United States following expropriation of Native lands for the benefit of settlers.[55] Potawatomi scholar Kyle Powys Whyte explains that settler colonialism is not an abstract concept; it involves "physical, material, and ecological excavation."[56] The literal excavation of Indigenous peoples' remains serves as a visceral and traumatic example.

THE UNITED STATES has a collection of laws and policies that protect ancestral remains and sites of cultural significance for federally recognized Native American tribes. The federal government places substantial limitations on tribal sovereignty, but it has also taken steps to create a legal duty to consult with federally recognized tribes on matters that affect their communities and homelands. Lumbees are excluded from these legal and political protections, or at least our inclusion is entirely up to the discretion of federal officials who oversee specific permitting actions or implementations of policy. So what are Lumbees missing?

The National Historic Preservation Act is a federal law that was initially designed to protect historical and cultural sites from "ever-increasing extensions of urban centers, highways, and residential, commercial and industrial developments."[57] Although the original version of the law, passed in 1966, did not mention Native peoples or their histories and cultures, updated legislation has clarified that the law intends to protect sites of historic and cultural significance to Indigenous peoples. Federal regulators sometimes describe these sites as "traditional cultural landscapes" to acknowledge that they are often larger and more diffuse than an individual delineated property such as a building or a battlefield.[58]

Section 106 of the National Historic Preservation Act requires federal agencies to consult, formally, with federally recognized tribes about traditional cultural landscapes or other sites that could be affected by the federal government's actions. These actions include things like construction on federal lands, direct federal spending on development activities, or issuing environmental permits to corporations. One prominent recent example of the Section 106 tribal consultation requirement is linked to the Dakota Access Pipeline. The project, undertaken by a private company, required a permit from the US Army Corps of Engineers to cross the Missouri River. The environmental assessment conducted by the Corps prior to issuing the permit triggered a requirement for the agency to consult with any tribes that may have cultural and historical ties to lands that would be affected by the pipeline's construction or operation.[59] In 2016, the Standing Rock and Cheyenne River Sioux Tribes brought legal action against the federal government on the grounds that the Corps did not consult meaningfully with the tribes prior to issuing the permit.

Section 106 of the National Historic Preservation Act entitles federally recognized tribes to consultation with federal agencies whenever the agencies conduct environmental reviews, but there are more expansive policies that require tribal consultation any time the federal government takes actions that could impact tribal peoples' lands. In 2000, President Bill Clinton signed an executive order directing federal agencies to "engage in regular and meaningful consultation and collaboration with tribal officials" on policies and actions that have implications for tribes.[60] The order emphasized the government-to-government nature of US-tribal relations, and it aimed to make sure that tribes had a seat at the table where important decisions might be made about them. The federal government has refreshed its policies on consultation multiple times since the 2000 executive order, most recently in 2021, when President Biden charged federal agencies with developing formal action plans to ensure that tribal consultation was embedded in federal policies and actions.[61]

Environmental permits like the one at the center of the Dakota Access Pipeline controversy represent only one example of federal actions that require government-to-government consultation between tribes and the United States. Any activity that requires federal authorization or funding and may impact the historic or present-day territories of federally recognized tribes triggers consultation. Many of these activities involve infrastructure; freeways planned and constructed with federal dollars trigger the consultation requirement, as do natural gas pipelines that require federal authorizations. Even the decommissioning of infrastructure—including the demolition of hydropower dams to restore rivers to their natural states—triggers consultation if the activities have implications for tribes.

Often, the trigger for tribal consultation on federally authorized projects traces to the National Historic Preservation Act, a law often associated with the preservation of colonial-era buildings or historic districts of some towns. The law certainly protects these kinds of sites, but it also recognizes other categories of historical significance, including properties that have cultural significance to Native Americans.

One key reason that tribal consultation is mandated under Section 106 of the National Historic Preservation Act is to ensure that sites are not overlooked that may be eligible for listing on the National Register of Historic Places, a list of places deemed worthy of preserving for their historic or cultural significance. The register was set up by the National Historic Preservation Act, and individuals or groups (including tribes) can nominate sites for listing on the register. Sites receive a modicum of protection, but it is quite slim compared to protections that accompany National Park or National Monument designation; it merely prompts additional scrutiny of the potential impacts of activities that use federal funding or require federal permits. Part of this scrutiny involves consultation with federally recognized tribes prior to making decisions about whether to expend federal dollars or issue permits for activities that could harm historically or culturally significant places.

In 1976, three years after the fire that consumed Old Main, state officials nominated the building's charred remains for listing on the National Register of Historic Places (figure 2.1).[62] Even in its ruined state, the building was

FIGURE 2.1 Old Main after the fire, 1973. Courtesy of the State Archives of
North Carolina.

accepted onto the list. No federally funded or federally authorized projects
threatened the building in the decades that followed, so there has never been
a test of the protections—meager as they are—offered by the building's listed
status. Today, Old Main is one of approximately one thousand properties on
the National Register listed because of their historic or cultural significance
to Native Americans. Another fifty or so have significance to Native Hawaiians
or other Pacific Islanders.[63] In total, the National Register includes more than
ninety-six thousand properties throughout the United States and its territories. These numbers mean that barely 1 percent of the list reflects properties
that tell the stories of Indigenous peoples. I can't help but keep these numbers in mind when I read the federal government's description of the National Register as "the official list of the Nation's historic places worthy of
preservation."[64]

Interestingly, the National Historic Preservation Act offers some protection
to culturally important sites even if they are not listed on the National Register.
The law requires consultation with tribal governments over eligible sites regardless of their listing status. Moreover, the Act recognizes categories beyond build-

ings and historic districts. These categories include cultural landscapes and traditional cultural properties—broader areas that, as a whole, have spiritual, cultural, or historic significance to Indigenous peoples. Sacred rock formations, sections of coastlines or rivers, and sweeping vistas are all examples of sites that may qualify under these categories. In 2010, the Keeper of the National Register determined that the entirety of Nantucket Sound (Massachusetts) was eligible for listing as a traditional cultural property because of its significance to the Mashpee Wampanoag and Aquinnah Tribes.[65]

Unfortunately, none of the federal requirements around tribal consultation apply to non-federally recognized tribes. The Lumbee Tribe is included here as a non-federally recognized tribe because of the restrictive language of the 1956 law, and the exclusion also applies to our Indigenous neighbors on the Coastal Plain who have state recognition but not federal recognition. These include the Coharie, Meherrin, and Waccamaw Siouan Tribes in the Coastal Plain and the Sappony, Occaneechi Band of Saponi, and Haliwa-Saponi Tribes in the adjacent Piedmont region. State-recognized tribes in Virginia and South Carolina also fall into this category, and so do completely unrecognized Indigenous groups like the Tuscarora Nation of North Carolina and the Chowanoke Indian Nation.

Instead of mandating tribal consultation with unrecognized tribes, the federal government issues nonbinding guidance that recommends engagement. The federal Advisory Council on Historic Preservation is one such group that has issued guidance in recent years to remind federal decision-makers about the "deep knowledge of the history and resources in their homelands" that is held, collectively, by unrecognized tribes. The council emphasizes that tribes, regardless of their recognition status, can enrich efforts to identify historic properties and to evaluate potential impacts on those properties due to federal actions. To be clear, the United States is legally bound to consult only with federally recognized tribes, but the council and other bodies strongly urge agencies to accommodate unrecognized tribes that could be impacted by federal permitting and decision-making.[66]

Despite encouragement from the Advisory Council on Historic Preservation, federal regulators routinely omit non-federally recognized tribes from decision-making about policies, permits, and other actions that impact tribal lands and communities. Chapter 4 of this book devotes substantial attention to this issue.

One of the tragic outcomes of the omission is that unrecognized tribes end up sidelined while decisions are made that either destroy their cultural resources or make it difficult to maintain their ties to culturally important places. At the same time, these cultural connections to place often form part of the voluminous evidence that tribes must assemble to petition for federal recognition. The tribes are caught in a tragic cycle of cultural decay.

North Carolina is an exceptionally important place to consider the implications of omitting Indigenous voices from decision-making; more than 130,000 people in the state identified as single-race American Indians in the latest census, which—by this very conservative measure—gives the state one of the largest Indigenous populations in the United States. There are eight state-recognized tribes with populations ranging from several hundred (Occaneechi Band of Saponi and Meherrin) to more than sixty thousand (Lumbee). The state recognizes four urban Native groups, which function as oases for individuals from all tribal nations (North Carolina-based or not) who find themselves living in the state's major urban centers.

The eight tribes and four urban organizations all hold seats on the North Carolina Commission of Indian Affairs, the collective intertribal voice in state government. Notably, the Lumbee Tribe is one of the ten largest tribes in the United States, even with its half measure of recognition. Only the Eastern Band of Cherokee, in the far western corner of the state, has full federal recognition in addition to state recognition. Tribes currently centered elsewhere claim parts of North Carolina as their ancestral home, and other tribal communities exist in the state without any formal recognition whatsoever. It is truly Indian Country, yet relatively little happens here in terms of meaningful tribal engagement in environmental decision-making.[67]

Tribal consultation is not a panacea—far from it. Evidence abounds that US consultation policies are merely box-checking exercises, as United Nations' Special Rapporteur Victoria Tauli-Corpuz described it in 2017 following visits to tribal communities throughout the western United States. Tauli-Corpuz documented their experiences with government-to-government consultation on energy project permits and related actions and found persistent communication breakdowns and a general failure of the government to engage in good faith with tribal nations. She reminded US officials, "The goal of tribal consultation is not simply to check a box, or to merely give tribes a chance to be heard. Rather, the core objective is to provide federal decision makers with context, information, and perspectives needed to support informed decisions that actually protect tribal interests."[68]

Tauli-Corpuz also reminded officials about the commitment to protect the collective rights of Indigenous peoples that had been made when the United States affirmed the United Nations' Declaration on the Rights of

Indigenous Peoples (UNDRIP). The declaration is a remarkable global framework that aims to empower the protection of—among other things — relationships between Indigenous peoples and the lands and waters that they call home. The preamble of UNDRIP recognizes that Indigenous peoples must have some control over their own territories "to maintain and strengthen their institutions, cultures and traditions."[69]

The declaration was initially ratified in 2007 by every U.N. member nation except the United States, Canada, Australia, and New Zealand—countries that have had especially fraught histories of settler colonialism. One of the key tenets of the declaration is the idea that nations should seek the free, prior, and informed consent of Indigenous peoples for decisions and actions that impact Indigenous territories and communities. UNDRIP sets an impressively high bar for nations to not merely engage with Indigenous peoples but to actually listen, to heed their advice, and to respect the rights of Indigenous collectives to actively shape their own futures. The right to self-determination embedded in UNDRIP is especially important for the survival of Indigenous peoples in a time of radical environmental transformation from climate change, deforestation, wetland loss, and unsustainable development.[70]

When the United States eventually adopted the declaration in 2010, federal officials clarified that they viewed it as aspirational and not binding.[71] The emphasis on free, prior, and informed consent (FPIC) was too extreme for the federal government—it ceded too much authority to tribes. The FPIC principles guarantee that Indigenous peoples determine what kinds of development activities occur in their territories—ancestral as well as present-day. The principles also affirm that governments must obtain consent rather than simply engage in discussion, and they should do it well in advance of any planned actions to ensure that Indigenous peoples have the necessary information and lead time to weigh issues and come to their own conclusions. It is a bold vision, and it is substantially stronger than the current US system of tribal consultation—a system that allows governments to ignore the advice, values, and preferences of tribal nations on decisions about climate and energy policies, pollution permits, and a host of topics that impact tribal territories and communities.

Together with self-determination, the principles of FPIC are central to the suite of Indigenous rights laid out in UNDRIP. But let's be clear: current policies in the United States dealing with tribal consultation and self-determination do not meet the bar set by UNDRIP. With that in mind, Lumbees and their non-federally recognized neighbors may be excluded from current policies—including the federal government's duty to consult with tribes—but all tribal nations are missing out on the full promise of UNDRIP.

What needs to happen in order for this situation to change? Sappony journalist Nick Martin offered a pointed answer in a 2021 essay in the *New Republic*, observing, "If there is any hope of ending the vicious cycle in which tribal nations are perpetually brushed aside in the name of America's domestic interests, the United States must willingly relinquish the political power it stole from this land's Indigenous people. Consultation, after all, is only meaningful when the entity consulted is allowed to give an inconvenient answer. The federal government—Congress, the courts, the White House—must steel itself for a day when the tribes can, and do, say, 'No.'"[72]

IF THE FPIC PRINCIPLES were actually observed in US decision-making, tribal nations would have the ability to exert substantial influence over individual development activities, and also over larger energy and environmental policies. Much of the nation's oil and gas infrastructure is situated on tribally held lands, as are large mining operations, power plants, and renewable energy sites. One could assemble an extensive list of facilities subject to Indigenous consent—even without counting facilities situated on treaty lands that are no longer under tribal control. It is hard to imagine a settler colonial state sharing so much power with tribal nations, but this level of participation—and power sharing—would go a long way toward addressing the grand challenges posed by climate change and unsustainable development in the United States and elsewhere.

The kind of power sharing and control embodied in the FPIC principles resemble the highest levels of public participation in decision-making described several decades ago by scholar and policy advisor Sherry Arnstein. In Arnstein's conceptual "A Ladder of Citizen Participation," published in the planning literature in 1969, each rung describes a different level of public participation in decision-making processes.[73]

Lower rungs on Arnstein's ladder represent various forms of nonparticipation in which governments and corporations simply tell the public what is happening—'splaining as some describe it today.[74] Middle rungs represent situations in which the public may have a seat at the table, but it is a token gesture with no real intent to act on public input. The highest rungs represent—in ascending order—partnership, delegation, and control. Tribal consultation as we know it in the United States did not exist when Arnstein published her conceptual ladder in 1969. However, it is noteworthy that her description of consultation—and her choice to situate it only midway up the ladder—meshes with current tribal consultation policies in the United States. Specifically, as Arnstein put it, consultation "offers no assurance that citizen concerns and ideas will be taken into account."[75]

Whether the issue is tribal consultation or general public participation in decisions about the environment, justice demands meaningful participation in decision-making by people on the front lines. In the United States, there is a long history of government agencies and corporations excluding tribal nations, racially marginalized groups, and poor people from decisions that saddle these communities with pollution, degrade the quality of their environments, and expose them to other harms. Environmental justice is the multifaceted struggle for remedies—remedies that address the immediate concerns of communities overburdened by pollution and hazards, and remedies that address the underlying issues of power, racism, and colonialism.[76]

The US Environmental Protection Agency defines environmental justice as the fair treatment and meaningful involvement of all people in environmental decision-making. The federal government aims to achieve environmental justice by directing federal agencies to identify and address the disproportionate impacts of their actions—including environmental permitting—on low-income and minority communities.[77] The directive flows from a 1994 Presidential Executive Order signed by Bill Clinton after years of advocacy and research led primarily by grassroots, religious, and civil rights organizations.[78]

One of the critical sparks in the environmental justice movement happened in North Carolina, not far from where I live. In the 1970s, a company in Wake County, where the capital city of Raleigh is located, disposed of thousands of gallons of polychlorinated biphenyl (PCB) waste by dumping it, illegally, along hundreds of miles of rural back roads at night.[79]

The perpetrators were caught and convicted, but the state government was left responsible for disposing of a massive amount of PCB-contaminated soil. State officials decided unilaterally to build a landfill for the contaminated soil in a predominantly African American community in Warren County. The decision sparked protest that united community members with national civil rights leaders and environmentalists. During these protests, the terms *environmental justice* and *environmental racism* were coined. In the years that followed, advocates worked tirelessly to focus national attention on racial and socioeconomic disparities in the siting of toxic and polluting facilities, and on the general lack of concern for poor and minority communities when it came to decisions about the environment.[80]

Environmental justice advocacy and scholarship have long focused on the inequitable distribution of pollution and other kinds of environmental harm. Protests erupted in Warren County not simply because community members had been denied a voice in the state's decision about locating the landfill; people protested because the landfill was yet another example of an African American community saddled with the burden of hosting a toxic facility. Advocates knew that these were not isolated incidents, and in 1987, a national report confirmed that, nationwide, hazardous and polluting facilities were more likely to be situated in minority communities than in white communities.[81]

In the decades that followed, a body of research emerged on racial and socioeconomic disparities associated with pollution and other kinds of environmental harm. Much of the work takes a conventional approach to evaluating distributive injustices that compares demographic characteristics (race, income, education) between two groups of people. One, the focal group, is a neighborhood, census tract, or other definable population that will experience harm from some activity. The other, the reference group, is a larger county, state, or region—often an area to which the focal group belongs. By comparing characteristics of the two groups, one can measure the disparity or disproportionality. The disparities usually focus on pollution and environmental harm, but they can also focus on environmental amenities such as urban tree cover or green space. These demographic-based methods are not unique to environmental justice research; they are commonly used by researchers in education, public health, and other fields to measure and track social disparities.[82] Environmental justice advocates work to raise awareness about various types of disparities and disproportionate impacts, and they also work to eliminate them. Chapters 4 and 5 of this book contain multiple examples of ways that researchers and advocates work together to quantify and raise awareness about disparities in the distribution of harm.

Political theorists point out that distributive injustices are underpinned by other societal factors, including recognition injustice, which David Schlosberg describes as "lack of recognition in the social and political realms, demonstrated by various forms of insults, degradation, and devaluation at both the individual and cultural level."[83] Schlosberg notes that lack of recognition can cause further harm to oppressed groups by excluding them from social and political processes that include environmental decision-making.

For Indigenous peoples in the United States, recognition justice involves persuading governments and corporations to acknowledge the brutal, oppressive, and unfair treatment of Native Americans by the United States and its colonial predecessors. For Native peoples of the Coastal Plain, the brutality includes war and violent aggression, but it also includes the white supremacist policies that emerged later on and sought to oppress, assimilate, and erase Native peoples as collective groups. The previous chapter of this book outlines some of the historical trauma that still haunts our communities, but these traumas are seldom acknowledged as factors that inform environmental decision-making, including decisions about where to situate hazardous waste and whether to continue building harmful and polluting infrastructure in communities that are still processing generations of oppression and disempowerment.

Today, some forty years after the Warren County protests and nearly thirty years after federal policies were enacted, environmental justice work has come to embody a vein of social advocacy, an area of public policy, and a topic of interdisciplinary scholarship. Much like policies on tribal consultation, environmental justice policies are largely aspirational. Moreover, policies around both tribal consultation and environmental justice suffer from epidemics of ignorance; decision-makers seem to understand relatively little about the aims and underpinnings of these policies.

Over the past several years, I have been asked repeatedly by attorneys, policy advisors, and others in positions of authority to explain the most basic concepts around environmental justice and tribal consultation. Few realize that disproportionality is a well-defined and quantifiable concept. Many believe that tribal recognition status is a litmus test for Indigenous peoples' connection to place. Some ask why I bother to acknowledge that disparities even exist. I field as many questions as possible, but I can't help but think that otherwise well-educated environmental experts should know better. Nevertheless, many of these decision-makers are grossly uneducated on tribal consultation and environmental justice. The ignorance may explain why both areas still receive similar treatment as "box-checking" exercises in state and federal decision-making.

In 2014, the North Carolina Commission of Indian Affairs invited me to join their newly formed committee on environmental justice as an ex officio member—an external technical advisor. I agreed to join, partly out of curiosity and partly out of an obligation to help tribal nations gain a clearer understanding of environmental justice policies and threats facing their communities. I was formally welcomed onto the committee by the Commission of Indian Affairs' chairwoman Mrs. Annie Ruth Locklear Revels—the same Ruth Revels who had advocated passionately for the preservation of Old Main decades prior.[84] Revels had long since retired from teaching, but she continued to serve tribal communities throughout North Carolina as chair of the Commission.

My work on the committee confirmed that distributive injustices are both pervasive and systematic; they are built into the fabric of decision-making. Individual actors may not have malicious intent, but the processes of environmental planning and permitting are nevertheless structured in ways that exclude marginalized groups from key decisions and—more often than not— leave them with the raw end of policies and permitting decisions.

My experience also taught me about the potential for meaningful tribal consultation—guided by the FPIC principles—to help tribal nations break free of the pervasive cycles of injustice that have plagued our communities for centuries. If Native people can break those cycles and ascend to the top of Arnstein's ladder, we can use our power and influence to help fashion more equitable systems of governance that improve the environment for everyone's benefit.

But before any of that can happen, we have to acknowledge the deep scars of colonialism and the infections of injustice that persist today. The next few chapters lay out the history of these scars on the Coastal Plain. The chapters also link these scars to present-day concerns about the inequitable burdens of pollution and environmental degradation placed on Indigenous peoples, barriers to tribal participation in decision-making, and a disregard for the deep cultural connections to our watery world.

CHAPTER THREE

Water in the Lumbee World

Refugia Transformed

QUESTION: The only trouble you have is that seven or eight men,
  who have been outlawed, have got into an inaccessible swamp,
  in which it is dangerous for men to pursue them, and where it is almost
  impracticable to pursue them.
ANSWER: Well, that does not state it exactly.
QUESTION: How is it, then?
ANSWER: It is just this way: These men have all forfeited their lives;
  they are entirely reckless. If you get a squad of men from the country,
  who have been impressed into that kind of service, when Henry Berry
  Lowry and his crowd shoot down two or three of them, you cannot
  get the rest to come up well.[1]

This exchange comes from a line of questioning between Senator Francis Blair Jr. of Missouri and Giles Leitch, an attorney from Robeson County. Leitch had been summoned to Washington in July 1871 to testify before the Joint Select Committee to Inquire into the Condition of Affairs in the Late Insurrectionary States. The committee filled several volumes that year with testimony about post-war racial violence in former Confederate states. Later known as the Ku Klux Klan Hearings of 1871, the committee's work focused mainly on the epidemic of anti-Black terror orchestrated by the Ku Klux Klan and other militant white supremacists.[2]

The hearings represented a watershed moment in the United States, a moment that historian Henry Louis Gates Jr. once described as "the closest that we've come in this country to a truth and reconciliation commission."[3] Although the hearings focus primarily on terror experienced by African Americans in the post-Civil War South, Leitch had come to Washington to relay a different story.

Senator Blair was perplexed by Leitch's testimony on that July day in Washington. Leitch spoke about rampant lawlessness in Robeson County, a sparsely populated backwater in North Carolina's Coastal Plain. The violence emanated from an area called *Scuffletown*, a swampland inhabited by people that Leitch had difficulty describing with the racial vocabulary at his disposal.[4] These people were the direct ancestors of present-day Lumbees, and Scuffletown was the name that outsiders had given to their main community on the Lumbee River, an ambiguously defined area some ten tortuous miles upstream of Lumberton.[5]

Several months before the hearing, the federal government had sent an entire company of troops to the area, but they had no luck whatsoever in quelling a guerrilla conflict that had raged on in the county for years following the end of the Civil War. The local sheriff had assembled a one-hundred-man posse to no effect, either. According to the testimony that the Senator heard that day, all of this drama boiled down to one man, an outlaw, Henry Berry Lowry, and his band of six or seven men who could not be extracted from a swamp not far from Scuffletown. How difficult could it be to put down a guerrilla campaign by seven or eight men, especially with federal troops and a large posse at the disposal of local authorities? What was so remarkable about the swamp where they hid? The Senator wanted answers. Leitch elaborated:

> Perhaps it would be well enough for me to describe that country down there, so you can understand it. . . . That swamp is about three-quarters of a mile wide on an average. It is not all swamp, but there are islands in it of an acre, or two acres, or five acres in extent. The swamp is about ten miles in length, of an average width of three-quarters of a mile. Upon those islands they have dens and caves in which they hide. Very few people traverse the swamp; there are few men who know where the islands are, or where their caves and dens are.[6]

Leitch's testimony epitomizes the frustrations that outsiders held toward the extensive wetlands that dominated the landscape upstream of Lumberton on the Lumbee River (map 3.1). Above the town, the main stem of the river could only be navigated by small rafts or canoes, and few outsiders ever ventured that way. The overland route between Lumberton and Scuffletown was scarcely any better; the north side of the river required travelers to cross several swamps—tributaries that flowed from the north and emptied into the Lumbee River's wide, forested floodplain. Back Swamp, nearly a mile wide, ran parallel to the river on its south side.

Travel was not impossible between Scuffletown and the outside world, but it was difficult. A wagon road—built over an older footpath called the *Lowry Road*—ran roughly parallel to the Fall Line and crossed the Lumbee River at a Native-run ferry and tavern near Scuffletown.[7] But the Lowry Road did not

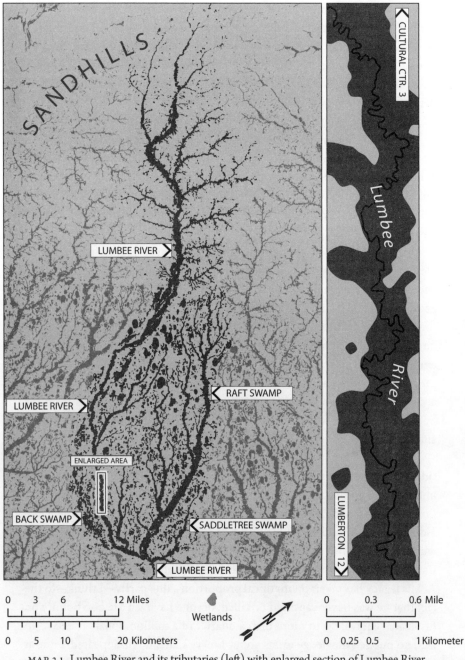

MAP 3.1 Lumbee River and its tributaries (left) with enlarged section of Lumbee River channel in the vicinity of historic Scuffletown (right). Signposts show prominent present-day locations. Signposts with arrows show directions and distances (in miles) to places located off the map. Map by author.

link up directly to Lumberton. Even though Leitch claimed to have been "born among" Lumbee ancestors and knew them "perfectly well," his Lumberton postal address made it unlikely that he visited Scuffletown very often, or at all, during his early years. In the years leading up to the Civil War, however, railroads finally began to bisect Robeson County, easing travel between Scuffletown and the outside world.

The swamps around Scuffletown were a different story altogether. As Leitch's testimony suggests, these wetlands were vast and disorienting, even after the advent of railroads. Back Swamp, where Henry Berry Lowry and his band reportedly laid out, was an especially confusing place for outsiders. Following Leitch's detailed testimony, Senator Blair probably came to realize why federal troops and local militiamen repeatedly failed to locate Lowry in what the Senator called a "jungle."[8]

One other detail of Leitch's testimony is worth examining in detail. Despite Leitch's detailed description, it is highly improbable that caves existed anywhere in the swamps of Robeson County. It is simply the wrong geological setting to find caves; there is no exposed bedrock in the area, and the sediments are too soft and sandy. But Leitch mentioned caves three separate times in his testimony that day. It seems to me that Leitch probably either embellished his sworn testimony, or he simply repeated rumors about a place that he himself had never visited. If Leitch, a lifelong Robesonian, could not accurately describe a prominent landform located only ten miles from his home, it is no surprise that soldiers and militiamen could not extricate Lowry and his band.

Lowry was—and still is—a larger-than-life hero to Lumbee people. We consider him a freedom fighter who, together with his band and with supporters in Scuffletown, fought injustice in Robeson County. During the Civil War, Lowry carried out raids and targeted killings directed at the Confederate Home Guard. After the war, his attention turned to local white supremacists, who still remained in positions of power. Lowry's band was multiracial, and he was admired by poor and oppressed people throughout Robeson County.

His legacy has taken on mythical proportions, due partly—I think—to the fact that he was never captured or killed, despite having a $12,000 bounty on his head—equivalent to more than a quarter of a million dollars in 2022.[9] In fact, no public knowledge exists about Lowry's fate; he disappeared without a trace a little more than six months after Leitch appeared at the Ku Klux Klan hearings. The combination of Lowry's skill as a fighter, the faithfulness of his comrades and community, the inaccessibility of the swamps around Scuffletown, and sheer luck meant that Lowry likely died a free man.

One of the stories circulated following Lowry's disappearance in 1872 is that he died of an accidental gunshot wound. In this telling, Lowry's companions buried his body in a secret location in the swamps around Scuffletown so that no one could claim the large bounty. To this day, Lumbees associate their namesake river and its swamps with Lowry, and many treat the river with the same sanctity that they would afford to a hero's grave.

While certain waters in Robeson County are more sacred than others, water is respected more generally because it defines where people can or cannot go, and it dictates where they can or cannot live. Even in relatively dry places, life in the county is a delicate balancing act between too much and too little water. A major storm or even a wet spell can saturate a farm or flood a homeplace. A dry spell could doom a crop.

The Lumbee River is the lifeblood of Lumbee people, and not only because its waters drain the soils of our communities and the strata of our past. The river also brings joy and solace to our people; it is a source of quiet refreshment and spiritual cleansing. Its tributaries surround and embrace the communities that Lumbee people call home. The river brings terror and destruction for sure; it ruins lives and keeps secrets. But in all of these ways, it is sacred. It is home. It is life.

The rest of this chapter examines the relationship that Lumbee people hold with the river that flows through our homeland. It highlights some of the ways—past and present—that settler colonialism has altered our relationship to the river. From early nineteenth-century attempts to market the river as a profitable business enterprise to twentieth-century efforts to eliminate the river's network of interconnected wetlands, settler society has worked hard to transform the river in ways that can ultimately harm Lumbee people and others who rely on the river in various ways.

ROBESON COUNTY IS NOT PART OF THE SANDHILLS, but pieces of the Sandhills slowly make their way into, and through, Robeson County. The Lumbee River and its blackwater tributaries gnaw incessantly at the grainy soils of the ancient coastal dunes, as they have ever since the primordial ocean receded eastward. The uppermost tributaries—the headwaters of the Lumbee—reach deep into the Sandhills, grasping for sediment to carry downstream. The entire network of blackwater streams is enclosed in densely forested wetlands, deep green ribbons that dissect the Sandhills and Coastal Plain.

Through countless millennia, sand grains have tumbled downstream, skittering and bumping along beneath the Lumbee River's dark current—a ceaseless procession of sediment. In some places, the riverbed is a disorganized mass; else-where, the interplay between moving water and sand creates ripples and dunes, organized bedforms that slowly migrate along the riverbed before dissipating and reorganizing anew. Here and there, gleaming beaches and sand bars grow, morph, and waste away. For the most part, the Lumbee River does not flow over solid, unmoving bedrock; the entire riverbed is an unconsolidated melange, slid-ing toward the Atlantic. Pressed along by the current of the Lumbee River, the Sandhills are returning, grain by grain, to the sea.

From a distance, the Lumbee River's stark white sandbars contrast sharply against the dark vitreous flow. Up close, however, a different picture emerges. Boaters, swimmers, and others who spend time in the river have experienced the infinite gradations between dark and light. From the vantage point of a canoe or kayak, one can sometimes see two or three feet beneath the dark surface of the water. I have pushed away from the banks of the Lumbee River countless times in canoes, kayaks, johnboats, and even atop stand-up paddle boards. Immediately, the white sand banks grade into rich golden hues, just below the waterline. Leaving relatively solid ground of the riverbanks behind, I engage the smooth dark current of my ancestral home.

To boat on the Lumbee River is to skim the boundary between two worlds. Overhead is a world of leaves and sky. A canopy of verdant foliage extends from each bank of the river; green branches stretch over the current, anx-ious to meet in the middle. The outstretched limbs belong mainly to short-statured birches and maples. Their trunks balance precariously on the banks, occupying the margin between floodplain and channel. Leaves and branches hang low, sometimes trailing in the water and waiting to chastise inattentive boaters. Trees occasionally fall during storms and block the river channel, either partly or fully. Known locally as *blowdowns*, their trunks and branches strain all manner of debris. They pose occasional hazards to boaters and swimmers but provide shade and cover to aquatic life.

High above the riverbanks loom massive bald cypress and pine trees. They cast shadows across the river channel and shade the floodplains that lie be-yond the riverbanks. The riparian forest is a world of sharp and unfiltered light and sound. Sun flecks illuminate bald cypress knees that poke up through dark, fibrous soil. Vines encircle tree trunks obscured in dim shadow. Bird-songs and hammering woodpeckers echo through the floodplain. Choruses of cicadas and frogs round out the soundscape.

The other world lies beneath. In the shallows, boaters glide over sub-merged dunes and ripples that are dappled in soft hues through translucent tea-stained water. The underwater features are especially clear where the surface of the river is perfectly smooth and unobstructed by downed trees or trailing branches. As the river deepens in these spots, boaters can see the features grow dim as the riverbed falls away. Sometimes the bedforms fade gently to black, but other times they disappear, abruptly, at the rim of a deep hole. Swirling eddies erode deeply into loose sediment and create these miniature abysses. Occasionally, the depths yield hints of a log or root or some other dark object. The world beneath the surface of the river is not inky black; it is a domain of filtered and muted light where fish, turtles, and other creatures cruise and creep. Ancient logs and waterlogged dugout canoes intermingle with marine fossils and the detritus of the Sandhills. With few exceptions, humans can only stare into this world from afar.[10] I have peered into this world many times from above, gliding over sun-strafed shallows and lightless depths in a boat made of plastic or fiberglass. I have never looked down, as my ancestors did, from the vantage point of a dugout canoe—a shallow draft of smoothed pine or bald cypress skimming the boundary between the worlds above and below. I hope to paddle the river in a dugout someday, but in the meantime, I take in both of these worlds as best I can.

I admit that my ancestors knew the river more intimately than I know it. The blackwater stream—and others like it—were defining features of the expansive homelands of Algonquian-, Iroquoian-, and Siouan-speaking ancestors of Lumbee people. My ancestors experienced the sights and sounds of the river free of the distant drone of traffic on Interstate 95, which crosses the river near Lumberton, and bisects one of my favorite reaches to paddle. My ancestors experienced a river free from pollution as well, including visible refuse and invisible contaminants—nitrogen, phosphorus, and pathogens that seep and spill into the stream through thousands of uncharted flow paths.

For millennia before automated monitoring stations arrived in the early twentieth century, Indigenous people kept tabs on the seasonal rhythms of the river. They carefully planned the locations of their temporary camps and permanent villages to avoid seasonal floods during winter and spring. They anticipated low flows during the summer and fall, planning extra travel time on the river to navigate sandbars and shallows. When the occasional hurricane swept through the region and brought widespread flooding, Indigenous people knew where to find high ground.

Indigenous people who lived in the Lumbee River basin prior to colonization were also active agents in shaping the riverine environment of their home. During the eighteenth century, Raft Swamp, one of the largest tributaries of the Lumbee River, differed from many of the other riverine wetlands in the Lumbee River basin. Most were floodplain forests, but Raft Swamp was a vast, open canebrake. One of the few settlers who pressed deep into the area during the mid-eighteenth century reportedly noted that "a person could stand on top of the hill on one side and see across to the other side."[11] Indigenous communities maintained canebrakes throughout the region by regular burning. Other canebrakes overtook croplands once they were left fallow. These carefully managed lands were hallmarks of Indigenous peoples who understood, through lived experiences, both the rhythms and idiosyncrasies of life in a watery world.

Periodic floods inject chaos into the seasonal rhythms of a river. On the Lumbee River, floods not only disgorge massive pulses of water up onto the floodplain, they also bring avulsions of sediment. Eruptions of sand, dislodged from the riverbed, occasionally burst free from the channel and bury low-lying areas in inches of sediment. In 2016 and 2018, when Hurricanes Matthew and Florence brought biblical rains to large swaths of the Coastal Plain, the Lumbee River spewed truckloads of white sand across neighborhoods of west Lumberton. Former floodplains, drained decades ago to make way for homes and businesses, were reclaimed by the river as a place to store its excesses of both water and sediment. In the aftermath of both hurricanes, piles of sand lined streets, sidewalks, and yards, bringing an eerie, snow-day feel to flood-ravaged neighborhoods. The sediment added to the tragedy and wreckage for people in Robeson County, but in the longer story of the Lumbee River, the two floods were part of the age-old interplay between the river's seasonal habits and its occasional quirks.

The Lumbee River floods periodically, in part, because it is a free-flowing stream. There are no dams or impediments to flow anywhere along the main stem of the river between its headwaters and the Atlantic Ocean. On other rivers, dam operators can modulate flows to avoid flooding of downstream areas following tropical storms or other heavy deluges. The Lumbee rises and falls with the weather. From its headwaters in the Sandhills, the river flows freely across Robeson County before entering South Carolina—a twisting, sinuous journey of more than one hundred miles. In South Carolina, it joins the Little Pee Dee River, a much shorter stream that lies immediately west of the Lumbee River. Below the confluence of the two streams, the intermingled waters flow for another sixty miles or so before joining the Great Pee Dee River. From there, the water flows some forty miles farther toward Winyah Bay, a shallow estuary where the Great Pee Dee River discharges into the Atlantic Ocean.

Water and sediment move unimpeded along the entire length of the free-flowing Lumbee River. Aquatic life moves freely too, both upstream and downstream. Shad, a fish that spends most of its time in the ocean, migrates upriver each spring to spawn in sandy reaches of the river. Sturgeon did too, before their populations were decimated by overfishing around the turn of the twentieth century. Previously, these massive prehistoric fish periodically visited their spawning grounds along the Lumbee other rivers in the region.[12] The Lumbee River was a conduit that connected people to the sea through these once-important sources of food. Through food and flood, the rivers gave and took. Lumbee ancestors likely understood this duality of water. Rivers sustained people with various physical and spiritual gifts—food, shelter, solace—but they could also lash out when provoked by the peculiarities of the weather. To understand and appreciate the duality is to respect water in the Coastal Plain.

Devoid of rapids, waterfalls, and other natural obstructions to flow, the Lumbee River's profile—a plot of riverbed elevation versus distance downstream from the headwaters—is a smooth curve, free of knick points and angles that appear on other profiles where streams encounter obstructions. The Lumbee River's smooth profile descends steeply out of the Sandhills and gradually flattens to a nearly imperceptible downhill slope on the Coastal Plain. Despite a lack of waterfalls and rapids, it has never been an easy river for outsiders to navigate. Sharp meander bends, multiple channels, and oxbow lakes create a maze of twisting passages. Some of these channels return travelers to the main flow, but others are dead ends. A few simply fade into endless bald cypress swamps.

Indigenous peoples of the Coastal Plain, who spent generations navigating the Lumbee River, were quite at home on the twisting, swamp-flanked channels of blackwater streams. Colonial surveyors, settlers, and military expeditions, however, were not. One of the earliest colonial accounts from the Lumbee River watershed is the 1712 diary of John Barnwell, the South Carolina military leader who led the first of two assaults on Indigenous people in eastern North Carolina during the Tuscarora War. Barnwell marched along the Fall Line from the Pee Dee River to the Cape Fear River and complained bitterly about a "very bad Road full of great Swamps" where his men pulled their horses out of the muck with ropes and brute strength.[13]

The Lumbee River is the main drainage between the Pee Dee and the Cape Fear, which means that Barnwell most certainly crossed the stream and its attendant swamps on his way to pillage Tuscarora towns and lay siege to Fort Nooheroka. As Barnwell traversed the Fall Line, his militia likely would have crossed the Lumbee River near its headwaters. There, in the Sandhills, the swamps are fewer and narrower than out on the Coastal Plain, in present-day

Robeson County. Despite Barnwell's complaints about the swampy lands between the Pee Dee and Cape Fear, his march could have been much more
vexing had he attempted to cross the even more expansive swamps farther
downstream.

Barnwell's journal is typical of colonial accounts of the Lumbee River basin; most accounts are transient stories of passing through the area en route
to more familiar—and drier—lands to the east and west. Prior to the Revolutionary War, only a handful of these accounts exist, mainly from those
who wandered into the basin to survey uncharted land or to chase fugitives.
Generations of historians and tribal advocates have scrutinized these records
to extract fragments of outsider information about Lumbee ancestors. These
sparse accounts are summarized and resummarized in a variety of academic
studies about Lumbee people, government reports scrutinizing our indigeneity, and public-interest pieces that play up the enigma of our existence.

There is a conspicuous absence of the river from the vast majority of records that were created by outsiders prior to the nineteenth century. In particular, the river is largely absent from maps created during the colonial period and
early statehood. For years, I puzzled over the fact that the Lumbee River—or
Drowning Creek as it was known by settlers prior to the early nineteenth
century—rarely appeared on colonial maps. After all, the river was not too far
from colonial population centers near the Atlantic Ocean, and it lay between
two well-traveled arteries of colonial commerce—the Cape Fear and the Pee
Dee Rivers. The few maps that showed the river prior to 1800 usually truncated its channel, cutting it off somewhere near present-day Lumberton. Maps
that included the headwaters of the river often appended them directly onto
other streams; they bypassed the truncated portion entirely.

Several years ago, spurred by curiosity and Lumbee oral history of Robeson County's swamps as refugia for Indigenous communities, I conducted a
detailed and systematic study of historic maps in the University of North
Carolina's digital collections.[14] The collections in Chapel Hill hold high-
quality digital scans of nearly one hundred historical maps, created between
the sixteenth century and the early twentieth century, that show the Coastal
Plain in sufficient detail to warrant including the Lumbee River and its
tributaries.

As part of the study, I created a rubric to score each map based on its topological representation of the Lumbee River basin. Topology, which is an area
of study concerned with the connection and arrangement of objects rather
than their geographical locations, allowed me to ignore the technological
limitations of colonial mapmakers who lacked sophisticated surveying equip-

ment and modern conveniences such as aerial photographs and GPS. Instead, a focus on topological accuracy allowed me to probe mapmakers' knowledge of the river as a network of connected places. This kind of knowledge—the arrangement and order of tributaries, river crossings, and settlements—requires familiarity with a river. A topologically accurate map is a traveler's map; it may not be drawn to scale, but important places are all shown, and they appear in the right order. Anyone who has navigated a modern subway network can attest to the utility of a good topological map.

The scoring exercise revealed that colonial mapmakers generally did a poor job of representing the topology of the Lumbee River prior to 1800. This may be surprising given that the river basin was surrounded by colonial populations and commerce routes; other Coastal Plain rivers were mapped fairly accurately long before this time. However, the river's twisting, wandering channel and the confusion created by its vast adjacent swamps likely deterred exploration by surveyors and other outsiders traveling either on foot or by boat upstream from South Carolina.

As a stand-in for outsider knowledge, the topological inaccuracies of pre-1800 maps suggest that colonial authorities or their stand-ins—surveyors, tax collectors, bounty hunters—knew little about the geography of the Lumbee River basin. It is no wonder that relatively few colonial accounts mention Lumbee ancestors, and those that do are surprised to find organized settlements of people "inclosed [*sic*] in great swamps" as one well-scrutinized record testifies.[15] This particular record, a militia report from 1754, reinforces one of the major inaccuracies of eighteenth-century maps; the report declares that Drowning Creek is situated at the head of Little Pee Dee River. It is not. Drowning Creek or the Lumbee River—by any name—flows out of the Sandhills and through the Coastal Plain for well over one hundred miles before joining the Little Pee Dee far downstream from the headwaters of the latter stream.[16]

People who traveled or lived along these waterways would have known that Drowning Creek belonged to a completely separate and much larger river system. With that in mind, the colonial official who filed the militia report from 1754 betrayed his unfamiliarity with regional geography. It seems that outsider maps and reports have more to say about colonial ignorance of the Lumbee River than about colonial knowledge of the region. Despite major reliability issues, the 1754 report and others like it continue to serve as authoritative records in histories about Lumbee people and their origins.

By the turn of the nineteenth century, settlers had infiltrated much of the Lumbee River basin, and their maps eventually corrected the river's misgrafted headwaters. Around this time, the interests of some settlers in the region turned to exploiting the region's dense swamp forests, even though most of Robeson County's swampland remained unsurveyed and unexplored by outsiders. Simplistic histories of the region claim that around this time, North Carolina's legislature changed the name of the river from Drowning Creek to Lumber River in 1809 to reflect a bustling timber industry.[17] Although the state legislature did approve the name change, the simple narrative is mostly false.

In reality, Drowning Creek had no bustling timber industry in 1809. The river basin was an enigma to most North Carolinians in the early nineteenth century. Although Revolutionary War veterans had laid out plans for a new town, Lumberton, on the banks of Drowning Creek soon after the war, the area was a relative backwater, tucked between the much more populous Cape Fear and Pee Dee River valleys to the east and west. Drowning Creek's expansive forests were mostly wetlands—vast swamps of bald cypress, inundated during wet weather and difficult to navigate, let alone clear-cut, under the best circumstances. Nevertheless, in 1809, six white settlers—recent immigrants to Drowning Creek—formed a private company to promote navigation and logging in the general vicinity of Lumberton. The group petitioned North Carolina's legislature for a charter to sell lottery tickets to fund the fledgling company.[18]

As part of their marketing, the men asked lawmakers to rename Drowning Creek. Records do not explain why, but I imagine that the name *Drowning Creek* was a liability to a company whose success hinged on marketing the swath of swampy land between the Pee Dee and Cape Fear Rivers. Perhaps they thought *Lumber River* would conjure up more lucrative mental images among would-be ticket buyers. In any case, lawmakers agreed, and the Lumber River Navigation Company began selling $2 lottery tickets in early 1810. The company promised a $1,000 payout and planned to use the remaining funds for their navigation project, which involved clearing blowdowns and dredging a navigation channel in the sediment-rich riverbed between Lumberton and the South Carolina state line. The company expected their project to spur economic development in the river basin—mainly through logging, milling, and floating goods downstream to the South Carolina coast.

Despite the marketable name, the Lumber River Navigation Lottery was a complete failure. After several weeks, only one-quarter of the tickets had been sold. The company ran newspaper advertisements nonstop to promote the lottery, promising that the navigation project would unleash "invaluable naval stores" from the river basin and that "never failing streams" would power sawmills in perpetuity. Advertisements claimed that the obscurity of this Coastal Plain backwater had sheltered its vast forests from colonial saws and axes, leaving the entire basin full of trees that were "equal if not superior in size and quality to any timber which is to be found in the Southern Section of the Union."

The company delayed the main prize drawing several times during 1810, and the lottery eventually paid out a few minor prizes. But by February 1811, no main prize drawing had occurred, and local authorities ordered the company to issue refunds to ticket holders. So ended the Lumber River Navigation Company. The simplistic narrative—that North Carolina's legislature renamed Drowning Creek to reflect the region's timber industry—is incorrect. The legislation was simply a marketing ploy by a group of settlers who hoped to exploit the river's wetland forests for economic gain. In the end, they were unsuccessful in creating a navigation corridor or spurring the promised economic development.

In the decades that followed, other settlers proposed similar economic development schemes for the river and its tributary wetlands. Each of them failed. In 1816, for example, lawmakers introduced legislation to provide public funding to improve navigation on the newly renamed Lumber River. Like the Lumber River Navigation Company before them, the lawmakers hoped to spur economic development in the region. State leaders, however, never committed funds for the project, and the idea languished.

In 1819, the state government began a decades-long feasibility study for an ambitious canal route to transport goods hundreds of miles from western North Carolina to Wilmington.[19] The plan called for connecting the upper reaches of the Pee Dee River—which drained much of northwestern North Carolina—with the Cape Fear River via an artificial canal.[20] Within months, surveyors had laid out a tentative route for the canal that approximated John Barnwell's march more than a century earlier. Where Barnwell complained about "great Swamps" in the Lumbee River headwaters, nineteenth-century surveyors saw feeder streams that could help maintain water levels in the proposed canal. In the end, however, the canal succumbed to the same lack of funding as projects that came before it. Prominent white residents in the area and lawmakers in Raleigh periodically called for state funding to complete the project, but funding never came. By the 1840s, railroads had rendered the canal obsolete, and the plan was dropped altogether. Had this major canal been built through central and eastern North Carolina, flow along the Lumbee River would have been radically altered—its headwaters diverted toward the Pee Dee River to the west and the Cape Fear River to the east.

Despite these various schemes, the Lumbee River and its swamp forests evaded destruction during much of the nineteenth century. Moreover, the river was temperamental; free-flowing sediment and blowdowns limited navigation to small boats and rafts. Unpredictable floods limited riverside development. Dense swamps continued to hinder incursions into the heart of the river basin. Thus, the swamps, and the sandy uplands that dotted the interstices, continued to serve as a refugia for Indigenous communities. But the expansion of railroads into the river basin and the advent of industrial machinery brought an end to the river basin's relative isolation and refuge.

By the turn of the twentieth century, the descendants of white settlers in the region supported a plan to dig a network of drainage canals throughout the Lumbee River basin. Their plan mirrored growing interests, nationwide, in publicly funded wetland drainage projects. Most of these projects promised to raise the value of marginal farmland—transforming waterlogged properties into productive cropland. In the Southeast, including Robeson County, wetland drainage projects also promised public health improvements. Swamps and other wetlands were viewed as sources of malaria and insect-borne diseases that affected both people and livestock. In 1906, a group of Robeson County citizens sued one of their neighbors for damming and flooding the largest Carolina Bay in the area, known locally as the Great Desert. The neighbor intended to use impounded water to power a gristmill. The complaint alleged that the flooded wetland coincided with an outbreak of "blind staggers" among local livestock. A local judge agreed, declaring the flooded landscape a source of "noisome odors and unwholesome fogs" and ordering the impoundment drained.[21]

In Robeson County, the largest and most sophisticated wetland drainage project was the effort to drain Back Swamp during the twentieth century.[22] Back Swamp was a large tributary of the Lumbee River that had served as a hideout for Henry Berry Lowry and his band during the 1860s and 1870s. By the early twentieth century, Back Swamp held a small but thriving community of Indigenous farmers, many of whom were sharecroppers, working marginal lands throughout the 22,000-acre drainage basin. The Back Swamp drainage project involved excavating a new artificial network of deep canals and intricate feeder ditches to lower groundwater levels and allow surface water to drain rapidly from soils. The United States Department of Agriculture, which helped design the project, speculated that the artificial drainage works would drastically improve crop yields. Meanwhile, timber interests in the region hoped that canals and ditches could be extended into dense swamp forests, finally allowing access to the prized stands of bald cypress that loggers had eyed for more than a century. In fact, out-of-state timber companies had been studying Robeson County for more than twenty years by the time the Back Swamp drainage project was first proposed in 1910.[23] The entire scenario echoed earlier schemes to exploit the Lumbee River and its tributary swamps; a proposal to alter the watery landscape promised economic development through infrastructure improvements.

In the end, the Back Swamp drainage project gave and took; it increased the amount of arable land in the basin, but at the cost of thousands of acres of wetlands. The destroyed wetlands—which included swamp forests, marshes, and pocosins—harbored fish and wildlife, and they protected downstream areas against flooding. The project's net impacts to Lumbee farmers are uncertain; some accounts contend that tax assessments associated with the project created an untenable burden for Lumbee landowners and spurred an exodus of Native farmers from Back Swamp. Other work fails to find evidence of declining Native property ownership in Back Swamp.[24]

In any case, the episode highlights the scale and complexity of public drainage projects that occurred throughout the Coastal Plain during the early twentieth century. These projects permanently transformed the ancestral homelands of Native peoples in the region, converting thousands of acres of wetlands into croplands. As the twentieth century progressed, additional drainage projects were planned and implemented in Robeson County. Today, Robeson County—and the Coastal Plain more generally—is enervated by a network of drainage canals and ditches. Although the network is actually not that old, three or four generations have come to depend on it for their livelihoods. Most of all, the network alters relationships that people have with water in places like eastern North Carolina. Some measure of respect for water's duality is lost when people believe they can shunt away water at will.

Indigenous peoples are not immune from the altered relationships to water brought on by artificial drainage networks. By the early twentieth century, most Lumbees —like other Native Americans in the region—had adopted farming practices tied heavily to commodity crops, including cotton, corn, and tobacco. Whether they owned their own farms outright or worked as sharecroppers, Lumbee farmers also depended, increasingly, on artificial drainage projects to sustain the acreage required for these crops.[25] Canals and ditches also alleviated some of the nuisance flooding that often stymied efforts to plant and harvest crops. Perhaps some farmers saw improvements in crop productivity and increased value of marginal lands.

However, one of the downsides of artificial ditching and draining is the elimination of flood protection for downstream areas. Landscapes crisscrossed with ditches and canals do not hold back floodwater effectively; the entire purpose of the drainage network is to route floodwater downstream as quickly as possible. Large drainage projects—including efforts like the Back Swamp project—can even exacerbate downstream flooding.

I commonly tell students in my environmental science classes that there is no free lunch. By this, I mean that efforts to modify and manage the environment always have consequences, often negative ones. The negative consequences are relatively clear for wetland drainage. They include not only loss of flood protection for downstream areas but also loss of fish and wildlife habitat and—for Indigenous peoples—loss of connections to the rhythms and idiosyncrasies of rivers that formed our communities, shaped our cultures, and influenced our histories. To reforge these connections may or may not require a radical replumbing of previously altered landscapes, but in either case, it will require a rekindling of respect for water as a force that both gives and takes away.

Indigenous studies scholar Dina Gilio-Whitaker has observed that "the origin of environmental injustice for Indigenous peoples is dispossession of land in all its forms; injustice is continually reproduced in what is inherently a culturally genocidal structure that systematically erases Indigenous peoples' relationships and responsibilities to their ancestral places."[26] The story is no different for Lumbee people and our Indigenous neighbors. The struggle for environmental justice begins and ends with the acknowledgment that our homelands have always been—and will always be—a watery world. Water dictates where we can and cannot live, it sheltered our ancestors, and it memorializes our heroes. To separate us from our watery world through wetland drainage, pollution, climate change, or any other factor is an insidious form of dispossession and cultural genocide in which we remain in place but the world transforms around us.

CHAPTER FOUR

This Is Indian Land
Pipelines and the Fight for Indigenous Visibility

Early one morning, well before dawn, a woman was driving through a remote part of Prospect, a community on the west side of Robeson County. The road meandered through a distant corner of her family's land near Bear Swamp. There, construction was underway for a new natural gas transmission pipeline. Progress on the pipeline had been slow because of wet weather; after days of rain, the water table had risen nearly to the ground surface. Soft soil bogged down sidebooms, dozers, and other heavy equipment. Trenches began to fill with groundwater as quickly as they were excavated. Diesel-fueled pumps ran throughout the workday to jettison water from the trenches and to keep them accessible for work.

Construction near Bear Swamp had dragged on for many days. Each morning pipeliners—specialized tradespeople who work on oil and gas pipelines throughout the country—commuted to Prospect from hotels in nearby cities. Their convoy of pickup trucks rolled past crop fields, cemeteries, and isolated country stores en route to the worksite. Each evening, the pipeliners loaded up their tools and themselves and commuted back, leaving behind only heavy machinery and stacks of steel pipe. They also left behind one pipeliner to watch over the worksite by night.

The woman who drove through predawn Prospect was a Lumbee Indian, and the pipeliners were working on land that her family had farmed longer than anyone could remember. Recently, government officials had declared the pipeline a public necessity, which gave energy companies legal rights to excavate on her land and the land of her neighbors. Construction crawled across Robeson County, and it left behind a swath of scarred earth—a reminder to everyone in Prospect about the energy company's right to their land.

As the woman approached the idle construction equipment and hulking stacks of pipe, she noticed a lone pickup truck amid the deep predawn shadows. A thin vapor rose from its tailpipe, a sign that the truck was running and likely occupied. Curious as to who else might be out so late (or so early), the woman pulled off the paved road for a closer look. Coarse gravel crunched under the tires of her sedan as she pulled up alongside the pickup truck. The woman barely made out the silhouette of a man behind the wheel. She nodded her head, slightly, in the general direction of the truck cab, and the silhouette bobbed in response.

The man was a pipeliner who had nearly completed the night watch. At the woman's beckoning, he lowered the truck window. The two exchanged brief introductions, and then the man relayed a remarkable story.

The pipeliner told the woman that while he sat in the cab of his truck, keeping watch over the worksite by night, he began to notice glowing orbs, the size of basketballs, rising up from the ground just beyond the perimeter of the worksite. He stared through the windows of his truck as the orbs danced around, illuminating the stalks of broom grass and goldenrod that grew just beyond the fringe of the gravel-strewn work area. After a time, the orbs drifted toward the line of trees near the edge of Bear Swamp. Then, the globes of light rose high into the air and faded away above the treetops.

The man's body still pulsed with adrenaline as he recounted the other-worldly experience. By the time he finished telling the story, the last stars had just disappeared from overhead. Pale grey dawn flooded the truck's cab, and the Lumbee woman could see the man's sleepless eyes. After a brief pause, the man confided that the experience had terrified him. He could not wait for construction to wrap up in Prospect. He would stay on the job, but he would never spend another night alone at that worksite.

The Lumbee woman laughed out loud and nodded, knowingly. The glowing orbs, she explained, were her ancestors. "They came to remind you that this is Indian land."

I FIRST HEARD THAT GHOST STORY in 2018. It circulated through Robeson County at a time when Native people throughout the region felt ignored amid the clamor over plans to build the Atlantic Coast Pipeline—one of the longest and most expensive natural gas pipelines proposed in the United States in recent memory.[1] The Atlantic Coast Pipeline, or ACP, was a massive infrastructure project designed by energy corporations to transport between one-and-a-half and two billion cubic feet per day of natural gas from fracking operations in shale basins of Central Appalachia over the Blue Ridge Mountains, through the Piedmont, and into the Coastal Plain.[2] The proposed pipeline's six-hundred-mile route crossed parts of West Virginia, Virginia, and North Carolina, and it ended in Robeson County. But the ACP was never built. By mid-2020, skyrocketing costs and multiyear delays forced the pipeline's developers to cut their losses. After six years of aggressive legal maneuvering, lobbying, and campaigning, developers quietly scrapped the project.[3]

The CEOs of Dominion Energy and Duke Energy—major companies behind the pipeline—announced the cancellation on July 5, 2020, via a press release that slipped into the turbulent flow of news about COVID-19 lockdowns, Black Lives Matter demonstrations, and fevered political campaigns.[4] The press release carefully avoided linking the cancellation to pressure from ongoing lawsuits, protests, and political actions by small community groups and large environmental organizations; instead, the CEOs chalked up the decision to "increasing legal uncertainty" over the future of fossil fuel infrastructure.

Within hours of the announcement, US Energy Secretary Dan Brouillette issued a statement of his own about the pipeline's cancellation, and he was much less discrete than the CEOs about laying blame. In a statement posted to Twitter by his staff, the Secretary scolded a group that he called "the well-funded, obstructionist environmental lobby."[5] Brouillette, himself a former lobbyist, may have believed that an organized and well-resourced lobby orchestrated the pipeline's demise, but the actual situation was much different.[6]

The ACP's size and scope had triggered widespread opposition from people who spanned a large geographic area and who despised the project for a broad spectrum of reasons. Grassroots organizations, community groups, and individual actors sprang up along the six-hundred-mile route to oppose the pipeline for reasons related to property rights, land and water conservation, climate change, endangered species, historic preservation, and environmental justice. Their reasons for opposing the pipeline were based on scientific consensus about the need to curb the global consumption of fossil fuels and on a litany of local harms related to the construction and operation of large oil and gas pipelines.

Together, the various groups formed a large but decentralized coalition of people who gave their time, money, and labor to ensure that the ACP would not be built. A handful of groups pursued lawsuits with the support of high-profile environmental organizations such as the Southern Environmental Law Center and the Sierra Club, but the ACP ultimately succumbed to countless uncoordinated acts of resistance and truth-telling by people who refused to be bullied, silenced, or bought by some of the largest energy companies in the United States.[7]

Indigenous people—individuals as well as tribal nations—featured prominently in resistance against the ACP. Developers had planned to route the pipeline through several tribal communities, and for Native people who called these places home, disengagement was simply not an option. The proposed route cut through landscapes and waterways that held cultural significance for Lumbee, Coharie, Haliwa-Saponi, Meherrin, Nottoway, Monacan and other tribes in the region. The route also ran directly through several large Native communities including Prospect. According to demographic data compiled by federal officials, nearly thirty thousand Native Americans lived along the pipeline route—mostly in North Carolina. It would be the largest Indigenous population ever impacted by a natural gas pipeline in the United States.[8]

With few exceptions, Native people did not participate in lawsuits against the ACP, and tribes certainly did not fit Brouillette's description of a well-funded environmental lobby. Still, Indigenous peoples resisted the ACP in their own ways. Tribal members and governments used regulatory filings, education and outreach activities, and media engagements to draw persistent attention to injustices associated with the project. Their efforts brought Indigenous issues to the forefront of public discourse about the pipeline, and they kept the issues alive despite corporate campaigns and government actions that downplayed the project's outsized impacts on Native people and lands. Pressure from Indigenous peoples also forced state and federal officials into serious discussions about weak (or nonexistent) policies around environmental justice and tribal engagement.

Not all efforts were well-coordinated or outwardly successful, but Indigenous peoples kept a spotlight on serious problems associated with the ACP and played a fitting role in the demise of the project, as journalist Nick Martin observed in the *New Republic*. Writing about the ACP's cancellation and about a major legal ruling against the Dakota Access Pipeline handed down the very next day, Martin noted, "Extractive projects which endangered the people in their path were in the end blocked specifically by the people who would be directly affected by them."[9]

I spent years working alongside tribal communities affected by the ACP, and I think Martin's observation is spot on. Martin, who belongs to North Carolina's Sappony Tribe, covered the ACP in depth and gave special attention to tribal perspectives on the project. He understood the nuances of state-tribal relations in North Carolina and the vast power imbalances between tribes and energy companies in the region. Martin's observation is informed by his insider perspective, and it also rings true in a way that Brouillette's big green boogeyman does not.[10] Perhaps Brouillette was unaware of the persistent undercurrent of resistance by individuals, communities, and tribes along the pipeline route. Or perhaps he knew and still chose to frame it as a coordinated effort by a powerful environmental lobby. I have no idea. But Brouillette's comment illustrates how easily Indigenous peoples can be erased from stories that are essentially about us and about our homelands.

The problem, of course, is not that Native peoples are excluded from political statements and press releases about canceled pipelines. The omissions merely point to deeper issues—ignorance, denial, stereotyping—that lead to the erasure of Indigenous peoples from major decisions about the places that they call home. And the absence is not accidental; it is a design feature of settler colonialism. In Robeson County and elsewhere on the Coastal Plain, erasure of Native peoples from environmental decision-making is the latest chapter in a centuries-old effort to separate us from our territories. Scholars Eve Tuck and Wayne Yang put it bluntly: "In order for settlers to make a place their home, they must destroy and disappear the Indigenous peoples that live there . . . Indigenous peoples must be erased, must be made into ghosts."[11]

There may be ghosts in the Coastal Plain, but there are also flesh-and-blood Indians who still care about the fate of their ancestral territories. This chapter examines what happens when they take action.

A CONSORTIUM OF ENERGY COMPANIES first announced the ACP in September 2014. A press release from Duke Energy, one of the project leads, touted the pipeline as an economic development engine and a surefire way to meet North Carolina's "rapidly growing demand for natural gas."[12] The press release did not mention that the state's "rapidly growing demand" for gas was driven almost entirely by Duke Energy's expanding fleet of gas-fired electric power plants; in fact, developers had reserved nearly 80 percent of the ACP's capacity for electricity generation at their own facilities. For all practical purposes, Duke Energy and its partners were their own customers.[13]

Early designs for the ACP placed the pipeline's southern terminus near Duke Energy's Weatherspoon power plant in Lumberton, but the final plans placed the terminus halfway across Robeson County along NC 710 in Prospect.[14] From the fortified industrial compound there, developers would be able to pump new supplies of Appalachian shale gas directly into a network of pipelines that fed power plants and industrial facilities throughout eastern North Carolina.

Supporters—many of whom had industry ties—praised the pipeline as welcome news for the region. Pat McCrory, a Duke Energy retiree who served as governor of North Carolina at the time of the pipeline's initial public announcement, hailed the project as a job creator and economic boon for the state.[15] Other pro-business advocates followed suit. The North Carolina Chamber of Commerce declared that the ACP would make North Carolina more attractive to relocating businesses, claiming that industries had "overlooked the state due to an inadequate supply of reliable natural gas."[16]

However, news of the ACP also drew harsh criticism. Environmental groups warned that the project would encourage fracking, exacerbate the climate crisis, and disincentivize clean energy investments. Communities protested the idea of hosting a large high-pressure pipeline, which they viewed as detrimental to public health, property values, and ecological integrity.[17] Industry watchdogs accused pipeline developers of self-dealing.[18] Other groups and individuals highlighted the pipeline's environmental justice implications, explaining that energy companies and their shareholders would reap most of the rewards, while marginalized communities would shoulder a disproportionate share of the burdens.

Throughout the United States, fossil fuel pipelines place disproportionately high and adverse burdens on marginalized groups, and the ACP would be no exception.[19] The chosen route cut a gash two hundred miles long through eastern North Carolina, running through counties with large minority populations, high poverty rates, and high levels of social vulnerability compared to the state as a whole. Early on, developers had considered a more westerly alternative for the pipeline that ran through the Piedmont before descending into Robeson County.[20] It was a straighter shot than the eastern route, but the western route needed much longer spur pipelines to reach company-owned facilities east of the Fall Line. Ultimately, ACP developers abandoned the western alternative, citing concerns over added costs and impacts that would likely come with the extra pipeline mileage due to the long spurs.[21]

Unlike the eastern route, which cut through some of the most economically distressed counties in North Carolina, the western alternative traversed some of the most affluent parts of the state. It grazed North Carolina's Research Triangle and passed within a few miles of Chapel Hill and Hillsborough in relatively wealthy Orange and Chatham Counties. According to data from the North Carolina Department of Commerce, household incomes were 18 percent higher in counties along the main stem of the western route than in counties along the eastern route.[22] The abandoned western route not only cut through wealthier parts of North Carolina than the eastern route, but populations along the western route tended to be whiter as well.[23] Developers may have abandoned the western alternative because of the additional mileage, but their decision also shifted environmental and public health burdens away from wealthier, whiter communities and into communities with less money, power, and privilege.

The route that developers ultimately chose for the ACP also impacted a large number of culturally significant streams and wetlands to Lumbees and other Indigenous peoples in eastern North Carolina. The pipeline would cross more than three hundred water bodies, and it would permanently alter or destroy nearly five hundred acres of wetlands.[24] The Robeson County portion of the route crossed several tributaries to the Lumbee River, including Big Marsh, Raft Swamp, Burnt Swamp, and Bear Swamp. Developers planned to clear-cut the swamp forests at each water body crossing, transforming the long green fingers of forest into shorter fragments bisected by pipeline crossings.

In Prospect, developers had already begun to acquire easements to install the ACP on privately owned lands. Easements placed a litany of restrictions on landowners, banning "houses, house additions, trailers, tool sheds, garages, poles, patios, pools, septic tanks, or other objects not easily removable" from a fifty-foot-wide swath around the buried pipeline.[25] Landowners could not re-plant trees in the easement, and in some cases, developers reserved the right to return to the land, year after year, to spray chemical herbicides that would ensure no trees or shrubs grew over the pipeline.[26]

Easements threatened to lower property values, and so pipeline developers sent land agents to negotiate one-time payouts to compensate landowners. But in Prospect and other places where Lumbee families occupied multi-generational homeplaces, the losses were difficult to quantify. How might the presence of a massive gas pipeline and its restrictive easement impact the long-term ability of a property to serve as a homeplace for generations of Lumbee people? What, if anything, was fair compensation for the uncertainty and risk?

The answer, it seems, was a little more than $4,000 per acre for land put into temporary or permanent easements. At least that is the value suggested by excise taxes levied on the first dozen ACP easement agreements filed at the Robeson County courthouse in late 2015. Eventually, hundreds of signed easement agreements and modifications would flow into the Robeson County Register of Deeds office between August 2015 and July 2020, when the pipeline was canceled. Many—if not most—of the landowners have recognizably Lumbee names.[27]

I have no idea how many Lumbee landowners negotiated for compensation or favorable route adjustments; I am not even sure how many of them knew that the process was open to negotiation. So far, no one has sought to answer these questions in any kind of systematic way. But accounts from other places along the ACP route suggest that some landowners had no idea that the easement terms were negotiable. Other landowners faced aggressive tactics, including lowball compensation offers and preemptive threats to seize easements using eminent domain—threats made before pipeline developers had even been granted those powers by federal officials.[28]

Pipeline easements limit what people can do with their land. They give strangers permission to access, alter, and despoil not only places of cultural significance but also spaces of private significance for individuals and families. Easements topple our grandparents' shade trees and uproot their grapevines. Easements for extremely large pipelines like the ACP also conceal serious risks of explosion that extend far beyond their nominal boundaries.[29] In all of these ways, easements transform homeplaces and the traditions of making and keeping homeplaces alive for future generations.

As the pipeline route eventually took shape, restrictive easements and other burdens seemed certain to concentrate in communities already marked by poverty and racial marginalization. In Prospect and other Native communities scattered throughout the Coastal Plain, people began to worry about the cultural harms of a pipeline that would tear through fields and swamps—felling trees, gouging the earth, and adding new kinds of injury to landscapes that have, for centuries, helped define our identities as Indigenous peoples.

PROSPECT HAS A HISTORY with natural gas pipelines that predates the ACP by decades. I am not talking about small pipelines that run beneath residential streets and deliver gas to homes and businesses; I mean massive gas transmission lines—the interstate highways of pipelines that transport natural gas over great distances. Some of the transmission pipelines beneath Prospect are larger than two feet in diameter, and they operate at very high pressures—several hundred pounds per square inch. Along with transmission pipelines, Prospect hosts aboveground infrastructure—fenced-in compounds where piping, valves, filters, and manifolds sprout from the earth. Gas hisses and squeals as it rushes through the tortuous maze. Occasionally, natural gas erupts from a faulty valve or fitting inside one of the compounds. When it does, a deafening roar travels for miles in every direction.[30]

Despite hosting all of this infrastructure, most people in Prospect do not have access to natural gas for their own use.[31] The closest residential gas service is in the town of Pembroke, several miles away. Of course, the lack of gas service in Prospect may not be a bad thing given that gas-fired appliances are major sources of indoor air pollution in the United States. One study found benzene, toluene, and a host of other toxic air pollutants leaking from natural gas stoves in Boston-area homes.[32]

People in Prospect may not have to deal with toxic leaks from natural gas stoves, but they still have to contend with pipelines that route millions of cubic feet of gas beneath the community each day. The situation is familiar for communities throughout the United States; transmission pipelines saddle rural communities with burdens while delivering fuel to faraway power plants and industrial facilities. In Prospect, most of the pipelines lead to power plants that supply electricity to large parts of North Carolina.

The tight connection between natural gas and electricity is relatively new in North Carolina. Before the shale gas boom of the mid-2000s, most of the state's electricity was generated by coal. Power plants consumed only a small fraction of the natural gas piped into North Carolina—between 5 and 10 percent, depending on the year. Back then, homes, restaurants, commercial buildings, and factories used most of the natural gas in North Carolina. The state's gas consumption hovered around 220 billion cubic feet per year throughout the 1990s and early 2000s.

The situation changed in the mid-2000s, when large-scale fracking operations began to release new supplies of natural gas that previously had been locked in shale deposits beneath the central Appalachian Mountains. Energy companies in North Carolina began to eye Appalachian shale gas—not quite on their doorstep, but close enough—as a possible replacement for coal in their electricity generation portfolios.[33] Coal was expensive to mine, it was dirty to burn, and it created a steady supply of toxic coal ash, which had been accumulating—for decades—in basins adjacent to riverside power plants.[34] Catastrophic coal ash spills in 2008 and 2014 polluted southeastern rivers with arsenic and other toxic metals, triggering a cascade of negative publicity and regulatory actions that pressured North Carolina's major energy company, Duke Energy, to stop burning coal and to do something about the ash basins adjacent to its power plants.[35]

As problems mounted with coal, and as markets flooded with supplies of shale gas, Duke Energy began to rely heavily on natural gas to replace coal in the company's generating portfolio. Gas was cheaper and came with fewer liabilities than coal—at least as far as Duke Energy's leaders were concerned.[36] Yes, fracking was a dirty business, and methane emissions certainly exacerbated the climate crisis, but those problems were far away and much easier to ignore than coal ash, which would eventually become a multibillion-dollar problem in Duke Energy's own backyard.[37]

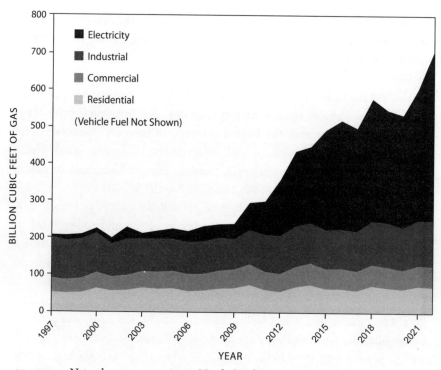

GRAPH 4.1 Natural gas consumption in North Carolina, 1997–2022. Data from "Natural Gas Consumption for North Carolina," US Energy Information Administration, April 2023, http://www.eia.gov/dnav/ng/ng_cons_sum_dcu_snc_a.htm.

Natural gas consumption soared in North Carolina as Duke Energy brought new gas-fired units online to replace coal-burning plants. The state's gas consumption doubled between 2009 and 2015 (graph 4.1). Beginning in 2015, electricity production consumed more natural gas than all other uses in the state combined.[38] Most years, North Carolina set a new record for natural gas consumption, a trend driven almost entirely by electricity generation. As natural gas consumption increased, so did the pressure to build new pipelines, compressor stations, and related facilities in places like Prospect.

Prospect became a hub for natural gas in the late 1950s, after a group of businessmen in Fayetteville took notice of the growing nationwide interest in natural gas as a heating source for homes and businesses. Much of that interest was driven by the opening of the Transcontinental Pipeline, or TRANSCO, in 1950. The pipeline delivered natural gas from the Gulf Coast to states along the Eastern Seaboard,[39] running from Texas to New York. At the time, TRANSCO was the world's longest gas pipeline, and it cut directly through North Carolina's

Piedmont. Charlotte and other nearby cities built short spurs that tapped into TRANSCO and supplied local gas utilities. But tapping directly into TRANSCO was not an option for cities in eastern North Carolina; they were too far away.[40]

To remedy the situation, the group of Fayetteville businessmen proposed a six-hundred-mile-long network of pipelines to carry natural gas from TRANSCO to cities and factories in eastern North Carolina. They organized a new firm, the North Carolina Natural Gas Corporation, or NCNG, to build and operate the pipeline network. The firm would recover investment costs and turn a profit by selling TRANSCO gas to municipalities and large industrial customers.

For technical expertise, the group recruited Volney H. Kyle Jr., an engineer from Houma, Louisiana, with decades of experience in the pipeline industry. Kyle grew up in Terrebonne Parish long before the area became a logistical hub for offshore oil and gas production. His father, Volney Sr., was a Confederate army veteran who moved to Houma in the 1880s and managed nearby sugar cane plantations. After graduating from Tulane, Kyle worked on—and eventually managed—large natural gas transmission pipelines in his home state of Louisiana and as far away as Colorado and Wisconsin. Among the major projects he worked on was a large transmission pipeline between Baton Rouge and New Orleans.[41] The pipeline carried natural gas that served as both fuel and feedstock for a booming petrochemical industry along an eighty-mile stretch of the Mississippi River later nicknamed "Cancer Alley."[42]

The Fayetteville company relied on Kyle's deep industry knowledge to plan the pipeline network and to help the group navigate the political and regulatory waters. In particular, NCNG would need authorizations from both the state utilities commission and the Federal Power Commission—predecessor to the current-day Federal Energy Regulatory Commission. One of Kyle's first objectives was to drum up support for natural gas in Coastal Plain cities through advertising campaigns and by promoting the fuel's benefits directly to local politicians and business leaders. The endorsements and alliances would improve the company's chances of gaining regulatory approval to build and operate the pipeline.

Kyle and other NCNG officers attended city council meetings and met with chambers of commerce, building hype around a "new natural resource" and kindling a fear of missing out among eastern North Carolinians if they did not support the project. The plan worked. Newspapers gushed over the NCNG proposal, repeating the company's claim that natural gas was sure to attract new industries to the region. One editorial opined that the pipeline would "broaden the horizons" of citizens. The chairman of the state utilities commission agreed with NCNG leadership, calling the pipeline "a tremendous thing" that would industrialize and invigorate the Coastal Plain's flagging economy.[43]

With enthusiastic support from state and local officials, NCNG received full approval from regulators in 1956 to supply eastern North Carolina with natural gas from TRANSCO.[44] The company set out to fine-tune the plan, which included finalizing the route. The initial plan called for the pipeline's main trunk to strike out east from TRANSCO, crossing the eastern Piedmont and Sandhills before cutting through NCNG's hometown of Fayetteville. From Fayetteville, long spur pipelines would deliver gas to Lumberton, Wilmington, Rocky Mount, and other parts of the Coastal Plain.

Near the end of the planning phase, sometime before fall 1958, NCNG altered the route of the main trunk pipeline. Instead of passing through Fayetteville, the site of NCNG's headquarters, the route of the trunk pipeline was relocated some twenty miles south to rural Robeson County. The new trunk would branch in Prospect, on the west side of Bear Swamp. The main line would continue southeast, toward Lumberton and Wilmington, and a major branch would run northeast, toward Fayetteville, Goldsboro, and cities in far eastern North Carolina.[45] Later on, the company would file maps with the state utilities commission showing the completed route with Prospect labeled as "Junction A" (figure 4.1).

In January 1959, NCNG held a groundbreaking ceremony for the much-anticipated project at an auspicious site near the Greene County community of Snow Hill. There, the northeastern branch of the pipeline would split into three separate lines running to New Bern, Rocky Mount, and Greenville. Kyle spoke at a luncheon before the guest of honor, Governor Luther Hodges, turned the first shovel of earth. Hodges pronounced the pipeline a boon to industry and one of eastern North Carolina's "great developments."[46]

At the time, the six-hundred-mile pipeline network was poised to be one of the largest utility projects in the state's history. Prospect and Snow Hill were separated by more than one hundred miles, and they were nowhere near the most distant points in the network, which covered more than ten thousand square miles of North Carolina. Both sites were strategic points in the network, but they were noteworthy for other reasons. Prospect, the site of Junction A, was—and still is today—a large and prominent Lumbee community that shares space with an ever-expanding tangle of gas pipelines and related infrastructure. The spot near Snow Hill where Hodges turned a shovelful of dirt, lies only a short distance from the site of Fort Nooheroka, where 246 years

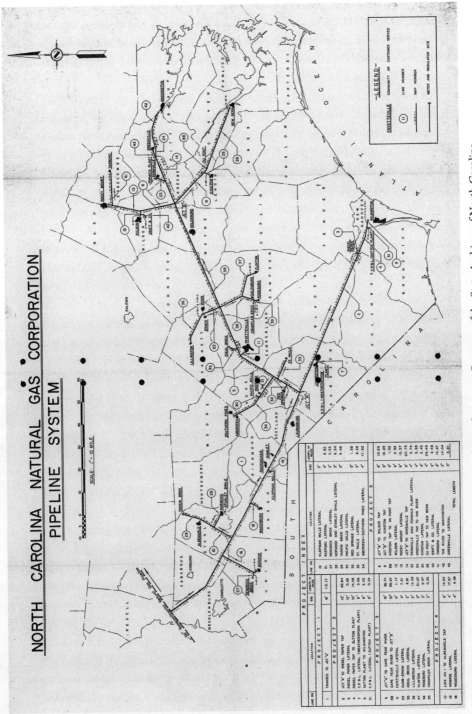

FIGURE 4.1 Natural gas infrastructure in eastern North Carolina, 1959. Courtesy of the State Archives of North Carolina.

earlier, Colonel James Moore ordered hundreds of Native people burned to death after his militia stormed the fort. The company's groundbreaking took place only a mile or so from the most horrific act of violence against Indigenous people in colonial North Carolina. Maps filed with the utility commission simply called it "Junction B."

In no way do I mean that Governor Hodges should have performed a land acknowledgment before the groundbreaking or that Volney Kyle Jr. should have invited tribal leaders to attend his luncheon. Those ideas are anachronistic and absurd. Native people enjoyed little or no power, visibility, or regard outside of their own communities during the 1950s, a time when Jim Crow policies sanctioned open racial discrimination against Native Americans and their African American neighbors. What I mean is this: when Indigenous people today say that fossil fuel projects plow through their lands without regard for the well-being of communities and cultural landscapes, they are not exaggerating; they are speaking from generations of lived experience. The NCNG project was a colonial endeavor, planned by and marketed to people who enjoyed the privileges of white supremacy.

After the groundbreaking, it took less than a year to complete the six-hundred-mile pipeline network. Once the project was finished in 1959, Junction A became a critical node in the newly completed network (map 4.1). From that date forward, most of the natural gas consumed on North Carolina's Coastal Plain flowed beneath Prospect.[47] A compressor station, powered by two large gas-fired engines, kept the pipelines pressurized so that gas would continue to flow. The engines ran around the clock for decades, belching exhaust from stacks that slowly turned brown with rust. Paint peeled from the metal sheds inside the compound. More infrastructure cropped up around the engines. Razor wire bloomed. Companies merged, and NCNG became Piedmont Natural Gas. Duke Energy acquired Piedmont.

In that time, Prospect has experienced a few near misses involving gas leaks. One of the largest occurred in November 2017, when at 4 A.M., a malfunctioning valve at the compressor station spewed gas violently into the night air. More than ninety minutes passed before technicians could reach the station and stop the leak. By then, two million cubic feet of gas had escaped.[48]

The leak began with a deafening roar that awakened residents for miles in every direction. Talford Dial, a Lumbee man who lived nearby, likened the noise to a large jet airliner taking off. Neither Dial nor anyone else in the area received any alerts about the potentially explosive leak. Residents suspected the compressor station, but they only learned of the leak from a Lumbee man

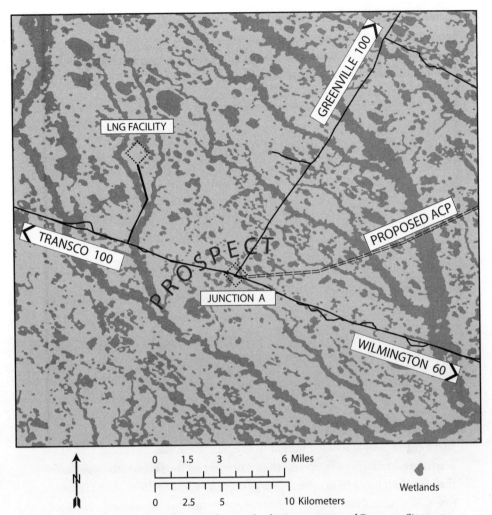

MAP 4.1 Present-day natural gas pipelines and infrastructure around Prospect. Signposts show prominent locations. Signs with arrows show directions and distances (in miles) to places located off the map. Map by author.

who walked from his home to the compound and spoke with the technicians. A company spokesperson reasoned that the leak never posed a safety issue, but people in Prospect did not share the company's confidence. Dial summarized the feelings of many residents when he told the local newspaper, "If that thing goes off, I cease to exist."[49]

WORD OF A NEW PIPELINE—the ACP—began to trickle into Prospect after the project was announced in late 2014. A handful of people were enthusiastic, some were ambivalent, and many were worried. Leaks, restrictive easements, and noisy industrial compounds were uneasy realities of life in Prospect, but the ACP raised new questions. It would be larger than any other pipeline in the region, and it would operate at much higher pressures. What additional stress and risk would come with the project? For a community already surrounded by pipelines, the ACP felt like overload.

Federal regulators seemed untroubled by the idea that the ACP would add to the burdens already experienced by people in Prospect. They also seemed unconcerned about the overrepresentation of Native Americans along the pipeline route through North Carolina, Virginia, and West Virginia. The Federal Energy Regulatory Commission declared as much in the draft environmental impact statement for the pipeline, released by the agency in late 2016. In the executive summary, regulators emphasized their conclusion that "environmental justice populations would not be disproportionately affected" by the ACP.[50]

The statement came as a surprise to people who knew anything about tribal nations in the region and were aware of the pipeline's proposed route. A glance at the ACP's corporate logo—which, conveniently, incorporated a stylized route map—showed the pipeline snaking through Meherrin, Haliwa-Saponi, Coharie, and Lumbee communities in North Carolina and other Native communities in Virginia.[51]

Datasets buried in the appendices of the environmental impact statement confirmed that Indigenous populations made up a disproportionately large share of the people living adjacent to the pipeline route. Lumbees and other Native Americans made up less than 1 percent of the three-state region, but they made up more than 5 percent of people living along the pipeline route—a five-fold overrepresentation of Native Americans in harm's way. In North Carolina, they made up more than 13 percent of people along the route—a more than ten-fold overrepresentation. The percentages sound small, but they translated into large numbers of people. Specifically, one in four Native Americans in North Carolina lived along the route—nearly thirty thousand people in all. Not even the Dakota Access Pipeline, which received international criticism and notoriety over its threat to the Standing Rock and Cheyenne River Sioux Tribes, affected such a large Indigenous population.[52]

I encountered the demographic appendix to the environmental impact statement and crunched the numbers myself in early 2017, a few days after regulators released the document to the public. Right away, I found a fatal flaw in the way that regulators had analyzed census data to come up with the assertion that no racial disparities existed. Their logic went something like this: For each census tract along the planned route, regulators asked whether the tract had a minority population that was disproportionately high compared to the surrounding county. If the answer was "yes," they tallied the census tract on one side of a ledger. If the answer was "no," they tallied it on the other side. Regulators asked the question over and over again, once for each census tract, and they updated the ledger accordingly.

To round out the analysis, regulators simply counted the number of census tracts on each side of the ledger. The environmental impact statement emphasized that because more tracts fell on the "no" side of the ledger than the "yes" side, the adverse impacts would not disproportionately impact marginalized groups in the region. But one of the problems with counting census tracts on opposite sides of a ledger is that the method is only informative if census tracts have roughly equal numbers of residents. Otherwise, large racial or socioeconomic disparities may go unnoticed. In pure mathematical terms, regulators computed a simple average when the issue called for a weighted average.

Census tracts along the ACP route varied wildly in population; the smallest had ten residents, and the largest had more than ten thousand. Under these circumstances, the demographic analysis employed by the agency was utterly useless as a decision-making tool. Worse yet, the environmental impact statement barely mentioned any affected tribes in North Carolina. These red flags prompted me to work throughout the spring of 2017 to catalog the problems for decision-makers. I submitted a technical report to federal regulators and tribal leaders, and *Science* magazine published a much-abbreviated version of the report a few months later.[53]

The ACP's impending impacts on Lumbee and other North Carolina tribes received some press coverage, especially after news broke that federal regulators had conducted their review without formally consulting any eastern North Carolina tribes or acknowledging the disparate impacts on Native Americans.[54] But attention waned after regulators authorized the pipeline in late 2017, issuing statements that doubled down on their original claims that poor and minority communities would not be disproportionately impacted by the project. By 2018, many of North Carolina's tribal leaders and community members sensed that they were being erased from yet another important decision about the future of land, water, and people in their territories.

That same year, the pipeline's lead developer, Dominion Energy, launched a massive advertising campaign—the largest in company history—to promote the project as an economic boon for communities in both North Carolina and Virginia.[55] The campaign included press releases, television and radio commercials, and social media posts. Public relationships staff trumpeted endorsements from labor unions, chambers of commerce, and others who hoped to benefit from the project. Campaign materials praised the federal government's favorable review of the project, ignoring the fact that regulators conducted the review with no input from tribal communities about the unique burdens they would likely face from the construction and operation of the ACP.[56] As the campaign sought to paint the project as an environmentally benign panacea for the Coastal Plain's struggling economy, contractors began felling trees and stockpiling sections of mint-green pipe along the pipeline's six-hundred-mile route. Early signs of activity along the route, together with the expensive multi-pronged advertising campaign, created a sense that the ACP was inevitable—a done deal.

The atmosphere of inevitability intensified feelings of marginalization and invisibility among Native people who, by 2018, already felt that developers and regulators cared little about Indigenous values or perspectives. Federal regulators had approved the pipeline over objections from tribal leaders in North Carolina who pleaded—unsuccessfully—for formal involvement in the environmental review.[57] One leader was Lumbee Chairman Harvey Godwin Jr., who months earlier—in 2017—had called on regulators to engage with his administration "in a way that acknowledges its status as a tribal government."[58] Godwin asserted that the 1956 Lumbee Act required federal regulators to consult with the Lumbee Tribe prior to finalizing the pipeline's environmental review.

Godwin's call for formal tribal consultation was bold; it was a demand for regulators to treat Lumbees as they would treat any federally recognized tribe in a similar situation. In other words, he called for agency officials to meet directly with Lumbee leaders and knowledge-holders to identify and address blind spots in the environmental impact statement. The blind spots were not trivial; the pipeline route cut through the heart of Lumbee territory and posed risks for between one-quarter and one-third of all tribal members.

Coharie and Haliwa-Saponi leaders issued similar demands for government-to-government consultation with the Federal Energy Regulatory Commission. No other Coastal Plain tribe had legislation like the 1956 Lumbee Act to bolster their demands, but they called for fair and ethical treatment as tribal nations anyway.[59] The Haliwa-Saponi Tribe went a step further and secured a resolution of support from the National Congress of American Indians. The mid-2017 resolution called for regulators to delay any decisions about the ACP until conducting an environmental review that "fully considers the concerns of affected Indian tribal nations."[60] The North Carolina Commission of

Indian Affairs weighed in with additional advice, noting, "Federal guidance documents pertaining [to] the National Environmental Policy Act and the National Historic Preservation Act encourage meaningful consultation between regulatory agencies and Indian tribes, even if those tribes are not federally recognized."[61]

Throughout 2017 and 2018, Godwin and other tribal leaders demanded government-to-government consultation with pipeline regulators, even though they knew the process was deeply flawed. In fact, the failures of tribal consultation policy had been on full display months earlier as procedural and legal disputes raged over efforts by an energy company to build the Dakota Access Pipeline through Oceti Sakowin treaty lands. For much of 2016, tribal leaders and community members in North Carolina followed news from half a continent away, where water protectors faced off against militarized law enforcement and private contractors on the plains overlooking the Missouri River.

Actually, North Carolina tribal leaders and Indigenous community members did much more than follow news about the Dakota Access Pipeline. In 2016, the Lumbee tribal council issued a resolution of support for the Standing Rock Sioux Tribe, and Lumbees sent an official delegation to Standing Rock to deliver ceremonial tobacco and to plant the Lumbee flag alongside flags of other tribal nations who stood in solidarity with water protectors.[62] In its resolution, the Lumbee tribal council specifically called out a lack of meaningful consultation between the tribe and the Army Corps of Engineers prior to the federal government's controversial decision to authorize the pipeline's Missouri River crossing. The Eastern Band of Cherokee tribal council passed a similar resolution and donated funds to the Standing Rock Sioux Tribe's legal effort on the same day.[63] If tribal consultation was not already a front-burner issue for tribes in North Carolina, Standing Rock ensured that it was.

In March 2017, shortly before North Carolina tribal leaders began to petition the Federal Energy Regulatory Commission about the ACP, the United Nations issued a scathing report on Indigenous rights and energy development in the United States. The United Nations' special rapporteur on the rights of Indigenous Peoples, Victoria Tauli-Corpuz, toured tribal communities throughout the western United States and reported, "Sadly, I found the situation faced by the Standing Rock Sioux Tribe is shared by many other indigenous communities in the United States, as tribal communities nationwide wrestle with the realities of living in ground zero of energy impact. The goal of tribal consultation is not simply to check a box, or to merely give tribes a chance to be heard. Rather, the core objective is to provide federal decision makers with context, information, and perspectives needed to support informed decisions that actually protect tribal interests."[64]

In March 2017, a few days after the release of Tauli-Corpuz's report, I summarized her findings for a group of tribal leaders and other professionals at the North Carolina Indian Unity Conference in Charlotte. Merging lessons from Standing Rock with insights from Tauli-Corpuz, I noted, "Your tribe may oppose or support a particular project, but consultation is an act of sovereignty that tribes should take seriously. Tribes can use their consultation status to ensure environmental justice for their communities—in other words, to ensure that our people do not receive a disproportionate share of pollution or other environmental burdens."[65]

The Dakota Access Pipeline underscored many problems with tribal consultation in the United States, and the United Nations' report placed the problems in a global context. By early 2017, tribal officials and other Native leaders in North Carolina knew the flaws of tribal consultation and were clear-eyed about the limits of consultation policies. Nevertheless, they insisted that the Federal Energy Regulatory Commission engage directly with them before finalizing the ACP's environmental review. Tribal leaders wanted to make sure that—at a bare minimum—the official record reflected their unique concerns about the pipeline's potential impacts on tribal territories—including the damages to culturally important landscapes, wetlands, and homeplaces. They viewed direct consultation with federal regulators as the only way to ensure that these concerns were incorporated into the decision-making process. The leaders also viewed consultation with pipeline regulators as a way to exercise the inherent sovereignty of their respective tribal nations.

Even if federal regulators did not plan to address the concerns raised by tribes, consultation would increase the likelihood that the concerns of Native people would appear in official records about the pipeline's impacts. Generations of Native Americans on the Coastal Plain had been ignored when it came to decisions that impacted their landscapes, waterways, and communities. Federal regulators were poised to continue that trend by leaving tribes out of yet another important decision. If nothing else, direct consultation would leave a paper trail describing how Native people had stood up for themselves and for future generations.

Direct government-to-government consultation could also force regulators to own up to the racial disparities involving Native Americans living in the path of the pipeline. Along the North Carolina section of the route, Native Americans were overrepresented by a factor of ten compared to their numbers in the rest of the state—an astonishing disparity that could not be ignored. Even using the agency's more restrictive reference area—specific counties crossed by the pipeline—Native Americans were overrepresented by 50 percent.[66] Formal consultation would give tribal leaders an opportunity to raise the issue of racial disparities and, hopefully, persuade regulators to acknowledge and address the pipeline's disproportionately high and adverse impacts on Native people.

GODWIN AND OTHER TRIBAL LEADERS never had an opportunity to consult directly with federal regulators on the Atlantic Coast Pipeline. Instead of heeding calls for consultation, the Federal Energy Regulatory Commission chose a much different strategy. In April 2017, soon after Godwin and other tribal leaders submitted requests to consult with regulators, the agency ordered energy companies—not federal officials—to work directly with North Carolina tribes to find out the locations of "tribal sites in the project area and the locations of natural resources that may be part of the tribes' traditional practices."[67]

The Federal Energy Regulatory Commission's directive essentially shut the door on meaningful consultation with tribes. Tribal officials had expected to work directly with federal regulators to update the environmental impact statement; they did not want their perspectives filtered through the lens of corporate representatives hoping for a favorable and expedient environmental review. Although the Federal Energy Regulatory Commission had a widespread reputation for "rubber stamping" natural gas pipelines, the agency could not approve a project without completing an environmental review.[68] Corporate sponsors of the ACP were banking on timely agency approval to meet their own deadlines, and they also believed that a favorable environmental review would help them build public support by framing the project as minimally invasive.[69]

Meaningful tribal consultation, however, was a potential wildcard—even a possible wrench in the works—from the standpoint of pipeline developers and federal regulators. If tribes insisted that the environmental impact statement include, for example, a full accounting of the racial disparities related to the pipeline route, regulators would need to put substantial time and effort into justifying the route's disproportionately high and adverse impacts on Native Americans. Similarly, if tribal consultation revealed concerns over impacts to cultural landscapes from pipeline construction and operation, regulators would have to describe those impacts and explain why the project should go forward anyway. Either scenario could delay construction or undermine the companies' efforts to portray the pipeline as environmentally benign. In reality, consultation only seemed like a wildcard at this stage because regulators had failed to engage with tribes at the beginning of the review process. By 2017, the agency was looking to wrap up the environmental review—not to introduce new concerns arising from consultation.[70]

Regulators found an easy way out. Because none of the North Carolina tribes had full federal recognition, the agency simply sidestepped their requests for consultation based on a minimalist interpretation of tribal engagement policies. Specifically, the National Historic Preservation Act, which plays a role in federal environmental reviews, requires that agencies consult only with federally recognized tribes. However, the Advisory Council on Historic Preservation, which issues guidance to agencies on how to carry out responsibilities under the law, recommends consultation with tribes regardless of recognition status. The advisory group issued a 2017 guidance document that warned regulators not to assume that recognition status is an indicator of a tribe's potential to hold deep historical or cultural significance to specific places. The group specifically noted that non-federally recognized tribes

> may also have important information about historic properties in the project area. For example, some non-federally recognized tribes still have ancestral ties to an area or still occupy their aboriginal territory. Members of non-federally recognized tribes may be direct descendants of indigenous peoples who once occupied an area affected by an undertaking, or can provide additional information regarding historic properties that should be considered in the review process.[71]

The Federal Energy Regulatory Commission simply ignored this guidance, although it would take more than a year for tribal leaders and community members to receive the official word that they had been snubbed. When federal regulators issued their directive to pipeline developers in April 2017, it was entirely unclear whether they still intended to consult with North Carolina tribes. After all, the directive contradicted the Federal Energy Regulatory Commission's own policy against delegating tribal consultation to third parties.[72] At that time, the Atlantic Coast Pipeline's environmental review was moving to completion, but it was not yet final. Tribal leaders still had a window of time to work directly with regulators to ensure that their concerns were adequately addressed in the final review documents—documents that would play a defining role in the agency's decision about whether to authorize the Atlantic Coast Pipeline. With such an important decision on the line, regulators would surely want to hear directly from tribes instead of having tribal concerns shuttled to them via pipeline developers. After all, the companies had no obligation to expand the narrow scope of the agency's directive or do anything else that might jeopardize the pipeline's favorable and expedient environmental review. But the agency never pursued direct consultation with any of the North Carolina tribes.

More than a year later, in August 2018, the Federal Energy Regulatory Commission issued a statement citing the tribes' recognition status as the motivating factor in their decision not to engage directly in consultation. In the statement, regulators claimed that even the Lumbee Tribe, which had partial recognition under the 1956 Lumbee Act, was ineligible for consultation.[73] The agency's assertion was bold, and it directly contradicted Lumbee tribal chairman Godwin's earlier claim that the Lumbee Act actually afforded the tribe consultation rights during the environmental review. Regulators never addressed this contradiction, and they neither cited precedent nor provided additional context to defend their actions.

The most generous interpretation of the agency's action is that the directive to pipeline developers was an attempt to meet North Carolina tribes halfway. But even if energy companies could set aside their conflicts of interest, the agency's narrow instructions—that companies learn locations of tribally significant sites and resources—closed the door to any substantive input from tribes on topics they had actually expressed concerns about in their letters to the agency. Ultimately, the directive snubbed tribes and confirmed the agency's reputation as a rubber stamp for the natural gas industry.

Regulators also set a harmful precedent that contradicted federal guidance and scholarly consensus on the subject of tribal consultation.[74] Specifically, by attempting to substitute corporate engagement for government-to-government tribal consultation, federal regulators twisted the meaning of consultation from a useful (and possibly transformative) step in their decision-making process into an easy task for pipeline developers to check off their to-do list prior to gaining regulatory approval. Worse yet, the agency's action continued the centuries-long practice of excluding these particular tribal communities from decisions about their territories; it perpetuated colonial practices of reshaping Native territories while silencing Native voices.

Quite apart from these issues, tribal leaders and community members were shocked by the nature of the directive; federal regulators wanted North Carolina tribes to disclose information about culturally sensitive sites directly to energy companies. Only a few months earlier, energy companies behind the Dakota Access Pipeline allegedly used culturally sensitive information to bulldoze sacred sites located in treaty territory near the Missouri River.[75] When water protectors attempted to stop the destruction, a North Carolina-based private security firm released attack dogs and pepper sprayed the group.

When I first saw headlines about these violent attacks at Standing Rock, I was preparing to present at a Congressional briefing on water security in the United States. It was my first time on Capitol Hill as a scientific expert, and I had been invited to speak at the briefing by the University Corporation for Atmospheric Research, an academic consortium that promotes earth system sciences and oversees the National Center for Atmospheric Research. The organizers had asked me to share examples of field-based research used to inform predictive models of flooding and drought. But as I prepared for the briefing, reports of violence against water protectors at Standing Rock gave me pause; I was a privileged academic with a rare national platform to speak about water. I felt obligated to remind federal decision-makers that Indigenous perspectives matter when it comes to creating policies and making decisions about water.

After seeking advice from colleagues and elders, I modified my remarks with strong support from the sponsoring consortium and from the other panelists. On the day of the briefing, I discussed field-based research, and I also spent a portion of my time addressing the need to respect Indigenous perspectives on water. A September 2016 press release for the briefing summarized my remarks: "Indigenous peoples across the United States are diverse, but one common theme is that water is sacred.... It's not only critical for life, but it is life itself. Beyond the tools, the models, and the management lies the knowledge of the original inhabitants of this nation that water binds us all to a common fate."[76]

I did not visit Standing Rock, but I followed the news closely as water protectors used their bodies and voices to reshape dialogue on the rights of Indigenous peoples. Their efforts drew widespread attention to the fact that colonialism thrives in the twenty-first century and continues to threaten Indigenous communities and cultures through extractive industries and associated infrastructure. The Dakota Access Pipeline dominated discussions in North Carolina's tribal communities just as it dominated discussions throughout Indian Country. Yet in the midst of the trauma, wonder, and incomprehensibility of Standing Rock, the Federal Energy Regulatory Commission decided to ignore tribal leaders' requests for direct consultation on the ACP. The decision was not only disappointing; it was utterly tone-deaf.

LEAD DEVELOPER ON THE ACP, Dominion Energy, eagerly took up the Federal Energy Regulatory Commission's directive to communicate with tribes about the company's project. In June 2017, a few weeks after the federal agency issued its directive, executives from Dominion Energy gave a public presentation to the North Carolina Commission of Indian Affairs during the group's quarterly meeting in Pembroke.[77] The meeting took place in a large gymnasium that is part of the Lumbee Tribe's Boys and Girls Club. One end of the gymnasium floor—a basketball court—held a makeshift boardroom with seating for twenty-one commissioners who represented the state's eight tribes and four urban Native organizations. Staff members and officials from several state agencies sat interspersed among commission members at folding tables. The tables faced a small lectern situated on the large tribal seal that adorned the half-court jump circle. An arrangement of blankets, shawls, and pottery adorned the lectern where speakers stood to address the commission.

Behind the lectern, on the opposite half of the basketball court, several dozen people occupied rows of folding chairs. Invited speakers, tribal members, journalists, and members of the public sat shoulder to shoulder in long rows, observing both the ceremony and the business of the commission meeting. The proceedings were amplified by a small PA system that mingled with the audiences' squeaking shoes, scooting chair legs, and not-so-hushed voices in a cacophony that reverberated from every surface in the gymnasium.

A handful of Dominion Energy executives, including the company's vice president, external affairs manager, and energy policy director, sat alongside other invited speakers in the first row of folding chairs. The meeting was a procession of individuals and groups that had business before the Commission: voter registration, census planning, community health programs. The summer morning streamed into the gymnasium through windows near the ceiling, and the meeting settled into a rhythm of presentation, discussion, and deliberation.

During their slot on the agenda, the energy company executives recited well-worn industry talking points about the economic benefits of pipelines in general, and about the benefits the proposed ACP in particular. They laid out an ambitious timeline for construction that involved groundbreaking later that year. The executives also emphasized their desire to understand tribal concerns as pipeline construction moved forward.

Unsurprisingly, the presentation utterly missed the mark for many of the commissioners and tribal members in the gymnasium that day. Months earlier, some of these commissioners—who were also tribal leaders—had raised alarms about the failure of the environmental impact statement to identify and address racial disparities involving Native American populations along the pipeline's route. These were the same tribal leaders who had expressed concerns about regulators' failure to consult with them about the pipeline's potential impacts in their communities and territories. The leaders had argued that until regulators addressed these deficiencies, it would be impossible for them to make a well-informed decision about whether to authorize the project.

Now, months later and with no response from regulators, energy company executives had arrived at the Commission meeting to announce that the environmental review was virtually complete and that construction would soon begin. Their presentation implied that federal regulators already had all of the information needed to approve the ACP, even with no input from tribes.

The idea that the pipeline's environmental review was complete stood at odds with the experiences of tribal leaders and members of tribal communities who had identified problems with the environmental impact statement earlier that year. In their view, these problems demonstrated that regulators were incapable of assessing the environmental and cultural impacts of such a project without the assistance of affected tribes.

The energy company executives missed this point entirely in their presentation. Despite statements about wishing to understand tribal concerns, the presentation revolved around the assumption that the project was inevitable. The presentation reinforced this assumption by emphasizing the aggressive construction timeline, years of preparation by the companies, and a dire need for natural gas to spur economic development in eastern North Carolina. With the exception of a few slides that summarized the status of archaeological work along the pipeline route, the presentation was geared toward a chamber of commerce or economic development club, not a gathering of tribal representatives awaiting responses from federal regulators. The executives drove home the pitch-like nature of their presentation by distributing brochures to commissioners that advertised employment and contracting opportunities related to pipeline construction.

Intentionally or not, the presentation set boundaries around the types of concerns that energy companies seemed willing to address. Issues that did not seriously affect their plans were negotiable, but questions about whether the pipeline should be built through tribal communities—or built at all—were out-of-bounds. Through it all ran a theme of economic development; the presentation touted cheap domestic energy in the long term and four thousand temporary construction jobs in the short term. Whatever the intention, the presentation communicated a message that tribal leaders would be crazy not to support the project, given the desperate economic conditions faced by their communities.

TO BE CLEAR, economic development matters to tribal nations. This is especially true in the Coastal Plain, where tribal communities still struggle with legacies of racial discrimination that limited education and employment prospects for generations of Natives and other people of color. Tribal elected officials and other community leaders face tremendous pressure to address chronic poverty, unemployment, and the constellation of hardships that surround these issues—food insecurity, mental illness, substance abuse, and more.[78] Corporations sometimes step into this space to offer solutions of their own, but these solutions are often motivated by companies' desires to profit from cheap land, cheap labor, or proximity to resources deemed ripe for exploitation.[79]

In the case of the ACP, the motivation was straightforward; the pipeline's sponsors wanted a new fuel supply for their emerging fleets of gas-fired power plants. Natural gas would allow the energy companies to move away from coal—which formerly dominated the region's electricity mix—without giving up fossil fuels entirely.[80] Fracking operations in the shale basins of Appalachia would supply the gas, and a dedicated pipeline would give the companies more control over the supply chain. The companies were happy to market any leftover gas as a solution to eastern North Carolina's flagging economy, but the ACP was principally for the companies' own benefit.[81]

It is possible, of course, for contrived solutions to benefit tribal members and the larger communities to which they belong. And the mere potential for economic benefit may explain why the ACP enjoyed limited support among Lumbees and other people throughout the Coastal Plain. A handful of supporters stood to profit from pipeline construction or held business ties to the energy companies, but most pipeline advocates simply hoped that the project would attract new industry to the region. Whatever their motivations, supporters tended to overlook the fact that the energy companies had reserved nearly 80 percent of the ACP's expected capacity for their own consumption.[82]

Energy companies behind the ACP also made no guarantees that surplus gas would end up driving economic development in Robeson County or anywhere else along the proposed route. Instead, corporate executives ambiguously dangled unused pipeline capacity as an attractive lure to garner the support of any community willing to take the bait.[83] The executives' presentation to the Commission of Indian Affairs typified this tactic—the claims were tantalizing, but they were vague enough that they did not constitute promises. The ambiguous messaging resonated with some people, including one Robeson County official, who justified his support to journalists in 2018: "We think it'll be a tool in our toolbox for recruitment."[84]

Pipeline developers occasionally made surprisingly specific claims about who might benefit from the project. Soon after the meeting in Pembroke, another Dominion Energy executive told a group of South Carolina business leaders that his company could deliver as much as two-thirds of the Atlantic Coast Pipeline's total capacity to their state. The Associated Press acquired a leaked recording in which the executive confided that North Carolina was not the pipeline's ultimate endpoint. He declared, "Everybody knows it's not going to end in Lumberton [sic]."[85] The executive did not explain how he could promise so much gas to South Carolina when 80 percent of the pipeline's capacity was already reserved for electricity generation in North Carolina and Virginia. Pipeline supporters chose not to question his calculations either.

Employment opportunities and vague promises of surplus gas are examples of manufactured solutions that pipeline developers sometimes offer to tribal nations in attempts to build support for their projects. Indigenous peoples may or may not actually benefit from these contrived solutions, but in any case, it is important to acknowledge that they are mainly side effects of a corporation's internally-motivated decisions repackaged as solutions to community needs. Such solutions are not always equitable, sustainable, or even useful to communities that host pipelines and other harmful or polluting projects.

When tribal communities raise cultural, ethical, or legal objections to a project as a whole, contrived solutions evaporate because they are tied to projects that communities do not want. Under these circumstances, corporate representatives—who say that they want to understand the concerns of Native peoples—should go back to their company's leadership and recommend a different course of action. At minimum, they should recommend a hiatus until the concerns are fully addressed. But in my experience, the odds are pretty slim that corporate representatives actually take these actions.

During another presentation to the North Carolina Commission of Indian Affairs by an entirely different consortium of energy companies, I had an opportunity to ask corporate representatives what would happen if tribal leaders fundamentally opposed their plan to build a large shale gas pipeline through tribal territories.[86] As a concrete example, I highlighted a pending pipeline project by the consortium and pointed out deficiencies in the environmental review that would likely lead regulators to underestimate harms to tribal communities. The representative was a tribal liaison for one of the energy companies, a job that I assumed involved bringing advice and recommendations from tribal nations back to corporate leaders. I specifically asked whether the liaison would—on the advice of tribal leaders—recommend to corporate leadership that the project not move forward until the deficiencies had been addressed. The tribal liaison paused for a moment and replied, "That's a difficult question."

The question may have been difficult for the tribal liaison, but it was not a hard question for the tribal leaders in the room that day whose communities would be affected by the pipeline. The leaders wanted regulators and corporations both to acknowledge and address the issues, even if it meant building the pipeline elsewhere or not building it at all. Tribal leaders expected, just as I did, that the liaison served as a direct line back to headquarters who could convey their concerns and recommendations back to corporate leaders. If officials from North Carolina tribes recommended against building a pipeline in their territories, why would a liaison have trouble relaying their concerns?

I suspect my question was "difficult" because the liaison had not come prepared to relay challenging tribal recommendations back to corporate leaders. Most likely, the liaison had been prepared to deliver a pitch and persuade tribal leaders to support the project. The liaison's presentation, which focused heavily on economic development and other contrived solutions, suggested as much.[87]

Corporate representatives can work against tribal interests when they prioritize building support for their projects over faithfully communicating tribal concerns and recommendations back to corporate leaders. In some cases, representatives and the companies they work for can even undermine tribal sovereignty and self-determination by promoting the idea that a project is moving forward no matter what tribes have to say about the impacts to their communities and territories. When corporations take this stance, knowingly or not, they resemble colonial powers dictating unilateral terms to Indigenous peoples. Tribal liaisons—of all people—should know that Indigenous peoples deserve to pursue economic development on their own terms, not on the condition that they support harmful and polluting projects that may include economic development as a side effect.

As the presentation to the Commission of Indian Affairs continued back on the floor of the gymnasium in Pembroke, one of the Dominion Energy executives listed several of the Atlantic Coast Pipeline's possible benefits to tribal nations. Among them was the company's willingness to train young Native Americans to work in the pipeline industry. The statement echoed through a suddenly silent room. The squeak of shoes and chairs against the floor quickly died down, and all eyes seemed to focus, laser-like, on the executive standing at the podium near half-court.

Why the silence? Thirty minutes earlier, everyone in the gymnasium—including the energy company representatives—had viewed a short documentary film about water protectors at Standing Rock and their resistance to the Dakota Access Pipeline. The film's creator, Lumbee attorney JoJo Brooks Shifflett, had spoken about the film only minutes before the energy company executives began their presentation.[88] Shifflett testified about a recent trip to Standing Rock, where she had witnessed violent actions levied against water protectors by militarized law enforcement officers who working to protect the pipeline company's interests. Shifflett had even carried back to North Carolina the same Lumbee flag that the tribe's emissaries had planted in North Dakota soil during the previous fall; it was tattered and smoke-infused after flying for months at the water protectors' encampment.

I read no malevolence in the executive's comment about training young Native people to work in the pipeline industry.[89] Most likely, the person simply failed to read the room. At any rate, the comment stuck with me as an example of the cultural gulf that can separate pipeline developers and tribal nations in discussions about fossil fuel projects. Representatives from energy companies appear before tribal councils or bodies like the Commission of Indian Affairs regularly, eager to explain the benefits of their projects and hopeful to build support. Sometimes their messages resonate with the audience, and other times they do not. I imagine that corporate representatives sometimes leave these meetings frustrated that tribal officials, elders, or community members failed to grasp the economic opportunities, strategic advantages, or geopolitical significance of their pipelines.

But here's the thing: we get it. Lumbees and other Native peoples of the Coastal Plain have—for generations—expertly navigated colonial systems that were designed for the convenience and enrichment of others. We survived military conflict, disenfranchisement, Jim Crow segregation, and more. Survival required us to identify economic opportunities and other advantages wherever we could. The histories of our tribes are filled with leaders who distilled benefits for their people from complex socioeconomic and political systems that were intended to harm, silence, and erase us. The purported economic benefits of pipelines are not lost on us.

What distinguishes our tribal nations from colonial entities is that we carry an additional burden of accountability to value systems that transcend the economic benefits of pipelines. The accountability calls us to weigh decisions, as best we can, against the risk of permanent harm to the places where we live—the places we come from.[90] Our collective identity as Indigenous people flows from cultures that are inextricably tied to these places.

The possibility of permanent cultural loss means that the stakes are incredibly high. Tribal leaders and community members must balance the risk of loss against any possible benefits of fossil fuel pipelines or other extractive projects. If we get it wrong, we perpetuate the cycle of cultural and environmental deterioration that has plagued our communities for centuries. I am not sure that energy company executives who say they want to understand the concerns of Indigenous peoples can actually do so unless they can grasp the emotional weight and social obligations carried by people who balance on the knife-edge of permanent cultural loss.

For Lumbees, the place we come from is the crazy quilt of blackwater streams, floodplain forests, and sandy uplands that all drain to the Lumbee River. It has been home to our communities since time out of mind. Nineteenth-century Lumbee hero Henry Berry Lowry aptly described it as "the only land I know."[91] Our collective homeplace has never been an especially easy place to live—as historic names like *Scuffletown* and *Drowning Creek* attest—but it belongs to Lumbee people all the same, regardless of who holds title to any given parcel. Just as Ruth Revels explained during the fight to save Lumbees' beloved university building, Old Main, "there is more than one way to own a thing. Some of the most precious things we all own were not bought and paid for with money."[92]

Fossil fuel pipelines and the industries attached to them cause permanent harm to the only land we know. They harm our lands directly—gouging wounds in the landscape, razing forests, kneecapping homeplaces, and endangering communities. They also do it indirectly—fueling hotter weather, intensifying floods, and attracting other polluting industries to our communities. Soon, these harms may render our collective homeplace unrecognizable. Who are Lumbees if we no longer recognize the only land we know?

If we lose our collective homeplace, what then? It is happening already to Native peoples who come from low-lying barrier islands along the Gulf Coast, from rapidly thawing parts of the arctic, and from other places.[93] Their territories are, in some cases, literally disintegrating. Lumbees and our Indigenous neighbors of the Coastal Plain are witnessing their own disintegration of a territory that has become dissected by pipelines, pockmarked with industrial livestock facilities, and deforested for a ravenous bioenergy industry. After centuries of stubborn resistance, is this how we ultimately succumb to colonialism—forced to assimilate because the places that sheltered us and shaped our identities no longer exist? Or perhaps when the crazy quilt finally disintegrates, we will simply "cease to exist," as Talford Dial put it.[94]

IMMEDIATELY AFTER THE EXECUTIVES' PRESENTATION, the Commission of Indian Affairs invited me to ask a list of questions that had been prepared by the environmental justice committee. The committee had formed a few years earlier, initially to advocate for roadside cleanups, recycling at pow-wows, and similar initiatives. Those activities were important, but the committee's early work did not align closely with the aims of environmental justice policy or the broader social movement. All of that changed by early 2017, when racial disparities at the heart of the Atlantic Coast Pipeline's route demanded the committee's close attention.

These disparities cut to the heart of federal environmental justice policy; according to the 1994 environmental justice executive order, regulators were required to acknowledge the disparities and, if possible, address them. But regulators had been absolutely silent on the issue of racial disparities associated with the ACP. Regulators had also ignored the closely linked issue of tribal participation in the environmental review, ignoring guidance from federal advisory bodies about engagement with non-federally recognized tribes.[95]

The ACP raised serious concerns not only about the inequitable distribution of harm but also about a regulatory process that could so easily ignore some of the largest tribal communities in the region. These two topics had dominated comments to federal regulators filed by tribal leaders earlier that year, and they were also among the top concerns raised by the Commission of Indian Affairs in its own letter to the Federal Energy Regulatory Commission. Together, the issues signaled that pipeline developers and regulators had not evaluated the route as carefully as tribal leaders and community members believed they should.[96]

In the lead-up to the June meeting in Pembroke, the Commission's environmental justice committee distilled the concerns of tribal leaders and community members into the list of questions that had been printed out and handed to me shortly before the meeting began. At the time, the committee knew that federal pipeline regulators were best qualified to answer the questions, but regulators had directed the corporations to deal with tribes instead. So we raised the questions as best we could with the visiting executives from Dominion Energy. Although they spoke at length about the Atlantic Coast Pipeline's purported benefits, the executives were either unprepared or unwilling to discuss racial disparities or other details about environmental justice and tribal consultation.

To their credit, the executives acknowledged that their visit to the Commission of Indian Affairs did not constitute any form of tribal consultation. For me, this was one of the most important takeaways of the meeting. Tribal consultation takes place between federal and tribal governments, and although corporations may have a stake in the outcome, their presence is not required in government-to-government consultations.[97] For outsiders—and even for tribal leaders who are new to these policies—it can be easy to mistake corporate engagement for tribal consultation. But the distinction is clear when one contemplates the goals of each activity. The objective of the former is usually to build support for a corporate plan; the objective of the latter (ideally) is to seek advice on whether and how a project should be authorized.

The energy company representatives left the meeting during the lunch break, soon after their slot on the agenda. I assumed they faced a long Friday afternoon drive back to Richmond, Virginia—250 miles north of Robeson County on Interstate 95. Later that day, in their absence, commissioners revisited the topic of the ACP. The group discussed the insufficiency of corporate engagement and decided to reach out once again to the Federal Energy Regulatory Commission in an attempt to broker government-to-government consultation on behalf of tribes in North Carolina. The Commission of Indian Affairs made an exceptionally convenient offer to federal pipeline regulators: the commission would organize and host a special meeting of all tribal leaders in the state later that summer. Pipeline regulators would only have to send representatives to a single meeting to consult with all tribal governments about deficiencies in the ACP's environmental review. All of the commissioners agreed to the plan on behalf of their tribes.

But federal pipeline regulators panned the offer, citing concerns over ex parte communications. The Federal Energy Regulatory Commission has quasi-judicial duties that officially begin during the environmental review process, and regulators feared that tribal consultation might violate their procedural rules. The situation was one that other tribes have encountered when dealing with the Federal Energy Regulatory Commission; the agency has a record of citing ex parte communication rules as a reason to forgo tribal engagement.[98]

The Commission of Indian Affairs still hosted the meeting of tribal leaders, even though regulators declined to attend. The scope of the meeting evolved from that of formal government-to-government consultation on the ACP into a statewide tribal leaders' summit on environmental justice. It was the first meeting of its kind ever held in North Carolina, and it predated the formation of North Carolina's statewide environmental justice advisory board by nearly a year.[99]

The summit, which was hosted by the Haliwa-Saponi Tribe in August 2017, featured testimonies from tribal leaders and community members throughout the state. Even the Eastern Band of Cherokee Indians, which does not always participate in matters affecting tribes in eastern North Carolina, sent a representative to observe and note the concerns of other tribes. Procedural issues related to the Atlantic Coast Pipeline's environmental review dominated the discussion, but the summit also included powerful testimonies about past injustices, including the illicit dumping of toxic polychlorinated biphenyls (PCBs) along rural roads in eastern North Carolina during the late 1970s. Members of the Haliwa-Saponi Tribe spoke about their personal encounters with the oily, toxic sheens that lined roadsides in their community. The state government's infamous decision to locate a dump for PCB-contaminated soils in the predominantly African American community of Afton actually launched the modern environmental justice movement in the United States, and Afton was only a few miles from the site of the tribal environmental justice summit at the Haliwa-Saponi tribal headquarters in Hollister.

State officials from the Department of Environmental Quality and federal officials from agencies without ex parte concerns listened to testimonies and gave feedback. The summit was open to the public, and ACP representatives appeared, even though they were not invited. When the corporate representatives asked for a slot on the speaking agenda, summit organizers denied their request, suggesting instead that they sign up for a two-minute speaking slot during the public comment period. The representatives declined the offer to give remarks alongside members of the public.

Later, one of the organizers explained that the summit's purpose was to amplify the voices and experiences of tribes. It was not intended as a promotional opportunity for pipeline developers. The representatives were entitled to speak as members of the public, but the agenda was reserved for conversations about environmental justice that promoted tribal sovereignty and self-determination.

Overall, the summit did not fulfill its original goal of formal consultation with federal pipeline regulators, but it was an unprecedented display of solidarity among tribal leaders in North Carolina who were tired of having their views ignored in permitting and policy decisions that affected their communities and territories. The summit also provided a modicum of closure to the question-and-answer session during the Commission of Indian Affairs meeting in June, which left many commissioners and attendees disappointed and unsettled.

I LEFT THE JUNE MEETING in Pembroke with an uneasy spirit. I drove from the gymnasium toward Lumberton, the county seat. On the way, I stopped at Lumbee Memorial Gardens, the cemetery where my maternal grandparents are buried. I pulled into the paved driveway and navigated progressively narrow lanes until I neared their graves. I opened the car door and welcomed the June air into the cabin. It was still early summer, and the air had not yet become oppressively hot and humid. Still, I could already feel beads of sweat forming around the cuffs and collar of the dress shirt that I wore to the Commission meeting that day. I had already shed my sport coat as I exited the gymnasium back in Pembroke. Before I left the shade of my car, I took off my necktie and unbuttoned my collar.

The cemeteries of Robeson County can be places of quiet reflection, and Lumbee Memorial Gardens filled that role on this day. I clambered from my car into sun-bathed stillness. A warm breeze pressed faintly against my face and neck, now liberated after hours of tie-wearing. I walked toward a row of gravestones and stepped off the narrow pavement.

The earth was soft, and I glanced down at my dress shoes. The contrast of stiff, shiny leather against dull sand and creeping grass reminded me of walking to church with my cousins when we were children. Sometimes, on Sunday mornings when the weather was just right, our parents would allow us—a compact horde of children—to walk the few hundred yards from our grandmother's house to Sandy Plains United Methodist Church. Our parents forbade us from walking on the pavement along Union Chapel Road, and so we stuck to the sandy, grass-studded shoulder—boys in penny loafers, girls in patent leather. My necktie clipped on back then, but it was just as uncomfortable as the hand-knotted tie that I had recently shed.

I continued down the row of stones, trying not to tread directly on any of the graves out of respect for the dead. My grandfather died several years before I was born, and I never met him. My grandmother outlived him by more than forty years. She passed away only a few years earlier. I stopped in front of their shared gravestone and remembered when only a birth date was chiseled into my grandmother's side of the granite slab.

My grandmother's funeral took place in late summer. Apart from the humidity, which is always oppressive at that time of year, late summer in Robeson County is normally quite dry. But the summer she died had been exceptionally rainy. Her graveside service at Lumbee Memorial Gardens was warm and bright, but the sandy soil was soft with moisture after weeks of rain. The water table was so high that the gap between her burial vault and the open grave had filled with dark water—to within inches of the surface. We did not stay to watch the machinery lower her vault into the watery stillness.

Lumbee Memorial Gardens occupies a sandy patch of land near the point where Moss Neck Swamp flows into Bear Swamp. It was fitting that my grandmother's remains were laid to rest here, near the mouth of Moss Neck. The farm where she was born, and where she spent most of her life, is situated only a few miles upstream on Moss Neck Swamp. Some of the groundwater that seeps through the sandy earth below the cemetery flows incredibly slowly—moving only a few inches per day. It flows from the general direction of my grandmother's land—from Union Chapel Road and Sandy Plains United Methodist Church.

I stood quietly for several minutes near my grandparents' gravestone taking in the warm breeze. Close by, a few artificial flower arrangements fluttered. I imagined groundwater seeping past, a few feet below my dress shoes. I wondered if I had seen any of that water firsthand when it fell as rain, decades earlier, on my grandmother's house. I wondered if my grandparents had seen or felt any of it fall as rain during their lifetimes. I wondered who the groundwater encountered as it seeped through the ancient soils of Robeson County, slowly making its way toward Moss Neck Swamp, Bear Swamp, and the Lumbee River. My unsettled feeling had long since passed. I turned and walked back down the row, still careful not to tread on any of the graves.

IN SEPTEMBER 2020, two months after cancellation of the ACP, the Lumbee Tribal Council unanimously passed CLLO-2020-0917-01, an ordinance mandating tribal consultation prior to issuing any permits for hazardous or polluting infrastructure. The ordinance applied to actions in the Lumbee Tribe's present-day territory, which comprises Robeson and three adjacent counties. The ordinance came shortly after tribal leaders met to discuss Duke Energy's latest plan—to build a one-billion-cubic-foot liquified natural gas processing and storage facility in Wakulla, a Lumbee community north of Prospect. The company had already obtained permits from the US Army Corps of Engineers to disturb wetlands in the area.

The ordinance did not mention the new gas facility at all; it looked at the deeper issue of state and federal agencies responsible for authorizing new sources of pollution and environmental degradation. The language of the ordinance targeted all state and federal agencies with environmental permitting responsibilities. It demanded that they engage in direct consultation with the tribe to "consider impacts upon the Lumbee tribal communities and, if permitted, how to mitigate such impacts." It named the Federal Energy Regulatory Commission, the Corps, and other actors who had a record of issuing environmental permits for harmful and polluting activities in the tribe's homeland.

The language of the ordinance was forward-looking; it called on regulators to "deny or suspend" permits for pending and future projects until overseeing agencies could fulfill their consultation duties toward the tribe. A clause warned that the tribal council would consider legal or administrative actions against government agencies that failed to comply. The ordinance refined the tribal government's prior statements on consultation by making it crystal clear that tribal leaders expected to be consulted prior to any major environmental permitting activity in Lumbee territory; their scope of interest was not limited simply to natural gas infrastructure.

The ordinance made no reference to the federal government's stipulation that only federally recognized tribes have a statutory right to consultation. As far as Lumbee leaders were concerned, this was a nonissue. To that end, the ordinance did not cite any of the federal government's consultation policies; it cited the United Nations Declaration on the Rights of Indigenous Peoples, where the principles of free, prior, and informed consent are laid out in detail. One particularly salient part of the declaration calls on governments to "consult and cooperate in good faith with the indigenous peoples concerned through their own representative institutions in order to obtain their free and informed consent prior to the approval of any project affecting their lands or territories and other resources, particularly in connection with the development, utilization or exploitation of mineral, water or other resources."[100] The ordinance came to remind state and federal officials—in no uncertain terms—that this is Indian land.

Pipelines and fossil fuel infrastructure expose key barriers to tribal participation in environmental decision-making on the Coastal Plain, but Indigenous peoples have responded to these barriers by exercising their inherent sovereignty in creative and powerful ways. In the case of the Atlantic Coast Pipeline, these were not meaningless exercises—a multibillion-dollar fossil fuel project was scrapped partly because of Indigenous resistance.[101] But in many cases, the economic and political power of an industry completely overwhelms a region—radically transforming land, water, and communities. The next chapter traces the radical transformation of the Coastal Plain by industrial livestock production—a recent arrival to our homelands but a powerful driver of change.

CHAPTER FIVE

The Smell of Money

Industrial Livestock and Racialized Environmental Harm

My father was raised by his grandparents, who were born in the late 1800s. His grandparents, my great-grandparents, were tobacco farmers and had a large family—thirteen children, not counting my father. When I was young, many of my great-aunts and great-uncles, who were essentially siblings to my father, were still alive. Our trips to Robeson County often included a daylong driving circuit to visit all of my aunts and uncles.

One of my favorite stops along the circuit was at the home of an aunt and uncle who farmed a patch of land near Lumberton until well into the 1990s. Their home was a clapboard affair—once a common dwelling in Robeson County, but rare today. Theirs was built in 1925. The house was planted in a small sandy yard framed by large pecan and cedar trees. Every now and then, a tuft of grass sprang from the bright-colored sand, but the yard was otherwise clean-swept. Sheets of russet-colored tin sloped down from the roof and across a wide front porch (figure 5.1). Rough wooden siding draped the exterior walls. The clapboards were ancient and the color of driftwood; I do not recall a time when they were any other color.

In spring and summer, flowers erupted from brick-lined beds around the home's foundation. During the fall and winter, wood smoke curled from the top of a stovepipe that jutted from the side of the house. Smoke lingered in the lifeless pecan branches or settled in the yard next to the house. Cement slabs formed stairs that led up from the yard to the porch. One slab wobbled and scraped on its stringers, announcing the arrival of visitors from the front yard.

My uncle raised truck crops—cucumbers, squash, melons, peppers, sweet corn, and a vast assortment of peas and beans—on a few acres that surrounded the farmhouse on three sides. A paved road ran along the fourth side—directly in front of the house. Across the road, my uncle grazed several head of cattle in a grassy pasture, and a handful of hogs lurked in a deeply shaded pen near the woods. The hog pen stank, but only up close.

Altogether, the farm where my aunt and uncle lived encompassed no more than twenty acres. It sat near the confluence of Bear Swamp and the Lumbee River, some ten miles downstream from Prospect. The Lumbee River was

FIGURE 5.1 Pickup truck parked next to Robeson County farmhouse, 1998.
Photo by author.

about half a mile away from their home, but Bear Swamp ran much closer to the house—less than one hundred yards. Because of its proximity to the yard, Bear Swamp was a place to explore with my cousin—the youngest child of my aunt and uncle—and with other children who lived nearby. We creeped through the brush along the edge of the swamp, armed against imaginary foes with pellet guns or river cane spears.

Truth be told, I rarely made it into Bear Swamp. More often, I never made it past the side yard, where my aunt kept a rotating cast of birds—a riot of poultry. Chickens ranged across the sand in a roaming flock of biddies that hunted insects and scavenged food scraps tossed along the edges of the adjacent crop fields. Turkeys roosted in low-slung pecan limbs that drooped over a large pen and coop. A shady alleyway of small hutches, coops, and sheds lined the backyard and hosted a menagerie of quail, pheasant, guinea fowl, and assorted chicks.

My aunt could do anything, and she seemed to do everything all at once. She tended to the poultry. She cooked and baked prolifically. She saved me from accidents involving sharpened river cane. One kitchen counter was perpetually adorned with multilayered cakes and meringue-covered pies perched on cake stands and dinner plates, or hidden beneath wrinkled foil. The smell of fried cornbread, collards, sausages, fatback, and chicken emanated from other parts of the kitchen.

Much of the food that my aunt prepared came from the farm, or from within a short distance. Pork, chicken, fish, and beef all came from nearby, and so did milk, eggs, vegetables, fruit, and nuts. Commodities like flour, sugar, coffee, and tea were some of the few things that did not originate close by. My aunt and uncle both worked incredibly hard and had an endless to-do list. But on some evenings, usually in the winter when dark came early, they held court in the main room of their home. Each sat in an upholstered chair that faced the flickering grate of a woodstove—the home's sole source of heat. The lighting was dim, and the high ceilings faded into dusk. Old photographs and calendars from a tobacco warehouse in Lumberton covered the walls. Gauzy curtains hung against yawning wooden windows.

Grown-ups flanked my aunt and uncle on sofas or wooden chairs carried in from the kitchen. Young people sprawled on braided rope rugs that covered the brittle linoleum flooring. A chihuahua, Little Bit, snored nearby in a wicker bed. Everyone was full of food, visitors came and went, and conversations waxed and waned. Grown-ups reminisced or shared the latest news; children had side conversations about basketball, movies, or river cane.

I remember these winter gatherings well into the 1990s. I do not know for sure, but I imagine that they resembled gatherings that took place in the house over more than half a century of winters. In some ways, change comes slow to Robeson County.

THE COASTAL PLAIN IS EVER-CHANGING. Sea level rises and falls over geological time scales, alternately drowning and exposing vast terrain. Lakes fill and drain; rivers dissect the landscape. Forests shift in structure, composition, and location. Changes play out slowly and across spans of times that are incomprehensibly long—even by the standards of Indigenous peoples who have been here for more than ten thousand years. But some changes come rapidly to the Coastal Plain. In a matter of days, massive wildfires reduce forests to charcoal and ash. In a few hours or days, colossal floods sculpt the soft earth into new landforms. Change can build slowly through time, or it can arrive suddenly. Change can also return, rhythmically, like the ebb and flow of tides along the barrier islands or the turning seasons in a riverine swamp.

Whether it plays out over eons or seasons, and whether it is gradual, unpredictable, or rhythmic, change defines the Coastal Plain. In recent eras, people have played major roles in those changes. Like Indigenous peoples throughout North America, the ancestors of Lumbee, Tuscarora, and other Native American groups on the Coastal Plain used fire to thin forests into open landscapes. And given the prevalence of ancient dugout canoes throughout the Coastal Plain, it is also possible that Native people modified rivers and streams to make navigation easier—perhaps by clearing logjams and woody debris to ease travel along these watery highways.

Colonialism brought rapid change to the Coastal Plain. Settlers transformed fire-managed woodlands into plantations that produced tobacco, cotton, and other commodities for export. They ditched and drained low-lying areas to make more cropland. Gas pipelines and other infrastructure fragmented wetlands and further dissected Coastal Plain landscapes. These changes affected Native peoples' lives in a variety of ways—sometimes by enabling people to grow more food or to earn a living in settler economies, and sometimes by disempowering people or exposing them to harm.

One of greatest drivers of change on the Coastal Plain in recent years (and possibly since the arrival of settlers) is the practice of industrial livestock production, a practice dominated by swine and poultry production in North Carolina. I use the phrase *industrial livestock production* to describe a vertically integrated technological system with several major parts. First, and most visibly, are the enclosed sheds that now sprawl across the Coastal Plain. The sheds are large buildings—some have acre-sized footprints—and are tightly packed with animals. The structures sit alone or in arrays, the largest of which contain more than forty animal sheds.

The system also includes slaughterhouses and meat packing plants—large industrial compounds that ingest livestock from the thousands of sheds that surround them on the Coastal Plain. Semitrucks, a critical part of the system, bring livestock into the compounds and carry away packaged meat. Trucks and trailers also haul away solid waste from production facilities, delivering it to nearby fields, where it is spread as fertilizer. Liquid wastes—swine feces from sheds and effluent from slaughterhouses—are not hauled away but are held nearby in lagoons or other structures before being sprayed on surrounding fields. Large sections of the Coastal Plain have become dumping grounds for the reeking and harmful wastes generated by the system of industrial livestock production. In only a few decades—since the 1980s—the industry and its waste products have radically altered lives and landscapes throughout the region.

Livestock sheds across North Carolina hold millions of hogs and tens of millions of birds. In less than forty years, the facilities have dosed the Coastal Plain with hundreds of billions of gallons of swine waste and millions of tons of poultry litter.[1] Each day, slaughterhouses and meat packing plants add millions of gallons of effluent to this number. Sprayfields for the liquid wastes occupy tens of thousands of acres on the Coastal Plain.[2]

The waste—whether solid or liquid—is loaded with nutrients and harmful pathogens. The industry and its regulators have agreed that disposal practices of spraying and spreading are acceptable due to the optimistic view that plants will absorb the nutrients, and a combination of sunlight and beneficial soil microbes will neutralize the pathogens. In reality, however, both nutrients and pathogens routinely end up in shallow groundwater beneath waste disposal fields. From there, the pollutants make their way into drinking wells or into surface waters. And when hurricanes or heavy storms occasionally sweep through the region, the entire Coastal Plain is awash, literally, in fecal waste.

The livestock industry's waste management practices are utterly unsustainable. Disposal methods rely too heavily on plants and soils to absorb nutrients and neutralize pathogens. Simply put, there are too many animals producing too much waste for the Coastal Plain to handle. Now, after nearly forty years of pushing the region to its limits, the Coastal Plain is groaning under an unbearable burden. Lagoons, sprayfields, and other parts of the industrial system not only reek; they create unbearable and unhealthy conditions for people who live nearby.[3]

It was only a generation ago that the livestock industry swept through the Coastal Plain. Within two decades, the number of large-scale swine operations (especially those with five thousand or more hogs) skyrocketed. Simultaneously, the number of small operations (i.e., those with two dozen or fewer hogs) plummeted.[4] Many of the small operations were diversified farms that raised a few hogs, a small poultry flock, and row crops. Some of these farms still exist, but they are far fewer now than they were a few decades ago. From an Indigenous perspective, the changes brought about by industrial livestock production have happened in the blink of an eye.

PROPONENTS OF INDUSTRIAL livestock production—large pork and poultry corporations and many of the independent contractors who operate concentrated animal feeding operations (CAFOs)—bill the system as a success story about feeding the world. Proponents frame criticism of the industry's waste disposal practices as a personal attack on farmers, and some view environmental researchers—including water scientists—with suspicion and contempt. Industry propaganda demonizes Waterkeepers and environmental advocates as "anti-agriculture activists."[5]

I am not a Waterkeeper, but I did experience the influence of the industry's campaign firsthand in 2018 when an industrial livestock proponent threatened to shoot me for collecting a water sample from a roadside ditch in Sampson County. The encounter occurred a few days after Hurricane Florence brought catastrophic floods to the Coastal Plain. I had traveled to Sampson County with Jocelyn Painter, a graduate student from my lab who belongs to the Winnebago Tribe of Nebraska. The two of us met up with friends from the Coharie Tribe, whose present-day territory included the part of Sampson County where we were working. We four Native people—two Coharies, a Lumbee, and a Winnebago—traversed still-sodden landscapes in a university van, filling sterile bottles with samples of reeking flood water and checking in on members of the Coharie community.

At one point that day, I left the other team members behind at our van parked along the highway, and I walked a short distance down the shoulder of the road to collect a water sample from a flooded ditch. Before I had a chance to collect the sample, I encountered the man, who told me that he believed water sampling threatened his livelihood. Lucky for me, he explained, my shirt—a bright red polo shirt with my university's logo—was the only reason he had not shot his gun at me.

The man, who was involved in various aspects of both swine and poultry operations, depended on the industries to make a living in a place where his family had lived for generations. He believed that water sampling had been weaponized against him and his neighbors in a way that could ultimately jeopardize their way of life.

I sympathized with the man. The encounter took place in a part of Sampson County where my ancestors had lived and farmed from before European contact until the middle of the nineteenth century. The roadside ditch, the road, and possibly even the nearby house where the man lived had all been part of my ancestors' territory.[6] I did not say any of this out loud; I only listened while he lectured me for fifteen minutes or so about the politics of environmental monitoring, the price of fertilizer, and more.

We parted ways, and I trudged back to the van, deflated. I did not feel that the two of us had connected in any meaningful way. I opened the driver's side door and hoisted myself inside. From their vantage point in the van, my companions could see that a serious conversation had taken place, but they were too far away to make out any details. I could tell by their silence that they knew the conservation had not gone well for me. I was actually thankful for the quiet interior of the van; it was a welcome respite after the man's threat and stern lecture.

I am not sure where it first began, but a few seconds after I closed the van door, giggles erupted from somewhere behind the driver's seat. In moments, the van burst into raucous laughter. The four of us sat on the side of the highway and laughed, without speaking, for several minutes. We were not laughing at the man; there was nothing funny about the conversation, and I had not yet told anyone about it. We were simply four Native people laughing together at the stressful day, the post-flood situation, or maybe life in general.

Lakota scholar and activist Vine Deloria Jr. observed, "When a people can laugh at themselves and laugh at others and hold all aspects of life together without letting anybody drive them to extremes, then it seems to me that that people can survive."[7] Laughter held together what was otherwise a difficult day. Not only was the work hot and tiresome, but seemingly every place we visited reeked of stagnant water and hog feces. Everyone we met shared heavy stories of weathering the immense rainfall and cleaning up the mess left behind by the flood.

That day sticks in my memory because of our shared moment of roadside laughter, but it also reminds me that industrial livestock production is a highly racialized activity in North Carolina. What I mean is that the vast majority of industrial livestock facility owners and operators are white. Recent agricultural census data from North Carolina show that white people make up over 90 percent of the state's swine and poultry operators.[8] This statistic is consistent with the demographic makeup of North Carolina's agricultural industry in general, which is also overwhelmingly white. At the same time, racial minorities make up an oversized share of the people who are exposed to air and water pollution associated with the industry's waste disposal practices.[9]

Intentionally or not, the livestock industry has created a textbook example of a distributive injustice in eastern North Carolina—people who have long suffered from racial discrimination, colonialism, and other forms of marginalization now endure environmental and public health problems created by a white-dominated enterprise.[10] It is impossible to discuss industrialized livestock production in North Carolina without considering racial disparities in who profits and who suffers from industry practices.

Corporations and the interest groups that represent them will go miles out of their way not to discuss the racial disparities endemic in the industry's waste management practices. Public relations campaigns, which include interstate billboards, newsletters, and websites, are filled with idyllic images that evoke positive images of rural farm life. Advertisements hint at nostalgia but include just enough modernity (a late-model pickup truck or a solar panel, for example) so that twenty-first century people can see themselves in the shoes (and overalls) of the families whose smiles beam down from billboards along Interstates 95 and 40, which run through some of the state's densest concentrations of CAFOs.

Lobbyists for the industry descend on Raleigh, armed with facts and figures that portray the industry as a crucial economic engine that deserves legislative protection and other special treatment. Based on these claims, lobbyists—and even legislators who have direct industry ties—have been extremely effective at creating CAFO-friendly legal and regulatory systems in North Carolina.

But regardless of any benefits that industrial livestock production brings to the region, the industry as a whole poses serious health and quality-of-life issues that fall disproportionately on racial minorities—African Americans, Latinos, and Native Americans—and on poor people throughout the Coastal Plain.[11]

The stakes are especially high for Lumbee people and our Indigenous neighbors in eastern North Carolina. Not only are we disproportionately exposed to pollution and intolerable living conditions—putrid odors, swarms of flies, roadsides littered with feathers—but we will likely have to deal with the mess long after the industry abandons its harmful practices or leaves our homeland altogether.

Of course, some Lumbee people and people from other tribal communities participate in the livestock industry—either as operators or in supporting roles as truck drivers, feed suppliers, or workers in meatpacking plants. However, most Native Americans in the Coastal Plain do not work in the industry. To be sure, Native people have farmed the Coastal Plain since time out of mind, but industrial livestock production bears no resemblance to our ancestral agricultural practices.

Let me be clear: mechanization and scale are not the characteristics of industrialized livestock production that truly differentiate it from our ancestral practices—or at least they are not the factors that I find objectionable. What I mean is that industrialized agriculture is an inherently colonial practice.[12] The industry operates on the assumption that the best use of land is to extract as much wealth as possible as quickly as possible. While this happens, the industry either ignores harms caused to people and to the environment, or it looks for evidence that its practices are not really harmful in the ways that people claim.

One alternative to the extractive philosophy that underpins industrialized livestock production is the mindset of stewardship that exists in the ways that Native communities on the Coastal Plain relate to the land. It is our homeland;

we have perpetual responsibilities to care for the Coastal Plain in ways that honor our ancestors and prepare future generations for success.

Individuals within the livestock industry may share values with Indigenous peoples—or they may be Indigenous people themselves—but that does not mean Indigenous values are reflected in the policies and practices of the industry. In fact, Indigenous perspectives and values are virtually absent from the industry today. The absence stems partly from a long-standing failure of the industry to engage meaningfully with tribal nations prior to implementing any of its plans. The same failure plagues government agencies who regulate the industry.

The livestock industry and government agencies both may claim to engage with the public, but their actions are largely perfunctory. Neither group seems open to the possibility that public engagement could lead to meaningful changes in policies or practices. It is mostly the kind of "empty ritual" that Sherry Arnstein used to describe the lowest levels of citizen participation in planning and decision-making.[13] Whatever the reasons behind government and corporate approaches to engagement, the result is that these institutions do not reflect Indigenous peoples' responsibilities to steward the Coastal Plain in perpetuity.

A SUSTAINABLE VISION OF STEWARDSHIP on the Coastal Plain must involve something akin to Lumbee agricultural practices, including the small diversified farms like the one that my aunt and uncle operated near the mouth of Bear Swamp. But Lumbee agriculture takes many different forms—household gardens, massive soybean fields, and everything in between. In Lumbee communities today, there are pasture-raised meats, vineyards, pecan groves, feedlots, organic farms, and more. Lumbee homeplaces sprout blueberry and pomegranate bushes, grapevines, and nut trees. Everywhere, kitchen gardens yield sweet corn, cucumbers, collards, field peas, peanuts, sweet potatoes, okra, beans, and more—enough to keep and enough to share. The need to raise—and share—our own food is a hallmark of Lumbee culture and identity. It stems partly from generosity and kindness, I am sure. But I also think it stems from the fact that we are age-old hosts to others in this land. Raising and sharing food is also a survival mechanism—a way that our communities traditionally helped those in need.

Indigenous peoples are the region's original family farmers.[14] Sixteenth-century prints, based on the watercolor studies of Elizabethan artist and colonial governor John White, show Algonquian towns on the outer Coastal Plain with clusters of homes amid fields sprouting corn, sunflowers, gourds, and sacred tobacco. Other prints show people fishing in the broad, shallow estuaries or hunting deer in the uplands. One series of images shows a man and woman first tending a rich corn and fish stew that simmers in a massive earthenware pot, then seated and dining on a cane mat. These prints reveal some of our ancestors' food traditions on the eve of colonization.

Colonization disrupted our ancestors' agricultural practices, but our people adapted. European settlers brought hogs, cattle, chickens, and new crops from abroad. Enslaved Africans brought seeds from their homelands and taught us some of their own foodways.[15] Eventually, these foods combined on Lumbee tables and mixed with older dishes, including foods like corn and fish that remain staples to this day. Our meals have evolved through time, but feeding ourselves from our own fields and waterways has always been a high priority for Lumbee people and our Indigenous neighbors.

In contrast to the diversified farms and gardens of Lumbee people, the business model for industrialized livestock turns on raising large numbers of animals to market weight as quickly possible. Companies have reached this scale through the interconnected system of livestock sheds and slaughterhouses that I described earlier. Robeson County lies about fifty miles away from the industry's densest concentration of CAFOs along the border of Sampson and Duplin Counties, but Lumbee territory still hosts a large share of this infrastructure, including two huge poultry slaughterhouses along Big Marsh in northern Robeson County. Nearby, just outside of Fayetteville along the Cape Fear River, sits the world's largest pork slaughterhouse, which is operated by Smithfield Foods and ingests more than thirty thousand hogs each day.

The corporations that own these slaughterhouses prescribe standardized materials and methods that are used by contractors who operate individual production facilities. These standardization practices allowed the swine industry in particular to grow explosively across North Carolina during the 1980s and 1990s. Smithfield Foods and other large vertically integrated meat corporations describe the period of explosive growth as economic salvation for the region's farmers and their families. During that time, the average size of a swine herd or poultry flock in North Carolina expanded astronomically, but the number of farms raising hogs or chickens tanked. For example, the number of chickens living in Robeson County increased more than thirtyfold between 1950 and 2017, exploding from approximately 220,000 to approximately 7 million (table 5.1). At the same time, however, the number of individual poultry operations in Robeson County has plummeted from more than seven thousand in 1950 to around one hundred in recent years. In a few decades, the average flock size has

TABLE 5.1 Robeson County livestock inventories in 1950 and 2017

Poultry	Number of Chickens (Approx.)	Number of Operations	Average Flock Size (Approx.)
1950	220,000	7,195	30
2017	7,000,000	114	61,400

Hogs	Number of Hogs (Approx.)	Number of Operations	Average Herd Size (Approx.)
1950	41,000	6,688	6
2017	330,000	32	10,300

Source: 1950 Census of Agriculture, Chapter B: Statistics for Counties https://agcensus.library .cornell.edu/wp-content/uploads/1950-North_and_South_Carolina-Table_of_Contents -1795-Table-03.pdf; 2017 Census of Agriculture, North Carolina https://www.nass.usda.gov /Publications/AgCensus/2017/Full_Report/Volume_1,_Chapter_2_County_Level/North _Carolina/

grown from a few dozen birds to tens of thousands of birds. Similar trends exist for hogs. This explosive growth has led to radical changes for Robeson County and other places where these industries have cropped up.

The scale of industrialization has generated substantial air and water pollution across large areas of the Coastal Plain, and it has also created unbearable living conditions for people nearby. Many of the problems stem from the livestock industry's practice of wastewater disposal. The most common practice, known as land application of wastewater, requires large tracts of land to absorb copious amounts of pollutants contained in liquid waste. Land application of wastewater is used by both swine and poultry industries, but in different ways. Operators of individual swine facilities flush feces into large open lagoons adjacent to sheds housing their hogs. There, bacteria partially decompose the waste, converting some of the nutrients into methane, ammonia, and hydrogen sulfide, gases that escape into the atmosphere. After a period of decomposition, swine operators pump wastewater out of the lagoons and through an irrigation system that sprays the waste onto nearby fields. There, soil microbes and plants—typically cover crops or animal feed crops—will ideally finish the job of breaking down the hog waste, absorbing liberated nutrients such as nitrogen and phosphorus, and neutralizing harmful bacteria and other pathogens remaining in the fecal waste. This arrangement is usually called a *lagoon and sprayfield system;* the lagoons are the holding pits where decomposition of fecal waste begins, and the sprayfields are the adjacent irrigated lands that receive the partially treated waste.

For the most part, poultry operators do not use land application of wastewater. Instead, they typically collect litter in a semi-solid form. They remove the waste from buildings and pile it beneath lean-tos meant to keep the piles from washing away or percolating into groundwater during storms. Eventually, the waste is hauled to nearby crop fields where it is spread as fertilizer.

Even though most poultry operators do not use land application of wastewater, the poultry industry relies heavily on land application elsewhere in slaughterhouses that can generate millions of gallons of liquid waste each day. The companies that operate these facilities sometimes opt for land application systems instead of on-site wastewater treatment plants. Wastewater treatment systems are more costly and receive more regulatory scrutiny than land application because the treatment systems usually fall under the purview of the Clean Water Act.

In contrast, land application systems are largely exempt from the National Pollution Discharge Elimination System, a federal program created by the Clean Water Act to limit pollutants flowing into wetlands and streams from municipal wastewater plants, factories, and other sources. The exemption is based on legal and regulatory assumptions that wastewater sprayed onto fields is not a direct source of pollution to waters of the United States, which include navigable rivers, their tributaries, and certain wetlands that drain into them.

Even though the law does not treat land application of wastewater as a direct source of pollution, there is clear evidence that wastewater spraying—both from individual swine operations and from large poultry slaughterhouses—has an impact on downstream surface waters. The physical mechanism is fairly straightforward; surface waters in the Coastal Plain are fed mainly by groundwater, which flows readily through porous soils and sediments beneath these facilities and their sprayfields. Groundwater also flows close to the surface—within two or three feet at some times of the year.

Wastewater that is sprayed onto crop fields immediately begins to infiltrate into the soil, and it eventually reaches the water table. When it does, two things happen. First, any pollutants still carried by the wastewater join the flowing subterranean mass that is groundwater. Flowing groundwater carries the pollutants to the nearest stream. Second, groundwater rises as wastewater percolates into soils and sediments. The same phenomenon happens during storms on the Coastal Plain, and sometimes—if the storm is heavy enough—the water table reaches the surface and floods the land in vast shallow pools. If the ground is even slightly sloping, pooled water will begin to flow downhill, carrying pollutants to wetlands and streams.

Technically, land application systems are designed so that contaminants are absorbed or neutralized before wastewater reaches groundwater. The systems are also designed so that the irrigation rate will never cause groundwater to reach the surface. (As a corollary, operators cannot spray wastewater when soils are already saturated.) State regulators scrutinize the plans for the systems, mainly to ensure that they will not saturate the surface and cause waste to flow along the surface and into wetlands or streams. They also review the plans to ensure that pollutants are not applied to the soil in volumes or concentrations that are too intense for plants and soil microbes to handle.

Some aspects of regulatory review seem performative, including numerical modeling studies that assume highly idealized (and unrealistic) conditions that usually portray land application systems or other activities in a flattering light. In 2015, I saw some of these assumptions firsthand when I reviewed the permit for a proposed land application system in Robeson County. The permitting documents, which were on file in the state regulator's office, described a land application system for a poultry slaughterhouse that expected to generate nearly 1.5 million gallons of wastewater each day.[16] The company purchased a sprawling assemblage of crop fields—a total of three hundred acres—on both sides of Big Marsh, a tributary of the Lumbee River. The plans included a large network of sprinklers to spray partially treated wastewater on the fields.

One of the main conditions of the permit was that wastewater irrigation could not cause an excessive rise in groundwater levels beneath the sprayfields. If groundwater came too close to the surface, wastewater would likely saturate the soil and flow across the land surface directly into Big Marsh. State and federal regulations expressly prohibit that scenario. In its permit application, the company used the results of a hydrological model to argue that this would not happen. This is a fairly typical use of hydrological modeling in the regulatory world.

The modeling exercise was largely self-fulfilling because the model's user-definable settings were tuned to settings that drastically reduced the likelihood that soils would become saturated under model scenarios representing the company's planned irrigation rate. The model made generous assumptions about hydraulic conductivity—a value that represents the permeability of belowground sediments. The settings allowed simulated groundwater inputs to drain away quickly, before they could mound up and reach the ground surface. The settings assumed that highly permeable sediments at the irrigation field's surface extended several feet down to the model's subterranean boundary. The assumption, however, ignored layers of relatively impermeable silt and clay that sat just below the surface of the field. These layers—remnants of ancient seafloor deposits—had exponentially lower hydraulic conductivities and were certain to saturate soils during heavy storms or under high irrigation rates. Because the field sloped gently toward Big Marsh, the saturated soils would allow pollutants to flow more rapidly toward the water body.

Another assumption built into the model was that it rained a small amount each day.[17] The assumption was utterly unrealistic, but it met the requirement from regulators that the model incorporate local weather conditions. The model met the requirement by adding an average amount of rainfall to each day's simulation. Over the course of a year, the daily averages added up to a realistic annual rainfall total. The assumption ignored the reality that storms arrive at random intervals and bring random amounts of rain.

The random—or stochastic—nature of storms influences groundwater levels, especially in the unconfined aquifer, which is the groundwater that lies closest to the surface and is readily affected by rainfall. Groundwater in the unconfined aquifer rises and falls in response to individual storms, and variability in storm characteristics (especially arrival time and amount of rain) can influence groundwater levels as much or more than the total amount of rain that falls during a year. Storm arrival times and rainfall amounts vary throughout the year in the Coastal Plain, and storms often bring groundwater very close to the surface. In Robeson County, it is this phenomenon—rising groundwater—that often leaves standing water in yards and fields after heavy storms.

Had the model scenarios actually incorporated these important characteristics of storms, irrigation would have been cut off for days at a time whenever storms brought simulated groundwater too close to the surface. And the model scenarios could not simply make up for lost time by spraying more water during dry periods; regulators limit the maximum daily irrigation rate to acknowledge the finite ability of plants and soils to absorb nutrients and neutralize pathogens.

So instead of incorporating realistic details about storms, the model simply made it rain a small amount every day. In the model scenarios, groundwater barely responded to these minuscule storms, and the extra irrigation water easily percolated into the earth without causing simulated groundwater to rise excessively.

The permitting documents for the land application system explained that the purpose of the model was "to support the recommended hydraulic loading by ensuring that a one-foot vertical separation is maintained between the [seasonal high water table] and the ground surface per North Carolina Administrative Code 15A NCAC 02T, Section .0505 (p)."[18] This is a complicated way of saying that the goal of the model was to strengthen the company's argument that wastewater would not saturate soils or flow across the surface and into Big Marsh. The model was set up to give the answer that the company wanted.

Despite the glowing model results, the company acknowledged that it could not spray wastewater every day given the unpredictability of storms. To that end, the company built a multimillion-gallon pond that could hold about two weeks of wastewater in reserve during wet weather. For their part, regulators made no comments at all on the model prior to issuing permits for the system. For years, I have shared the story of this modeling study with my hydrology students. We use it as a case study to examine the complexity of soils and the inadequacy of models to represent that complexity.

But the ultimate lesson from this case study is not that this model (or any other model) is useless; the lesson is that models must be folded into larger experiments that can answer relevant questions. And modeling experiments (like laboratory experiments) require more than a single observation to produce defensible results. My students learn that by running the model hundreds or thousands of times while also randomly varying conditions such as rainfall magnitude or soil hydraulic conductivity, modelers can build an ensemble of results to answer questions that are actually useful for regulatory purposes—questions such as, "How often will this system saturate the soil in a typical year?" or, "Might the system need to scale back irrigation rates under future climate conditions?" These questions are much more meaningful to regulators than, "Did a single model scenario support the company's argument?"

Even in well-engineered land application systems, nutrients and pathogens seep continuously through soils and mingle with groundwater. Water samples collected from wells on or near sprayfields routinely show elevated concentrations of nutrients and harmful bacteria.[19] Inevitably, contaminated groundwater makes its way into swamps and streams. It eventually drains into coastal waters. Some of this pollution contributes to harmful algae blooms and fish kills. Waste irrigation and spreading activities send droplets and solid particles of fecal waste drifting across rural landscapes. Particles settle on yards, homes, and anything left outdoors. Breezes that once brought respite from summer heat are now infused with stenches of ammonia and hydrogen sulfide. At times, people who live nearby cannot go outdoors. Regulatory frameworks have failed both people and ecosystems in the Coastal Plain.

Industrial livestock production causes real harm to people and ecosystems, but Lumbees and our Indigenous neighbors are resilient. Generations of oppression and discrimination have made us this way. The self-sufficiency of my aunt and uncle on their farm near the mouth of Bear Swamp, and the self-sufficiency of other farmers like them serve as powerful illustrations of our resiliency, but the story goes back much further.

BOTH OF MY PARENTS GREW UP on small tobacco farms in Robeson County. My father grew up on a farm in Saddletree, a predominantly Lumbee community several miles north of Lumberton. After spending much of their lives as turpentine laborers and tenant farmers, my great-grandparents—who raised my father—purchased land on the rim of Robeson County's largest Carolina Bay, the Great Desert.

Just beyond the Great Desert's ancient shoreline, my great-grandfather, who was also a brickmason, built a small house and several outbuildings—all from cinder blocks. The family raised tobacco in the surrounding fields and kept hogs in a pen on the edge of the woods. They had a shallow well, about thirty feet deep, that my great-grandparents augered into the sandy soil adjacent to the house. The well water was clean; land on that side of the Great Desert had never been heavily fertilized or exposed to other sources of pollution. On Sundays, worshippers from a tiny church across the road would walk over to my great-grandparents' house to pump water from their well—the nearest source of drinking water.

My mother lived in a multigenerational farmhouse with her parents and grandparents. Her grandparents owned land in the Sandy Plains community, a spit of sand across Bear Swamp from Pembroke. They farmed tobacco and other crops on approximately fifteen acres in the upper headwaters of Moss Neck Swamp, a narrow green vein that was heavily ditched, drained, and channelized during the early twentieth century. Their homeplace was anchored around a two-story wooden house where my mother lived with her parents, siblings, and grandparents. Several of my mother's aunts and uncles lived nearby, and the extended family shared responsibility for the fifteen acres of cropland.

Eventually, my mother's family built a house of their own on one edge of the fifteen-acre field. My own parents followed suit, building a house next door when they were first married. By then, the homes of extended family members had nearly hemmed in the fifteen-acre field.

My parents' families were privileged to own land at a time when relatively few Native Americans in Robeson County could say the same. The racialized hierarchy of Jim Crow segregation made it difficult for Native Americans and their African American neighbors to buy land or to keep it. But land owner-ship was only one of many ways that segregation affected the lives of my par-ents and other Lumbees. Both of them attended and graduated from Native-only schools in Robeson County that were overcrowded and under-resourced compared to nearby white schools. African Americans in Robeson County experienced similar or even worse discrimination in schooling. Robeson County's policy of triracial segregation was omnipresent in public spaces—shops, theaters, train stations, and other public spaces. Even though segregation ended in Robeson County several years before I was born, its memories are imprinted on me by stories from my elders about hateful speech and actions directed at them, opportunities lost, and rights denied.[20]

Farming was one of the few livelihoods accessible to Lumbees living in Robeson County during segregation. As a practical matter, farming was one of the few livelihoods accessible to anyone living in Robeson County during that time. In 1950, the year my parents were born, Robeson County had more than eight thousand farms and some 450,000 acres in crop or pasture—nearly three-quarters of the county's total land area was under cultivation. By this time, the county's major wetland drainage projects had been completed and operating for decades. Virtually every acre dry enough to farm was farmed.

In 1950, Native Americans and African Americans made up two-thirds of Robeson County farmers, but they controlled less than half of the county's farmland. Only about 20 percent of Native American and African American farmers owned the land that they farmed compared to about 45 percent of white farmers.[21] The vast majority of non-white farmers were tenants or sharecroppers. Many of these sharecropping families leased their fields and rented clapboard shacks that were dilapidated, drafty, and overcrowded. Their farm leases renewed annually, which meant that eviction notices could follow any given year's harvest. Sharecropping itself was an oppressive system that perpetuated poverty and despair regardless of race, but the system dis-proportionately affected Native American and African American farmers in Robeson County.

A generation earlier, during the Great Depression, federal agents visited Robeson County to assess living conditions among Native American farm-ers. The lead agent, John Pearmain, interviewed dozens of Lumbee farmers, documenting intense poverty, overcrowding, and oppression under the sharecropping system. Most of the farmers were one-third sharecroppers—meaning that the landlord kept two-thirds of the annual cash crop sales, and the farmer was left with the remaining one-third to settle debts and pay expenses. An acute housing shortage saw families living in partially finished shacks, multiple families living in two- and three-room houses, and families living in tobacco barns. The housing shortage was accompanied by a shortage of farming leases, and the general consensus among those interviewed by Pearmain was that the shortages stemmed from a concerted effort by white landlords to recruit white tenant farmers from the Piedmont—tobacco growers who worked the clay-rich soils at the feet of the Appalachian Mountains.

Poverty and shortages of both houses and farms were compounded by predatory lending in Robeson County. Lumbee sharecroppers sank further into debt to lenders who charged 10 percent interest on groceries and supplies. For Lumbees who owned their farms, foreclosure was a perpetual threat. Pearmain noted one particular lender who had an especially voracious appetite for foreclosure. He observed of this individual, "Nothing would satisfy the debt but the land."[22]

Amid the unhappiness and desperation evident in his interviews with Lumbee farmers, Pearmain also recorded a hopeful description of the ideal farm from S. M. Bell, a sixty-year-old man from the Bethel Hill community.[23] Bell, who had farmed in Robeson County since twelve years of age, theorized—with striking precision—that a proper Lumbee farm should include eight and one-half acres of cotton or tobacco to sell at market, fourteen and one-half acres of subsistence crops—corn, wheat, sugar cane, potatoes, and beans—two acres each of hog and cow pasture, two acres of oats and one and one-half acres of beans for animal feed, and a one-half-acre kitchen garden. Bell also recommended ten acres of woodland for firewood and construction. All told, Bell's ideal farm included just over forty acres of land—a highly diversified farm that met most of the food and income needs for the average Lumbee household, which Bell placed at eight people.[24]

By 1950, the year my parents were born, a little more than one thousand Robeson County farms were fully or partly owned by either Native American or African American farmers. The average size of these farms was forty-eight acres. Most of the land was devoted to cash and subsistence crops with a few acres left over for pasture. No detailed data exist on Lumbee farms in particular, but it seems that Bell's ideal had been largely achieved by 1950, at least for Lumbees who were fortunate enough to own their own farms. Most Lumbee farmers at this time, however, still did not own their land.

Four thousand additional farms in Robeson County were operated by Native American and African American tenant farmers and sharecroppers in 1950. Tenant farmers, who leased their lands and homes but owned their own plows, tools, and other supplies, typically had more autonomy than sharecroppers. But both groups worked smaller farms, on average, than those who owned their own land.[25] Inequity, however, ran deeper than farm size. Tenants and sharecroppers remained beholden to landlords, they faced the uncertainty of one-year leases, and they continued to sink into debt. In 1950, a full 80 percent of the combined population of Native American and African American farmers in Robeson County remained tethered to this extractive system.

As long as tenant farming and sharecropping have existed in Robeson County, the negative impacts of these arrangements have fallen disproportionately on Native American and African American farmers. At the very same time, the benefits of the system accrued to landowners and lenders who were overwhelmingly white. The system itself was reinforced by Jim Crow policies that institutionalized white supremacy and erected barriers to ensure that Lumbees would never achieve S. M. Bell's dream of the ideal farm. The policies fed forward, too; through my parents' generation, Jim Crow segregation posed formidable roadblocks to any Lumbee who aspired to a career besides farming, teaching, or preaching. Even now, decades later, it is impossible to understand current issues around wealth, land ownership, and race in Robeson County without acknowledging the lagging harms of exploitative practices around tenant farming and sharecropping.

Those arrangements were not always exploitative—at least not overtly so. My aunt and uncle did not own the property where they lived and farmed near the mouth of Bear Swamp; they were tenants who leased the farm from a prominent white family that operated tobacco warehouses in Robeson and Sampson Counties. By all accounts, my aunt and uncle had an amicable relationship with their landlord, and they leased the farm for more than twenty years. Even under friendly terms, however, tenant farmers do not own land to bequeath to their children. And today, the house near the mouth of Bear Swamp stands vacant, the once-sandy yard overgrown, the menagerie silent. The driftwood-colored clapboards and russet metal roof are still as ageless as ever.

RESEARCHERS AND ADVOCATES have spent years evaluating the environmental justice implications of industrialized livestock production—including the fact that waste disposal practices disproportionately impact Native Americans and African Americans living in the Coastal Plain. The health and environmental impacts of industrial livestock production are so well-documented and widely reported that I have no need to catalog them here. Instead, I think it is important to consider the ways in which various groups respond to information about the industry's impacts on people and the environment.

In particular, I want to briefly examine the responses of industry proponents and government regulators to the environmental justice implications of industrialized animal production. I am also interested in the responses of impacted communities. Industry proponents and regulators are uniquely positioned to address the concerns of communities that are disproportionately impacted by industrial livestock production, and their reactions to community concerns are revealing.

Regrettably, corporations and advocates largely ignore allegations that racially marginalized groups are disproportionately impacted by industry activities, including air and water pollution from land application systems, and odors and emissions related to manure spreading. When asked informally about the chronic stench of ammonia and hydrogen sulfide that hangs in parts of the Coastal Plain, industry proponents often deflect criticisms by changing the subject. Sometimes, proponents offer some chestnut about it being the "smell of money."[26]

Witticisms notwithstanding, the industry has faced legal challenges in recent years related to the accumulation of its negative impacts on marginalized communities. Several years ago, more than twenty high-profile nuisance lawsuits were lodged against Murphy-Brown, a division of the world's largest pork company, Smithfield Foods.[27] The cases were brought by more than five hundred people living near industrial swine facilities in North Carolina's Coastal Plain. Most of the plaintiffs were African Americans, a sign of the industry's outsized impact on the well-being of rural Black communities in the region. However, even after juries awarded staggeringly high damages to plaintiffs in each of the lawsuits that went to trial, there is no evidence that the legal actions spurred the industry to reflect on its disproportionate harm to racially marginalized communities and other vulnerable groups. Instead, proponents and state legislators closed ranks and passed laws to shield the industry from further lawsuits.

At the first hints that the lawsuits were forthcoming, the North Carolina Pork Council and North Carolina Farm Bureau—major industry groups—preemptively advocated for upgrades to North Carolina's so-called Right-to-Farm Law, a 1970s statute that shielded hog operations from nuisance lawsuits.[28] The statute hinged on the belief that complaints arise mainly from people who move into areas where activities such as swine production are already underway, but that situation did not actually apply to the communities who brought the string of nuisance lawsuits against Murphy-Brown. Soon after the first cases were decided in 2018, state lawmakers—most of whom were sympathetic to the industry—amended the "Right-to-Farm" law once again to cap legal damages and impose major restrictions on nuisance claims by communities living near these facilities.[29] The move to amend state law rather than confront the substance of the nuisance complaints is telling; it suggests that neither the livestock industry as a whole nor the state legislature is ready to take seriously claims about the disproportionate impacts of industrial livestock production on marginalized groups.

In 2020, a federal appeals court ruled that the amended "Right-to-Farm" law did not retroactively apply to the five jury awards already handed down. In the appeals case, the Pork Council and Farm Bureau, together with their national counterparts, filed an amicus brief that further emphasized the industry's defensive stance and refusal to acknowledge some of its most harmful practices. The brief declared the lawsuits a "war on farmers" levied by outsiders who were ignorant about "rural communities or the agricultural way of life."[30] It also contained the familiar refrain of the industry as economic salvation for the Coastal Plain as tobacco and other cash crops waned toward the end of the twentieth century. The brief never mentioned the substance of the complaints, including the plaintiffs' experiences with swine waste: the pervasive stench, particulate fecal matter, ubiquitous flies and vultures, increased truck traffic, and other issues that transformed daily life near the facilities.[31]

For the most part, the livestock industry in North Carolina avoids any discussion about racial disparities linked to environmental and health impacts of industrial livestock production. In 2018, however, the North Carolina Pork Council released a five-page special report in its quarterly magazine, *NC Pork Report*, that represented a rare attempt to tackle these racial disparities head-on.[32] The Pork Council issued the report in response to research by scientists at the University of North Carolina showing that industrial hog operations were disproportionately concentrated in rural African American, Native American, and Hispanic communities.[33] The work relied on a standard method of computing demographic disparities, which involves comparing proportions of marginalized populations living near a pollution source to proportions living in a reference area.

The university study concluded with statistical rigor that each of the demographic groups was significantly more likely than whites to live within three miles of an industrial hog facility. Advocacy groups cited the study in a Title VI Civil Rights complaint against state regulators filed with the US Environmental Protection Agency. The complaint alleged that regulators had permitted the industry to expand in ways that led to the racial disparities. The Environmental Protection Agency signaled that it would take the complaint seriously—a rare step for the agency.

The Pork Council issued its special report directly in response to the Civil Rights complaint and to the university study that backed it up. On the first page, the special report highlighted to readers of the magazine, "If you read no further, you should know this: The allegation is patently false." The remainder of the special report stumbled through a reinterpretation of the university study, first criticizing the study's choice of reference area (all rural North Carolina counties with swine operations), and then attempting to reanalyze the demographic data.

The Pork Council's reinterpretation consisted of a single map showing top hog-producing counties alongside counties with large African American populations, and a set of tables showing demographic characteristics of populations at various radiuses around swine operations in North Carolina. The Pork Council's map highlighted non-overlapping areas between major urban areas (which have large African American populations because they have large populations in general) and counties where hog operations are located. It was mainly a display of urban and rural counties that lacked any interpretive value. Their tables, however, revealed nearly the exact same results as the university study—African American populations were overrepresented in nearly all of the concentric radiuses compared to populations in other rural parts of North Carolina. The tables did not include any reference populations for comparison, so the Pork Council could not draw any conclusions about racial disparities surrounding swine operations. Instead, the special report could only conclude that African Americans did not make up a majority of the population surrounding these facilities. That is an accurate statement, but it did not contradict the university study's findings about the overrepresentation of African Americans near swine operations compared to other rural areas.

Ultimately, the Pork Council's special report fell flat because its authors did not address the basic concept of disparity—a concept at the heart of the 1994 federal executive order on environmental justice. The executive order's mandate to identify and address disproportionately high and adverse impacts on poor and minority populations requires knowledge about demographic disparities—differences in population proportions between a study group and a reference group. The university study defined both groups and gave rigorous arguments to support the definitions. Doing so allowed the researchers to quantify disparities in the racial makeup of populations surrounding swine operations. The Pork Council's special report criticized the university researchers' choice of reference population but never suggested an alternative. Neither the map nor the tables attempted to identify reference populations or compute disparities; without this information, their criticisms were meaningless.

Perhaps proponents of industrial livestock operations are ignorant or dismissive of demographic disparities and other technical concepts related to environmental justice because federal policy does not yet carry the weight of law. I do not know. But communities are clearly exploring other options to seek relief from the harmful impacts of these operations. Nuisance lawsuits against corporations and Title VI Civil Rights complaints against regulators are two of those options, although the state legislature has moved quickly to defang the former remedy.

And although state regulators have made a few meek efforts to acknowledge the decades-long buildup of industrialized livestock operations around African American, Native American and, increasingly, Hispanic communities, the acknowledgment is largely performative. The efforts have created no obligation to address inequities by removing sources of harm or by seeking other remedies. One example of this kind of performative acknowledgment is an interactive online map that state regulators developed in recent years to juxtapose pollution sources, waste facilities, and marginalized communities.

Before state regulators created the map, I asked agency officials what they hoped to achieve through the exercise. One responded that the map would help potential permit applicants learn where tribes and other vulnerable communities are located. "So they can avoid these areas?" I asked. The response was basically the opposite—so that permit applicants could connect with communities early on to inform them about their proposed projects. It was a disappointing answer, and it revealed the agency's position (or at least this official's opinion) that environmental justice policies are more about letting people voice their concerns and less about stemming the flow of harmful and polluting industries into their communities.

One of the greatest concerns of communities living near industrial livestock operations is that the facilities will persist, indefinitely, into the future. Their concerns are beginning to materialize now that energy companies have begun to collect waste methane from lagoons to inject into the pipeline network that feeds gas-fired power plants and industries throughout the region. The communities have spent years asking Smithfield Foods to honor its twenty-year-old commitment to upgrade waste-handling technology in order to eliminate air and water pollution.[34] But instead of listening to these communities, the company has plowed ahead with unasked-for plans that only address one portion (the profitable portion) of the serious waste disposal challenges that plague the industry as a whole. Community advocates have voiced their concerns for decades, and they are skeptical that the methane-collection scheme will provide relief from ongoing air and water pollution issues. As an environmental scientist, I agree.[35]

As a Lumbee person, I am also dismayed and concerned about two particular issues stemming from industrial livestock production. First, I lament the radical transformation of portions of our ancestral territory into massive waste disposal facilities. As a descendant of agriculturalists who have worked this land since time immemorial; I find the desecration galling, and the problem continues to grow as a new wave of industrial poultry operations overtake the original surge in swine operations during the 1980s and 1990s. Our homelands will take generations to heal from this harm.

Second, I am concerned about the lack of self-awareness by the industry and its regulators around the colonial aspects of industrial livestock production in eastern North Carolina today. Colonialism extracts value from people and place, and that is exactly what industrial livestock production has done to the region over the past four decades. The Coastal Plain is losing access to clean air, clean groundwater, and clean surface water because of industry practices. As conditions deteriorate, people are losing their sense of connection to places that convey deep historical, cultural, and personal significance. Those losses put Lumbees and other Native peoples one step closer to being erased from their homelands.

In North Carolina, tribal governments and Native organizations have been fairly quiet when it comes to raising concerns about the environmental harms of industrial livestock production. Perhaps it stems from a fear of criticizing a politically powerful industry that provides steady work for Native people in slaughterhouses or as truckers hauling animals and their waste. Or maybe the reluctance to speak out stems from present-day entanglements with industry or from lingering reactions to the not-too-distant era of tenant farming and sharecropping. My sense is that if Lumbees and other Native peoples of the Coastal Plain do not soon find ways to inject their cultural values into high-level discussions about the future of industrial livestock production, the industry's polluting and unsustainable practices will eventually squeeze us out of our homelands. The situation is already serious, but as the next chapter explains, climate change raises the stakes even higher.

CHAPTER SIX

Flood

Climate Change in a Watery World

Standing in hip waders at the edge of Lake Waccamaw, a wide shallow bowl of water located some twenty-five miles inland from North Carolina's southernmost beaches, I can barely make out a cluster of docks and houses on the opposite shore, some two miles distant. Lake Waccamaw is a nine-thousand-acre oval that, from space, resembles a giant thumbprint pressed into the pliable Coastal Plain soil. Today, at ground level, it is a vast rippling surface of dark water that extends from the distant docks all the way to a gentle lapping against the green rubber toes of my waders. The shoreline beneath me is a tangle of living grass, shriveled leaves, and detritus from a recent storm.

Not quite two weeks earlier, in September 2018, Hurricane Florence trudged across North and South Carolina, dousing the eastern half of both states with sheets of rain, hour after hour, for three days. When the sky cleared, more than twenty inches of rain had fallen on North Carolina's southeastern corner, the epicenter of the storm. A few weather stations in the Coastal Plain recorded more than thirty inches, a near-Biblical amount of rain, as the storm meandered through the Southeast before veering off toward New England.

In the days that followed the deluge, rivers and streams swelled far beyond their banks and spilled across the flat, low-lying Coastal Plain. Typically quiet, stagnant swamps became roiling, frothing torrents. Sluggish rivers expanded into liquid superhighways that inundated—indiscriminately—pine forests, crop fields, industrialized livestock facilities, and neighborhoods. Streets and highways became eerily angular lakes. Occasionally, automobile roofs or antennas broke the dark surface. In the days after Hurricane Florence, water nearly swallowed the Coastal Plain whole.

On this day, nearly two weeks after the storm, my view across the lake caps a long day of collecting post-hurricane water samples in and around Waccamaw Siouan communities near the lake. The communities—Buckhead, St. James, and Council—are part of the Waccamaw Siouan Tribe's traditional territories, which also include the lake itself and the vast wetlands that surround it. I am part of a team that will analyze the water samples to determine what pollutants are present in the stew of floodwater. We suspect harmful bacteria from industrial livestock waste and septic tank effluent, but we are also curious about nutrients, which can fuel algal blooms, and other contaminants flushed into the wider world by the three-day deluge.

Another faculty member from my university department, Katie Martin, has spent the day riding next to me in a university van. The van's rear seats cradle red-and-white plastic coolers filled with assorted bottles and chunks of rapidly melting ice. The bottles, our bounty, hold water samples dipped from recently inundated swamps, canals, and floodplains in Waccamaw Siouan communities that spread across Columbus County, north of the lake.

Because it is the end of the day, the van's floor has devolved into a jumble of hip waders, coiled rope, and scattered Ziploc bags. The bags, originally packed with clean examination gloves, have become transparent pillows stuffed with wadded paper towels, balls of tape, and bits of purple nitrile gloves. At some point in the day, rogue Sharpies began to skitter across the floor of the van at each turn in the road. Despite the best efforts of the van's air-conditioner, an aroma of rubber, algae, and dampness has overtaken the vehicle by late afternoon.

For much of the day, Katie and I have tailed a dark Toyota Camry around the back roads of Columbus County. The Camry belongs to Pamela Young-Jacobs, vice-chairwoman of the Waccamaw Siouan Tribe and our de facto guide to sampling locations on several streams and swamps that are of interest to the Tribe. Undistracted by navigation apps or paper maps, Katie and I talked between sampling stops. Over the drone of the van's air-conditioner, we discussed hurricanes, water pollution, and culture. "I call her *Ms. Pamela* instead of *Ms. Jacobs* as a sign of respect," I said at one point, watching the Camry signal a left turn ahead. Indeed, *Mr. or Ms. "first name"* is a common way to address elders in tribal communities throughout North Carolina.

Outside, the day has been sweltering. In the wake of the storm, the heat and stagnant water proved to be perfect incubators for gallinippers, the 747 of mosquitoes. At every stop, fresh swarms of the quarter-sized insects attacked our exposed arms and faces. Katie and I were defenseless, our hands preoccupied with sample bottles or note pads. Ms. Pamela mercifully fanned the air around all three of us while we worked, her determined face framed by a large pair of bejeweled sunglasses. Despite her best efforts, however, the gallinippers prevailed. They pierced fabric and skin, drawing blood and raising welts. Late in the afternoon, we parted ways with Ms. Pamela. Katie and I motored toward Lake Waccamaw to collect one more set of water samples.

Back on the lake shore, I scribble the time, latitude, and longitude displayed on my smartphone into a small field notebook—the kind with waxy waterproof pages and a hard yellow cover. The open page is a record of all the sites we have visited that day. Katie, meanwhile, wades into the shallows with empty bottles in her gloved hands.

Lake Waccamaw is the largest of all Carolina Bays, the ubiquitous ellipses that dot the Coastal Plain.[1] The lake is culturally important to Waccamaw Siouan people, who call themselves *People of the Falling Star*. That name derives from a Waccamaw Siouan account of the lake's creation. In their telling, a ball of fire fell from the sky and crashed into the earth sometime in the distant past. The violent impact formed Lake Waccamaw.

One interpretation of the story is that an ancient meteor impact left a giant depression on the Coastal Plain. Lake Waccamaw formed as the depression filled with water. In the early twentieth century, earth scientists held the same interpretation for the formation of Carolina Bays. They raised this idea after the first aerial photographs were collected over the Coastal Plain following World War I. The Carolina Bays' repetitive shapes and angles of orientation made it easy to imagine that a swarm of meteor impacts had created the features. Most earth scientists abandoned that explanation after they failed to find meteorite fragments or clear evidence of a high-speed, high-temperature impact.

The Waccamaw Siouan account of the lake's creation predates aerial photography. It highlights the depth of knowledge about a place that accumulates over many generations—perhaps over many centuries—as people observed, mapped, and analyzed the terrain around themselves. Like Lumbees, Waccamaw Siouans have survived centuries of oppression in various forms, including voicelessness on issues of their identity as Indigenous people of the Coastal Plain.[2] The survival of this story about Lake Waccamaw is a testament to the persistence of Indigenous oral traditions and to the resilience of Waccamaw Siouan people.

I am still thinking about ancient meteor showers when Katie wades back to shore, arms laden with full sample bottles. We double-check the times and identification labels on the bottles against the notes in my yellow-bound notebook and place the bottles in a red-and-white cooler. We climb into the van and are greeted by an even stronger smell than before of rubber and algae. I crank up the air-conditioner and turn the van northward, back toward the university some two hours' drive away.

IN THE WAKE OF HURRICANE FLORENCE, Katie Martin and I, together with several other colleagues, crisscrossed eastern North Carolina in teams of two, collecting samples of residual floodwater from swamps, canals, floodplains, and ephemeral pools left behind after the deluge. We—along with everyone else traversing the Coastal Plain—dodged roadblocks and navigated detours around flooded freeways and back roads. One of the most prominent was a multicounty closure of Interstate 95, the Eastern Seaboard's main north-south highway. In the days after the storm, state officials hastily blocked entrances to the interstate using convoys of old motor-pool vans, parked end to end along exit ramps.

Officials barricaded access to Interstate 95 through much of North Carolina after the Lumbee River surged through Robeson County and overwhelmed the bridge where Interstate 95 crossed the river at Lumberton. There, the river rose sixteen feet above the threshold at which flooding poses a serious hazard to people and property.[3] The interstate remained impassable for ten days. State officials advised east-coast travelers to avoid the Coastal Plain entirely and to follow an hours-long detour through the Piedmont.[4]

The interstate closures affected emergency response, commerce, and other travel on the Coastal Plain, but the temporary shutdowns only scratched the surface of infrastructure vulnerability to flooding. The storm wreaked havoc on public waterworks throughout the region. Heavy rain and floodwaters contaminated water supplies and compromised municipal sewer systems. Power outages disabled industrial sewage pumps. Tens of millions of gallons of raw sewage poured into Coastal Plain waterways.[5]

In Robeson County, artificial drainage and flood control infrastructure also failed or underperformed. The Lumbee River inundated large parts of southwestern Lumberton when the river exceeded the protective limits of the city's levee. In rural parts of the county, artificial ditches and canals, some a century old, could not keep up with the deluge. Some were choked with silt or overgrown with vegetation, but even clear and well-maintained ditches were simply not designed to accommodate twenty or more inches of rain in a single storm. As a result, wetlands that had been drained a century earlier briefly refilled. Water pooled and spread in low-lying areas and cut off road access to some areas. Flooding inundated crop fields, homeplaces, and neighborhoods that were all developed on early twentieth-century promises that drainage infrastructure would convert swamps into safe and productive working lands.

During Hurricane Florence, ditches and canals that functioned as intended probably worsened flooding in Lumberton and other downstream parts of the watershed. Well-maintained ditches shunted excess rainfall directly into the Lumbee River and its tributary streams. In some cases, the concentrated floodwaters flowed so furiously through tributaries of the Lumbee River that they washed away culverts, bridges, roads, and utility lines.

From there, floodwaters flowed rapidly downstream and arrived—seemingly all at once—in Lumberton. Without artificial drainage, abundant wetlands located upstream would have held back much of the floodwater, temporarily, before releasing it, slowly, over the course of a few weeks. To be sure, Lumberton still would have experienced a flood but probably not the surge that occurred in the aftermath of Hurricane Florence.

With that in mind, artificial drainage places Robeson County in a catch-22. If the infrastructure drains sluggishly during a large storm, flooding affects upstream communities that depend on ditches and canals to dry up their land and keep swamps at bay. If the infrastructure performs efficiently, it can intensify flooding in Lumberton and other downstream communities.

Catch-22 or not, the amount of rain that fell during Hurricane Florence created the worst of both scenarios—floods devastated both upstream and downstream communities. Canals and ditches were not engineered to carry so much water in so short a period of time. Even well-maintained drainage infrastructure drowned under twenty inches of rain. Similarly, Robeson County's intact swamps, Carolina Bays, and other wetlands could store only a fraction of the water. Wetlands, canals, and ditches overflowed and flooded upstream areas, but they simultaneously—and rapidly—disgorged water into the Lumbee River. Downstream, Lumberton experienced the largest flood ever recorded.

The Lumbee River's tea-colored water poured into southwest Lumberton a few days after Hurricane Florence drenched the upstream watershed with several months' worth of rain in three days. Lumberton flooded despite the presence of Jacob Swamp Dike, a two-and-a-half-mile-long levee built during the 1970s to protect low-lying lands adjacent to the Lumbee River.[6] The protected area, which is really part of the Lumbee River's floodplain, lies across the from Lumberton's older, wealthier, and whiter neighborhoods. Those neighborhoods are situated on a natural bluff opposite the river from the levee. Several other river towns on the Coastal Plain share this general characteristic: wealthier (and usually whiter) neighborhoods on the high side of the river; poorer (and often minority) neighborhoods on the low side.[7]

Jacob Swamp is the name of a tributary that formerly meandered through the floodplain on the south side of the Lumbee River. As Lumberton grew and expanded during the twentieth century, industrial development, housing, and other construction gradually crept into the floodplain and encroached on Jacob Swamp. By the 1960s, regular river flooding and poorly drained soils—completely normal and expected in a floodplain—had become a nuisance to businesses and residences. City planners pitched the idea of combining a levee with an extended drainage system—the Jacob Swamp Drainage Project—to dry out the floodplain and protect developed lands from future floods. The project took most of the 1970s to finance and build.

From its inception, the Jacob Swamp Drainage Project suffered from a common problem faced by flood control infrastructure worldwide—it was designed to protect against the kind of flooding experienced in the past, not the future. The levee's designers touted its level of protection as "two feet higher than the worst flood on record."[8] However, what the planners of the 1970s knew to be the largest floods on record were barely half the magnitude of the flood that followed Hurricane Florence.[9]

In the days after Hurricane Florence, the residents, business owners, pastors, and workers of southwest Lumberton braced as the river climbed steadily toward the benchmark of two feet higher than the worst flood imagined by planners of the 1970s. As the water level surpassed that fateful elevation— 122.8 feet above sea level, to be precise[10]—the river poured into the city through a relatively small gap beneath Interstate 95. At that spot, the CSX railroad passes underneath a bridge that carries the interstate. Here, Interstate 95 ascends a massive earthen berm leading up to the bridge over the railroad tracks. For all practical purposes, the interstate berm extends the Jacob Swamp Dike a few hundred extra yards—until it reaches the railroad gap.

As the Lumbee River poured through the gap, it flooded more than a square mile of homes, businesses, and churches in southwest Lumberton. The ordeal was tragic enough, but it was worsened by the fact that the same thing had happened less than two years before.

In October 2016, Hurricane Matthew tracked sluggishly through the Coastal Plain. Matthew dumped slightly less rain overall than did Hurricane Florence in 2018, but the results were similarly tragic for Robeson County. The Lumbee River poured through the same railroad gap and flooded the same part of Lumberton. Upstream, undersized and neglected canals and ditches caused wetlands to reappear in places where they had been drained a century earlier. Everywhere in Robeson County, flooding was likely exacerbated by soils that still held water from heavy storms that crossed the region a month earlier—a one-two punch that magnified the later impact of rainfall from Hurricane Matthew (figure 6.1).

Hurricane Matthew—the first of the two recent floods—served as a wake-up call to the realities of climate change on the Coastal Plain. A warmer atmosphere and warmer ocean waters increase the likelihood that slow-moving, moisture-laden tropical storms will drop twenty or thirty inches of rain— several months of rainfall in an average year—in two or three days. When this

FIGURE 6.1 Washed-out road crossing at Saddletree Swamp following Hurricane Matthew, 2016. Photo by author.

amount of rain falls on relatively flat and low-lying places, the results can be disastrous—especially for people who have grown comfortable living under the protection of levees and artificial drainage systems. Climate change is rapidly rendering this kind of infrastructure obsolete.

IN SEPTEMBER 2018, while rivers in the Coastal Plain were still near their peaks, I was scrounging around the university campus in search of a few last pieces of gear for our floodwater sampling campaign. I was also on the hunt for an autoclave—a giant scientific steam cooker. The research team needed it to sterilize dozens of sample bottles used to look for harmful microbes in floodwater. Until recently, most of my lab's research had focused on questions about the movement of water: How much? How fast? How long? I had spent far less time studying the water's content. As a result, my laboratory was not equipped with an autoclave or many other items needed to study microbes in water.

My collaborators, however, had more expertise and more specialized equipment for studying water quality. We had gathered nearly everything for the water sampling campaign—everything but an autoclave. That afternoon, in mid-scrounge, I received an email from a journalist at the *News & Observer*, the flagship newspaper in Raleigh. It was an inquiry about water contamination during post-hurricane flooding. Although my group had yet to collect any samples following Hurricane Florence, I had some idea of what to expect based on water quality samples that we collected and analyzed after Hurricane Matthew, which hit the region less than two years earlier.

Later that day, the journalist and I connected by phone. I acknowledged that it was hard for the public to focus on water pollution given the sheer amount of water inundating eastern North Carolina at that moment. And rightly so—dozens of people died during the storm or in the immediate aftermath. Dramatic photos and videos circulated on social media of normally quiet swamps swollen into churning blackwater torrents—dark whitewater. Images from Lumberton and other Coastal Plain towns documented rescue efforts by volunteer groups.[11] The Southeastern Emergency Relief Group—a scrappy and informal group of Native volunteers—roamed Lumberton in a high-clearance vehicle, rendering aid, giving out supplies, and sharing information about road conditions via Facebook live stream.

The journalist and I spoke against this backdrop of liquid carnage. I warned, "We focus on the drama on how high the water is. But there is a complete other dimension, too—what the water contains."[12] I explained that floodwaters were likely to be a hazardous soup of pathogens, nutrients, and other contaminants picked up and spread across Coastal Plain landscapes. The entire region was littered with pollution sources that could easily mingle with floodwaters—residential septic systems, wastewater treatment plants, and industrial livestock operations. Even before the flood, I explained, industrial livestock operators regularly disposed of liquid waste and manure by spraying or spreading it onto fields. Many of the same fields had been inundated by floodwaters in recent days, allowing bacteria-laced water to drain into ditches, then into swamps, and ultimately into rivers. Even fields with no visible flooding conveyed waste and pathogens to streams via shallow groundwater connections.

As the floodwaters rose, they also imperiled livestock confined to industrial sheds in low-lying areas. On the same day that I spoke to the journalist, North Carolina's Agricultural Commissioner—normally a proud booster of the state's industrial livestock operations–issued a grim press release estimating that more than three million chickens and turkeys and more than five thousand hogs had already succumbed to the flood.[13]

Floodwaters also risked spreading pollution from coal-fired power plants in the Coastal Plain. Large ponds of coal ash—power plant waste laced with arsenic, selenium, and other metals—perched, precariously, near the edges of major rivers in the region. Soon after the journalist and I spoke, reports emerged of multiple coal ash spills into flood-swollen rivers.[14]

Eventually, the water samples that our group collected bore out some of these concerns. We focused mainly on identifying pathogens in water samples collected during and soon after Hurricane Florence flooded the region. Early results were intriguing. Collaborators who mainly studied food-borne illnesses set out to look for *Campylobacter* in samples that we collected, but their cultures turned up an entirely different species of bacteria, *Arcobacter*, which is often found in poultry guts. My colleagues found *Arcobacter* in three-quarters of the water samples that we collected during the flood. Those samples also contained *Listeria, E. coli,* and other pathogens.[15]

A growing body of research exposes the relative ease with which pollutants can disperse across flooded landscapes. Long-standing dogma holds that this type of widespread contamination is unimportant because the shear amount of floodwater dilutes the pollutants.[16] However, even at dilute levels, pathogens can cause illness to people who are exposed to floodwaters, and both nutrients and pathogens can accumulate downstream and wreak ecological havoc, especially in warm, shallow coastal waters.

To add insult to injury, many of the flooded areas reeked of hog and chicken shit. Just prior to collecting samples in Waccamaw Siouan territory,

I spent a day collecting floodwater samples with members of the Coharie Tribe. The Great Coharie River—their namesake stream—drains dense areas of industrial livestock production. A graduate student, Jocelyn Painter, and I traveled through the watershed that day with our two Coharie friends, haunted by the blistering stench of manure that diffused from the river and emanated from recently inundated surfaces. As Jocelyn and I headed back to campus to process the samples we collected, my feelings of gratitude for a day of fieldwork with an all-Indigenous crew were tinged with heartbreak for the river and its people.

HURRICANE MATTHEW AND HURRICANE FLORENCE brought profound flooding to the Coastal Plain twice in two years.[17] The floods were traumatic—partly because their magnitudes exceeded the worst floods either in living memory or in the record of monitoring stations distributed throughout the region. And as far as I know, no oral traditions describe flooding like this. For all practical purposes, the two floods fell beyond the envelope of human experience on the Coastal Plain—for Indigenous peoples and settlers alike.

I am not alarmed by the idea that floods can exceed the experiences and memories of humans in any given location. Hydrologists acknowledge this possibility whenever we estimate flooding probabilities and similar statistics using historical data. Our calculations account for the fact that historical records never capture the largest possible storm, flood, or other event.[18] As a hydrologist, I know that a more extreme flood than we have ever seen always looms beyond the horizon of our scientific gaze.

Similarly, as a Lumbee person, I am not surprised that Hurricanes Matthew and Florence brought floods that exceeded human experience—even the deep experience of Indigenous peoples. Lumbees have deep affection for our namesake river, but we also acknowledge its power. The river is a source of life, renewal, and recreation, but it also demands respect. We know that the river is capable of destruction and ruin.

As much as I am unsurprised by the Lumbee River's potential for destruction, I am saddened that the river's fits of rage are intensified by human activity. People dug canals and ditches to drain wetlands and replumb the landscape in order to move water quickly and efficiently downstream. People built levees and other protective infrastructure that allowed us to overtake floodplains— the river's active domain. Our ceaseless emissions of greenhouse gases have warmed the atmosphere and ocean, conditions that increase the likelihood of catastrophic storms and floods.

Floods are not the only hazards associated with climate change faced today by Lumbees and others on the Coastal Plain. The region is no stranger to hot and humid weather during the summer, but extreme heat is worsening. Summer daytime temperatures reach or exceed 95 degrees more often in recent years than in decades past, and summer nights are not as cool as they once were. Recently, North Carolina's Department of Health and Human Services has begun to raise concerns about the impacts of this weather on human health. Heat-related illness and hospital visits are already on the rise—especially in the Coastal Plain—and the trend will likely continue given humanity's current pace of fossil fuel emissions.[19]

Climate change not only threatens human health, but it also endangers Coastal Plain environments. Extreme summer heat stresses plants and increases their demands for water. This is true for crops and also for plants growing in pine savannas, swamps, and other natural ecosystems. Coastal Plain soils, usually flush with moisture, can dry out in extreme heat. Groundwater levels fall, and less water is available to recharge rivers and streams. Floodplains dry out, wells run dry, and plants wither. A handful of Coastal Plain ecosystems are equipped to handle these extreme summer conditions, but many are not. In particular, the swamp forests that flank the Lumbee River and its tributaries—the very ecosystems that made present-day Robeson County a refuge for Lumbee ancestors—are vulnerable to the dry conditions that come with extreme heat.[20]

All told, climate change has turned the Coastal Plain into a place of extremes. It is becoming hotter and drier, and yet the risk of another catastrophic flood looms on the horizon. Decision-makers simultaneously face the challenges of planning for droughts and floods—a frustrating and unenviable situation.

Floods, droughts, and other challenges associated with climate change on the Coastal Plain raise concerns about environmental justice because the harms connected with these phenomena do not affect everyone equally. Neighborhoods in southwest Lumberton, for example, are much more vulnerable to flooding than areas of town on the north side of the Lumbee River. At the same time, the neighborhoods in southwest Lumberton have high social vulnerability—a metric that combines data on socioeconomic status, housing security, education attainment, and access to health care into a single metric that attempts to capture a community's ability to recover from natural disasters or other adverse situations. High social vulnerability means that a community has little capacity to deal with additional harm. Floods will always come to Lumberton and to other parts of the Coastal Plain, and communities that are least equipped to deal with the aftermath are often most impacted. The imbalance between impacts and abilities represents one of the core inequities associated with climate change.

Floods are not alone in driving inequity on the Coastal Plain. Extreme heat also has an outsize impact on socially vulnerable communities. High daytime temperatures and lack of nighttime cooling means that natural shade, passive ventilation, and electric fans—sufficient remedies for oppressive summer heat a generation ago—can no longer stave off exposure to dangerously hot weather. At the same time, air-conditioning equipment and power bills are expensive— especially when it comes to cooling poorly insulated trailers and mobile homes found in socially vulnerable communities throughout the Coastal Plain.[21] Extreme heat disproportionately affects farm workers and other outdoor laborers, and droughts affect those who rely on crops—as commodities to sell, as feed for their own livestock, or as food for their own tables.

Climate-related problems build on one another to the extent that Robeson County—by the end of this century—will probably incur more economic damages from climate change than any other county in North Carolina. The damages, estimated for a national study published a few years ago in the academic journal *Science*, will likely exceed 10 percent of Robeson County's gross per capita income. The key takeaway from the study is that increased energy and medical bills, lost income, and other climate-related damages add up to what is essentially a hefty fine levied on people throughout the United States. The fines, however, change from place to place, and they are felt more severely in places like Robeson County—where communities are least equipped to deal with climate extremes or the related economic fallout. By comparison, the same study estimated that climate change will cost the entire state of North Carolina about 3 percent of its gross income—an annual bill of some $18 billion in present-day value. The amount may be stunning, but the study predicts a relatively higher cost for Robeson County when accounting for the county's per capita income.[22]

The disparity in potential economic damages from climate change is striking, especially considering that wealthier, whiter counties—which are expected to see much smaller proportional damages—are the seats of power for corporations and governments that make most of the decisions about fossil fuel pipelines, power plants, and other sources of climate-warming emissions in the state.[23] Close scrutiny of disparities between those responsible for climate change and those who suffer from it is central to climate justice, an area of study and practice that focuses on, as environmental scholar Rob Nixon describes, "inequities between those who have grown rich off hydrocarbon culture and the predominantly poor people . . . who are low-level hydrocarbon consumers but at greatest initial risk from the climate crisis."[24] And although climate justice is often framed as an international issue of wealthier nations emitting most of the greenhouse gases while poorer nations deal with most of the consequences, similar disparities also exist within national borders. The disturbing estimates for Robeson County's likely damages from climate change serve as a powerful example.

Undoubtedly, Lumbees, Waccamaw Siouans, and others who live in low-lying areas of the Coastal Plain will shoulder disproportionately large economic burdens stemming from climate change. Indigenous peoples, however, will also incur other damages that are difficult (or impossible) to express in dollars. Lumbees and other Indigenous peoples who live in the Coastal Plain still dwell in our ancestral territories. Our lands are vastly diminished and constantly threatened by pollution, land-use change, and unsustainable development, but we have survived for three centuries on the exact parcels of land that gave our ancestors refuge from disease, enslavement, murder, and dispossession. Generations of our homeplaces, farms, and settlements look out over the same swamps that settlers once deemed to be impenetrable, festering wastelands. Not only did we survive, but our communities grew and flourished, and the interstitial spaces—the marginal lands—became beloved.

Of course, Lumbee people understand that we hold even deeper connections to these places—the landscapes and waterways of the Coastal Plain—through ties forged by our ancestors. We Lumbees and our Indigenous neighbors are committed to revitalizing these connections. The process is painstakingly slow and meticulous, and other cultural revitalization efforts suggest that the process may require collaborations with colonial institutions that have done much harm to Indigenous peoples.[25]

Lumbee connections to place stem from the refugia of the past three centuries and from time immemorial. In truth, the two timescales are part of a single historical arc that shifted into a new phase in response to colonialism. The entire arc matters. But for now, Robeson County is the center of the cultural universe for Lumbee people. Our ancestors may have lived throughout a much larger region, but as a nation, we are defined by this place alone. Lumbee people persist today as a living Indigenous collective in large part because we have a recognizable Robeson County to call home. Other tribal nations in the region hold similar connections to place—Waccamaw Siouan people have Buckhead and other communities; Coharie people have Shiloh, New Bethel, and so on; and the story continues for Meherrin, Haliwa-Saponi, and others.

For that reason, climate change poses an existential threat to the continued existence of Indigenous peoples in eastern North Carolina. Flood, drought, and heat—the direct threats of climate change to the region—affect people and ecosystems separately, but they have the unique and terrifying ability to amplify other hazards. One clear example is the way in which climate change magnifies the environmental impacts of industrialized agriculture. Floods disperse animal waste, pathogens, and other pollutants across large regions. Even subtle changes in storm patterns—unrelated to hurricanes—exacerbate pollution risks from industrial livestock practices such as land application of wastewater.[26]

Climate change also impacts Robeson County through indirect channels. In particular, governments and corporations often respond to climate change in ways that pose dire risks to the landscapes that shape Lumbee identity. The decision by energy companies, for example, to replace coal with natural gas in their electricity portfolios was driven partly by concerns about coal's greenhouse gas footprint.[27] However, the decision to construct new transmission pipelines and gas processing infrastructure in the county has led to destruction of cultural resources and has introduced new sources of pollution into Lumbee communities.

Climate policies that encourage bioenergy as an alternative to fossil fuels introduce similar threats. Forests in Robeson County and in other parts of the Coastal Plain are transformed into wood pellets to satisfy the voracious appetite of European bioenergy markets. The pellets are prized by industry as a carbon-neutral energy source, a claim that scientists have pushed back against.

Elsewhere, companies plan to offset harmful emissions of fossil fuels by capturing methane produced by industrial swine lagoons. Energy corporations and meat processors have already teamed up on pilot projects to capture and condition methane from swine lagoons before blending it with natural gas that flows through transmission pipelines. The move seems helpful at face value, but it will likely prolong our reliance on natural gas by creating a regulatory system that treats blended gas as a carbon-neutral fuel.[28] At the same time, the move will make it harder to find a sustainable alternative to the current practice of storing industrial swine waste in unlined lagoons and using large tracts of land to dispose of the effluent.[29] In the end, a policy aimed at reducing carbon emissions will further entrench two of the most harmful and polluting industries in the Coastal Plain.

What these policies typically overlook is that energy sources can be renewable and yet profoundly unsustainable—a sentiment I shared with Barry Yeoman, a journalist who has written extensively on contentious energy projects in Robeson County. In 2022, Yeoman and I spoke about the state's decision to authorize an air pollution permit for a Lumberton power plant that has a long track record of air quality violations. The plant burns a mixture of poultry litter and wood, and the operator is called *North Carolina Renewable Power*—a nod to the state policy that considers the mixture a "renewable" source of energy. The facility sits on the south side of the Lumbee River in an area protected by the Jacobs Swamp Dike. The surrounding population—most exposed to pollution from the facility—is overwhelmingly African American.

"Renewability and sustainability are not fully overlapping concepts," I told Yeoman during an interview over Zoom.[30] I sketched out a larger view of the issue that accounted for the power plant's role in supporting industrialized poultry operations that currently wreak havoc on Coastal Plain ecosystems and communities. Beyond the fence line, the project is decidedly unsustainable for the people of Robeson County; the power plant itself exposes people living nearby to air pollution, and the poultry facilities that supply the plant imperil populations and ecosystems dispersed over a much wider area. In a larger sense, the same problems exist in policies that promote carbon neutrality and in many other proposed solutions to the climate crisis. The policies often promote solutions based on factors that do not include the values and perspectives of marginalized people—people who suffer first and longest when these policies go into effect.[31]

Indigenous peoples face seemingly endless obstacles to protecting their lands and waters from climate change. Regrettably, some of the obstacles stem directly from efforts to address the climate crisis through policies that inadvertently promote or prolong unsustainable practices around food, energy, and more. With so much at stake—including our continued existence as distinct peoples—we have no choice but to press forward through these obstacles.

The struggle to protect land, water, and relationships to sacred places requires that Indigenous people engage in discussions about why certain policies—climate-related or otherwise—may prove harmful. At the same time, we must begin to imagine our ancestors' values sprouting anew from the distressed landscapes of the twenty-first-century. To envision such a world is the first step in bringing it into being.

My friendship with elders from the Coharie Tribe—the two elders who guided us around the Great Coharie River after Hurricane Florence—has given me a glimpse of what it looks like to envision a world that revolves around the protection and healing of a culturally important place. During the past several years, the Great Coharie River—their river—has become a focal point for cultural renewal, environmental restoration, and community well-being. Through hard work, vision, and creativity, Coharie people have managed to rebuild long-dormant connections to their river. The next chapter tells the story of their struggles and accomplishments, providing an example of what it looks like for Indigenous communities to exercise sovereignty and strengthen connections to the places they call home.

CHAPTER SEVEN

Hope and Healing

Cultural Renewal on the Great Coharie River

Greg Jacobs and Philip Bell are elders and friends of mine. The two men belong to the Coharie Tribe, an Indigenous community of about three thousand people centered some fifty miles northeast of Pembroke in present-day Sampson County. A small portion of the Coharie community lives to the west of Sampson in present-day Harnett County.

Coharie people share some aspects of their history and culture with other Indigenous peoples of the Coastal Plain. Like the Lumbee, the Coharie Tribe is an amalgamation of Native people who survived disease, enslavement, warfare, and land dispossession during the early eighteenth century. By their own account, Coharies descend primarily from the Neusiok people, an Indigenous group whose territory included the lowest reaches of the eponymous Neuse River and its estuary.[1] The mouth of the Neuse River lies approximately seventy-five miles due east of the present-day Coharie tribal center in Sampson County. Few oral traditions remain, and colonial records dwell little on Neusioks, but from what little survives, we know them as Iroquoian peoples, allied with Tuscaroras, and part of the Native coalition that tried and executed John Lawson in 1711. They were among the groups that launched raids against settlers along the lower Neuse River and suffered uncounted loss during the military expeditions led by Barnwell and Moore in 1712 and 1713.[2]

Coharies, like Lumbees, share their name with a river that flows through their homeland. Coharie people adopted their name from the ancient river during the twentieth century, but their ancestors have occupied these lands—northeast of the Sandhills and just below the Fall Line—for centuries. Much like Lumbee territory, Coharie homelands consist of broad sandy uplands dissected by a network of densely vegetated swamp forests. The swamps drain directly into the Great Coharie River or into nearby streams, all of which eventually flow into the aptly named Black River. The Black River—a dark meandering stream—weaves across the southern Coastal Plain for miles.

The country surrounding the Black River and its tributaries is full of pine plantations, industrial livestock operations, massive crop fields, and other signs of intensive land management, none of which is visible from the level of the river. These blackwater streams flow through corridors of densely forested swampland that grow wider moving downstream. On the main stem of the Black River, this swampy corridor blocks out nearly all signs of development. Only the occasional highway bridge, boat launch, or riverside cabin reminds travelers that people live and work nearby. The Black River eventually empties into the Cape Fear a few miles upstream of a brackish estuary near the port city of Wilmington.

The Great Coharie River flows through the heart of the tribe's present-day territory, and it drains much of north and west of Sampson County—a county that is only slightly larger than Robeson County at about 960 square miles. For centuries, the stream and its swampy tributaries have provided Coharie people and their ancestors with fish and game, places to recreate and socialize, and space to worship or simply enjoy solitude. Those traditions continue today—although the face of recreation has evolved to take advantage of plastic kayaks, fiberglass canoes, and inflatable paddle boards. On any given day when the weather is clear and the water level is right, it is not unusual to find a flotilla of brightly colored kayaks drifting down the river. Playful voices dance across the surface of the dark water. Paddle-splashes glitter in sunbeams that penetrate the bald cypress canopy overhead. Smiles beam from paddlers' faces, half hidden by straw hats and baseball caps in warm weather or framed in trapper hats and toboggans in cold weather.[3] And on any given day, Greg and Philip are either leading the colorful procession or bringing up the rear.

From a Coharie perspective, connecting with their river involves—first and foremost—experiencing the river up close. Nowadays, the tribe has a fleet of modern recreational kayaks to help tribal members and visitors enjoy and bond with the river. Bank fishing and simply sitting by the water are also popular activities. Today, much of the Great Coharie River is open and accessible to boaters and others who want to experience this intimate blackwater stream.

But the Great Coharie River's accessibility did not come easily. For almost a decade, Greg and Philip led a remarkable effort by the tribe to secure access to the river and to ensure that kayaks and canoes could navigate the water. In doing so, they helped restore cultural ties to the river, sparked a new generation of advocates for the Great Coharie River, and inspired a passion for rivers among Native people from many tribes. Along the way, the tribe has grown successful at grant writing and fundraising. They have forged meaningful partnerships with nonprofit groups and government agencies, and they have accolades for their conservation efforts.

Coharie people overcame serious obstacles to reach this point. Most recently, the tribe had to deal with years of neglect by the state, which manages thousands of acres of land along both sides of the river. Hurricanes toppled entire trees into the river and swept woody debris through the narrow channel, where logjams formed. Invasive plants filled the gaps left by blown-down trees. Beaver populations grew, unchecked, along the river and augmented the logjams with their own dams and lodges. The woody gauntlet blocked the river's flow, flooded nearby farmland, and left the entire river corridor unnavigable by boat and inaccessible by foot. Nearby, industrial swine operations boomed, threatening to pollute the river with nutrients and pathogens from hog waste. These ills pushed the river toward a tipping point.

Swine operations aside, it may be tempting to think of a river blocked by blown-down trees or beaver dams as simply nature's way of reclaiming what is hers, but Coharie people view it differently. For Coharies (and other Indigenous peoples), nature and humanity are not concepts that separate neatly from one another. A healthy river is one that sustains a community and meets all of their needs—physical, mental, and spiritual. The river is a place where people can paddle, fish, hunt, or simply be themselves in a way that takes comfort in the knowledge that their ancestors knew the same sights, sounds, and smells of this specific place. A healthy river is one that people can navigate in canoes or kayaks, free of beaver dams and blowdowns, which limit accessibility by elders and other people who cannot manage strenuous portages or complicated maneuvers. A healthy river also has good overland access to boat landings, sand beaches, and fishing holes. From a Coharie perspective, wood-choked channels and trackless, sodden floodplains are signs of a river in distress.

Greg and Philip are among the people who watched the Great Coharie River closely during this time. They witnessed the changes that threatened to tip their ancestral stream into new and unfamiliar territory. The men responded by spearheading an effort to restore health to the river as best they could. What began as a handful of volunteers using hand tools to saw, chop, and drag debris from the river channel has evolved into teams of contractors wielding power tools and heavy equipment. Philip, who personally oversaw much of the early work, used to measure the tribe's river-clearing progress in feet per day; now he tracks his contractors' progress in miles per week. Paddlers these days may round a bend in the Great Coharie River and encounter work crews dissecting riverwide log jams using chainsaws and hauling debris using skid steers and winches.

FIGURE 7.1 Philip Bell collecting a water quality measurement on the Great Coharie River, 2020. Photo by author.

The two men also lead the tribe's efforts to monitor the river's health using high-tech measurements of water quality and other river characteristics. My research group helped install basic monitoring equipment on the river to record water level, temperature, and specific conductance (i.e., the total amount of material dissolved in the water). We not only coordinated with Greg, Philip, and others from the tribe to collect post-hurricane water samples, we also helped them develop strategies to monitor water quality more broadly across the Great Coharie River watershed (figure 7.1). To date, the river has not been a high priority in state and federal water-monitoring efforts, which tend to focus on larger rivers or on urban streams.

For Coharie people, this work is integral to the health of a river that is so much more than a landform that drains one small piece of the Coastal Plain. The Great Coharie River is a living relative that connects Coharies to their past, sustains them in the present, and ensures the continuation of their lifeways and communities into the future. The work of cleaning out channels, securing access to the river, and monitoring water quality are some of the ways that Coharie people care for their watery kin. The work also involves teaching youth to be good stewards of the river. Lastly, the work includes efforts to make sure that the entire Coharie community has access to the river that helps shape their identity as Indigenous people. Coharies and, increasingly, everyone else call their collective work the *Great Coharie River Initiative*.

My friends Greg and Philip have an inspiring vision for their tribe and for the river they call home. They envision a healthy, thriving community that is centered around the river and other aspects of Coharie culture—including the tribe's generations-old farming practices and food traditions. Their vision acknowledges the importance of both water and land (and places in between) in preserving and strengthening cultural traditions. In the world they envision, Coharie people also play a prominent role in decision-making about the place they call home.

Their vision would be ambitious for any tribal nation, but Coharies face the additional challenge of accomplishing all of this without federal recognition. Although the tribe was finally recognized by the State of North Carolina in 1971, Coharies have never been recognized formally by the United States. Like other Coastal Plain tribes in North Carolina, Coharies face an uphill battle when it comes to tribal consultation and other forms of meaningful engagement around environmental decisions and policies. Still, the tribe has been able to accomplish many of its goals without statutory protections and other resources provided by federal recognition. Coharie people have also accomplished these goals within a generation or two of harsh racial discrimination that gripped the region during the Jim Crow period. Through the Great Coharie River Initiative, the tribe has modeled protection and stewardship of sacred places in the face of intertwining legacies of colonialism and discrimination that still affect land, water, and people on the Coastal Plain. Their story is inspiring, but it is also instructive. It is a hopeful image of the successful exercise of inherent sovereignty in a world that seeks to erase, ignore, and deny the rights of Indigenous peoples.

US HIGHWAY 421 CARRIES much more traffic than its two narrow lanes suggest that it should. The road is a main thoroughfare through the Coharie Tribe's territory, and it traces an old route along the high sandy ground in between swampy arms of the Great Coharie River in Sampson County. Tractor trailers, pickups, and passenger vehicles pulse, steadily, along the highway day and night, completing a circuit between the town of Clinton, Sampson's county seat, and Dunn, the seat of nearby Harnett County. In the time before interstate highways, US 421 was also a major route from Sampson County to the Piedmont Triad cities—Greensboro, Winston Salem, and High Point—and to the Appalachian Mountains beyond.

I add to the traffic on US 421 whenever I travel to Sampson County to meet with Greg and Philip. My route usually crosses the Fall Line on Interstate 40, and then it enters a tangle of byways in northern Sampson County where I exit the interstate near the small town of Newton Grove. I tack back and forth on rural roads before they eventually dump me into the flow of vehicles on US 421 several miles from the tribal center where Greg works. Greg has been the Coharie Tribe's administrator since the 1970s, and the Coharie tribal center is a stately white cinder block structure that faces the highway. A sandy drive loops in front of the building and offers a modest buffer between the front doors and the traffic nearby.

The tribal center first opened in 1943 as the East Carolina Indian School, a segregated campus for Native American students living in Sampson and surrounding counties. The school was funded and built through a combination of state appropriations, community fundraisers, and sweat equity. Coharie people oversaw operations for the school, which served Native students from eastern North Carolina tribes that did not attend Lumbee schools in Robeson County.[4] Coharie families even provided room and board during the week for students who traveled from other Native communities—some from as far away as Person County, one hundred miles to the northwest.[5] The East Carolina Indian School spanned elementary grades through high school. But it was more than a schoolhouse; it was a cultural institution and guide star for Coharie people.

When I travel to Coharie territory, my first stop is usually Greg's office at the school-turned-tribal center. The walls that surround his large wooden desk are adorned with photos taken on the Great Coharie River. Some reveal verdant landscapes, and others show people smiling from the cockpits of kayaks—sunlight glinting off the surface of the dark water that surrounds them. Unmistakable joy radiates from every face. In one corner of the room, an easel supports a large situation map of the river and its watershed. Hand-drawn arrows and labels adorn the map, and brightly colored sticky notes draw attention to noteworthy places. Signs of the river sprawl throughout the office.

For years, Greg's office has served as the backdrop for countless meetings to discuss the river's health and plans for its future. Some meetings are formal gatherings with state officials, funding partners, or delegations from visiting tribes. But other meetings are preludes to impromptu conversations about food, family, and history. No matter the audience, the meetings are infused with stories about the old days at the East Carolina Indian School, which Greg and Philip both attended when they were boys. Usually, they tell stories tag-team style, with Greg's deliberative baritone complemented by Philip's rapid-fire recollection of facts and anecdotes.

Together, the men weave rich narrative tapestries that shuttle back and forth across Sampson County, intertwine with nearby Robeson County, and reference places beyond. They tell about basketball games, tobacco farming, and the pace of life in a small, tight-knit tribal community situated in the midst of much larger non-Native populations. Many of their stories draw in other figures from the Coharie community, and some of the storylines play out over centuries. In these tales, Greg and Philip are the latest narrators in a story arc that spans generations. Other conversations focus on the present—visitors to the river, meetings with state officials, recent weather. At some point, nearly every discussion turns to the river. Nostalgic talk distills into concrete conversations about what it means to protect and preserve the Great Coharie River in the twenty-first century. If it is an especially good day, we make our way out of Greg's office and toward the water.

State and federal agencies refer to the Coharies' river in the diminutive, labeling it Great Coharie Creek on maps and in official records. But for Coharies and others who know the stream well, the term *creek* does not do justice to the strong dark current that cuts through present-day Sampson County. The term *creek* evokes a small stream or tributary. In the local vernacular, it also refers to any of the braided back channels or oxbows that flow parallel to the main river. And although some creeks are beautiful to behold, the implied message is that rivers are larger and more powerful bodies of water than creeks. The Great Coharie may be small compared to its downstream waters—the Black River and the Cape Fear River—but it is impossible to understate its power as a cultural symbol and identity marker for Coharie people. The river is their tribe's lifeblood; to call it a creek diminishes its significant and ancient role in creating and sustaining the Coharie Tribe as a distinct group of Indigenous people.

A few miles down US 421 from the tribal center, the river splits into three separate channels, and the highway crosses three bridges in quick succession. Here, green road signs announce Great Coharie Creek. There is a parking lot nearby and a footpath down to a narrow canoe launch that sits almost beneath one of the three bridges. Near the water and beneath the roar of traffic on the bridge above, a copse of bald cypress and gum trees shades the water and muffles most of the road noise. The is one of the spots where I often go with Philip, Greg, or others to take a quick look at the river. The dark water snakes past the canoe launch, and sometimes I think about the story of the rattlesnake in the nearby Neuse River tributary—the story that John Lawson heard firsthand but only recorded in brief out of a duty to spare his readers from the "strange ridiculous Stories these Wretches are inclinable to believe."[6] I imagine what all I would give to hear the original story, told in full.

Both Greg and Philip grew up on the Great Coharie River, and they take pride in showing off the river to visitors. Today, a kayak can put in at the three bridges launch and float downstream for several miles, all thanks to the tribe's efforts to clear out the main channel. In the early days of their work, Greg and Philip shepherded visitors down the river using borrowed boats from a local group, Friends of Sampson County Waterways. But in recent years, the tribe has acquired its own fleet of recreational kayaks, paddles, and other gear. Soon, the tribe hopes to launch a culturally informed ecotourism operation to combine river trips with meals, farm tours, and other experiences that teach visitors about Coharie history and culture. The venture make sense; the river is sublime on most days, and Coharies have an important story to tell about Indigenous survival in the Coastal Plain today.

Coharies—like other Indigenous peoples who call the Coastal Plain *home*— were heavily affected by generations of racial discrimination and marginalization. Philip and Greg are a generation ahead of me—the last generation of North Carolinians to grow up under Jim Crow segregation. The white supremacist polices of that era determined where Coharies, Lumbees, and other Native people could attend school, where they could socialize, and with whom. But for Coharie people, the river was a refuge from marginalization, a place to escape Jim Crow laws—even if temporarily. Narrow footpaths through the forested floodplain led to oak-shaded banks where Coharies gathered freely to worship, to wade in the water, and to fish.

Coharie people fished extensively for subsistence up until a few decades ago. Fishing was also a social event. Some of the stories that Greg and Philip tell involve Coharies who traveled in large groups to the river. Nearly everyone carried cane poles or seining nets. A few used their bare arms to noodle for fish in submerged logs. In these stories, sandy river banks are comfortable and inviting places. Deep water brings respite from hot and toilsome fields. People gather at the river's edge to sing hymns, to joke and play, and to fry fish.

Coharie elders tell about these times in ways that fill in the details of what it means to live close to the river. For them, the river is not an abstract concept; it is the backdrop to their lived experience as Native people in the twentieth century. It is also the one place on Earth that connects them to their ancestors and to their oral traditions. No wonder so much of the tribe's efforts focus on restoring and protecting the Great Coharie River and its surrounding environment. As Greg once put it, "The River has always taken care of us. And now it's calling out for help, and we've got to take care of it."[7]

During the late twentieth century, Coharie people were not in a position to focus much attention at all on their ancestral river. Between the mid-1960s and the early 1980s, the tribe struggled to assert its identity following the loss of the East Carolina Indian School, a focal point for Coharie community and culture. The school was not simply a place to educate children; it was a community center, a networking hub, and one of the only institutions that provided visibility for Coharie people in a region where they held little political power or influence.

The school closed in 1965, after Sampson County ordered the desegregation of its schools. As part of its plan—and with no input from Coharie people—the county shuttered the East Carolina Indian School. The campus closed for good at the end of fifth grade for Philip and sixth grade for Greg. The next fall, Coharie students dispersed to Sampson County's now-integrated schools. Up to this point, school had been an immersive experience for Coharie children—they were surrounded all day by other Native students and teachers. They even learned about life in other tribal communities. After desegregation, many of the children became the only Native students in their classrooms. They were instantly minorities in schools that were integrated but far from welcoming or affirming of Coharie identity. The East Carolina Indian School's closure was a tremendous loss for the tribe.[8]

The local Board of Education took over the Coharie school's campus, and one year later, they relocated Sampson County's technical institute to the East Carolina Indian School property.[9] Later renamed *Sampson Community College*, the technical institute taught sewing, cosmetology, and other vocational courses in the main building of the former Indian School. The gymnasium and outbuildings were used for masonry practice and to store heavy equipment. A decade later, the Board of Education moved the institute to a new campus that was funded by a $500,000 taxpayer bond. Meanwhile, the board retained ownership of the now-vacant property, and Coharies watched as their beloved school buildings and grounds fell into disrepair.

Coharie leaders hired Greg as the tribal administrator in the 1970s, and one of his first tasks was to negotiate the return of the vacant school property to the tribe. Coharie people considered the school to be their institution, even though the tribe had never held the deed to the property. (The State of

North Carolina had purchased the land and provided a modest amount of funding to launch the school in the 1940s.) Coharie people had advocated for the school in the first place, and their efforts—which included substantial sweat equity—had sustained it through twenty-two years of operation. Just as Lumbees in nearby Robeson County viewed Pembroke State as a Lumbee institution no matter who held the deed, Coharies viewed the East Carolina Indian School as part of their tribe's legacy and cultural heritage.[10]

By Greg's own account, negotiations for the school's return began poorly. Administrators at the technical institute turned him away, explaining that the institute wanted to reserve the former Coharie school for possible storage needs in the future. Greg next spoke to the county commissioners, one of whom strongly opposed any plan to help the Coharie Tribe regain ownership of their school. The commissioner dismissed Greg's request on the grounds that Sampson County would not aid a "discriminatory group." Incredibly, the commissioner's implied message was that Coharies were discriminatory because all of the tribe's members were Native Americans.

Greg talks unhurriedly; every word is deliberate, and so is every pause. His story about meeting the county commissioner is no different. When he describes this decades-old encounter, Greg pauses after the words "discriminatory group." The silence is long enough to recall that only a few years before that meeting, some of the same officials had fervently upheld racist policies that forbade Coharies—including Greg—from attending white-only schools in Sampson County. The story confirms that allegations of reverse discrimination are nothing new, and that white supremacy adapts quickly to the language and norms of the day.

With a host of tribal members and allies supporting Greg's work and toiling behind the scenes, the tribe changed tack and slowly built political support, eventually persuading county officials to relinquish their claims to the property. In 1977, Governor Jim Hunt signed an order to convey the old East Carolina Indian School back to the tribe.[11]

The main building at the Coharie tribal center still bears the hallmarks of a 1940s country schoolhouse, both inside and out. The front steps funnel visitors into a wide hallway that branches into two yawning corridors. One can almost hear the shuffle of children's shoes on the hardwood planks and the echoes from the stark cinder block walls and high ceilings. Near the entryway, a rack of wooden bins offers free seasonal produce from the tribe's garden. Beyond them, large doors open into a former assembly hall, which now serves as a multipurpose meeting space and art gallery. Inside, the white cinder block walls are adorned with nearly life-sized oil paintings of Coharies and members of neighboring tribal communities—a permanent art installation at the center.

Elsewhere in the building, classrooms serve as administrative offices and repositories for tribal records and artifacts. Sunlight streams in through banks of tall windows that line the walls of classrooms. Along the rear of the building, large windows peer onto former courtyards and ball fields that now comprise a medicine garden and powwow arbor. Coharie people are reclaiming, repurposing, and renewing the East Carolina Indian School to suit their administrative, cultural, artistic, and practical needs in the present.

In its reimagined role as the Coharie tribal center, the East Carolina Indian School is once again a focal point for Coharie community and culture. It is a hub for community programs that pass on traditional knowledge around farming, quilting, and other practices. The center houses offices for energy assistance and other aid programs. In the summer and fall, it becomes a distribution point for vegetables harvested from the tribe's community garden. And it is the nerve center for the Great Coharie River Initiative. Appropriately, the front doors of the tribal center face east—the direction of the river. But the river is not visible from the tribal center, even though it is only half a mile away. The view is blocked by dense forests that slope down away from the sandy spit of land that holds the tribal center and US 421.

The Great Coharie River may be invisible from the tribal center, but it is stunning from the vantage point of a canoe or kayak. Even though the surrounding landscape is dominated by massive row-crop fields and studded with industrial livestock operations, the river itself is embedded in a corridor of dense swamp forest. Where it flows beneath US 421, a few miles south of the tribal center, the Great Coharie is notably smaller than the Lumbee River near Pembroke. Here, tree limbs extend from each bank nearly to the center of the stream. The meeting branches fully enclose the river in a living tunnel of wood and leaf. Elsewhere, the river splits into multiple channels that weave around sandbars or diverge around massive half-sunken logs. Along some sections of the river, beaver dams are everywhere. The dams span the main channel and cause the river's tea-stained flow to spread across the entire floodplain, shin-deep. The flooding can extend into adjacent pastures and crop fields, turning their soils into muck.

Like the Lumbee River, the Great Coharie rises and falls with the seasons. Fall is usually the driest time of the year, and—barring tropical storms—the river level drops several feet to reveal high banks of sand and silt laced with living tree roots. The layers of sediment that hold the roots are reminders of the Coastal Plain's watery history—first submerged beneath seas, then gouged by wind and waves, and now sculpted by meandering rivers. The river also holds evidence that Indigenous peoples have lived on and around the Great Coharie for millennia.

The most dramatic signs of the deep historical connections between people and water—on the Great Coharie and elsewhere on the Coastal Plain—are ancient dugout canoes that periodically emerge after centuries of hiding beneath the dark current. The canoes were sunken—accidentally or deliberately—and lodged on the riverbed, where they were entombed by the ceaseless tumble of sand and silt.[12] Sometimes, extreme droughts cause the river level to drop dramatically. During these times, silhouettes of canoes—real or imagined—are visible against the bright sand of the riverbed. At other times, powerful floods scour away riverbed sediments and dislodge ancient vessels. The canoes are utilitarian vessels, unembellished and each shaped from a single log. Simple as they are, these resurrected watercraft are powerful reminders of the skill and knowledge that allowed Coharie ancestors and the ancestors of other present-day Coastal Plain Natives to thrive in this watery world.

LIKE LUMBEE, COHARIE is not the name of a precolonial tribe, but instead it is a geographic name that the community chose for itself around the turn of the twentieth century. Both Coharie and Lumbee names commemorate places where our ancestors sought shelter and forged collective identities as survivors and refugees in the remotest parts of our ancestral territories. Although many of Greg's stories are lighthearted and entertaining, one particular story holds somber reminders of the tribe's history of survival. The story has been part of Coharie oral tradition for generations, and Greg related to me in the following way.

Coharie ancestors encountered a time in which they were forced to flee from colonists who threatened them with kidnapping and death. During that time, Greg explained, "our mothers hid their children in the woods and shushed them with fingers over their mouths." When he told me this part, Greg placed a finger to his lips and made the universal sound for "quiet."

For Coharie people, Greg explained, the sound evokes the wind whispering as it blows through the branches of pine trees that grow throughout the uplands of the Coastal Plain. When people hear the whisper of wind in the pine trees, they should remember the mothers who hid with their children and quietly shushed them. When enemies approach, the people of the whispering pines survive by becoming as quiet as possible. This is why, Greg explained, Coharie people call themselves *People of the Whispering Pines*.

As an Indigenous scholar, I am reminded by Greg's story of the desperate pleas encoded in the wampum belts that Tuscarora people delivered to Pennsylvania in 1710, just before the war that culminated in the mass death and enslavement of so many Coastal Plain Natives. I still can hear the shushing mothers in the wampum belt that represented the cries of "children born, & those yet in the womb." I imagine the crouching mothers, cradling their children, in the wampum belt that called for an end to "murdering & taking" that left them sorely "affraid [sic]of a mouse, or any other thing that Russles the Leaves." Perhaps the Coharie story of the whispering pines carries an echo of the deep trauma endured by a people who were hunted, killed, and enslaved so that settlers might have room to spread across the Coastal Plain.[13]

The story also hits close to home because I am an Emanuel. Although I belong to the Lumbee Tribe, my Emanuel ancestors were Coharies from Sampson County. They left North Carolina in the late nineteenth century to travel with other Lumbee and Coharie families to Georgia, where they sojourned as laborers on a large turpentine plantation.[14] Families from the two Native communities intermarried and raised a generation of children in Georgia. The sojourners thrived for a short time before they were hit by the decline of the turpentine industry, by World War I, and by the 1918 influenza pandemic. By 1920, most of the survivors had abandoned Georgia and returned to North Carolina. Many of them—including my Emanuel ancestors—returned to the home communities of their Robeson County kin. So Lumbees and Coharies are close relatives, and my Emanuel family forms one of the ligaments that knits our two tribes together. The Coharie oral tradition resonates with me because I share ancestry with the People of the Whispering Pines.

Not all of my Emanuel relatives left Sampson County for Georgia. One of my uncles, Enoch Emanuel, stayed behind. He was a fierce advocate for education at the turn of the twentieth century. He managed to secure modest government funds to support elementary schools for Coharie people decades before the East Carolina Indian School was established. Although I am not a Coharie by tribal membership, I am a relative to Coharie people and consider myself an ally. Even today, some fraction of the water in the Great Coharie River washes around and through the remains of my ancestors who lie buried in its watershed.

Our shared ancestry is one of the reasons why, in 2014, I responded enthusiastically when Philip asked if I would paddle a section of the Great Coharie River with him. The two of us met on a damp, gray morning in November in the narrow driveway between the serenity of the tribal center and the diesel-fueled chaos of US 421. Philip brought kayaks—twelve-foot recreational boats that were appropriate for navigating the river's narrow upper reaches. I spent my twenties paddling whitewater streams throughout the southern Appalachian Mountains—Tellico, Tallulah, Ocoee, Nolichucky, Nantahala, and a host of other rivers in the Carolinas, Tennessee, Virginia, and farther afield. Here, the water sucked, pumped, and pulsed through slots and over ledges. It frothed and boiled over submerged crags and slabs of stone. Streams threaded their ways through boulder fields at the bottoms of steep-sided valleys, lush with hemlocks. I enjoyed those years of paddling in the mountains, but I was only a visitor. By 2014, I was old enough to know the difference between loving a place as a visitor and longing for home.

Although I had never boated the Great Coharie River, it felt like a homecoming to paddle alongside Philip. We left a vehicle at the takeout and rode together back upstream to the three bridges. Our paddle strokes and the wakes of our boats were the only disturbances to the water's smooth surface that day—a nearly perfect reflection of gray sky and shadowy tree limbs. A handful of branches still held colorful leaves; maples and sweet gums dangled red and yellow branches over the quiet water. Holly trees and river cane added a green hue to the otherwise dull floodplain.

Philip narrated as we paddled. He explained that in recent decades, Coharie people had been largely cut off from the beaches, landings, and access points along the river where they formerly gathered to fish, swim, and worship. Much of this occurred in the wake of large land transfers between pulp and paper companies, conservation groups, and the State of North Carolina. In the mid-twentieth century, paper companies purchased large tracts of land in the Great Coharie River's floodplain. They clear-cut swamp forests and sent the logs to mills near the coast. Loggers could not reach every tree in the floodplain, and some ancient sentinels survived. Below the Great Coharie River where roads are fewer and floodplains are broader, a sheltered pocket of ancient bald cypress trees survived in the sinuous swamps along the Black River. The oldest trees stand in Three Sisters Swamp, a semi-submerged cove of bald cypress trees that are more than 2,600 years old—the oldest living trees in eastern North America.[15] Their lower trunks are thickened by buttresses that stabilize the giants in the floodplain silts where they are rooted. The treetops do not taper or branch gracefully; they are shorn and ragged, but still elegant. The ancient trees have stood over the southern watches of the Black River since time immemorial.

Apart from Three Sisters Swamp and a few other isolated spots, paper companies were fairly thorough in the work of deforesting the floodplains of the Great Coharie River and other tributaries of the Black River. Logging activities permanently altered the floodplain—where dense riparian forests had once stood—and other parts of the river system. Not only were the stately bald cypress, black gum, and bluff oak trees gone, but heavy equipment had compacted fragile soils, lacerated the terrain, and sloughed sediment into the river.

Some paper companies even carved off belowground mineral rights from the deeds to their properties. They did this on the chance that at some point in the future they might wish to sell the land but keep the right to extract iron ore or other mineral wealth below the surface. Weyerhaeuser, one of the largest companies operating in Sampson County during this period, separated the belowground mineral rights from at least five thousand acres in the county. The company did not limit this practice to Sampson County; across North Carolina, Weyerhaeuser separated mineral rights from surface rights for an estimated 155,000 acres of forestland.[16] Other companies followed suit. Although the anticipated mineral exploitation never occurred, the aboveground and belowground rights for most of these properties had not been rejoined as of the 2010s.[17]

Native people have always known that healthy rivers and healthy communities depend on intact wetlands. But it took major policy shifts in the late twentieth century before environmental managers, regulators, and developers in the United States took widespread actions to protect these environments. Many actions followed the federal government's policy of "no net loss"—implemented during the 1980s to curb rampant dredging and filling of wetlands.

The policy was rooted in the federal government's authority to regulate wetlands under the Clean Water Act. The law brings some wetlands under federal jurisdiction as Waters of the United States.[18] Although the "no net loss" policy did not truly stop wetland destruction, it did pave the way for market-based solutions that promised to restore and protect wetlands in compensation for what was lost.

State and federal regulators crafted policies to allow developers of highways, neighborhoods, and other projects to purchase credits to offset wetland destruction. The credits represented real acreage in wetlands that had been restored, enhanced, or—in some cases—created. Restrictive easements protected real acreage in perpetuity. Conservation groups, environmental firms, private investors, and universities supplied wetland credits to land developers, transportation agencies, energy companies, and others. Credit suppliers established wetland mitigation banks—each storing hundreds or thousands of acres worth of wetland credits.[19]

Mitigation banks arose as a clever solution to the federal government's "no net loss" policy on wetlands. Banks were usually established on properties that were former wetlands; the lands had been ditched, drained, and converted to other uses long before the policy was established. Technically, the properties were not wetlands at the time the federal government declared an end to "net" wetland loss. By purchasing the properties and restoring them to some semblance of a wetland, bank owners created—at least on paper—new surpluses that they could sell to offset wetland destruction elsewhere.[20] If a highway widening project threatened to fill in several acres of wetlands, the Department of Transportation could purchase credits in a nearby bank to offset the losses. A landowner who could not develop their property without destroying a fraction of an acre of wetland could do the same.

Regulators ensured that buyers purchased credits from banks containing the same types of wetlands that were harmed or destroyed. Regulators also imposed premiums on wetlands deemed to have especially high environmental value to discourage their destruction.[21] High-value wetlands included those that played significant roles in mitigating water pollution, preventing downstream floods, or harboring rare plant communities.

In North Carolina, wetland-destroying parties could also pay a fee to a state-run initiative, the Ecosystem Enhancement Program, instead of buying credits in a nearby mitigation bank. The fund was established in the early 2000s, mainly to compensate for wetland impacts due to state highway construction and widening. The North Carolina Department of Transportation had conducted much of its own mitigation in the form of wetland restoration projects throughout the state, and it spent tens of millions of dollars annually on these efforts. The Ecosystem Enhancement Program was created, in part, to take over Department of Transportation wetland mitigation efforts and similar efforts by other agencies. In lieu of selling credits in an actual wetland mitigation bank, the program would collect fees from the Department of Transportation—or from anyone else who needed to purchase credits. The fees funded a portfolio of restoration and protection efforts throughout the state, often targeting sites that had special environmental or cultural significance.[22]

The jury is still out on the overall success of programs put in place to ensure "no net loss" of wetlands. Metrics such as the overall area of wetlands restored versus wetlands lost paint the programs as successful, but closer scrutiny of differences in quality, location, and other factors between lost and protected wetlands have led some researchers to criticize the programs as less effective than they seem at first glance.[23]

THE CONSERVATION TRUST of North Carolina helped manage the Ecosystem Enhancement Program during the early 2000s, identifying candidate properties across the state for preservation and restoration.[24] Some properties were formerly logged floodplains that had been owned for decades by pulp and paper companies. Those companies now hoped to unload properties where tree regrowth was painfully slow and where regulatory oversight had increased following the federal government's "no net loss" policy. In fact, this is how four thousand acres of formerly logged lands along the Great Coharie River came to be owned by the State of North Carolina. Years ago, conservation groups identified a string of interconnected floodplain properties along the Great Coharie River owned by pulp and paper companies. In 2004, conservationists negotiated the purchase of several parcels of land using funds from the Ecosystem Enhancement Program. The groups then placed restrictive easements on the land and deeded all four thousand acres to the State of North Carolina.

The purchase ensured that the Great Coharie River's floodplain would never again be clear-cut or developed. The arrangement not only protected expansive riparian wetlands, but it also protected the river itself—providing a buffer against water pollution from industrial livestock operations located nearby. This buffer helped to protect water quality downstream, in places like the treasured Three Sisters Swamp. The entire project was made possible by funds paid into the Ecosystem Enhancement Program to compensate for wetland losses elsewhere.

As our two kayaks glided across the surface of the Great Coharie River on that gray November day, Philip and I passed patches of floodplain forest that seemed to have been spared from the chainsaws of pulp and paper companies decades ago. Likely, they were places that were too wet or too remote for loggers to reach. Elsewhere, the floodplain bore scars of logging from earlier decades—scrubby and stunted trees, choked by vines, now inhabited large chunks of what was once a vast contiguous forest, a ribbon of green that sheltered the Great Coharie's dark current.

While we paddled, Philip explained that Coharie people were largely forgotten during recent conservation efforts. The tribe had little involvement in the land transfer or the watershed management plans that were developed afterward. The tribe barely appears in the watershed's 2014 management plan, which lays out formal recommendations for improving the river's overall health.[25] A consortium of local and state decision-makers developed the plan over a five-year period and emphasized the importance of community engagement in the planning process.

Despite this emphasis, the management plan hardly mentions the Coharie Tribe or its priorities related to the river. The tribe is simply named alongside a generic "agricultural community" as a group that values the river and its watershed.[26] Philip recalled learning about the plan for the first time only a short time before it was finalized and released to the public. To be clear, Philip and other Coharies are pleased that the river and its floodplain are protected by conservation easements and that a management plan exists to guide future development and conservation efforts in the watershed. But the state's vision for conservation has not always aligned with the values and priorities of Coharie people, especially when it came to dealing with blowdowns, woody debris, beaver dams, and other obstacles that prevented people from paddling the river or even accessing its banks.

Philip told me about beaver dams while we paddled and—as if on cue—the flow widened and slackened as a small dam came into view. I never encountered beaver dams when I paddled whitewater, and I was surprised by the structure's stability—the mass of wood and sediment flexed only slightly as our boats crossed the broad crest and slid down the two-foot slope on the opposite side. With virtually no water velocity to push us along, we had to coax our boats over the prickly ledge.

Officials at North Carolina's Department of Environmental Quality were initially reluctant to authorize the Coharies' plan to clear out logjams and other obstructions in their river. Large portions of the state-owned land acquired through the Ecosystem Enhancement Program were off-limits to the public—marked with No Trespassing signs. The department had leased much of the river's floodplains to a private hunting club, and the club's members held exclusive rights to access the state-owned land. Department officials even rebuffed Philip when he simply requested permission for tribal members to cross the floodplain in order to reach sand beaches and other historically significant sites spread throughout the four thousand acres. At the time, Coharies could only reach a few spots along the river where highway bridges provided public waysides with water access. Many of the tribe's historic fishing, boating, and gathering spots, however, were on lands that the state had leased for hunting.

Eventually, the tribe secured permission to access some of these sites, which created options for planning canoe and kayak trips of varying lengths; distant highway bridges were no longer the only access points for boating. Little by little, Greg and Philip sought permission from state officials to expand the work. First, they asked to clear some of the strainers and logjams that prevented canoes and kayaks from navigating the stream. Success. Next, they sought permission to cull the massive beaver population that had overtaken the river and floodplain on the state's watch. Success again.

Slowly, state officials came to see the tribe's vision of stewardship for the Great Coharie River. The change of heart happened around the time of my river trip with Philip. By then, both he and Greg were seasoned advocates for the river, and it was their persistence that opened the eyes of state regulators. It took substantial time and resources on behalf of the tribe to convince the Department of Environmental Quality to green-light their efforts, but the state eventually allowed the tribe to hire contractors to clear the channel and trappers to cull the runaway beaver population.

Globally, conservation efforts have often excluded and dispossessed Indigenous peoples in the name of establishing wilderness areas, preserves, or other protected places. The practice, sometimes called *fortress conservation*, treats humans as visitors to protected lands (or bans them altogether). At the core of fortress conservation is some variation on the theme that nature must be protected from humans. It is certainly—and increasingly—true that people misuse and abuse nature; however, by excluding Indigenous peoples from their own lands, fortress conservation promotes the colonial myth that settlers arrived in various places to discover pristine wildernesses, devoid of people.[27]

Coharies did not occupy farms or homes on the four thousand acres of land that conservationists placed into the Ecosystem Enhancement Program, but the action still restricted Coharie peoples' access to the river by making them trespassers in floodplain forests where they had walked, fished, and hunted for centuries. To be sure, the Ecosystem Enhancement Program did not set out to harm or inconvenience Coharies or anyone else, but there is also no evidence that state officials or conservationists ever accounted for Coharie peoples' rights to access their traditional lands when they added the Great Coharie River's floodplain to the program's inventory of land.

In North Carolina as in other places with deep histories of settler colonialism, Indigenous peoples and their priorities are rarely considered in plans for watershed management, compensatory wetland mitigation, or ecological restoration. Even though the Coharie Tribe is not federally recognized and does not benefit from federal laws and policies meant to foster tribal engagement and consultation, the tribe has been recognized by North Carolina for decades. However, the Coharie experience shows just how little this recognition mattered (at the time) in the state's decision-making.

The situation is slowly changing in North Carolina, mainly due to advocacy by tribes themselves and not self-awareness on the part of state government. Still, the unfortunate reality is that Indigenous peoples' values simply do not factor into the vast majority of environmental planning and regulatory efforts, even when those efforts focus on places that have exceptional cultural or historical significance. This is especially true for tribes in the Coastal Plain. Federal officials overlook Coharie and other Coastal Plain tribes because they lack federal recognition. And even though these tribes have state recognition, state officials have no formal policies to guide tribal engagement.

In the end, North Carolina's failure to include Coharies in their initial plans to protect the Great Coharie River and its wetland forests created setbacks for the tribe, but it did not derail the tribe's plans entirely. Thankfully, Greg, Philip, and others had the experience, tact, and persistence to convince the Department of Environmental Quality to approve their culturally motivated work on the river. But the story of the Great Coharie River Project does not end there.

In the years since Philip and I first paddled together on the Great Coharie River, the tribe has secured funding to pay for much of the channel-clearing work. In recent years, the tribe has worked with a Lumbee contractor whose work crews carefully extricate downed trees and other debris from the channel using a combination of hand tools, chainsaws, and other equipment. The tribe has partnered with conservation groups and other organizations to prioritize and purchase culturally significant tracts of land along the river. One recent acquisition included a large sandy beach—a point bar—on a stretch of river several miles downstream from the three bridges. The property has vehicle access from the highway, and the point bar provides easy entry for people and boats into the river's dark flow. Unlike the rugged or sodden trails that wind through other parts of the floodplain, this is a place where elders or those with limited mobility can easily reach the water. It is a place that makes it easy to fish, boat, or simply feel close to the river.

Now that long stretches of the river are open to canoes and kayaks, the tribe is beginning to map out strategies for ecotourism. The venture is a natural fit; Greg, Philip, and others are gracious hosts on the water and are both endless wells of factual stories and tall tales. Tourism and microentrepreneurship experts from North Carolina State University helped the tribe organize and promote river trips for the general public. The first two trips sold out quickly and generated rave reviews. Greg and Philip have also brought on board a younger tribal member, Kullen Bell, to work out the details of what it might look like for the Coharie Tribe to own and operate a culturally engaged ecotourism business.

To support its work on restoration and ecotourism, the tribe recently invested in basic water monitoring equipment. After disastrous flooding from Hurricane Florence in 2018, Greg Jacobs and Philip Bell approached me with an idea to monitor water conditions in Great Coharie River's headwaters. They were most interested in water quality, but they also recognized the importance of monitoring water levels for paddling trips and for documenting future floods and droughts. The US Geological Survey operates a network of stations throughout the country that serves these purposes, but no such station exists on the Great Coharie River. In fact, the nearest station is far downstream on the Black River. The Black River monitoring station can only give an approximate view, at best, of conditions on the Great Coharie River or any of its tributaries. Moreover, because the station lies so far downstream, any information that it records about flooding or water pollution in the headwaters is both delayed and attenuated.

By early 2019, we had agreed on a location and technical specifications of the monitoring station. We wanted basic observations that included water level (i.e., the height of river water above a certain reference elevation), water temperature, and specific conductance—a measure of the total amount of material dissolved in the water. Specific conductance cannot tell the difference between different chemical species (e.g., nitrate and chloride), but the technology is much more reliable and much less expensive than sensors designed to measure concentrations of any particular chemical.[28] We installed the station later that year with help from Jeff Currie (the Lumbee Riverkeeper) members of my research group, and a small aluminum boat.

One of the best decisions about the monitoring station was the acquisition of hardware that allows remote access to data from the station using a cellular phone network. Greg and Philip now have remote, real-time access to the station's data on their smartphones, and so do I. We spent an afternoon together, in Greg's office, installing phone apps and configuring them to communicate with the station. The ability to view real-time water-monitoring data has been around for decades, but I still geek out over the ability to take a remote peek at data from the station that we built together, as a community.[29]

Whenever any of us connects our phone to the station, there is a momentary anxiety while waiting for the latest numbers to appear. My heart rises into my throat as the phone screen fades into a spinning digital wheel accompanied by the message, "connecting . . ." The feeling is the same whether I am one mile away from the station or one hundred miles away; the anxiety does not scale with distance. Without fail, though, the numbers always appear within a second or two. I am always excited to digest the latest information, but before diving in, I pause for a moment to appreciate the passion and motivation that underpin the entire enterprise.

THE COHARIE TRIBE'S WORK is inspirational, but it is more than a feel-good story. Until recently, the tribe was invisible in many spaces where decisions are made about land, water, and communities. And long before that, Coharie people faced overt racial discrimination in nearly every aspect of their lives. But in recent years, Coharies have gained visibility as stewards, protectors, and healers of the river through the Great Coharie River Initiative.

In doing so, the tribe has also gained respect from the non-Native neighbors, from other tribes, and from various entities involved in decision-making about the environment. The tribe has developed an especially close relationship with Friends of Sampson County Waterways, a local group that promotes river recreation and healthy streams. Other tribes in the region cite the Great Coharie River Initiative as an example of self-determination; what they mean is that Coharies have found ways to achieve their cultural and environmental goals, and they have done it in spite of their tribal recognition status.

In 2019, the North Carolina Wildlife Foundation—one of the state's premier conservation groups—named the Coharie Tribe *Water Conservationist of the Year* as part of its annual Governor's Conservation Achievement Awards program. The award citation read, in part, "Native American leaders marshaled grant funding, community involvement, academics and scientists to help clear the river for small-scale boat navigation, and reconnect the tribe to its ancestral waters. Bringing together cultural, historical, and natural assets, the tribe dedicated three years and 5,000 volunteer hours to restore access to the river."[30]

The award is well-earned, and it highlights the tribe's incredible efforts to protect the Great Coharie River. However, another recent event strikes me as a profound testament to the level of respect and honor that is now accorded to Coharie people in their homelands. In 2018, the North Carolina Office of State Archaeology recovered a 650-year-old dugout canoe from a river in Sampson County. The canoe may have been dislodged from the riverbed by floodwaters following a recent hurricane, and then exposed during low flow later on. The twelve-foot-long boat was carved and burned from a single massive log—charred wood and marks from stone tools still visible along its length.

Four days after the canoe's discovery was first reported by a Sampson County resident, the State Archaeologist's office reached out to the tribe to discuss a possible plan for preservation and repatriation.[31] It is likely that a conversation like this would not have happened even a few years earlier—or at least it would not have happened at an appropriately early stage. But in 2018, the Coharie Tribe was well-known to state agencies, largely through the persistence of Greg, Philip, and others who advocated for their vision of a healthy river.

The canoe's discovery also occurred in the midst of controversy over the failure of state and federal regulators to consult with tribes prior to approving permits for the Atlantic Coast Pipeline. Perhaps it was a sign that state officials were becoming attuned to expectations that tribes should have a say in cultural and environmental affairs in their homelands.

Coharies were quick to speak publicly about the canoe's cultural importance to the tribe. Philip summarized the tribe's sentiment in the local newspaper, explaining that the dugout was "important to sharing the story of the Coharie people's past" and hailed it as a sign of the tribe's resilience.[32] Philip's assertion was clear; the canoe was part of the tribe's cultural heritage, and its rightful place was with the Coharie people. Moreover, it should not be locked away in a repository or archive; it should be on display to remind everyone about the age-old connection between Native people and their rivers on the Coastal Plain.

After meeting in person with tribal officials, the Office of State Archaeology agreed to send the ancient canoe to a laboratory near Wilmington so that it could be preserved prior to repatriation and permanent display at the Coharie tribal center. The preservation process would take more than a year. The tribe asked, if possible, for the state to return the canoe in time for their fall powwow the following year.

In the late summer of 2019, outside the assembly hall of the former East Carolina Indian School, the 650-year-old dugout returned home to the Coharie people. Rows of careful hands carried the canoe indoors and into the hall. The hands gently placed the dugout on a rough wooden platform staged against one of the white cinder block walls. The platform held the canoe's hulking mass at waist height, and a woolen trade blanket cradled its weight and protected it from the platform's rough wooden ribs. Native eyes peered down at the canoe from the enormous oil paintings that lined the walls of the room. Their expressions seemed to signal approval.

Throughout the powwow weekend, individuals and small knots of people drifted in from the outdoor festivities to see the canoe. Some prayed over the charred hull and lovingly dropped fragments of tobacco and cedar inside. Others gently touched the boat's interior, as black as if it had been burned and scraped yesterday. Still others stood silently and took it all in.

The assembly hall would not be the canoe's permanent home; the room lacked the required climate control. Philip was already reviewing plans to convert one of the old classrooms into a space to permanently house the canoe alongside educational displays featuring the Great Coharie River. State officials agreed to hold the canoe until the permanent space was ready, and so the powwow display was only temporary.

I visited Greg and Philip immediately after the powwow weekend—a few days before state officials would come back to retrieve the dugout. The two men led me into the assembly hall and gave me a wholly undeserved moment alone with the 650-year-old canoe. I had no words. I touched the charred wood and tried to imagine the people who fashioned and handled the boat centuries before. My hands gently acknowledged the worn spots along the rails and inside the hull. I stared at the offerings of tobacco and cedar left behind by others. My mind wandered. The canoe had lain in sediments at the bottom of a Coastal Plain river for centuries—probably since the 1300s. I imagined what the boat missed while it was sleeping in the river—all that had happened to the Coastal Plain and its people until hurricane-fueled floods dredged it up from the depths. Philip and Greg walked over to me, and the three of us stood, quietly, near the canoe. Finally, someone broke the silence, "Why don't we go down to the river?"

CHAPTER EIGHT

Recommendations

Indigenous Environmental Justice in a Transformed World

Academics sometimes use the term *Lumbee English* to describe the unique dialect spoken by Native Americans in Robeson County.[1] Lumbees in and around Robeson County have always talked differently from their Black and white neighbors. Scholars have put forward a few different ideas about the origins of our dialect, but most agree that Lumbee speech reflects the depth and intensity of colonialism, which has erased nearly all signs of our ancestral languages after more than ten generations of sustained contact with settlers. The erasure is not surprising. Linguist Clare Dannenberg, who studied Lumbee English, observed that under the pressures of colonialism, Native American languages "can be lost without a trace within three generations."[2]

With that in mind, Lumbee English bears little resemblance to our ancestral languages, be they Siouan, Algonquian, or Iroquoian languages. Our ancestors were exposed to English-speaking colonists for centuries—as long as any other Indigenous peoples in the Southeast. And by the mid-eighteenth century, English had replaced all of our ancestral languages as the common tongue of trade, diplomacy, and survival in the Coastal Plain.

A few interesting figures of speech emerged, however, as Lumbee ancestors forged new lives and created new communities in our corner of the Coastal Plain. One such phrase is "on the swamp." It simply means to be in the neighborhood or around the community. The phrase is not literal—Lumbee communities are not actually located in swamps; they occupy higher ground nearby. To be "on the swamp" means to be around Prospect, Saddletree, Burnt Swamp, Sandy Plains, Back Swamp, or one of the myriad other Lumbee communities arrayed across the Lumbee River basin. The phrase is a reminder about the powerful connections that Lumbee people have to these communities. Our communities orient us; they are stars in the verdant and watery firmament that we call home.

I spent much of my childhood "on the swamp" in Robeson County, but I also grew up in Charlotte, a city two hours away from Robeson County. As a result, I did not inherit my family's distinctive Lumbee dialect—one of the downsides of living in the city. My parents brought Lumbee speech and customs with them to Charlotte in the 1970s; both of them had attended segregated, Indian-only schools and had spent most of their lives up to that point among other Native people who spoke like them, looked like them, and shared many of the same life experiences of growing up in rural Robeson County. Through my parents, I heard Lumbee English spoken at home every day. I was immersed in Lumbee English whenever we traveled to Robeson County, which occurred at least monthly until I went to college. But for a variety of reasons, Lumbee speech did not rub off on me.

Instead, I took on the linguistic melange of a booming southern city in the late twentieth century. My classmates and teachers came from rural and urban neighborhoods, and the classrooms of my formative years were racially, ethnically, and culturally diverse. By the time I started school in the early 1980s, Charlotte-Mecklenburg Schools—the state's largest school district comprising both the city of Charlotte and the surrounding county—had spent years working out the kinks of a plan that made the district a national exemplar of school desegregation.[3] Charlotte-Mecklenburg Schools gave me opportunities that were inaccessible to my parents and unimaginable to my grandparents, and I am forever grateful for the experiences and privileges that I gained through my schooling.

At the same time, I missed the day-to-day cultural immersion experienced by Lumbee children who grew up "on the swamp." Their classrooms, playgrounds, and school buses were full of Lumbee people. In contrast, I was the only Lumbee—and usually only Native student—in my classes and one of a small handful of Native students at my school. A few hundred other Native students (less than 1 percent of the district's population) were similarly dispersed in classrooms and schools across a system that served nearly one hundred thousand students at the time I graduated. From our teachers and peers, we learned harmful stereotypes and settler myths about our own tribes or about Native Americans in general. At times, we were tokenized or saddled with the burden of educating our peers and teachers about our communities and cultures. Mostly, however, our identities were ignored altogether in curricula that focused heavily on narratives of the South as a racial binary of Black people and white people.[4]

Native American families petitioned Charlotte-Mecklenburg Schools to do something about the isolation, stereotyping, and other challenges faced by Native children in the school system. Specifically, they asked school district leaders to take advantage of a new federally funded program designed to aid Native students in public school systems. The Indian Education Act, passed by Congress in 1972, had authorized the creation of support programs in school districts across the United States.[5] Charlotte, the families argued, had a critical mass of Native students to justify its own federally funded Indian education program.

District officials agreed, and within a few years Charlotte-Mecklenburg Schools had launched an Indian education program. The district tapped Mrs. Rosa Revels Winfree, a Lumbee educator who lived in Charlotte, as the program's director. "Mrs. Rosa," as we all knew her, traveled regularly from school to school, checking in with individual Native students and giving presentations to classes and school assemblies. She strode gracefully into our elementary school classrooms or gymnasiums to deliver culturally appropriate lessons about Native peoples, laboring to undo harmful stereotypes and erasure. In upper grades, she arranged to meet with Native students all at once, in a counselor's office or quiet space where we could spill our guts about the challenges of maintaining cultural identity in a large urban school system. Mrs. Rosa had the ease and authority of an experienced classroom teacher, and she did not hesitate to follow up with teachers, administrators, and district officials on issues related to the erasure of Native peoples from society.

Thus, instead of being cast adrift in the state's largest school district, we Native students knew that Mrs. Rosa kept an eye on us and had our backs. Behind the scenes, Mrs. Rosa and a cadre of parents and community members advocated fiercely for resources and policies to help Native students overcome the barriers of cultural isolation and colonial stereotypes.

Under Mrs. Rosa's leadership, the Indian Education Program in Charlotte-Mecklenburg Schools graduated a generation of urban Native students who were culturally competent and prepared to serve their people in various ways. Some took jobs working with tribes or Indigenous organizations, and others diffused into public service or the private sector. Still others took up roles in their churches and communities. Wherever they ended up, students who participated in the Indian Education Program remained connected to their cultures and became part of a large network of Indigenous people with ties to Charlotte and Mrs. Rosa. Certainly, some students would have made these connections without Indian Education, and the program did not pull every Native student into its orbit. But in a school district where Native students made up less than 1 percent of the population, Indian Education was a powerful force against erasure of Indigenous peoples.

Native students who grew up in Charlotte had different experiences from our kin back home in our tribal territories. Even though Native North Carolinians were largely spared from federal policies that relocated Indigenous peoples to major cities such as Minneapolis, Seattle, and San Francisco, we share many common experiences with urban Natives elsewhere.[6] Among these experiences was the feeling that cities were ephemeral outposts from which we orbited and periodically intersected our true homes—our tribal communities and homelands. Our families may have spent a generation or two (or even three) in the city pursuing work or education, but Native children carried the expectation that someday we—or perhaps our descendants—would return home. Our families didn't move to the city in an attempt to reach escape velocity; we only wanted a clearer view of home.[7]

Together with advocates like Mrs. Rosa, our families made sure that we received every possible privilege of living in the city, but without compromising our identities as Indigenous people. They taught us the intricate process of what many Native people call "walking in two worlds" or what Mi'kmaw elder Albert Marshall more appropriately describes as "two-eyed seeing."[8]

In my case, life in between Robeson County and Charlotte helped me to see the myriad ways in which Lumbee people and our Indigenous neighbors remain rooted to our ancestral lands and waters despite centuries of attempts to erase, talk over, and assimilate us. I have shared these observations and lessons with my own children, Laurel and Reed, who were raised in an urban Native community in Raleigh but understand what it means to be rooted to a place like Robeson County. And they have taught me a great deal about what it means for young Indigenous people to maintain and express their cultural connections to place in the twenty-first century.

The fact that Lumbees have remained in our homelands is no trivial matter in a region where Indigenous peoples were targeted, for centuries, by colonial policies aimed—ultimately—at our expulsion and extermination. Many Lumbee people—including tribal leaders and elders—describe our collective identity in terms of a strong sense of kinship and community belonging. I think that our kinship networks and community structures remain strong in part because they still occupy the template of our ancestral homelands—the patchwork quilt that binds together Prospect, Saddletree, Pembroke, and all of the other places that collectively define Lumbee people as a tribal nation. And all of it—the mosaic of communities, farmland, and swamps—persists today because the Lumbee River held us close while colonialism swept through the Coastal Plain.

In *Strike at the Wind!*, a long-running Lumbee outdoor drama about Henry Berry Lowry, the fictional narrator tells the audience, "The greatest thing is not to possess, but to belong." This line is an apt summary of our relationship to our homelands. Lumbees belong to the landscapes and waterways that preserved us and molded our culture, just as we belong in community with one another. Our collective identity is inextricably bound to this place.

I have trouble imagining how Lumbee people could survive as a distinct nation of people if we became permanently separated from the rural landscapes and waterways of Robeson County.[9] After all, this place has been our home since time out of mind. It is the only land we know, regardless of who holds legal title to it, as the words of both Henry Berry Lowry and Ruth Revels remind us. And while our homelands on the Coastal Plain have always experienced environmental change, colonialism has shifted both the tenor and pace of those changes. Instead of slow and sustainable changes meant to preserve Lumbee communities for the benefit of future generations, colonialism has spawned rapid changes that aim to extract as much wealth as possible (and as quickly as possible) from Robeson County and from the homelands of other Indigenous peoples.

Often, the extraction involves exploiting places like Robeson County for waste disposal, as in the case of industrial livestock operations. Other times, extraction involves sacrificing Lumbee homeplaces for hazardous and polluting infrastructure like natural gas pipelines. Sometimes extraction involves the large-scale destruction of intact ecosystems, as in the case of wetland drainage and deforestation. In all of these cases, Lumbee lands, waters, and communities are permanently altered—and usually for the worse. Our shallow groundwater is overloaded with nutrients and pathogens that seep into tributary swamps of the Lumbee River. Vast contiguous swaths of forest have been razed and fragmented until only ragged vestiges remain. High-pressure natural gas pipelines dissect rural communities en route to distant cities and power plants.

To be sure, some Lumbees have benefited from extraction. Lumbee people were among those who acquired newly drained and cleared wetlands for farms or found work in slaughterhouses and industrial plants. But Lumbee people have had little, if any, collective say in what takes place in our homelands. Extraction and sacrifice, imposed by outsiders, are the intergenerational legacies of colonialism, racial discrimination, and assimilation policies levied against Indigenous peoples on the Coastal Plain. With that in mind, perhaps a better way to say that Lumbees benefited from extraction is to acknowledge that we were dealt a sorry hand and still managed to beat the odds.

Until recently, beating the odds meant drawing from the deep well of cultural capital woven into the crazy quilt of swamps and interstitial uplands dotted with Lumbee homeplaces and communities. But in the twenty-first century, Robeson County's landscapes and waterways are transforming at a furious pace. The energy sector's insatiable desire for cheap fuel and the live-stock industry's lust for cheap protein drive much of the transformation. At the same time, climate change compounds the situation by permanently altering the reality of where people and our nonhuman relatives can live and thrive.

Thriving in Robeson County has always been about finding balance be-tween water and land, wet and dry, too much and too little. Lumbee people found the sweet spot in between the sandy pine forests and the sodden bald cypress swamps, and we thrived. Today, however, this narrow zone of habit-ability is shrinking. Climate change causes rivers and swamps to expand and contract unpredictably, altering ecosystems and disrupting centuries-old knowledge about how close we can live to the river without imperiling lives or property. Today, the river warns us to back away. Opposite the river on higher ground—where our ancestors farmed and lived—massive livestock opera-tions, slaughterhouses, and wastewater sprayfields now create noxious zones of pollution that warn people to back away. Gas transmission pipelines and processing plants cut wide swaths through our forests and fields with signs that warn people to back away.

Lumbee people and our Indigenous neighbors have been backing away for centuries—adapting and making do with the hands we were dealt. As a result, our homelands feel a little less like home, in some ways, with each passing year. Lumbee communities are shrinking safe havens. Flooding from human-caused climate change threatens communities from one side and industrial-ization from the other. The last vestiges of our formerly expansive homelands are caught in the squeeze of extraction and sacrifice. It is a perilous place to be, but we remain. We belong.

SO FAR, LUMBEE PEOPLE have had virtually no collective voice in the scope or pace of Robeson County's sacrificial transformation. The situation is simi-lar to that of Indigenous peoples across the Coastal Plain and around the world. The present voicelessness—borne of our erasure from society—is es-pecially frustrating given that state and federal governments often name envi-ronmental justice and Indigenous rights as values worth upholding. Even corporations, many of whom act as modern-day agents of colonialism, claim environmental justice and human rights among their operating values.[10]

But words are cheap; governments and corporations operating in the Coastal Plain and elsewhere have little to show when it comes to acknowl-edging and addressing their past and present roles in transforming Indigenous homelands. The situation is unfortunate, because justice begins with the acknowledgment of harm.[11] Until governments and corporations acknowledge the impacts of colonialism and pursue meaningful actions to reverse the erasure of Indigenous voices, policies on environmental justice ring as hollow as many of the institutional land acknowledgments that have emerged in recent years—eloquent but devoid of systemic change needed to set things aright.

But the situation is evolving, even as governments and corporations continue to sidestep systemic change. Lumbee people and their neighbors on the Coastal Plain have begun to take matters into their own hands, taking steps to protect sacred places and to eliminate disparities in the distribution of pollution and other environmental harms. In North Carolina, these steps include a series of formal statements issued in the past few years by tribal governments and by the state's Commission of Indian Affairs. The documents—including resolutions and ordinances—call out government agencies for their failures to engage tribal nations in key decisions to allow fossil fuel infrastructure and other unsustainable projects in tribal communities. The documents are framed around the principles of environmental justice and Indigenous rights, reminding governments and corporations about the values that they claim to uphold.

Some of the issuances by Indigenous leaders in North Carolina call on government officials to rescind decisions made in the absence of free, prior, and informed consent by tribal nations—echoing language from the United Nations Declaration on the Rights of Indigenous Peoples (UNDRIP). Even if the United States considers the declaration "aspirational" rather than legally enforceable, the adoption of this language signals that tribal nations are watching expectantly to see what, if anything, "aspirational" actually means.[12] Other resolutions from North Carolina tribes call out specific corporations for alleged offenses that include the "disturbance and desecration of unmarked ancestral burials" during the development of new industrial facilities to support North Carolina's transition to natural gas as a primary source of electricity.[13] Here, too, tribal leaders in North Carolina have signaled their expectation that corporations will own up to actions that harm cultural heritage.

The various resolutions and ordinances from tribal leaders in North Carolina are important for at least three reasons. First, at the heart of these statements is a demand that governments and corporations shift, seismically, in their posture toward our communities and homelands. The statements challenge the inequitable status quo in which tribal nations are typically ignored or—if they are lucky—afforded the same input as garden clubs, chambers of commerce, or other special-interest groups. Neither case recognizes the deep insights that tribal nations can bring to environmental decision-making based on centuries of accumulated knowledge about the places we come from. As a result, the decisions that governments and corporations make about the Coastal Plain are incomplete, if not at odds with Indigenous views about our homelands and their futures.

Governments and corporations must center Indigenous views and values in their decisions if we are to preserve the landscapes and waterways of our homelands for the benefit of future generations—Native and non-Native alike. The Haliwa-Saponi Tribe's 2017 warning to state regulators about the proposed Atlantic Coast Pipeline exemplifies these values applied for everyone's benefit: "With the rising threat of climate change, investing in a massive, new infrastructure project that will foster continued reliance on carbon-intensive fossil fuels will likely harm future generations."[14] More broadly, Indigenous values push back against the notion that North Carolina's Coastal Plain remains ripe for colonial exploitation—an idea that lies at the heart of the region's environmental ills and is at least as old as John Lawson's 1709 travelogue.

Second, resolutions and ordinances by tribal leaders in North Carolina illuminate the definition of environmental justice for places like the Coastal Plain. To acknowledge that Indigenous peoples still exist and deserve collective voices in governance are powerful expressions of both recognition justice and participatory justice for peoples who have suffered for centuries under successive waves of colonialism. These acknowledgments also link environmental justice to Indigenous rights; Lumbee people and our Indigenous neighbors belong to inherently sovereign tribal nations with rights to determine what kinds of development activities take place in our homelands.[15]

Third, the various statements by tribal leaders set a minimum standard for respecting Indigenous rights in twenty-first-century North Carolina. In a nutshell, these statements call for an end to the sacrificial transformation of sacred landscapes and waterways, and they call for Indigenous participation in decisions about these places from now on. The statements are rooted firmly in ethical expectations that flow not from current state or federal law, but from the United Nations declaration, from our tribal constitutions, and from other Indigenous governing principles. These statements draw on values that differ—sometimes sharply—from colonial notions of exploitation that continue to underpin environmental decision-making in the United States.

If governments and corporations were to take these statements seriously, we would see a radical shift in environmental governance that prioritizes sustainability and reciprocity over exploitation and profit. In the long run, such a shift would benefit everyone who lives on or loves the Coastal Plain, and it would also help ensure that Lumbee people and our Indigenous neighbors survive the squeeze of colonialism in the twenty-first century.

How can governments and corporations embody the principles embedded in these statements, and how can they work alongside tribal nations to promote environmental justice and Indigenous rights in the Coastal Plain? For starters, governments must resist the temptation to conflate environmental justice with public engagement and outreach. Recently in North Carolina, environmental regulators have begun to reframe state-level policy on environmental justice as a promise to improve public outreach and communication during environmental permitting. For example, regulators have committed to hold additional public meetings, issue multilingual communications, and generate demographic reports about communities on the receiving end of adverse impacts from recent permitting decisions. These types of commitments can support efforts to advance justice, but in the absence of actions to avoid disproportionate harm, public meetings, multilingual materials, and demographic reports cannot promote environmental justice on their own.

Disappointingly, top regulators in North Carolina have gone on record in recent years to say that environmental justice has no formal role in their decisions to issue permits for hazardous or polluting projects.[16] In other words, despite stated commitments to environmental justice, state regulators do not reject environmental permits on the grounds that regulated activities will perpetuate or intensify harm in overburdened communities. Environmental regulators who value outreach but are unprepared to act on behalf of tribal nations or other marginalized groups do not merely talk out of both sides of their mouths; they also undermine environmental justice by reinforcing a harmful status quo in which disparities emerge and grow stronger under the guise of bureaucratic neutrality.[17] Regulators and other government officials must acknowledge and address the existing disconnect between their stated values and the inequitable status quo, especially in North Carolina. Until either the state or federal government enacts meaningful environmental justice legislation, the state's top policy advisors and regulators must take responsibility for avoiding and eliminating disparities through actions that go far beyond public outreach and communications.

Similarly, corporations must stop treating the concerns of tribes and marginalized communities as public relations issues. Allegations that corporate actions add to the harms experienced by overburdened communities are serious, and they are usually backed by strong evidence. Corporate responses, however, rarely address these allegations head-on. Most often, these responses ignore or dismiss community concerns out of hand.[18] When corporations do respond to allegations, they often attempt to explain away racial or socioeconomic disparities—an attempt at reputation management. More often than not, however, this strategy backfires and reveals a poor grasp of fundamental environmental justice concepts, including disproportionality, privilege, and colonialism.[19]

Worse yet, some corporations attempt to redefine environmental justice to align with their own public relations narratives around job creation or product affordability (especially when their products are energy or food). In some cases, corporations may go so far as to claim that the exact projects opposed by overburdened communities actually "restore" justice by creating economic opportunities for the same communities.[20]

Of course, it is possible that new jobs or cheap energy may help offset disproportionately high and adverse burdens borne by communities, but the benefits and burdens do not cancel one another simply because corporations claim that they do. Environmental justice advocates have spent decades warning against the use of economic incentives to justify saddling already-overburdened communities with new forms of pollution and environmental degradation.[21] Corporate leaders should heed these warnings and avoid making unilateral claims about the extent to which economic incentives can mitigate harm. These claims exploit power imbalances between corporations and communities, they entangle communities with extractive and unsustainable industries, and—in some cases—they prevent tribes from exercising their sovereignty.[22] Unilateral corporate claims of justice cannot replace community perspectives about what is equitable and just.[23] Impacted communities, not corporations, determine environmentally just outcomes. To claim otherwise is ignorant or disingenuous.

In light of the present situation, how can corporations promote justice? First, instead of treating environmental justice as a public relations issue or redefining justice in ways that simply paint corporations in a positive light, corporate leaders must own the harms that their past and present activities have caused for tribal nations and marginalized communities.[24] Corporations must commit to formally acknowledging harm, and they must cede responsibility for defining just outcomes to impacted communities. And when communities articulate their views of justice, corporate leaders must be prepared to act accordingly. Otherwise, corporate environmental justice policies are little more than "thoughts and prayers" to frontline communities.

Perhaps policies that privilege community perspectives on environmental justice are too extreme for corporate leaders who are accustomed to setting their own ground rules. Perhaps the temptation to redefine environmental justice is too great, particularly given the lack of enforceable environmental justice statutes in the United States.[25] Nevertheless, corporate leaders can no longer assume that vulnerable communities will acquiesce to hosting pipelines, wastewater sprayfields, and other harmful or polluting projects. Networks of tribal nations and other communities are growing throughout the United States, and they are drawing attention to long-standing issues around disparities in the placement of these projects and around issues of consultation and consent. Whether they work through legal, political, or other channels, these networks have demonstrated the ability to sustain multi-year campaigns to substantially delay or even defeat harmful and polluting projects.

Both corporate and government actors need to become better educated about the tribal nations in whose territories they operate. Over the past several years, this point has become exceedingly clear for regulated industries in the Coastal Plain. Even though the region is home to several tribal nations and has one of the largest Indigenous populations in the United States, corporate representatives and government officials have been caught off guard, repeatedly, when they learn that tribal communities would experience disproportionately large negative impacts from regulated activities. In my experience, the issue is not that corporate and government decision-makers believe that the activities are risk-free; instead, they are incredulous that Indigenous communities have remained so intensely rooted to their ancestral homelands and care so deeply about the future of these places. Decision-makers seem especially blindsided by the idea that the collective fate of an Indigenous group could hinge on the sacrificial transformation of culturally important landscapes. But such are the connections to our ancestral lands and waters.

Many corporations and government agencies have teams of attorneys and policy analysts at their disposal, yet they appear to have little or no understanding about the histories, cultures, and political frameworks that tie Indigenous peoples to our homelands and define us as peoples. For the situation to change, corporations and agencies will need to build up a coherent base of relevant knowledge about Indigenous peoples—likely by training existing staff or by hiring new individuals.

Some corporations have already made mild attempts to address the deficiency by creating new positions within their organizations. Sadly, many of these positions—often called *tribal liaisons*—are held by individuals who have no professional training or relevant expertise related to tribal governance, Indigenous rights, or environmental justice.

Well-trained tribal liaisons have the potential to help corporations pursue activities that actually advance tribal sovereignty and promote environmental justice. Often, however, liaisons focus on promoting predetermined corporate agendas or recruiting new employees from tribal communities. The former activity is better described as public relations, an area that can help corporations build relationships with tribes but does not—by itself—advance tribal interests or promote justice. Recruitment activities could benefit Indigenous peoples in the long run, but only if a sufficient number of tribal members advance through the ranks into positions where they can influence corporate policies around environmental justice and Indigenous rights.[26]

At bare minimum, tribal liaisons can better serve both their employers and tribal communities by relaying tribes' perspectives, values, and concerns to corporate leaders. Liaisons must champion opportunities for their employers to uphold Indigenous rights, and they cannot hesitate to highlight threats to tribal sovereignty. My experience, however, is that tribal liaisons rarely take on these responsibilities. In some cases, this is because liaisons do not clearly understand the basics of tribal sovereignty or Indigenous rights. For example, I once asked a tribal liaison to explain how his company's effort to obtain air pollution permits for a swine biogas facility in the Coastal Plain could impact the ability of a nearby state-recognized tribe to exercise its sovereignty. The liaison responded by insisting that the question was irrelevant, because his employer did not engage in political lobbying for or against tribal federal recognition. After some probing, I realized that the liaison's understanding of tribal sovereignty was limited to the idea that sovereignty and federal recognition were wholly synonymous. He had not considered that his company's pursuit of pollution permits might have lasting impacts on a tribe's ability to exercise sovereignty over its homelands.

When I pointed out to the liaison that state regulators had not obtained free, prior, and informed consent from the nearby tribe, and that the company had not encouraged regulators to seek consent either, the liaison explained that he was not a legal expert but believed that Indigenous consent was not necessary. The conversation left me wondering whose interests are served by tribal liaisons who do not center tribal sovereignty and Indigenous rights in their work.

Even if tribal liaisons have the training and experience to engage with complicated issues around tribal sovereignty and Indigenous rights, they may still face headwinds from employers who do not value tribal liaisons as essential members of strategic planning and decision-making teams. At present, companies tend to deploy tribal liaisons after they have already decided where they will site pipelines, power plants, or other environmental threats.[27] The tragedy is that tribal liaisons have the potential to help steer their corporations toward projects and policies that promote tribal sovereignty and rectify historic injustices, but instead they are often merely corporate mouthpieces who happen to spend time in tribal communities. Instead of persuading corporate leaders to listen to Indigenous peoples, tribal liaisons persuade Indigenous peoples to take a positive view of their employers. They are merely influencers who give corporations bragging rights for having boots on the ground in tribal communities. This situation is likely why the tribal liaison in chapter 4 thought the idea of challenging corporate leaders posed a "difficult question." Until the situation changes, tribal liaisons will do little to repair harm or build meaningful relationships between tribal nations and corporations.

Finally, governments and corporations both must acknowledge that marginalized communities can face multiple environmental calamities at once. This is especially true in the Coastal Plain. Here, Indigenous peoples are not only overburdened by industrialized livestock operations and fossil fuel infrastructure, but they are also threatened by climate-related disasters—floods, droughts, and extreme heat. The current regulatory framework compartmentalizes these issues during environmental permitting. In other words, it matters little that Robeson County is already crisscrossed by gas pipelines and dotted with poultry facilities when regulators review a permit for a new source of pollution; in most cases, regulators ignore these prior sources of harm. Few corporations voluntarily consider existing levels of pollution in communities where they seek permits, and most are happy to follow the lead of regulatory agencies that allow permit applicants to downplay or ignore the accumulation of air pollution, safety hazards, and other environmental harms in communities.

In an encouraging move, the US Environmental Protection Agency has begun to study regulatory measures that could address multiple environmental threats faced by communities all at once—cumulative impacts. Perhaps future regulatory frameworks will find meaningful ways to acknowledge that lived experiences matter and that life is rarely compartmentalized in ways that are conveniently digested by corporate boards or permitting agencies.

CORPORATIONS AND GOVERNMENT REGULATORS have much ground to cover, but in the meantime, tribal nations can take actions on their own to promote justice and to assert sovereignty needed to protect their communities and homelands. For tribes in the Coastal Plain, bids for federal recognition

are important steps, but federal recognition is not the only path to meaningful tribal participation in environmental governance.[28] In North Carolina
specifically, formal relationships between tribes and the state government
are sorely underutilized when it comes to environmental permitting and
decision-making.

As a legal framework, state-level tribal recognition has existed in North
Carolina for more than a century, yet the state government still has no formal policy on tribal consultation. State agencies and tribal governments
have not agreed on the terms of tribal engagement, nor have they agreed on
the circumstances that should warrant formal consultation. Recently, however, the Lumbee Tribal Council has articulated some of its expectations
in the form of an ordinance (i.e., tribal legislation) that affirms the tribe's
right to participate meaningfully in decisions involving water quality and
other environmental permits sought by corporations working in the tribe's
state-designated territory. In particular, the ordinance defines meaningful
consultation in the context of UNDRIP's free prior and informed consent
provision, and it demands that such consultation take place prior to any
regulated activity in the tribe's territory. The ordinance goes on to demand
denial or suspension of governmental authorizations granted without meaningful consultation.[29]

The Lumbee ordinance is an important step toward defining the terms of
meaningful engagement; it calls for state and federal regulators conduct
government-to-government consultation prior to issuing permits. It also requires regulators to formally acknowledge and address racial disparities and
cultural impacts to Native peoples as a substantive part of permitting. Far
from grandstanding, the tribal ordinance seeks to fill a policy vacuum; tribal
leaders have essentially handed state leaders a draft policy that lays out—in
no uncertain terms—the Lumbee Tribe's values and expectations around collective participation in environmental decision-making. State leaders should
be grateful for such clarity, and they should immediately formalize state-tribal
consultation policies that adopt these values and expectations.

I do not know whether the Lumbee Tribe's present consultation ordinance
will be legally enforceable in state or federal courts. But regardless of its en-
forceability, the legislation is a template for other tribal nations, particularly
those lacking the statutory right to consultation that accompanies federal recognition. If other tribes follow the Lumbees' lead, and if state officials take
these tribal consultation mandates seriously, then state-tribal consultation
could become a fruitful area of cooperative decision-making and stewardship
that benefits everyone who lives in or near tribal territories.

Meanwhile, tribal governments and officials need to prepare for a future of state-tribal engagement by creating and funding environmental protection and historic preservation staff positions. In most cases, these positions will have substantial overlap given the sanctity of Indigenous homelands; our sacred landscapes and waterways tie us to our ancestors and allow our cultures to continue into the future. These places belong to Indigenous peoples not because we hold legal title to them, but—as Occaneechi elder Vivette Jeffries-Logan eloquently points out—because the soils of present-day North Carolina literally contain the dust of our ancestors.[30] These are the places we come from—the places that sheltered and protected us since time out of mind. And if we are fortunate, our bodies will return to our ancestral soils one day. We will become part of our descendants' homelands.

Tribes throughout the Coastal Plain of North Carolina share cultural and familial ties but many lack resources to establish their own environmental and historic preservation offices. These tribes should join forces—even if temporarily—to create intertribal offices of environmental protection and cultural preservation. The offices can serve as official points of contact for regulators and other decision-makers who want to pursue meaningful engagement but do not know where to begin. Such offices can eliminate some of the ambiguity that currently hinders efforts at meaningful tribal engagement in North Carolina.[31]

There is strength in numbers, and threats to our shared homelands are evergreen. Threats emerge through pollution, climate change, unsustainable development, and general ignorance about the important role of Coastal Plain landscapes and waterways in shaping and preserving the identities of tribal nations. These threats supersede cultural and political barriers that historically prevented tribal nations from working together. A time may come when individual tribes may form offices of their own, but even then, intertribal offices of environmental protection and cultural preservation could prove useful for addressing regional threats to the Coastal Plain.

Currently in North Carolina, the state historic preservation office represents the interests of non-federally recognized tribes (including the Lumbee) when it comes to legal and regulatory issues around cultural resources and environmental permitting. The office, which is housed in the Department of Natural and Cultural Resources, can help tribes to establish an intertribal historic preservation office. The state's new American Indian Heritage Commission, conveniently housed in the same department, can assist as well. One of the duties of the new commission is to advise the department and its secretary on matters relevant to tribal nations; surely this includes advising the department on how it can assist tribes in creating a historic preservation office capable of identifying and working to protect cultural landscapes.

Even before tribes establish historic preservation offices, they can secure a modicum of protection for their shared ancestral homelands by petitioning to list cultural landscapes on the National Register of Historic Places or by seeking congressional designation for a portion of the Coastal Plain to be listed as a National Heritage Area—defined by the National Park Service as an area "where natural, cultural, and historic resources combine to form a cohesive, nationally important landscape."[32] The National Register is no panacea, but listed sites may receive an added layer of scrutiny by regulators and corporations who may have no other knowledge about the cultural significance of the region.

In addition to the steps described above, the Lumbee Tribe can take at least one additional measure to help protect its homelands. Specifically, the tribe can pursue federal Wild and Scenic River designation for the remaining undesignated reach of its namesake river. When federal officials added the Lumbee River to the National Wild and Scenic Rivers system in 1998, they omitted a thirty-four-mile stretch of the river that runs through the heart of Lumbee tribal territory, including areas around Maxton, Red Banks, and Pembroke. Officials declared the stretch ineligible not because it lacked the outstanding qualities of the remaining eighty-one miles of river, but because it lacked a nonfederal entity to oversee the river's management and protection. The Lumbee tribal government, which did not exist in its current form when the Wild and Scenic Rivers study took place, is now in a position to take on the role of nonfederal caretaker for the remaining river miles. Lumbee ancestors stewarded the river for countless generations; the least our tribal leaders can do is take an active role as present-day stewards through the National Wild and Scenic Rivers program.

Although none of these designations can ultimately protect culturally significant landscapes from pollution or degradation, they do provide additional funding for cultural preservation and additional oversight during major permitting actions.[33] But more importantly, these designations have the ability to raise public awareness about Indigenous peoples' connections to the Coastal Plain. They can also rally support around a common vision of the Coastal Plain as a place that is culturally sacred, ecologically significant, and worth preserving for everyone's benefit.

These are only some of the steps that tribal nations can take to protect culturally significant landscapes and waterways of the Coastal Plain—even before tribes achieve full federal recognition. The programs listed here were not originally intended to advance the priorities of tribal nations, but they meet two important criteria: they already exist, and they are currently accessible to non-federally recognized tribes and intertribal alliances. They also align with shared values of eastern North Carolina tribes, including stewardship, sacrifice, and the preservation of home. Given the severity of the Coastal Plain's transformation by climate change, pollution, and unsustainable development, tribal governments should look seriously at every possible way to protect the places that shape our collective identities and bind us together as Native peoples. The work of restoring justice to the Coastal Plain and its people begins with us.

Tribal governments have collective responsibilities to act on behalf of their people, but individual tribal members also have responsibilities, especially when tribal governments fail to act in ways that protect our communities and homelands. Individual tribal members can complement efforts of their tribal governments through grassroots advocacy or by joining larger nongovernmental organizations. In recent years, many of these organizations have begun to reckon with their histories of centering Euro-American perspectives on nature and wilderness. Indigenous people may find that the doors of influential organizations swing open more easily now than in decades past; however, individual tribal members must decide for themselves whether these organizations deserve Indigenous involvement and leadership. If they do not, an emerging crop of Indigenous-led nongovernmental organizations awaits our attention.

Individual Native people can also raise their voices when tribal governments are silent on issues involving environmental protection or cultural preservation. Besides joining grassroots organizations, Individual Native people can advocate through public comments to regulators, through letters and opinion pieces to newspapers, and through other actions to raise public awareness about Indigenous peoples and their lasting connections to specific landscapes and waterways. Along the eastern seaboard, where Native peoples are still erased and ignored, and where state and federal regulators insist on treating tribal nations as disaggregated individuals, it is especially important for Native people to remind decision-makers and the general public that we are still here.

Individual members of tribal nations in the Coastal Plain must also do a better job of voting for public officials to represent Indigenous perspectives in Raleigh and Washington. There is great room for improvement here, and Lumbees in particular have failed to turn out in large numbers during recent elections. Despite rampant punditry about recent Lumbee voting tendencies, fewer than 60 percent of Native American registered voters in Robeson County participated in the 2020 US presidential election—an election that was widely hailed by news outlets as the "most consequential" election of our lifetime. In comparison, the same election saw record-breaking turnout across North Carolina (75 percent) and nationally (67 percent). Overall, Robeson County tied for last place in turnout among North Carolina counties, with only 62 percent of registered voters of all races casting ballots. Even worse, when voter registration rates are taken into account, it appears that the majority voting-age Lumbees in Robeson County did not vote at all in the 2020 election.[34] Lumbee people must do better if we truly care about political representation.

THE ENVIRONMENTAL CHALLENGES facing tribal nations in the Coastal Plain feel insurmountable at times, but I am encouraged by the opportunities for change that are open, even now, to institutions and to individuals. Our nations have occupied the Coastal Plain since time immemorial, and although our ancestors were subjected to centuries of trauma, they survived. The present-day tribal communities of eastern North Carolina are indelibly marked by colonialism, and colonial practices persist still today in the form of extractive industrial practices and policies that ignore Indigenous knowledge, perspectives, and values in key decisions about our homelands. One of the most insidious characteristics of twenty-first-century colonialism is the assumption that tribal communities and their homelands can be sacrificed in the name of economic development.

But tribal nations are equipped, increasingly, with resources and expertise to push back against practices and policies that incentivize the sacrificial transformation of our ancient home on the Coastal Plain. Our intellectual resources include scholars who work in (and across) diverse disciplines— breaking down silos within academic institutions and between academia and communities. We also have non-Indigenous allies, including students poised to become tomorrow's corporate executives, federal regulators, and decision-makers. Building up expertise and allyship is a long game, and it is intellectually and emotionally taxing. But the work is essential to chip away at stereotypical depictions of Indigenous peoples and mythological notions of how the United States came to be.

Some of our homegrown expertise comes from initiatives like the federal Indian Education Program that supported Mrs. Rosa Winfree's work back when I was a student in Charlotte-Mecklenburg Schools. When Mrs. Rosa died in 2017, hundreds of people from across the United States packed the sanctuary of her church in Kannapolis, North Carolina, for a memorial service—a testament to her impact not only with Indian education but also as a member of President George H. W. Bush's advisory committee on Indian education and founder of a national advocacy group, American Indian Women of Proud Nations.[35]

In her last years, Mrs. Rosa suffered from terminal cancer, and her once-bold voice had grown frail and soft. She continued to attend cultural events, often draped in a blanket or shawl and seated in a wheelchair. Despite her illness, she always greeted me by grabbing both of my hands, looking directly into my eyes, and declaring, "I love you, Ryan." I knew that Mrs. Rosa meant the words with all of her heart. I also knew that the sentiment applied to everyone she taught, mentored, and championed through the course of many years.

I delivered one of several eulogies during Mrs. Rosa's memorial service, and I closed with a request for all of her former Indian Education students to stand. Throughout the sanctuary, dozens of adults rose to their feet. Her students had grown into working professionals, scholars, parents, cultural teachers, and engaged community members. And those in attendance were only a small fraction of the lives she touched through a career aimed at building a corps of Indigenous leaders capable of meeting the challenges of twenty-first-century colonialism. Perhaps the best news of all is that educators and advocates like Mrs. Rosa exist all across Indian Country.

In my own path as an educator, I have been privileged to walk alongside students and colleagues from Lumbee, Coharie, Waccamaw Siouan, Meherrin, Haliwa-Saponi, Sappony, Occaneechi, Nottoway, Cherokee, Catawba, Hopi, Potawatomi, Navajo, Winnebago, Lakota, Swinomish, Lummi, Narragansett, Tuscarora, Pascua Yaqui, and many other native nations and Indigenous communities who received similar instructions—to gain all the education and privilege that we can, and to refashion it for the survival of our nations. Each of our paths is unique, but they intersect in ways that inspire and remind me that the work of protecting our homelands, strengthening tribal sovereignty, and promoting environmental justice is not a solo effort.

Conclusion
On the Swamp, April 2022

A little more than five years after I visited Prospect to take in the February chill and to the ponder the glinting razor wire along NC Highway 710, I am back again with the same colleague. We are visiting her family homeplace—the farm at the end of the dirt driveway that is wedged in between Bear Swamp and the sprawl of pipeline infrastructure. It is mid-April—the height of spring in Robeson County. Already today, I have walked as deep into Bear Swamp as possible without tall boots. The swamp is alive; sweet gum, tupelo, and poplar leaves unfurl everywhere. Bald cypress trees bristle with tender needles. Down below, dragonflies alight on woody cypress knees. Dogwoods dropped their blossoms a week ago or longer, and a few white petals still float atop small pools of dark water. Fat tadpoles dart beneath the petals.

I am only a few steps in, but I can feel Bear Swamp vibrate with the greenness of spring and the hum of new life. Everything rises to meet the light, water, and warmth of April in Robeson County. The brow-sopping humidity and ravenous mosquitoes of summer are still a few weeks away, and so I stand perfectly still and quiet, enchanted, if not content. I wonder about the names that my ancestors gave to the water, the spreading leaves, and the darting tadpoles. I ask them aloud, in English, what they want to be called. The sound of the foreign words momentarily tinges my wonder with guilt.

The dull thud of helicopter rotors breaks the enchantment altogether and reminds me that the natural gas compounds are only a few hundred yards away. The rotor sounds come from the southeast, and they grow louder. I look up in time to see a Bell 407 approaching from across Bear Swamp. The blue and white aircraft swoops into Prospect, close enough to read its registration number emblazoned on its rear quarter and the word PATROL spelled out on its belly. It belongs to Duke Energy, the parent company of the utility that owns the natural gas pipelines and nearby compounds. The helicopter's flight path roughly traces the route of one of the transmission pipelines that strikes out from Junction A—the original branching point for the Coastal Plain's expansive pipeline network, now surrounded by razor wire, floodlights, and surveillance cameras. The helicopter banks and circles the company's two compounds. It flies back toward the southeast, along the clear-cut through Bear Swamp that marks the pipeline easement. The thud dissolves, overtaken by the green hum of spring in Prospect.

THE SHEET-METAL SHED and gas-fired compressors no longer sit inside the compound in Prospect; the company decommissioned the compressors sometime after the major gas leak in November 2017. Since then, however, the compound has nearly doubled in size, evidenced by an expanded perimeter of razor wire. Inside the compound, massive knees of pipe sprout from the gravel. Some pipes are topped with valves, and others have vents, sensors, or various protrusions. Across NC 710, the new natural gas compound has similarly expanded and sprouted new steel growth. The compounds are separated from the rest of Prospect by barbed wire, floodlights, and surveillance cameras. Helicopter patrols add to the inescapable feeling that the compounds are twenty-first-century versions of settler fortifications in the heart of Indian Country.

In recent years, Robeson County has become a metaphorical battlefield in the struggle over sustainable energy in the United States. Energy companies canceled the Atlantic Coast Pipeline in 2020 and gave up their plans to pipe fracked gas directly into North Carolina. At the same time, the owner of North Carolina's major electric utilities, Duke Energy, has leaned even harder into natural gas as an energy source. The company not only increased its capacity in recent years to burn gas for electricity, but it also invested $250 million in a gas liquefaction and storage facility on six hundred acres of land in the Lumbee community of Wakulla—only a few miles away from Junction A in Prospect. The project required the company to install new pipelines through Prospect and Wakulla to connect the facility to their existing gas network. In doing so, they extracted property easements from Lumbee families, cut through Long Swamp, and further dissected this section of our ancestral homelands.

The gas pipelines are Hydra-like; whenever one project is canceled, two new ones seem to spawn in its place. The pipelines are fueled not by supernatural strength but by government and corporate policies that prop up society's addiction to fossil fuels. More often than not, Robeson County or another socially vulnerable area shoulders the burdens that come with these policies.[1]

The situation is dire, but today I am hopeful. Today I am in Prospect with a group of Indigenous scholars. They are experts in environmental science, public policy, American history, Indigenous education, data science, and other fields. Some are graduate students, and others are postdoctoral researchers—most are just beginning their careers as scholarly advocates for their people. Together, we occupy virtually every career stage and span a wide range of academic disciplines.

We are here to walk the land near Bear Swamp, to put our hands into the soil, to speak with people who live nearby, and to imagine how our work together might promote justice and fight erasure of Indigenous peoples. Prospect was one stop on a daylong visit to Robeson County. Earlier, we visited the university in Pembroke and toured the Museum of the Southeast American Indian, located in Old Main. The museum director, Nancy Strickland Fields, is one of Mrs. Rosa's former Indian Education students, and we grew up together in Charlotte.

Nancy led our group through the museum and pointed out highlights from the permanent collection, including an ancient dugout canoe and a patchwork quilt—sewn around the turn of the twentieth century by Maggie Lowry Locklear, daughter of "swamp outlaw" Henry Berry Lowry—that inspired the pinecone design that adorns contemporary Lumbee powwow regalia and tribal insignia. Nancy also guided us through a temporary exhibit of sixteenth-century prints that were among Europe's first published accounts of the Coastal Plain. We gathered around softly lit images that showed Roanokes, Secotans, and other Algonquian-speaking peoples fishing and working the land. Nancy noted the title of the temporary exhibit—*Wuskitahkamik Miyai: Intersection of Worlds.*[2] She explained the title as a pivot away from the condescending mythology that Europeans "discovered" Indigenous peoples on the Coastal Plain. Instead, she chose a name that emphasized the confluence of societies embodied in the images and in the events that they depict.

Back on the edge of Bear Swamp, the afternoon grows warm, and we all migrate to the shade of a large magnolia tree near the house with the bright white siding. My colleague reminisces about the old days. She points out landmarks that tell the story of her family's homeplace in Prospect. We carry on for awhile, talking about ditches, pipelines, ghosts, and dreams. We joke about helicopters and surveillance cameras.

Before long, we leave Prospect to meet with other Lumbees, including Wendy Moore, a member of tribal council. Soon, the tribal council will announce the formation of a new department of agriculture and natural resources. Moore championed the department's creation, and we are excited to learn more about how we might support its work. She asked to meet us at Hayes Pond, site of the 1958 rout of fifty Ku Klux Klansmen by hundreds of Lumbees and their allies (figure C.1).

On the way to Hayes Pond, we meet up with Jeff Currie, the first Lumbee to work as a Riverkeeper, and the first Riverkeeper based in Robeson County. We form a small convoy and follow Jeff on a circuitous path through the county. Jeff leads us by the cultural center near Red Banks. A handful of

FIGURE C.1 Hayes Pond, April 2022. Photo by author.

people fish in the blackwater stream below the earthen dam that creates the cultural center's lake. After Hurricane Matthew, floodwaters severely damaged the dam and its spillway; the tribe recently finished repairs and refilled the lake. Today, fish are biting below the new spillway; it is this spring's "honey hole"—the sweetest spot for fishing. The main stem of the Lumbee River lies a few hundred yards downstream; I stare through the swamp toward the river, even though I know it is too far to see. Jeff asks about the fishing, and we take a few photos of bald cypress trunks protruding from the now-filled lake. We press on toward Hayes Pond and our meeting with councilwoman Moore.

The early career scholars are hungry for justice; I knew it already, but the day's conversation makes it crystal clear. No matter where we come from, our people need healthy landscapes, waterways, and communities to survive. But climate change, pollution, and unsustainable practices threaten the places we come from—the places that inform our identities as Indigenous peoples. All of us are driven by some version of the same fear that I have—that I will be part of the last generation of Lumbees to look across our homeland and see what our ancestors saw: landscapes and waterways unspoiled by colonial notions of exploitation and extraction and communities not haunted by the looming threats of climate change.

The exact threats differ from one tribal community to another, but we all recognize the severity of the situation and the need to do something about it. Today's trip to Robeson County is a stark example of homelands imperiled by policies and practices that ignore Indigenous perspectives and values. At the same time, Indigenous peoples are still here, and we take comfort in the fact that we can face these threats together—as small convoys of scholars, as collections of sovereign nations, or as members of a global community that share a vision of Indigenous peoples as the original and permanent stewards of the places we come from, the only lands we know, and the places worth fighting for.

Acknowledgments

In October 2016, right after Hurricane Matthew swept through Robeson County, my grandmother, Vernice Emanuel Hughes, came to stay at my house in Raleigh. She was in her eighties and still living on her own at the Emanuel family homeplace. But without electricity, water, or phone service in the wake of the hurricane—and with the Lumbee River still rising—she packed a bag and traveled back to Raleigh with me.

In the days that followed, I mostly worked from home, and the two of us spent time at the kitchen table telling and retelling stories. At one point, my grandmother reminisced about walking behind her mother—my great-grandmother—down footpaths into Saddletree Swamp to visit my great-grandmother's favorite fishing holes and berry patches. I had heard similar accounts before from other relatives, but this time the story landed differently. Around that time, the Lumbee River was cresting in Robeson County—engulfing southwest Lumberton and permanently transforming lives. The juxtaposition of my grandmother's tranquil memory with the disaster unfolding back in Robeson made me uncomfortable in a way that was hard to describe in the moment. So I wrote about it.

I typed something rough, probably about the duality of water in the Lumbee world, or about water as a powerful force that gives and takes, or about Lumbees as people of the river—in good times and bad. Whatever it was that I wrote, I printed it the next day and shared it with my grandmother as we sat at the kitchen table. She read it once over, and we carried on with the day. And I kept writing for the next few days, picking out a paragraph or two each day to print and share with my grandmother during our kitchen table conversations. Those were some of the earliest parts of this book, written to my grandmother.

I wish that I could tell all of the metastories—the stories of how the stories in this book came to be—but that would be impractical. Instead, I will acknowledge some of the institutions and people who are part of the stories behind the story of this book. I am extremely grateful to the National Humanities Center for providing world-class resources and the luxury of time to work on this project as a Fellow during the 2020–21 academic year. The William C. Friday Fellowship and the class of 2020–2022 Fellows challenged me to write in a way that builds relationships with future readers. Along the way, I have been privileged to work in academic units—the College of Natural Resources at North Carolina State and the Nicholas School of the Environment at Duke—that value transdisciplinary research and have been supportive intellectual homes in which to conduct this work. I am deeply indebted to the University of North Carolina Press and the staff who helped bring this book to fruition—especially Lucas Church, a phenomenal editor and a steady source of advice, encouragement, and instruction from our first meeting onward.

The most important story behind this book is the story of my family's support and encouragement. I am incredibly grateful to my wife, Cayce, who has been my strongest advocate, closest confidant, and inspiration. My daughter, Laurel, and my son, Reed, kept me afloat with their love, humor, patience, and daily reminders of why this work matters.

My parents, Pam and Laney Emanuel, answered dozens of questions and read numerous drafts. My mom, in particular, was the first person to read and give feedback on a complete draft of the book manuscript. My brother, Joey Emanuel, was an important sounding board for early chapter ideas during our trips to western Washington to attend the Vine Deloria Jr. Symposium at Northwest Indian College. Many of my relatives shared stories and supported me in too many ways to count. I deeply appreciate and love all of you.

I am indebted to my other relatives—elders, tribal leaders, and community members— who shared their stories and diverse perspectives. I am grateful to Jeff Anstead, Jennifer Revels Baxter, Danny Bell, Kullen Bell, Philip Bell, Jennifer Brewer-Young, Reggie Brewer, Evon Bullard, Donna Chavis, Lana Dial, Harvey Godwin, Robie Goins, Tony Hayes, Cecil Hunt, Eudora Hunt, Greg Jacobs, Vivette Jeffries-Logan, Adrienne Kennedy, Mac Legerton, Kaya Littleturtle, Senora Lynch, Louise Maynor, Eddie Moore, Wendy Moore, Freda Porter, Jorden Revels, Greg Richardson, Beth Roach, Kara Stewart, Patrick Suarez, John Whittemore, Pamela Young-Jacobs, and many others. I look forward to spending more time with all of you in our shared homelands.

A large number of other experts—scholars and technical professionals—weighed in at various stages with valuable advice and constructive feedback that improved the book tremendously. I especially appreciate the encouragement and mentorship of Malinda Maynor Lowery. I would also like to express my sincere thanks to Marcelo Ardón, Todd BenDor, Emily Bernhardt, Matthew Booker, Martin Doyle, Rob Dunn, Nancy Fields, Jane Flowers Finch, Emily Grant, Seth Grooms, Jim Igoe, Mary Ann Jacobs, Stan Knick, Lawrence Locklear, Ryke Longest, David Lowry, Katie Martin, Michelle Montgomery, David Neal, Emma Norman, Danielle Purifoy, Diego Riveros-Iregui, Louie Rivers, Erin Seekamp, Steve Semken, Vickie Sutton, Sherri White-Williamson, Ulrike Wiethaus, David Wilkins, Shelly Wilkins, Cedric Woods, Barry Yeoman, and others. I am especially grateful to Jefferson Currie II, whose vast knowledge of all things North Carolina is paired with an even greater spirit of generosity. Thank you, Jeff, for your constant feedback and friendship.

I also want to thank the students, postdocs, and staff who have been part of my research program throughout this project. Your insight and enthusiasm helped to shape this book. I also appreciate the support and curiosity of my collaborators and colleagues—particularly the cadre of hydrologists who check in on me from time to time.

Notes

Preface

1. "New Exhibits at American Indian Resource Center," *The Robesonian*, January 15, 2009.

2. I made the following calculations in January 2020 while preparing a talk for the annual meeting of the American Historical Association in New York. While this thought experiment did not appear in that talk, a brief review can be found in R. E. Fulton, "What's the Big Deal with the Anthropocene?," *Perspectives on History*, April 27, 2020, https://www.historians.org/research-and-publications/perspectives-on-history/may-2020/whats-the-big-deal-with-the-anthropocene-reflections-from-aha20.

3. For a general overview of archaeological time periods in North Carolina, see Ward and Davis, *Time before History*, 1–6.

4. C. S. Ellis, "The Nineteenth Century," *Weekly Standard*, June 24, 1857.

5. "Splaining" occurs when people from dominant groups attempt to explain (or explain away) issues of oppression to people who have experienced (or are currently experiencing) oppression. See Johnson et al., "It's Not in Your Head," 1031. These 'splained beliefs are among the "multiple simultaneous and conflicting messages about Indigenous peoples" described in Tuck and Yang, "Decolonization Is Not a Metaphor," 9.

Introduction

1. Throughout this book, I refer to the river that flows through Robeson County as the *Lumbee River* in deference to an ordinance passed by the Lumbee Tribal Council in 2009. Local, state, and federal governments refer to the same river as the *Lumber River* for reasons that I cover in chapter 3. See "CLLO-2009-0625-01: Reclamation of the Lumbee River's Ancestral Name (June 25, 2009)," Lumbee Tribe of North Carolina, accessed April 13, 2023, https://3aa0349e-a4c3-4857-8f0a-2e7e416fac87.filesusr.com/ugd/269399_93813671119d417fac2525afdbfcc43e.pdf

2. There are few written records from the colonial era that focus on present-day Robeson County, especially western parts of the county where Prospect and several other historic Lumbee communities are located. Chapter 3 includes a detailed explanation of how environmental conditions may have led to a dearth of written documentation about these areas. Whatever the reason for the lack of colonial records, the result is that Lumbee ancestors seem to be some of the most poorly documented Indigenous people of the Southeast. A dearth of records, combined with the fact that Lumbee ancestors had already adopted English as a common language by the mid-1700s (nearly two hundred years after English colonizers first arrived in the Coastal Plain), means that historians, anthropologists, ethnographers, and genealogists have had difficulty pinpointing the exact tribal affiliations of Indigenous people who coalesced along the middle reaches of the Lumbee River and

its swampy tributaries in what is now Robeson County. Despite these limitations, the consensus among researchers and Lumbee knowledge-holders is that Lumbees descend from Siouan-speaking peoples who migrated from the Inner Coastal Plain and Piedmont (e.g., Cheraw, Saponi) as well as from Algonquian-speaking peoples who migrated from the Outer Coastal Plain (e.g., Hatteras). See Lowery, *The Lumbee Indians*, 16–58.

3. This assertion is supported by Lumbee oral traditions and complemented by a quantitative analysis of maps that I conducted and described in Emanuel, "Water in the Lumbee World," 33–38.

4. Letter from James Merrell to US Congressman Charlie Rose, October 18, 1989. Vine Deloria Papers.

5. Historian Malinda Maynor Lowery gives a detailed explanation of where Lumbee ancestors came from and how they ended up in isolated communities in present-day Robeson County. See Lowery, *The Lumbee Indians*, 16–58.

6. Tuscarora political identity has been a hot-button issue among Native people in North Carolina for decades. The controversy centers partly on the political ramifications of formally recognizing Tuscaroras as a tribal nation in present-day North Carolina—specifically recognizing them as a people distinct from their Lumbee relatives. That form of recognition is opposed by the Lumbee government, which has long viewed North Carolina Tuscaroras as a splinter faction within the larger Lumbee community. In recent years, leaders of the federally recognized Tuscarora Nation in New York have also opposed recognition of North Carolina Tuscaroras, even though the groups were allied at times during the Red Power Movement in the late 1960s and early 1970s. In 2019, the North Carolina Commission of Indian Affairs, which reviews petitions for state tribal recognition, recommended that North Carolina Tuscaroras not be recognized as a separate tribe due in part to objections by Lumbees and New York Tuscaroras. The North Carolina Tuscaroras and their advocates often criticize Lumbee opposition as hypocritical because Lumbee leaders have worked to derail Tuscarora recognition while simultaneously complaining about efforts by Cherokee political leaders to derail full federal recognition for the Lumbees. In any case, it is impossible to fully understand the controversy outside of federal acknowledgment policies, which promote easily digestible accounts of tribal origins over the complicated realities of post-contact survival. During the 2019 Commission of Indian Affairs hearings on state tribal recognition for the North Carolina Tuscarora, Gerald Sider, an expert on Indigenous political identity in Robeson County, attributed the fracture between Lumbees and North Carolina Tuscaroras to different strategies for survival in the face of oppression and exploitation. Sider noted that such factionalization was not uncommon, testifying to the Commission, "Native communities necessarily split . . . often antagonistically." Sider's statement is a reminder that living tribal nations may experience irreconcilable political fractures—including the formation of new tribal entities. Gerald Sider's testimony as well as statements by the North Carolina Tuscarora about themselves are accessible at *Transcript of the Public Hearing on Tuscarora Nation of North Carolina Petition for State Recognition: North Carolina Commission of Indian Affairs* (July 26, 2019), https://files.nc.gov/ncdoa/Public-Hearing_Condensed-Transcript-of-7-26-19_Tuscarora-Nation-of-NC-2019_0726_MINI.pdf. See also Lowery, *Lumbee Indians in the Jim Crow South*, xi (note 1), 220.

7. Robeson County has the lowest median home value and mortgage payment in North Carolina according to a National Association of REALTORS dataset analyzed by Madison

Troyer of *Stacker* and published by WNCT News. "Counties with the Lowest Home Prices in North Carolina," June 22, 2021, https://www.wnct.com/on-your-side/consumer-watch/counties-with-the-lowest-home-prices-in-north-carolina/.

8. The desecration of burial mounds is both horrific and galling, and it is completely consistent with practices that occurred elsewhere in the United States. It is a sinister form of erasure, but optimistic perspectives do exist. Thomas Fibiger, a scholar of Arab and Islamic studies, studied urbanization in Bahrain, which has destroyed a large number of burial mounds in an ancient necropolis. Fibiger observed that the destruction of a burial mound or sacred site is "not necessarily erasure of its significance as heritage" but can lead to a site that is "transformed and even reinforced as heritage." I want to share Fibiger's optimism, but I also do not know what kind of "heritage" can replace something as basic as knowing where our ancestors' remains were laid to rest. See Fibiger, "Heritage Erasure."

9. Lowery, *Lumbee Indians in the Jim Crow South*, 5.

10. The owner of the station, Piedmont Natural Gas (a company later purchased by Duke Energy), reported emissions to state regulators most recently in 2010. That year, the company estimated that the compressor station emitted 1,743 tons of carbon dioxide, 5.1 tons of nitrogen oxides, 1.3 tons of carbon monoxide, and 1 ton of sulfur dioxide, as well as smaller amounts of particulate matter. See "North Carolina Criteria and Toxic Air Pollutant Point Source Emissions Report" for Piedmont Natural Gas–Pembroke Compressor Station, NC Department of Environmental Quality, accessed July 15, 2022, https://xapps.ncdenr.org/aq/ToxicsReportServlet?ibeam=true&year=2010&findfacility=5413.

11. North Carolina's largest gas customers, by quantity, are far and away the electric power plants owned by Duke Energy. (Note that Duke Energy purchased Piedmont Natural Gas in 2016 and operates the gas utility as a subsidiary company.) The amount of gas consumed by electricity generation exceeded all other uses combined in North Carolina every year starting in 2015. "Natural Gas Consumption by End Use," US Energy Information Administration, accessed July 1, 2020, https://www.eia.gov/dnav/ng/ng_cons_sum_dcu_snc_a.htm.

12. The general narrative of the Dakota Access Pipeline is outlined in a 2017 essay by Whyte, "The Dakota Access Pipeline," and described in much greater detail in a 2019 book by Estes, *Our History Is the Future*. Note that in 2020, more than three years after the height of the events at Standing Rock, federal courts ruled that the pipeline's environmental assessment was inadequate and must be replaced by a more thorough environmental impact statement. See "Standing Rock Sioux Tribe Wins a Victory in Dakota Access Pipeline Case," *New York Times*, March 25, 2020.

13. In August 2019, Malinda Maynor Lowery observed on Twitter (@malindalowery) that "when someone wants to profit off of human suffering, they locate their crimes in #RobesonCounty where they don't think anyone is looking." Lowery's tweet referred to an unlicensed facility in Robeson County used to house migrant children separated from their families, but her point applies to pollution as well. https://twitter.com/malindalowery/status/1158041253247934464.

14. "Executive Order 12898 of February 11, 1994, Federal Actions to Address Environmental Justice in Minority Populations and Low-Income Populations," National Archives, accessed April 14, 2023, https://www.archives.gov/files/federal-register/executive-orders/pdf/12898.pdf.

15. See Bullard, "Dismantling Environmental Racism."

16. See Bullard et al., "Toxic Wastes"; Wilson, "Environmental Justice Movement."

17. See Champagne, "UNDRIP"; Gilio-Whitaker, "Idle No More"; and Miller, "Consultation or Consent."

18. For a creative and insightful explanation of these inextricable links, see Whyte, "Way Beyond the Lifeboat."

19. Brayboy, "Tribal Critical Race Theory," 429.

20. Brayboy, 427.

Chapter One

1. Some of the key criticisms of institutional land acknowledgments are summarized in Stewart-Ambo and Yang, "Beyond Land Acknowledgment"; Hailu and Tachine, "Black and Indigenous Theoretical Considerations"; and Red Shirt-Shaw, "Beyond the Land Acknowledgement."

2. Institutional land acknowledgments are sometimes published on university websites or read at prominent campus events. I have seen at least one land acknowledgment embossed on a plaque on display at a campus in North Carolina. Most simply acknowledge the prior presence of Indigenous peoples in the area, but a few elaborate on the theft of land and subsequent displacement of Native peoples by settlers. On rare occasions, these statements acknowledge both the theft of Indigenous lands and the exploitation of enslaved African Americans, a brutal combination that taints the histories—and the endowments—of many universities. Where I now work, at Duke University, Native and Indigenous students have offered "healing statements" in lieu of land acknowledgments to highlight the need for institutional actions to accompany institutional words.

3. See Pieratos, Manning, and Tilsen, "Land Back."

4. Deloria, *Custer Died for Your Sins*, 5.

5. I do not mean to say that web-based resources for identifying tribal territories are useless or have bad intentions. One popular resource, native-land.ca, opens with a prominent disclaimer that the tool's boundaries are imperfect and that users should consult actual Native nations about their own territorial claims. This is an important warning, but few users heed it. As a result, the website has caused a proliferation of erroneous information that has never been vetted or authorized by any tribal nation. For example, native-land.ca formerly mismapped the traditional lands of the Catawba Nation, erroneously labeling the entire eastern half of North and South Carolina as Catawba territory. The Catawba Nation, however, describes a very different traditional territory on its public-facing website. I contacted the creator of native-land.ca in 2020 and requested a correction after educators throughout eastern North Carolina began tweeting the website's incorrect claims about Catawba territory. I pointed out that the website had misinterpreted the color legend on a decades-old map published by the Smithsonian Institution. Indigenous territorial claims are complicated and always require context (e.g., what time period does a claim represent?), but in this case, the website developers had simply misread someone else's research. This anecdote highlights another peril associated with web-based resources that attempt to represent Indigenous territorial claims over an area as large as North America. When errors or disagreements inevitably arise, individual Indigenous

educators, scholars, and advocates become unpaid fact-checkers, interpreters, and context-givers. The labor is often unwanted and unexpected, but it is necessary because the websites are treated as authoritative (disclaimers notwithstanding), and Indigenous people recognize the websites as sources of misinformation and confusion that impede our own outreach and education efforts.

6. For a detailed exposé on land grant universities and the tangible benefits that they received from Native lands, see Robert Lee and Tristan Ahtone, "Land Grab Universities," *High Country News*, March 30, 2020.

7. See Stein, "Truth before Reconciliation."

8. Jennings, "Indian Trade," 406.

9. Emanuel, "Water in the Lumbee World," 35.

10. See the idea of an American "origin myth" discussed in Dunbar-Ortiz, *An Indigenous Peoples' History*, 46. Related to this idea is the criticism of land as a "pristine sanctuary" as described in Cronon, "Trouble with Wilderness," 7–8.

11. Deloria, *Custer Died for Your Sins*, 52.

12. Deloria, 52.

13. Deloria, 52.

14. Environmental justice scholar David Schlosberg has emphasized that misrecognition or malrecognition of oppressed or marginalized groups underpins many commonly observed injustices. Schlosberg situates recognition among other factors that are required to promote justice, noting, "justice, in political practice, is articulated and understood as a balance of numerous interlinked elements of distribution, recognition, participation, and capability." Schlosberg, *Defining Environmental Justice*, 12.

15. Here, I call on readers to "listen" in the sense that Deloria warned about the price of not listening to Native people when he counted the environmental costs of non-Native land exploitation, development, and expropriation in Deloria, *We Talk, You Listen*, 195.

16. Sociologists link these phenomena to ongoing health disparities, interpersonal violence, food insecurity, and barriers to cultural resurgence in our communities. Research in this area is sometimes linked to fundamental cause theory, which aims to explain how and why health disparities persist for long periods of time across categories of race, ethnicity, and socioeconomic status despite efforts to address the proximal causes of poor health. One key tenet is that power differentials influence access to knowledge, money, and other resources that can influence human health. Fundamental cause theory was introduced in Link and Phelan, "Social Conditions." Examples of applications related to historical and cultural trauma include Evans-Campbell, "Historical Trauma"; Bowen, Elliott, and Hardison-Moody, "Structural Roots"; and Subica and Link, "Cultural Trauma."

17. The histories of Indigenous peoples in this region were not isolated on the Coastal Plain. They interacted with Native groups farther inland, on the Piedmont and in the Appalachian Mountains. They interacted with people to the far north (e.g., the Great Lakes) and south (e.g., present-day Florida) as well. However, these interactions fall beyond the scope of topics covered in this chapter.

18. Sea level rose and fell, repeatedly, across the Coastal Plain during the Pliocene and Pleistocene epochs of geologic time. Multiple periods of rising sea level (called *transgression* by geologists) and falling sea level (called *regression*) occurred, and the Fall Line represents the highest of all the transgressions. For more detailed chronologies of transgression and

regression during the Pliocene and Pleistocene epochs, see Ward, Bailey, and Carter, "Pliocene and Early Pleistocene Stratigraphy," 274.

19. Robeson County lies entirely east of the Sandhills, although it is sometimes lumped into a sociopolitical region of North Carolina named *Sandhills*. The Sandhills themselves occupy a fifteen-to-twenty-five-mile-wide swath along the Fall Line, but the sociopolitical groupings tend to be much larger. For one example, see "AIG Regions and Local Plan," North Carolina Department of Public Instruction, accessed April 9, 2023, https://www.dpi.nc.gov/aig-regions-and-local-plans.

20. The distance across the Coastal Plain from the Sandhills to the present-day Atlantic Ocean is approximately one hundred miles. Farther north, beyond the Sandhills, the Coastal Plain presently extends approximately 150 miles from the Fall Line to the barrier islands, a distance that includes the wide estuary that separates the string of islands from mainland North Carolina.

21. See Platt and Brantley, "Canebrakes."

22. For a fuller description of this distinct landform, see Kaczorowski, *The Carolina Bays*.

23. Geologists in the 1930s coined the term *Carolina Bay* to describe this particular landform, but local residents have called the landforms *bays* since at least the 1890s. See Kaczorowski, *The Carolina Bays* and also the discussion of Lake Waccamaw, the largest Carolina Bay, in chapter 6.

24. Forest managers and researchers have long held that the word *pocosin* is an Algonquian-dialect word that translates to "swamp-on-a-hill." Pocosin wetlands may, indeed, occupy higher ground than their surrounding landscapes, but there is absolutely no linguistic or anthropological evidence to support this translation. To date, no one has ever cited an Indigenous source for this translation, and the oldest non-Indigenous source cited by anyone is an 1899 journal article by linguist William Wallace Tooker. Tooker, however, makes no such claim in that article or in any of his other work. The translation may be poetic but does not appear to be historically accurate. Instead, a cursory review of the technical literature suggests that the translation appears to have been invented sometime between the 1950s and 1970s. Despite any lack of evidence for this translation, "swamp-on-a-hill" references can be found throughout research literature on wetlands and throughout science communication materials, including public-facing websites of state and federal science agencies. See Tooker, "Adopted Algonquian Term 'Poquosin.'"

25. The largest lake in North Carolina's Coastal Plain, Lake Mattamuskeet, may have been formed or enlarged by an extremely large peat fire several thousand years ago. The potential for peat fires to alter the elevation of the landscape is visible today as well. Large wildfires during recent droughts (2008 and 2011) ignited organic soils in the general vicinity of Lake Mattamuskeet and burned more than one foot of soil from the ground surface in some places. The entire region surrounding Lake Mattamuskeet is no more than a few feet above sea level, so even a change of one or two feet in elevation can drastically alter the landscape. See Mickler, Welch, and Bailey, "Carbon Emissions "; Rodriguez, Waters, and Piehler, "Burning Peat."

26. For details on the formation and geomorphology of the estuary and barrier islands, see Stutz and Pilkey, "Open-Ocean Barrier Islands"; Mallinson et al., "Barrier Island and Estuary Co-Evolution."

27. The Coastal Plain today remains one of the world's biodiversity hotspots according to Noss et al., "Global Biodiversity Hotspots."

28. Historic records and geographic place names suggest bison were at one time abundant in the Southeast, including parts of the Coastal Plain. For example, one of several North Carolina streams named *Buffalo Creek* is located in Scotland County, part of the Sandhills and located adjacent to Robeson County. Evidence of bison may also appear in one of the earliest depictions of Coastal Plain Native people by Europeans: a sixteenth-century drawing by Englishman John White of a *weroance*, or leader, of an Algonquian-speaking group along the coast of present-day North Carolina. In the drawing, an object that resembles a bison's tail hangs from the rear of the weroance's apron. Art historians have described the object as the tail of a puma (i.e., cougar or mountain lion), but a distinctive tuft suggests that the tail could have come from a bison instead. See Sloan, *A New World* for an art historian's perspective on the drawing, which is held by The British Museum (Museum number 1906,0509.1.12) and can be viewed at https://www.britishmuseum.org /collection/object/P_1906-0509-1-12. For additional information on the presence of bison in this region, see Rostlund, "Geographic Range."

29. Numbers derived from Noss et al., "Global Biodiversity Hotspots."

30. Documentary evidence suggests that southeastern Native peoples really did view their society as an interconnected network. The "Catawba Deerskin Map" is one example of this evidence. The map shows Native towns and other polities of present-day North and South Carolina represented as nodes in a network, with trading paths as links between nodes. The map is topological, meaning that its main purpose is to describe relationships between nodes (i.e., various peoples) rather than to show the precise geographic location of each town or polity. Several of the groups shown on this map are Siouan-speaking peoples who banded together to become the Catawba Nation. One group recorded in this network, the Cheraw (written as *Charra* on the map), are Lumbee ancestors. For additional discussion of the Catawba Deerskin Map, see Tim St. Onge, "Celebrating Native American Cartography: The Catawba Deerskin Map," *Worlds Revealed: Geography and Maps at the Library of Congress* (blog), November 30, 2016, http://blogs.loc.gov/maps/2016/11/celebrating -native-american-cartography-the-catawba-deerskin-map/. For more on topological networks in general, see Emanuel, "Water in the Lumbee World," 36–37.

31. Most of these peoples belonged to the Woodland culture, but there is evidence that Mississippian culture was present in parts of the Piedmont and Coastal Plain through the sixteenth century. See Perdue, *Native Carolinians*, 11–12.

32. For more on the cultural and linguistic diversity of the region at the time of European contact, see Oberg, "Tribes and Towns"; Wallace, *Tuscarora*, 59.

33. Historian Michael Oberg suggests *Ossomocomuck* (and its translation) as the term used by Algonquian-speaking peoples to describe their shared homelands in what is now coastal North Carolina. Oberg's argument clarifies earlier efforts by scholars to interpret English records from the attempted colonization of Roanoke Island in the 1580s. See Oberg, *Head in Edward Nugent's Hand*, 3.

34. An interdisciplinary group from Virginia Tech has recently proposed a map of "Eastern Siouan Speaking peoples" during the seventeenth century. The map shows how various Siouan speakers across the region may have formed a constellation of towns and roads that stretched from the Atlantic coast across the Piedmont and into the Appalachian Mountains, covering parts of the present-day states of North and South Carolina, Virginia, and West Virginia. See David Fleming "A New Map Reconstructs the Social Landscapes of

Southwest Virginia Prior to European Arrival," *Virginia Tech News*, November 15, 2021, https://vtx.vt.edu/articles/2021/11/cnre-eastern-siouan-mapo.html.

35. Robin Wall Kimmerer and Frank Kanawha Lake describe the widespread use of fire by Indigenous peoples of North America for clearing land, felling trees, hunting, and more. In their words, "fire was a ubiquitous tool" that fundamentally altered the nature of ecosystems throughout North America over the course of many centuries. See Kimmerer and Lake, "Indigenous Burning," 38.

36. For more on cultivation of alluvial floodplains, see Perdue, *Native Carolinians*, 8.

37. See Mt. Pleasant, "Three Sisters Mound System."

38. A highly stylized version of Native agricultural fields on the Coastal Plain can be seen in Plate XX from Thomas Hariot's *Briefe and True Report*. The plate shows the layout of Secota, a large town near the site of present-day Bath, North Carolina, during the 1580s. Clearly visible are the Three Sisters, pumpkins, sunflowers, tobacco, and other crops. For a more specific description of Indigenous medicinal knowledge passed down to Lumbee people by their ancestors, see Boughman and Oxendine, *Herbal Remedies*.

39. Yaupon is the only caffeinated drink made from a plant that is native to the present-day borders of the United States.

40. Whelk shells were also used to craft white wampum beads. See MacKenzie et al., "Quahogs."

41. See "Canoe Hull Shape Defined," Paddling.com, accessed April 27, 2021, https://paddling.com/learn/canoe-hull-shape-defined.

42. During a severe drought in 2000, approximately one hundred dugout canoes were discovered in a dried lakebed in central Florida. They ranged in age from five hundred to five thousand years old, and the longest canoe exceeded thirty feet. Despite thousands of years between the oldest and youngest canoe, they all exhibited relatively similar characteristics and construction styles. See Wheeler et al., "Archaic Period Canoes." The largest dugout canoe discovered in North Carolina, was a thirty-six-foot-long craft recovered at Phelps Lake on the far eastern edge of the Coastal Plain. Radiocarbon dating suggests the canoe is more than four thousand years old. See https://www.ncparks.gov/pettigrew-state-park/history.

43. Perdue, *Native Carolinians*, 10–12.

44. MacCord, "McLean Mound" and Perdue, *Native Carolinians*, 10.

45. Knick, "Because It Is Right."

46. Stated directly in the title of Hariot, *Briefe and True Report*.

47. Green, *The Lost Colony*, 6–7.

48. Recent research found that redface was deemed more socially acceptable than blackface by many people in the United States, partly because most people do not believe Native Americans exist as members of modern society. See Lopez, Eason, and Fryberg, "The Same, Yet Different."

49. Oberg, *Head in Edward Nugent's Hand*, 73–78.

50. Oberg, x–xi.

51. Green, *The Lost Colony*, 5.

52. Lawson, *New Voyage to Carolina*, 159.

53. "Atlantic Sturgeon, NOAA Fisheries," National Oceanographic and Atmospheric Administration, accessed January 19, 2021, https://www.fisheries.noaa.gov/species/atlantic-sturgeon.

54. It is also important to acknowledge that tribal nations in western Washington were fighting legal battles in the 1970s for treaty rights that were codified more than a century earlier. The experience of tribes in western Washington shows that even though treaties are the "supreme law of the land" in the United States, Native peoples must always be prepared to reassert their treaty rights in various ways. See Brown, "Treaty Rights."

55. Lawson calls Natives "careless and negligent of their Health" and lists numerous examples, including "wading in the water." Lawson, *New Voyage to Carolina*, 223.

56. In this specific example, Lawson attended a meeting in which various nations compared their records and agreed that the Pamlico Sound had frozen over precisely 105 years earlier. Interestingly, Lawson does not record the year in which he attended this meeting, so the Indigenous timekeeping precision is lost, and we are left with an approximate date for the freeze of around 1600. The traditional use of decaying materials like cane or grass to record history—especially in the humid climate of the Southeast—is a reminder that the Coastal Plain was (and still is) a place where physical records can be easily lost. With this in mind, once our ancestral languages fell out of use, it is no surprise that Native peoples of the Coastal Plain have suffered so much cultural loss. See Lawson, *New Voyage to Carolina*, 181.

57. Lawson, 213.

58. Lawson, 213.

59. Lawson, 45, 235.

60. Lawson, 17.

61. The original 1704 complaint appears to be written in Powell's own hand, which includes numerous flourishes. As a result, *Souther* is often transcribed as *Louther*. Either (or neither) transcription may be correct. A digital scan of the original document can be found in the Albemarle County Papers, 1678–1714, Document VC_46_4_Page056_01, accessed May 6, 2021, https://digital.ncdcr.gov/digital/collection/p15012coll11/id/1904. Regardless of the spelling, other mentions of Souther's story can be found in Garrow, *The Mattamuskeet Documents*, 18; La Vere, *The Tuscarora War*, 60.

62. I am obviously comparing Powell to the memetic "Karen" explained by Ashitha Nagesh in "What Exactly Is a 'Karen' and Where Did the Meme Come From?," *BBC News*, July 31, 2020, https://www.bbc.com/news/world-53588201.

63. Lawson was notably concerned that Native people vastly outnumbered settlers in the Coastal Plain during the first decade of the eighteenth century. In the notes accompanying his travelogue, he welcomes a pending influx of Swiss settlers, "especially when we have more Indians than we can civilize." Lawson, *New Voyage to Carolina*, 206.

64. See Ridgely, *Nineteenth-Century Southern Literature*, 13. Note, however, that historian James Merrell describes Lawson's work as more than a "promotional gimmick." According to Merrell, Lawson went to great lengths to make the Carolinas seem like a familiar and comfortable place to European readers. See Merrell, *The Indians' New World*, 6.

65. Angela Calcaterra notes that Lawson and other writers of his era "wrote themselves into already established Native activities and archives, but our literary history frequently relies upon Eurocentric time periods that exclude or minimize Native contexts." I think we can both value Lawson's writing and criticize it because of the trauma it helped to inflict. Calcaterra, "Bad Timing," 94.

66. Alice Gregory, "How Did a Self-Taught Linguist Come to Own an Indigenous Language?," *New Yorker*, April 12, 2021.

67. The eight pleas of the Tuscarora emissaries were delivered orally before Haudeno-saunee and colonial officials, and the pleas were also represented visually and materially by eight wampum belts. Although the ultimate fate of eight belts is unknown (personal correspondence with Rick Hill, Sr., February 23, 2021), the eight specific pleas were documented in a report by colonial representatives John Ffrench and Henry Worley, Minutes of the Provincial Council of Pennsylvania, 533–34.

68. Stephen Feeley discusses some of the land conflicts between Native people and colonists during the first decade of the eighteenth century. Many of them dealt with colonial objections to Native fire management practices. See Feeley, "Before Long," 143, 146.

69. Gallay, *The Indian Slave Trade*, 23–30, 48.

70. In his paper with Daniel Coleman, Tuscarora elder Rick Hill, Sr. writes that "Wampum belts, made from small tubular shell beads woven into symbolic designs, were essential elements in Hodinöhsö:ni' treaty-making, which was based on the belief that wampum could capture the words and pledges made in its presence. This belief made the use of wampum critical in maintaining the oral memory of treaty-making." Thus, in addition to currency, wampum is a powerful form of communication. It is also painstaking to manufacture (I have tried and failed miserably). See Hill and Coleman, "Wampum-Covenant Chain Tradition."

71. Minutes of the Provincial Council of Pennsylvania, 533.

72. Minutes of the Provincial Council of Pennsylvania, 533.

73. Colonial Virginia authorities, in particular, encouraged both murder and kidnapping of eastern North Carolina Natives by enforcing the terms of treaties with Indigenous peoples living adjacent to colonial settlements. These "tributary Nations" included the Chickahominy, Pamunkey, and other groups. One purpose of the treaty was to buffer settlers against "strange Indians" (i.e., Native peoples not from "tributary nations"), including the Tuscarora and other groups living beyond the settler government's sphere of influence. The treaty terms were largely unfavorable toward all Native peoples, regardless of whether they were parties to the treaties. This is because "tributary nations" were required to police their territories, capturing any "strange Indians" and delivering them to the colonial capital in Williamsburg, where they could be enslaved. "Tributary nations" were obliged to join military expeditions against other Native peoples, and to show good faith toward colonial officials. Native leaders gave their children as "hostages" for colonial education and indoctrination at the newly chartered College of William & Mary. Virginia officials attempted to expand their sphere of influence and stave off an impending war by offering a similar treaty to a coalition of Tuscarora people in 1711 (note that at the same time that they were negotiating with the Tuscarora coalition, Virginia officials demanded that Chickahominy and Pamunkey leaders continue to capture Tuscarora people found within the territories of the two "tributary nations"). When, after several months, the Tuscarora coalition had not accepted their treaty terms, Virginia officials enforced a strict trade ban against all Tuscarora people, set colonial militias on high alert in every colonial jurisdiction, and ordered men from "tributary nations" to accompany the militias as a demonstration of their loyalty to the colony. In his discussion on the enslavement of Native people, historian Edmund Morgan characterizes the relationship at this time between Virginia colonial officials and Tuscarora people as "friendly." This is a mischaracterization of the relationship based on Virginia's actions toward Tuscarora people at this time. Instead, Virginia's offer to

bring Tuscarora people into the colony's sphere of influence through slave trading suggests a proposed relationship that was more coercive and exploitative than friendly. See Executive Journals of the Council of Colonial Virginia, 285–304; Morgan, *American Slavery, American Freedom*, 330.

74. Lawson is often held up as a progressive thinker among colonial writers of his time because he observed of Indigenous people, "They are better to us than we are to them . . ." See, for example, Dowie, *The Haida Gwaii Lesson*, 41. But despite positive framing of Lawson's views, his work as a whole unapologetically supports colonial exploitation.

75. Scholars of this conflict agree that Lawson was executed by Tuscarora people and their allies (see Feeley, "Before Long," 143–45; La Vere, *The Tuscarora War*, 65–68; and Wallace, *Tuscarora*, 67–70). The obvious implication—which is not often articulated in academic writing but worth noting here—is that Lawson was held accountable for his misdeed under the Indigenous justice system that still prevailed in the Coastal Plain at that time.

76. Stephen Feeley raises the possibility that these raids could have been part of a larger strategy not to drive out Europeans from the Coastal Plain but to force a more orderly coexistence in what had been a seemingly chaotic series of colonial expansions near the mouths of the Neuse and Pamlico Rivers. See Feeley, "Tuscarora Trails," 154.

77. Alan Gallay notes that Governor Hyde incentivized assistance by offering thousands of Indian slaves to "whoever came to the colony's rescue first." Gallay, *The Indian Slave Trade*, 278.

78. See La Vere, *The Tuscarora War*, 113–35.

79. Anthony Wallace also discusses the relationship between these "killing fields" and the multigenerational trauma experienced by present-day Tuscarora people in New York. See Wallace, *Tuscarora*, 107.

80. At the urging of Virginia's governor, North Carolina's colonial government installed a Tuscarora named Tom Blount as "king" over all Native people in eastern North Carolina. This move made Blount accountable for all of the actions of Native people under his nominal leadership. The terms were most convenient for the colonial government; North Carolina could hold a single individual responsible for the actions of several different groups of Native people. See Executive Journals of the Council of Colonial Virginia, 333.

81. In 1713, Virginia colonial officials were surprised to find a large number of Tuscarora people—"a great body of that Nation"—living along the Roanoke River above the Fall Line in the Virginia Piedmont. They offered the group tributary status, but only if they promised to relocate more than one hundred miles farther north, beyond the James River. There, the governor had predetermined that they could serve as a buffer community against the colony's real or imagined enemies. See Executive Journals of the Council of Colonial Virginia, 357–68.

82. Hirschberger, "Collective Trauma."

83. Bennett and Provan, "What Do We Mean by 'Refugia'?"

84. Lowery, "Telling Our Own Stories," 499.

Chapter Two

1. The date and location are given on the building's 1976 nomination paperwork for the National Register of Historic Places, accessible online at "North Carolina SP Old Main,

Pembroke State University," National Archives, accessed April 9, 2023, https://catalog
.archives.gov/id/47721974. See also Dial and Eliades, *The Only Land I Know*, 166.

2. Adjusted for inflation, the state's allocation for the construction of Old Main would be
approximately $750,000 in 2021 dollars.

3. Lumbee identity is so intimately tied to physical presence in a specific place that
Lumbee people living outside of the tribe's jurisdictional territory (Robeson and certain
adjoining counties) cannot enroll as tribal members without demonstrating meaningful
connections to tribal territory. The tribal government has implemented this requirement in
various ways, including interviews with enrollees, written questionnaires, and mandatory
classes—all of which center around knowledge of specific Lumbee communities and places
of historical or cultural significance. For a detailed discussion of processes and politics surrounding the so-called contact criterion. See Hite, "Whoz Ya People?"

4. Lowery, *Lumbee Indians in the Jim Crow South*, 25; Lowery, *The Lumbee Indians*, 44.

5. Hamilton McMillan considered himself an expert on the group's origins and published a pamphlet to advance his ideas about their origins. See McMillan, *Sir Walter
Raleigh's Lost Colony*.

6. Although school desegregation sought to end the white supremacist philosophy of
"Separate but Equal," the process was opposed by some Lumbees because it forced them to
surrender what little control they had over substandard, but Native-led, schools. See Lowery,
The Lumbee Indians, 94–102. See also Ben A. Franklin, "Indians Resist Integration Plan in
Triracial County in Carolina," *New York Times*, September 13, 1970.

7. Dial and Eliades, *The Only Land I Know*, 90–91. See also "North Carolina SP Old
Main."

8. "The Croatan and Their Improvement," *Weekly Observer*, July 19, 1888.

9. The 1885 legislation recognized the tribe under the name *Croatan Indians*, which
reflected a belief by various outsiders and Native people that the Indigenous people of
Robeson County descended principally from the survivors of the failed Roanoke colony
and the Native people of Croatoan, who may have absorbed them into their community
sometime between 1587 and 1590. Dial and Eliades, *The Only Land I Know*, 2–5; Lowery,
The Lumbee Indians, 26; and Perdue *Native Carolinians*, 45.

10. This is especially true between the time Old Main was constructed and the early
1960s, when Lumbee churches began to replace small wooden buildings with much larger
brick sanctuaries. See Smith and Smith, *The Lumbee Methodists*; "Interview with Danford
Dial," August 1, 1972, Lumbee Oral History Collection.

11. In a 1972 letter to *The Robesonian*, Ruth Revels highlighted the building's poor condition and charged that Old Main and other buildings constructed for non-white institutions
were "poorly constructed" and "not properly maintained." Annie Ruth (Locklear) Revels,
"Relates Saving 'Old Main' to 'Acting with the Heart,'" *The Robesonian*, January 19, 1972.

12. A handful of Lumbee students attended Carlisle Institute, including my great-
grandfather, J. C. Oxendine, who arrived at the school in September 1911 and ran away a few
weeks later, making his way back to Robeson County—covering four states and a distance
of 450 miles. For many years, Oxendine and other Lumbees were misidentified by the
Carlisle archives as belonging to the Cherokee Nation. In 2017, I brought the issue of
Lumbee misattribution to the attention of staff at Dickinson College's Digital Resource
Center, where the Carlisle archives are held. After I explained the situation, and after

receiving similar requests from other Lumbees, the Digital Resource Center agreed to update the metadata in my great-grandfather's record and in the records of other Lumbee students who attended the boarding school. Records of students who attended the Carlisle Institute can be found at "Carlisle Indian School Digital Resource Center," Dickinson College, accessed April 9, 2023, http://carlisleindian.dickinson.edu.

13. Pratt was a military officer credited with the maxim "Kill the Indian, save the man." Although the entirety of Pratt's career is often summarized in this quote, Lomawaima and Ostler challenge the view of Pratt as the "human face of inhumane, authoritarian oppression" and present a fuller portrait of Pratt and his relationship to the Native American boarding school period. See Lomawaima and Ostler, "Reconsidering Richard Henry Pratt."

14. Decades later, Lumbee Helen Scheirbeck played an instrumental role in founding a consortium of tribally controlled colleges that would eventually follow in Pembroke's footsteps as Native-controlled institutions offering degrees to Native Americans. Scheirbeck, a federal education official, drafted federal legislation to establish the American Indian Higher Education Consortium. See Stein, "American Indian Higher Education Consortium."

15. By the early 1970s, Pembroke State had also become a predominantly white institution. US Indian Claims Commissioner Brantley Blue (Lumbee) cited this demographic shift in a front-page interview published by *The Robesonian*. See Delores Briggs, "U.S. Aide Blasts N.C. Officials on P.S.U. Dispute," *The Robesonian*, February 6, 1972.

16. See "Change in PSU Curriculum Emphasis is Needed: Jones," *The Robesonian*, November 11, 1971; Dial and Eliades, *The Only Land I Know*, 166.

17. Gene Warren, "PSU President Certain He's Right on Old Main Demolition Question," *The Robesonian*, January 16, 1972.

18. Gene Warren, "Sacrifice Claims Said 'Not True,'" *The Robesonian*, January 16, 1972.

19. Gene Warren, "Sacrifice Claims."

20. A few groups, including the Lumbee-dominated alumni association, supported the administration's plan. At one point, President Jones offered a compromise involving a small-scale replica of Old Main placed under glass in the entryway of the new performing arts center. Preservation advocates panned this idea. See Gene Warren, "PSU President Certain He's Right"; Olin Briggs, "'Save Old Main' Supporters Reject Jones' Replica Plan," *The Robesonian*, January 18, 1972.

21. James M. Locklear, "'Old Main' Symbol of Progress by Indians," *The Robesonian*, January 16, 1972.

22. See Dial and Eliades, *The Only Land I Know*, 167; "Interview with Danford Dial." Danford Dial also led local protests to save Old Main and was known for carrying a large Stop sign. See Currie, "Laying the Foundation."

23. Dial and Eliades, 169.

24. Grassroots efforts to preserve Old Main may or may not have represented a majority opinion among Lumbee people. No formal polls or surveys were ever conducted on the issue, but if Danford Dial's seven-thousand-signature petition was any indication, the grassroots position that he represented was a prevalent, if not a majority, opinion.

25. "Interview with Danford Dial."

26. Bill Norment, "Restoration of Confidence Seen in House Appointment," *The Robesonian*, March 18, 1973.

27. Dial and Eliades, *The Only Land I Know*, 169–70.

28. Wind information is based on historic records from the nearest climate station, located at the airport in Fayetteville, NC, approximately thirty miles from Pembroke. See "Fayetteville, NC Weather History," Weather Underground, accessed April 9, 2023, https://www.wunderground.com/history/daily/KFAY/date/1973-3-18.

29. C. E. McLaurin, "Old Main, Grocery Destroyed as Robeson Fires Continue," *The Robesonian*, March 19, 1973.

30. C. E. McLaurin, "Old Main, Grocery Destroyed"; Dial and Eliades, *The Only Land I Know*, 170.

31. "Governor Meets Indian Leaders," *Daily Times-News*, March 24, 1973.

32. Karen Vela, "Old Main Funding Committed," *The Robesonian*, October 31, 1976.

33. Annie Ruth (Locklear) Revels, "Relates Saving 'Old Main' to 'Acting with the Heart,'" *The Robesonian*, January 19, 1972.

34. It is important to acknowledge that one of the key leaders and advocates for the Native-led institution was W. L. Moore, a neighboring Waccamaw Siouan Indian who lived and worked in Robeson County, and who married a Lumbee woman. Moore was also a prominent Methodist minister and much revered among Lumbees. So respected was Moore that his portrait was displayed prominently in some Lumbee homes, including the home of my great-grandparents. See Smith and Smith, *The Lumbee Methodists*, 105.

35. The Haudenosaunee introduced the concept of Seven Generations thinking, one interpretation of which is the idea that decisions made by people today should be made in deference to the well-being of seven generations into the future. See, for example, King, "The Value of Water," 457, note 22. The point of this note is not to suggest that Lumbee ancestors thought explicitly about the Seven Generations concept when they founded Croatan Normal School; it is simply to point out the general practice among Indigenous peoples of making decisions that sustain the collective for generations to come.

36. In contrast, the average public law passed by the 84th Congress (1955–56) occupied approximately 1.8 pages in the Federal Register according to a report by the Brookings Institution, "Vital Statistics on Congress," The Brookings Institution, accessed April 9, 2023, https://www.brookings.edu/wp-content/uploads/2016/06/Vital-Statistics-Chapter-6-Legislative-Productivity-in-Congress-and-Workload_UPDATE.pdf.

37. Senator Daniel Inouye included this quote from Deloria in a letter to US tribal leaders dated November 25, 1991. Vine Deloria Papers. See also Emanuel, "Sovereignty's Cycle."

38. The quote is included in a timeline of Lumbee federal recognition milestones assembled by the Lumbee Sovereignty Coalition, a grassroots group that formed in 2010 during a recent bid to amend the 1956 Lumbee Act. See "Federal Recognition: Lumbee Tribe's One Hundred Twenty-Two Year Quest," Lumbee Sovereignty Coalition, accessed January 1, 2022, https://lumbeesovereigntycoalition.files.wordpress.com/2010/04/lumbee_recognition_timeline4.pdf.

39. Deloria, *Spirit and Reason*, 267.

40. Lowery, *Lumbee Indians in the Jim Crow South*, 191.

41. Lumbee Act of 1956, Pub. L. No. 84–570, 70 Stat. 254 (1956). See also Transcripts, Lumbee Indians of North Carolina, Senate Hearing on Bill H.R. 4656, February 20, 1956, (Section 002, Item 002.011.013, MS 170), Costo Papers.

42. See, for example, the Rancheria Termination Act of 1958, Pub. L. No. 85–671, 72 Stat. 619 (1958).

43. Barton, Bruce, "As I See It," *Carolina Indian Voice*, November 7, 1974.

44. The exemplar is the Federal Energy Regulatory Commission, which cited the 1956 Lumbee Act in its formal decision to exclude the Lumbee Tribe from decision-making about the now-canceled Atlantic Coast Pipeline. Interestingly, Lumbee leaders also cited the 1956 Act in their formal petition to participate in the Federal Energy Regulatory Commission's decision. The fact that opposite assertions cite the same legislation highlights the contradictory nature of the 1956 Lumbee Act. See chapter 4 and also Wilkins and Emanuel, "Breaching Barriers," 9, 24.

45. By 1830, Lumbee ancestors lived in places deemed too remote and too wet for settlers to exploit for timber or crops. To be certain, the bloody uprooting of Indigenous peoples from their homelands by the Indian Removal Act was traumatic, but damages inflicted by policies of the era extended farther than forced uprooting and relocation. Native peoples of the Coastal Plain who were not evicted by military actions were those who, according to Roxanne Dunbar-Ortiz, "remained, without land, without acknowledgment, until the successful struggles of some of them for recognition in the late twentieth century." Dunbar-Ortiz, *An Indigenous Peoples' History*, 110.

46. Malinda Maynor Lowery has written extensively about Lumbee identity in the context of white supremacist systems in the American South. See especially Lowery, *Lumbee Indians in the Jim Crow South*, 19–54.

47. Several harrowing examples are summarized in Emanuel and Bird, "Stories We Tell."

48. Emanuel and Bird, "Stories We Tell."

49. John Kirkpatrick, "Cumberland Fair," *Weekly Observer*, November 19, 1860.

50. Regardless of whether Pearsall actually took the preserved drink from a burial mound, that he was willing to make such a public spectacle of his grave robbing highlights the normalcy of such a macabre activity during this time period. The story was apparently popular enough that it was retold two years later in a different North Carolina newspaper. See "Echoes of Convention: What North Carolina Editors Are Saying about Press Association Meeting at Wrightsville Beach," *Wilmington Morning Star*, June 19, 1910; "A Box from Pender," *Evening Chronicle*, April 4, 1912.

51. Daniels was implicated as a leading mouthpiece and supporter of white supremacist rhetoric associated with the Wilmington Race Riot of 1898, an incident in which a violent white mob overthrew the city government and targeted black citizens with violence, killing dozens. See "Race Riot Commission Report," North Carolina Department of Cultural Resources, accessed June 10, 2021, https://digital.ncdcr.gov/digital/collection/p249901coll22/id/5339.

52. The "opening" of Native burials was a widespread practice in the United States during the nineteenth and twentieth centuries, and partnerships between local guides and distant researchers created a situation in which museums across the United States acquired collections of Native remains, sometimes from remote locations. For this example, see MacCord "The McLean Mound"; Stewart, "Human Bones Recovered." For general background, see Midtrød, "More Than Human Vengeance," 313.

53. I have attended several talks where Jeffries-Logan made this statement, but this quote comes directly from a doctoral dissertation written by another member of the Occaneechi Band of Saponi Nation. See Jeffries, "Whole Indian," 105.

54. See Midtrød, "More Than Human Vengeance." Midtrød raises a related issue, which cannot be discussed in great detail here, that involves systematic underreporting of post-contact

Indigenous archaeological sites, a practice that researchers in California warned has the potential to "obscure the realities of lived experience and the element of power inherent in the process of colonialism." Panich and Schneider, "Categorical Denial," 664.

55. Anthropologist Anthony Wallace believes that Fort Nooheroka may have been built around a Tuscarora burial mound, and that some of the noncombatants slain during the 1713 assault on the structure may have been Tuscarora refugees attempting to collect their ancestors' bones as they fled from North Carolina. Because the South Carolina militia burned the fort and its occupants, Wallace speculates that the unusually high body count for such a small structure—more than nine hundred slain—may have been a miscalculation of those killed during the assault plus the disinterred human remains intended for transport to New York. Given the wave of grave robbing in the centuries that followed, perhaps the departing Tuscarora were wise to take their ancestors' bones with them. See Wallace, *Tuscarora*, 71.

56. Whyte, "Indigeneity and US Settler Colonialism," 96.

57. National Historic Preservation Act, 54 U.S.C. § 300101 (1966, amended 1996). Quote from title and policy declaration of original legislation, 16 U.S.C. § 470 b5.

58. "Traditional Cultural Landscapes | Advisory Council on Historic Preservation," Advisory Council on Historic Preservation, accessed July 24, 2022, https://www.achp.gov /indian-tribes-and-native-hawaiians/traditional-cultural-landscapes.

59. There are many excellent resources on controversies surrounding tribal engagement and the Dakota Access Pipeline, particularly the Standing Rock Syllabus, "#StandingRockSyllabus," accessed July 24, 2022, https://nycstandswithstandingrock.wordpress .com/standingrocksyllabus/. However, I think one of the most powerful and insightful resources comes from Phyllis Young, who in 2014 was a member of the Standing Rock Sioux Tribal Council. In a 2014 speech given during a meeting between pipeline company representatives and the tribal council, Young explained the long history of troubled relations between her people and the federal government, and she cited Section 106 of the National Historic Preservation Act as a step toward tribal empowerment to reverse generations of harm. An audio recording of the full meeting was published by the Standing Rock Sioux Tribe in 2016 after the CEO of the pipeline company claimed that his company had no prior warning about the tribe's opposition to their project. See "Sept 30th DAPL Meeting with SRST," Standing Rock Sioux Tribe, accessed July 24, 2022, https://www.youtube.com /watch?v=ZlwdtnZXmtY.

60. "Consultation and Coordination with Indian Tribal Governments," Exec. Order No. 13,175, 65 C.F.R. 67249 (Nov. 6, 2000).

61. "Memorandum on Tribal Consultation and Strengthening Nation-to-Nation Relationships," The White House, accessed January 26, 2021, https://www.whitehouse.gov /briefing-room/presidential-actions/2021/01/26/memorandum-on-tribal-consultation -and-strengthening-nation-to-nation-relationships/.

62. The nomination form described the property as "ruins" and a "work in progress." See "North Carolina SP Old Main."

63. Data downloaded and analyzed for "Native American" and "Pacific-Islanders"—two categories used by the register to list significance to Indigenous peoples. Data source: "National Register Database and Research," National Park Service, accessed June 6, 2021, https://www.nps.gov/subjects/nationalregister/database-research.htm.

64. "What Is the National Register of Historic Places?," National Park Service, accessed June 7, 2021, https://www.nps.gov/subjects/nationalregister/what-is-the-national-register .htm.

65. "Determination of Eligibility Notification for Nantucket Sound," United States Department of Interior, January 4, 2010, accessed June 7, 2021, https://www.achp.gov/sites /default/files/2018-05/National%20Register%20of%20Historic%20Places%20determina- tion%20of%20eligibility%20of%20Nantucket%20Sound.pdf.

66. "Guide to Working with Non-Federally Recognized Tribes in the Section 106 Process," United States Advisory Council on Historic Preservation, accessed August 1, 2017, https://www.achp.gov/digital-library-section-106-landing/guide-working-non-federally -recognized-tribes-section-106.

67. The Eastern Band of Cherokee are the exception to this statement, because they are entitled to federal-tribal consultation per their recognition status.

68. "End of Mission Statement by the United Nations Special Rapporteur on the Rights of Indigenous Peoples, Victoria Tauli-Corpuz of Her Visit to the United States of America," United Nations Office of the High Commissioner on Human Rights, accessed March 10, 2017, https://www.ohchr.org/en/statements/2017/03/end-mission-statement-united-nations -special-rapporteur-rights-indigenous.

69. "United Nations Declaration on the Rights of Indigenous Peoples (UNDRIP), Reso- lution 61/295," United Nations General Assembly, October 2, 2007, https://www.un.org /development/desa/indigenouspeoples/wp-content/uploads/sites/19/2018/11 /UNDRIP_E_web.pdf.

70. For an explanation of Indigenous survival as "cultural continuance," see Whyte, "Justice Forward," 518–20.

71. McCulloch, "Free, Prior, and Informed Consent," 243.

72. Nick Martin, "Indian Country's Right to Say No," *New Republic*, November 1, 2021.

73. Arnstein, "Ladder of Citizen Participation."

74. Johnson et al., "It's Not in Your Head," 1031.

75. Arstein, "Ladder of Citizen Participation."

76. This definition of environmental justice is a highly compressed summary of the seventeen principles of environmental justice adopted during the First National People of Color Environmental Leadership Summit, which took place in October 1991 in Washing- ton, D.C. The principles set an ambitious agenda for the growing environmental justice movement, and it served as a guide for federal policies, which emerged in a much more di- lute form, following Bill Clinton's 1994 Presidential Executive Order. The Summit was sponsored by the Racial Justice Commission of the United Church of Christ. The seven- teen principles can be found on the Church's website: "Principles of Environmental Justice," United Church of Christ, accessed April 13, 2023, https://www.ucc.org/what-we -do/justice-local-church-ministries/justice/faithful-action-ministries/environmental -justice/principles_of_environmental_justice/.

77. "Office of Environmental Justice in Action (Fact Sheet)," Environmental Protection Agency, accessed April 14, 2023, https://www.epa.gov/sites/default/files/2017-09/documents /epa_office_of_environmental_justice_factsheet.pdf.

78. For a general chronology of the movement, including the important role of the First National People of Color Environmental Leadership Summit (1991), see Bullard,

"Environmental Justice in the 21st Century." For the text of Executive Order 12898, see "Executive Order 12898 of February 11, 1994: Federal Actions to Address Environmental Justice in Minority Populations and Low-Income Populations," National Archives, accessed April 14, 2023, https://www.archives.gov/files/federal-register/executive-orders /pdf/12898.pdf.

79. Bullard, "Environmental Justice for All."

80. See Bullard et al., "Toxic Wastes"; Vasudevan, "Performance and Proximity."

81. Commission for Racial Justice, *Toxic Wastes and Race in the United States.*

82. See, for example, Skiba et al., "The Color of Discipline"; MacMillan and Reschly, "Overrepresentation of Minority Students."

83. Schlosberg, *Defining Environmental Justice*, 14.

84. Annie Ruth (Locklear) Revels, "Relates Saving 'Old Main' to 'Acting with the Heart,'" *The Robesonian*, January 19, 1972.

Chapter Three

1. "Report of the Joint Select Committee to Inquire into the Condition of Affairs in the Late Insurrectionary States, Testimony of Giles Leitch, July 31, 1871," Civil War Era NC, accessed April 10, 2023, https://cwnc.omeka.chass.ncsu.edu/items/show/277.

2. For a general overview of the Ku Klux Klan Hearings of 1871, see Wright, Carr, and Gasek, "Truth and Reconciliation."

3. "Henry Louis Gates, Jr., Live at America's Town Hall," *We the People Podcast*, National Constitution Center, May 9, 2019, accessed July 1, 2022, https://constitutioncenter.org /interactive-constitution/podcast/henry-louis-gates-jr-live-at-americas-town-hall.

4. When Senator Blair asked Leitch if the people in Scuffletown were African Americans, Leitch responded, "Well, sir, I desire to tell you the truth as near as I can; but really I do not know what they are; I think they are a mixture of Spanish, Portuguese and Indian. . . . I was born among them, and I reckon that I know them perfectly well." See "Report of the Joint Select Committee." To be crystal clear, Leitch was talking about the ancestors of Lumbee people. His self-contradictory response suggests confusion (or ambivalence) toward Lumbee identity; Leitch grew up among Lumbee ancestors and knew them "perfectly well," and yet he admitted to having no clear idea about their racial identity. Leitch's response illustrates why it is important to carefully scrutinize late nineteenth-century claims about Lumbee identity made by outsiders—including non-Native people who lived in Robeson County at the time. Like Leitch, they may not actually know what they are talking about.

5. Lowery, *The Lumbee Indians*, 55.

6. I have taken some license with the order of Leitch's responses in this section. The block quote here is actually testimony given by Leitch to Senator Blair earlier in the day, before the exchange at the beginning of this section. Senator Blair did ask Leitch to describe the swamp later that day (as narrated in the main text), and Leitch repeats much of the information from this block quote, but his later response rambles much more than the quote here. Thus, even though the block quote is not chronologically correct in the order of the day's testimony, it contains essentially the same information that Leitch relayed earlier in the day. See "Report of the Joint Select Committee."

7. Lowery, *The Lumbee Indians*, 33.

8. "Report of the Joint Select Committee."

9. Evans, *To Die Game*, 25–30.

10. In the late summer of 1954, the Lumbee River was at an exceptionally low level due to drought. While the water level was low, fossil hunters found a trove of shark teeth exposed in a section of riverbank near Lumberton. See John Gause and Webster, "Evidence of Fossil Remains Found along Lumber River," *The Robesonian*, December 1, 1954. The US Geological Survey stream gaging station at Boardman confirms the exceptionally low water level; it recorded flows of less than one hundred cubic feet per second during this period. Such low levels occur approximately once per decade. See "Lumber River at Boardman, NC—02134500," US Geological Survey, https://waterdata.usgs.gov/monitoring-location/02134500/.

11. The settler's observation is remarkable given that it is nearly impossible to see across Raft Swamp today; the floodplain lying between the low bluffs (the settler's reported "hills") now comprises a dense swamp forest. See "Nearly Forgotten Communities Flourished in Robeson before Present Towns Grew Up," *The Robesonian*, February 26, 1951.

12. Today, Atlantic sturgeon are protected by the Endangered Species Act in waters of the United States. In addition to overfishing, dam construction on other rivers have cut off access to spawning grounds for many sturgeon populations along the Atlantic coast. See "Atlantic Sturgeon | NOAA Fisheries," National Oceanic and Atmospheric Administration, accessed January 19, 2021, https://www.fisheries.noaa.gov/species/atlantic-sturgeon. Note also that west of the Lumbee River, farther up the main stem of the Pee Dee River, stone fishing weirs are still visible in the shallows below Blewett Falls Dam—a hydroelectric dam that inundated a fertile river valley more than a century ago. See "A Powerhouse on the Pee Dee River," Duke Energy, accessed January 19, 2021, https://illumination.duke-energy.com/articles/a-powerhouse-on-the-pee-dee-river.

13. See Barnwell, "Journal," 392.

14. For a detailed explanation of the study and its quantitative results, see Emanuel, "Water in the Lumbee World," 33–39.

15. See "Report Concerning the Militia in Each County of North Carolina," Documenting the American South: Colonial and State Records of North Carolina, 1754, accessed June 28, 2021, https://docsouth.unc.edu/csr/index.html/document/csr05-0072.

16. Often, moving downstream from the confluence of two tributaries, the longer tributary gives its name to the downstream river. There are notable exceptions to this convention, of course—the Missouri is much longer than the upper Mississippi River, yet the river is Mississippi below the confluence in St. Louis. The convention requires, though, prior knowledge of both tributaries' lengths. The river below the confluence of the Lumbee and the Little Pee Dee was named the *Little Pee Dee* by European settlers, even though the Lumbee River is the much longer tributary. It is possible that the unconventional naming decision reflects settlers' mistaken belief that Drowning Creek was attached to the headwaters of the Little Pee Dee. In their minds, this would have made the Little Pee Dee a much longer and more substantial stream than the Lumbee River. See Emanuel, "Water in the Lumbee World," 33–39.

17. See, for example, the official history of the Lumber National Wild and Scenic River: "Lumber River, North Carolina," National Wild and Scenic Rivers System, https://www.rivers.gov/rivers/lumber.php.

18. Lawmakers were tight with public funds during early statehood and frequently issued charters for private parties to operate fundraising lotteries for a variety of projects that

would be considered public works today—roads, bridges, and navigation channels, to name a few.

19. At this time, nearly all river commerce in the western part of the state flowed into South Carolina, mainly via the Catawba and Pee Dee Rivers. Lawmakers viewed the situation as lost revenue. See "Extract from Mr. Couty's Report on the Lumber River Canal," *Weekly Raleigh Register*, May 28, 1819.

20. The legislative committee charged with planning the canal noted, however, that "The grounds between those two rivers have not been surveyed, and your committee cannot therefore speak with confidence, as to the practicability of opening such a communication." See "Report on Inland Navigation," excerpt in *North-Carolina Star*, December 27, 1816.

21. See "Injunction Sought against Operator of Dam at Outlet of 'Desert' Pond," *The Robesonian*, April 5, 1939. Prior to the development of insecticidal sprays, one alternative to draining impoundments was to spray petroleum oil into the wetlands, coating the surface of the wetland in an oil slick. It seems that state officials had implemented this solution on Roanoke Island to control mosquitoes around the amphitheater where Paul Green's outdoor drama, *The Lost Colony*, had recently opened, and citizens of Robeson County wondered openly why the same measures could not be employed for their own mosquito problems. See D. G. McMillan, "The Great Desert and Malaria Control," *The Robesonian*, August 10, 1938.

22. For a detailed analysis of this project, see Maxwell, "Back Swamp Drainage Project."

23. An 1888 briefing in *Scientific American* laid out, clinically, plans by Michigan-based partners to ditch and clear-cut portions of the Lumbee River watershed. The lumbermen planned to use steam shovels and dredges to dig their way into the vast swamp forest via a network of new canals. The canals would serve as conduits to float logs out of the swamp and into the river, where they could be rafted and floated farther downriver. The plan was pitched as a way to finally "solve the cypress problem" in eastern North Carolina. Notably, the briefing discusses the perspectives of local people using overtly racist language. See "How to Utilize a Cypress Swamp," *Scientific American*, March 10, 1888.

24. Maxwell discusses Gerald Sider's claim that the Back Swamp Drainage Project led to Lumbee land loss as well as counterevidence that the project actually facilitated Lumbee land ownership. See Maxwell, "Back Swamp Drainage Project," 19.

25. At the same time, most Lumbee farm families kept "kitchen gardens"—separate plots for growing beans, vegetables, potatoes, and other crops for home consumption. See Pearmain, *Report of John Pearmain*.

26. Gilio-Whitaker, *As Long as Grass Grows*, 36.

Chapter Four

1. These superlatives are based on a 2019 report released by BTU Analytics. "Gas Pipeline Costs Run Higher, Again," BTU Analytics, February 1, 2019, https://btuanalytics.com/natural-gas-pricing/costs-run-higher-ii/.

2. Developers initially sought authorization to build a pipeline that would carry 1.5 billion cubic feet of gas per day using three compressor stations, but they indicated that the same pipeline could actually carry up to 2 billion cubic feet per day by adding additional compressor stations. See Federal Energy Regulatory Commission, *Final Environmental Impact Statement*, 2–57.

3. The *Washington Post* once described ACP developers' activities as a "sophisticated political campaign" to win support for the pipeline, citing evidence from a slide presentation given by Dominion Energy's senior energy policy director. The director's slides describe the campaign partly as an effort to draw out a "silent majority" of pipeline supporters through messaging, advertising, endorsements, and other means. See Gregory S. Schneider, "'Campaign to Elect a Pipeline:' Va.'s Most Powerful Company Ran Multi-Front Fight," *Washington Post*, November 29, 2017.

4. "News Releases: Dominion Energy and Duke Energy Cancel the Atlantic Coast Pipeline," Dominion Energy, accessed July 5, 2020, https://news.dominionenergy.com/2020-07 -05-Dominion-Energy-and-Duke-Energy-Cancel-the-Atlantic-Coast-Pipeline.

5. Secretary Brouillette's full statement was first tweeted by his press office account (@EnergyPress) on the evening of July 5, 2020. See https://twitter.com/EnergyPress /status/1279905955334021121. But Brouillette personally tweeted about the pipeline cancellation too. After sitting for a brief interview the following morning on the Fox Business program "Varney & Co.," he tweeted a link to the interview from his individual government account (@SecBrouillette). See https://twitter.com/SecBrouillette/status/1280258745117835267.

6. "Revolving Door: Dan Brouillette Employment Summary," OpenSecrets, accessed July 9, 2022, https://10.33.1.124/revolving/rev_summary.php?id=13726.

7. I do not mean to say that the ACP did not have any support. In fact, the project enjoyed strong support from those with connections to the oil and gas industry and from pro-business individuals and entities, many of whom believed the pipeline would bring economic opportunities to struggling communities. Developers often mentioned that the pipeline enjoyed widespread public support, but the claims were based on developer-sponsored surveys, including surveys that seeded questions with pro-industry talking points. Derek Sideman, a researcher for the corporate and government accountability group Little Sis, posted a detailed analysis of a 2016 survey sponsored by ACP developers at "Atlantic Coast Pipeline Corporate Backers Fund Faulty Pro-Pipeline Poll," Little Sis, accessed July 1, 2021, https://news.littlesis.org/2017/05/16/atlantic-coast-pipeline-corporate-backers-fund -faulty-pro-pipeline-poll/.

8. For more details and citations to demographic data, see Emanuel, "Flawed Environmental Justice Analyses."

9. Nick Martin, "The People Killed the Pipelines," *New Republic*, July 6, 2020.

10. The phrase *big green boogeyman* is inspired by the title of a 2011 *Orlando Sentinel* article on fear mongering by Florida businesses against environmental regulations. See Scott Maxwell, "Big Biz Creates 'Big Green' Boogeyman to Scare You," *Orlando Sentinel*, October 8, 2011.

11. Tuck and Yang, "Decolonization Is Not a Metaphor," 6.

12. "Duke Energy, Piedmont Natural Gas Select Dominion to Build 550-Mile 'Atlantic Coast Pipeline' to Transport Natural Gas from West Virginia to Eastern North Carolina," Duke Energy, accessed July 1, 2022, https://news.duke-energy.com/releases/duke-energy -piedmont-natural-gas-select-dominion-to-build-550-mile-atlantic-coast-pipeline-to -transport-natural-gas-from-west-virginia-to-eastern-north-carolina.

13. The ACP developers' arrangement to purchase gas from themselves was nothing new in the pipeline industry. Watchdog groups have long criticized what they describe as a practice of self-dealing by energy companies that look to build natural gas pipelines. The general

process went something like this: Pipeline-proposing energy companies signed contracts to deliver future gas supplies to themselves (or to their wholly owned subsidiaries), and federal regulators long treated these contracts as sufficient evidence that market demand warranted federal authorization of a pipeline. Federal authorization allowed developers to seize easements using eminent domain, and it also guaranteed an unusually high return on equity for pipeline owners. (At the time the ACP was proposed, the guaranteed return was around 14 percent.) In 2021 (after the ACP had been canceled), the DC Circuit Court of Appeals ruled that federal regulators could no longer rely solely on self-dealt contracts to justify the authorization of natural gas pipelines due to the ease with which developers could manipulate the system to their advantage. For more information on natural gas pipeline authorizations and self-dealing, see Lorne Stockman and Kelly Trout, "Art of the Self-Deal: How Regulatory Failure Lets Gas Pipeline Companies Fabricate Need and Fleece Ratepayers," Oil Change International (with Public Citizen and Sierra Club), accessed July 1, 2022, https://priceofoil.org/2017/09/19/how-gas-pipelines-fleece-ratepayers/. For additional analysis, see the post by Jennifer Danis on Columbia University's Climate Law blog, "D.C. Circuit Decision: Pipeline Developers Can't Self-Deal in the Public Interest," *Climate Law* (blog), June 22, 2021, https://blogs.law.columbia.edu/climatechange/2021/06/22/d-c-circuit-decision-pipeline-developers-cant-self-deal-in-the-public-interest/. See also Bell and Macbeth, "Putting the Public Back."

14. Early designs, including early route plans, appear in the supplemental information to a draft version of "Nationwide Permit 12, Pre-Construction Notification–Joint Permit Application," figure 10.8.1-1. The document is archived online at https://edocs.deq.nc.gov/WaterResources/DocView.aspx?id=493098&dbid=0&repo=WaterResources&searchid=20dfd3f2-293d-4d40-beac-f06e2981cc69.

15. "Duke Energy, Partners to Build $5B Gas Pipeline from WV to NC," WRAL Business News, accessed June 1, 2022, https://www.wral.com/duke-piedmont-natual-gas-move-ahead-on-5b-pipeline/13942896/.

16. The Chamber of Commerce statement did not specify which companies or industries had overlooked North Carolina due to issues related to natural gas. For a copy of the full statement, see "NC Needs the Atlantic Coast Pipeline," North Carolina Chamber of Commerce, accessed June 5, 2022, https://ncchamber.com/2017/07/13/nc-needs-atlantic-coast-pipeline/.

17. Environmental groups began to criticize the ACP less than twenty-four hours after the project was announced. For example, the Sierra Club's Virginia Director sharply criticized the project as a boon for fracking operations, and within a few days, newspapers began to publish letters from the public expressing concern over land rights, climate impacts, and environmental degradation. See, in particular, an article by Aaron Applegate and Carolyn Shapiro, "$5B Natural Gas Pipeline May Run through Virginia," *Virginian-Pilot*, September 3, 2014, and another by Bruce Dorries, "Pipe Up, Underdogs, Pipe Up," *News Leader*, September 6, 2014.

18. Analysts at Oil Change International claimed that regulators were "asleep at the wheel" when it came to evaluating actual market demand for new natural gas pipelines, and the costs of lax evaluation criteria would ultimately fall on ratepayers (i.e., the general public). See Stockman and Trout, "Art of the Self-Deal."

19. Together with a group of social scientists, I laid out empirical evidence to support the assertion that natural gas gathering and transmission pipelines disproportionately burden

vulnerable groups in the United States. See Emanuel et al., "Natural Gas Gathering and Transmission Pipelines."

20. The western route is visible in "Nationwide Permit 12," figure 10.8.1-1.

21. "Nationwide Permit 12," figure 10.8.1-1.

22. Economic data on North Carolina counties come from 2015, which is the same time period that figure 10.8.1-1 in "Nationwide Permit 12" was released. See "2015 North Carolina Development Tier Designations," North Carolina Department of Commerce, Labor and Economic Analysis Division, accessed June 1, 2021, https://files.nc.gov/nccommerce /documents/files/2015-Development-Tier-Rankings.pdf.

23. Demographic data on North Carolina counties come from the 2020 US Census as aggregated by the state government. See "NC Complete Count Committee," North Carolina Office of State Budget and Management, accessed June 5, 2022, https://ncosbm .opendatasoft.com/pages/nc-complete-count-committee/.

24. "Comments from Southern Environmental Law Center to Jennifer A. Burdette, NC Department of Environmental Quality, on Section 401 Certification for the Atlantic Coast Pipeline, August 18, 2017," Southern Environmental Law Center, accessed June 5, 2022, https://www.southernenvironment.org/wp-content/uploads/legacy/words_docs /Comments_on_NC_401_Certification_Application_for_ACP.pdf.

25. Federal Energy Regulatory Commission, *Final Environmental Impact Statement*, 4–350.

26. One typical example of legal paperwork filed with the Robeson County Register of Deeds specified that the pipeline developer could apply herbicide before reseeding the easement and could also "conduct spot application of herbicide on woody and invasive plants on an ongoing basis." Robeson County Register of Deeds, "Modification of Easement Agreement for Pipeline no. AP 2 and Tract 24–071," Book 2160 Page 696, January 7, 2019.

27. Compensation amounts are typically not shown on publicly filed easement agreements, but using the current excise tax rate of $1 per $500 of compensation, it is possible to back-calculate total compensation from the amount of excise tax paid at the time of filing with the Robeson County Register of Deeds. Drawings attached to each agreement show the dimensions and total acreage for temporary and permanent rights-of-way, which make it possible to compute compensation on a per-acre basis. I am grateful to Jane Flowers Finch for teaching me about this back-calculation method using public records. Records are available online at https://robeson.bislandrecords.com/index.php.

28. News media and academic researchers have reported on shady practices by land agents working on behalf of Atlantic Coast Pipeline developers in North Carolina and Virginia. Here are a few specific examples: A 2016 law review article by Rebecca Ewing summarized evidence that Dominion Energy had threatened legal action against landowners who refused to allow the company's surveyors onto their property. A 2018 study led by Mary Finley-Brook listed some of the lawsuits in Virginia arising from these actions. Journalists working for *IndyWeek* and *NC Policy Watch* have covered similar lawsuits in North Carolina, where one of the main land agents working on behalf of pipeline developers was not even licensed to operate in the state. The study by Finley-Brook and colleagues describes threat of legal action (and the associated expense) as a tactic used by pipeline developers to gain access to private property. They write, "Using the courts and team of

attorneys, [Atlantic Coast Pipeline] forced entry on private lands against the will of land-owners, even lands held in conservation trust." Officials in Nelson County, Virginia even wrote to federal regulators about citizens who they claimed had been strong-armed into signing easement agreements "under threat of eminent domain." See Ewing, "Pipeline Companies Target Small Farmers"; Lisa Sorg, "Landowners in the Path of Proposed Atlantic Coast Pipeline Look to Federal Judge for Relief," NC Policy Watch, March 15, 2018, https://ncnewsline.com/2018/03/15/landowners-in-the-path-of-proposed-atlantic-coast-pipeline-look-to-federal-judge-for-relief/; Finley-Brook et al., "Critical Energy Justice"; and Nick Cropper, "Nelson Board Endorses Letter to Federal Agency Regarding Land Easements," *Nelson County Times*, April 18, 2021.

29. The ACP's route threatened properties beyond legal easement boundaries. In particular, the pipeline's large diameter (thirty-six inches along the Robeson County portion) and extremely high operating pressure (nearly 1,500 pounds per square inch) endangered people and property for several hundred feet on both sides of the easement. Anyone or anything within this zone risked incineration in the event of a major gas leak. Explosion risks were not hypothetical either. In 2018, a similar natural gas pipeline ruptured and exploded following a landslide in West Virginia. When the accident occurred, the pipeline was not even six months old and had been advertised as having "best-in-class" safety features. See the August 2017 report prepared by Oshin Paranjape, Hope Taylor, and Ericka Faircloth, "High Consequence Areas, Blast Zones and Public Safety along the Atlantic Coast Pipeline," Clean Water for North Carolina, accessed June 1, 2021, https://cwfnc.org/wp-content/uploads/initialpdfs/High-Consequence-Areas-Blast-Zones-Public-Safety-along-the-ACP.pdf. See also Anya Litvak and Karen Kane, "Officials: W. Va. Explosion Was along Newly Installed Natural Gas Line," *Pittsburgh Post-Gazette*, June 7, 2018.

30. See "Gas Leak Makes Noise in Prospect," *The Robesonian*, November 21, 2017.

31. Natural gas service is generally unavailable in Prospect due to the high cost of tapping into transmission systems and running new distribution pipelines in an area that lies beyond municipal utility service areas. One notable exception is Prospect Elementary School. Robeson County authorized natural gas service for the school at the urging of state school officials who were concerned about the rising cost of coal, which at the time was used to heat nearly all rural Robeson County schools. In 1970, county school leaders agreed to begin switching the school heating systems from coal to natural gas. They started with Prospect Elementary, probably because the school was located only five hundred yards away from a large transmission pipeline. A short time after converting their heating systems, schools in Robeson County faced possible winter closures because of natural gas shortages during the 1970s energy crisis. See "Natural Gas, Oil Heat Recommended for Schools," *The Robesonian*, August 5, 1970; David Shelley, "FPC Approval of Emergency Gas Predicted to Halt Area Industry, School Cutbacks," *The Robesonian*, January 14, 1977; and Virginia B. Simkins, "Eyeing Education," *The Robesonian*, January 17, 1977.

32. Michanowicz et al., "Home Is Where the Pipeline Ends."

33. During the mid-2000s, coal-fired power plants generated nearly half of Duke Energy's electricity. Nearby, in Virginia, burning coal supplied more than a quarter of Dominion Energy's electricity. These figures are based on statements from the two companies. See Duke Energy, *Connected: 2014 Sustainability Report*; Dominion Energy, *2018 Sustainability & Corporate Responsibility Report*.

34. The CEO of North Carolina-based Duke Energy, Lynn Good, once put it this way: "Storage of ash should be thought of as part of the provision of electric service. . . . You build the power plant, you operate it, you decommission it, you store the waste associated with it. And all of us benefit from that stream by using the electricity." See Good's full remarks in "Duke Energy CEO Talks Big Investments, Nukes, Jobs, Substations," *Citizen Times*, August 4, 2017.

35. The 2008 spill occurred at a Tennessee Valley Authority site on the Emory River in Tennessee, but the 2014 spill occurred at a Duke Energy site on the Dan River, along the North Carolina–Virginia border. The 2014 spill polluted a seventy-mile swath of the river with selenium, arsenic, and copper, and by one researcher's account caused nearly $300 million in ecological damages to the river. See Lemly, "Damage Cost."

36. An April 2016 press release authored by Good, the Duke Energy CEO, emphasized the role of natural gas in her company's long-term plan, explaining, "Today, natural gas is growing rapidly—it is more affordable than coal, with half the carbon emissions. Due to the shale gas boom, we have an abundant supply of this flexible fuel source that we can adjust, as needed, to meet daily fluctuations in demand." See "Solving the Lower-Carbon Puzzle," Duke Energy, April 7, 2016, https://news.duke-energy.com/releases/releases-20160407. Note that Good's assertion that the carbon emissions of gas are half the emissions of coal is based on combustion efficiency alone. The claim ignores methane emissions from gas wells, pipelines, and other parts of the natural gas supply chain. As a result of these additive emissions, the greenhouse gas advantage of gas over coal is completely erased once the cumulative (i.e., fugitive) methane emissions exceed about 3 percent of the total gas supply. For calculations, see Alvarez et al., "Assessment of Methane Emissions."

37. After the sovereign-wealth fund of Norway divested from Duke Energy in 2016 over ethical issues surrounding coal ash, the *Wall Street Journal* reported that Duke Energy was "disappointed" because the fund had not accounted for the company's recent retirement of dozens of coal-fired units. Duke Energy credited natural gas and renewables with the rapid pivot away from coal. That year, however, only 1 percent of the company's electricity had been generated by renewables, according to the company's own reporting. Thus, Duke Energy's pivot away from coal was almost entirely due to natural gas. See "Norway's Sovereign-Wealth Fund to No Longer Invest in Duke Energy; Sovereign Fund Cites Utility's Environmental Record," *Wall Street Journal*, September 7, 2016; Duke Energy, *Bringing the Future to Light*.

38. The US Energy Information Administration publishes data on natural gas consumption in North Carolina by year and sector. See "Natural Gas Consumption by End Use," US Energy Information Administration, accessed June 1, 2021, https://www.eia.gov/dnav/ng/ng_cons_sum_dcu_SNC_a.htm.

39. Later on, TRANSCO would multiply into several parallel pipelines moving billions of cubic feet of gas along the East Coast each day, but in 1949, TRANSCO consisted of a single pipeline.

40. Information about TRANSCO comes from a document distributed to local governments and other groups alongside promotional materials for Williams' Atlantic Sunrise Pipeline. I found these materials posted on the Lancaster County, Pennsylvania, website as "Atlantic Sunrise," accessed July 13, 2022, https://www.co.lancaster.pa.us/DocumentCenter/View/2525/Atlantic-Sunrise.

41. My sketch of Kyle's background comes mainly from three documents—a 1928 announcement of his wedding in Amarillo, TX; his father's 1929 obituary; and a 1957 profile

published by a Rocky Mount, NC, newspaper. Note also that Kyle's father—not his grand-father—was a Confederate veteran. Kyle's actual grandfather—the father of Volney Sr.—died before the Civil War but had owned a sugar cane plantation in Madison County, Mississippi, where enslaved African Americans likely worked. Thus, within three genera-tions of Kyle's family, there can be found a slaveholder, a Confederate soldier, and a gas pipeline engineer—a surprisingly compressed timeline. See "Miss Virginia Chandler and Mr. Volney Kyle Are Joined by Beautiful Ring Ceremony," *Globe-Times*, September 28, 1929; "Volney H. Kyle," *Times-Picayune*, March 11, 1929; and "Kyle Will Head Natural Gas Co.," *Rocky Mount Telegram*, March 28, 1957.

42. Allen "Cradle of a Revolution?," 116.

43. Quotes taken from "Council Discusses Gas Controversy," *The Robesonian*, June 4, 1956; "Attraction to Industry," *The Robesonian*, May 7, 1957; "Eastern N.C. Cities to Get Natural Gas by Pipelines," *Daily Times-News*, March 2, 1957.

44. A competing company, Trans-Carolina Pipeline Corporation, also applied in 1956 for regulatory approval to pipe gas into eastern North Carolina via a connection to TRANSCO in South Carolina. The Federal Power Commission reviewed the competing plans and chose to approve NCNG after finding Trans-Carolina's plan deficient in several areas. See "Trans-Carolina Pipeline Corp.: Notice of Application for Certificate of Public Conve-nience and Need," Fed. Reg. 21(101), 3466, May 24, 1956; Federal Power Commission Reports 17, 1956, 360–62.

45. "Natural Gas Pipeline Routing Promises Earlier Local Fuel," *The Robesonian*, September 3, 1958.

46. "Eastern Residents to Get Gas Soon," *Daily Times-News*, January 9, 1959.

47. I found no documentation to explain why NCNG rerouted the pipeline (and Junc-tion A) from Fayetteville to Prospect. In 1957, NCNG signed an agreement to supply gas to a large electric power plant in Lumberton as a backup fuel to its normal supply of coal. It is possible that the agreement prompted the company to move the main trunk closer to Lum-berton, but this is pure speculation on my part. For information on the agreement to supply gas to the power plant, see "CP&L Contracts for Excess of Natural Gas Piped Here," *The Robesonian*, October 11, 1957.

48. Before dawn on the day of the incident, I received messages from people in Prospect who witnessed the leak. It was a school day, and I was up early fixing lunches for my children. Later that day, I summarized the concerns in an email to state environmental officials, who referred the matter to their division of air quality regulators for investigation. During the investigation, Duke Energy estimated the amount of gas lost during the inci-dent but underestimated the leak by nearly 50 percent! Heather Carter, the air quality compliance coordinator, copied me on all of her email correspondence with Duke Energy, which allowed me to point out the company's error. The compressor engines were decom-missioned soon after the incident. For reporting on the leak—including quotes by Talford Dial below—see "Gas Leak Makes Noise in Prospect," *The Robesonian*, November 21, 2017. For follow-up analysis of the incident—including links to the formal complaint—see Lisa Sorg, "The Natural Gas Compressor Station That Leaked? It Operates without a Permit—Legally," NC Policy Watch, November 28, 2017, https://pulse.ncpolicywatch.org/2017/11/28/natural-gas-compressor-station-leaked-operates-without-permit-legally/.

49. "Gas Leak Makes Noise in Prospect."

50. By "environmental justice populations," regulators and decision-makers usually mean racially marginalized people, poor people, or both. See Federal Energy Regulatory Commission, *Draft Environmental Impact Statement*.

51. No state or federally recognized tribal nations presently occupy territory in the state of West Virginia.

52. Emanuel, "Flawed Environmental Justice Analyses."

53. Emanuel, "Flawed Environmental Justice Analyses."

54. One of the first media outlets to cover the racial disparities in ACP routing was WUNC, the public radio station for much of central and eastern North Carolina. In July 2017, WUNC ran a news brief about the disparities on "Morning Edition" and then aired a longer segment on the midday news program "The State of Things." A summary of the segment and an archival recording are accessible on the WUNC website. See "Are Native Communities Being Overlooked in Atlantic Coast Pipeline Process?," WUNC, accessed March 4, 2022, https://www.wunc.org/show/the-state-of-things/2017-07-27/are -native-communities-being-overlooked-in-atlantic-coast-pipeline-process.

55. Sarah Rankin, a journalist with the Associated Press, reported on March 8, 2018, that Dominion's multifaceted campaign included direct mailings, advertisements (television, radio, and print), community meetings, donations, helicopter tours, dinners, and other activities. One Dominion executive told journalists, "If you want fair media coverage you need to pay for it." See "Documents Reveal Immense Outreach on Atlantic Coast Pipeline," AP NEWS, accessed March 1, 2022, https://apnews.com/article/bb9e146130c94891a25e00332f5c3fbb.

56. As part of their larger advertising and outreach campaign, energy companies created an online entity called the EnergySure Coalition (energysure.com). The entity included a website and social media accounts used to disseminate promotional materials about the ACP. Promotional materials included testimonials and infographics, many of which were framed as educational materials, leading off with phrases such as *Did you know?* or *The Facts*. Some of the infographics parroted mainstream oil and gas industry talking points (e.g., natural gas is required because wind and solar are intermittent), but other material rehashed overtly disingenuous tropes with long-standing connections to climate change denialism, including the claim that pipelines have a smaller physical footprint than wind or solar installations and are therefore better for the environment. (This particular trope traces to a publication by Steve Goreham, *The Mad, Mad, Mad World of Climatism*, which the Heritage Foundation distributed to science faculty throughout the United States more than a decade ago.) EnergySure also released non sequiturs, including an infographic that implied the environmental review process was of high quality because it contained 150,000 pages of documentation—as tall as a five-story building, as an accompanying tweet put it (https://twitter.com/EnergySure/status/898297144460931074). For a more general discussion of industry talking points around natural gas, see Delborne et al., "Dueling Metaphors, Fueling Futures."

57. Together with Lumbee political scientist David Wilkins, I assembled and analyzed a full timeline of corporate, regulatory, and tribal actions related to the Atlantic Coast Pipeline. See Emanuel and Wilkins, "Breaching Barriers."

58. "Lumbee Tribe of North Carolina Submits Comments re the Atlantic Coast Pipeline Project et al under CP15–554 et al," Federal Energy Regulatory Commission, accessed April 10, 2023, https://elibrary.ferc.gov/eLibrary/docinfo?accession_number=20170417-0013.

59. The demands were not unreasonable considering that federal policy guidance recommends meaningful engagement with tribes regardless of their recognition status. Key guidance can be found in National Environmental Justice Advisory Council, *Guide on Consultation and Collaboration*; Advisory Council on Historic Preservation, *Guide to Working with Non-Federally Recognized Tribes*.

60. "Federal Energy Regulatory Commission to Fulfill Its Obligations to Indian Tribes in Pipeline Permitting," Resolution #MOH-17-054, National Congress of American Indians (2017).

61. "North Carolina Commission of Indian Affairs Submits Comments re the Atlantic Coast Pipeline Project et al under CP15–554 et al," Federal Energy Regulatory Commission, accessed April 10, 2023, https://elibrary.ferc.gov/eLibrary/docinfo?accession_number=20170418–0013.

62. Kaya Littleturtle, personal communication, March 2022. See also "Standing in Solidarity with Standing Rock," Lumbee Tribe of North Carolina Resolution CLLR-2016-0906-01, September 6, 2016.

63. Anthony Brown, "Council Approves $50,000 to Support Standing Rock Sioux," *Cherokee One Feather*, September 6, 2016.

64. "End of Mission Statement by the United Nations Special Rapporteur on the Rights of Indigenous Peoples, Victoria Tauli-Corpuz of Her Visit to the United States of America," United Nations Office of the High Commissioner for Human Rights, accessed April 10, 2023, http://www.ohchr.org/EN/NewsEvents/Pages/DisplayNews.aspx?NewsID=21274.

65. This quote is taken from a prepared speech that I delivered at the 2017 North Carolina Indian Unity Conference on March 9, 2017, in Charlotte, NC.

66. Regulators provided the raw data needed to compute these disparities. However, the data tables were buried in an appendix of the environmental impact statement, and regulators never computed racial disparities as advised by recent federal policy guidance on environmental justice. See the 2016 report by Federal Interagency Working Group on Environmental Justice & NEPA Committee, "Promising Practices for EJ Methodologies in NEPA Reviews," United States Environmental Protection Agency, March 2016, https://www.epa.gov/sites/default/files/2016-08/documents/nepa_promising_practices _document_2016.pdf.

67. "Letter Requesting Atlantic Coast Pipeline, LLC et al to File a Response within 20 days re the Environmental Information Request for the Atlantic Coast Pipeline Project et al under CP15–554 et al," Federal Energy Regulatory Commission, accessed April 10, 2023, https://elibrary.ferc.gov/eLibrary/docinfo?accession_number=20170411–3007.

68. Major environmental groups, individuals, and even the US House Committee on Oversight and Reform have referred to the Federal Energy Regulatory Commission as a "rubber stamp" for the natural gas industry because of the agency's overwhelming record of approving natural gas projects. A 2020 investigation by the House of Representatives found that the agency had failed to authorize only six out of more than one thousand natural gas projects reviewed in twenty years. For examples, see April 2018 reporting by journalist Tom Johnson, "FERC, Called a 'Rubber Stamp' by Critics, Begins Policy Review for Approval of Natural Gas Pipelines," StateImpact Pennsylvania, https://stateimpact.npr.org/pennsylvania /2018/04/23/ferc-called-a-rubber-stamp-by-critics-begins-policy-review-for-approval-of -natural-gas-pipelines/, as well as 2020 press releases: "Feds Rubber Stamp Another Fracked Gas Pipeline," Sierra Club, https://www.sierraclub.org/press-releases/2020/06/feds-rubber

-stamp-another-fracked-gas-pipeline and "Press Release: Subcommittee Releases Prelimi-nary Findings Showing FERC Pipeline Approval Process Skewed against Landowners," US House Committee on Oversight and Reform, https://oversight.house.gov/news/press-releases/subcommittee-releases-preliminary-findings-showing-ferc-pipeline-approval.

69. Sure enough, immediately after regulators finalized the environmental review, EnergySure released a celebratory statement that began, "After almost three years of exten-sive study by the Federal Energy Regulatory Commission (FERC) and other agencies, we are encouraged by the favorable conclusions of the final environmental report released today. Never before has an infrastructure project in our region received so much scrutiny by so many agencies and offered so many opportunities for public input. We have total confidence in the process, and we are convinced the project will be built with all necessary protections for the environment and public safety." This statement, together with follow-up social media posts praising the environmental review process, confirms that pipeline developers used the favorable review in their efforts to build public confidence around the project. For an example of how other industry interests amplified the EnergySure message, see "EnergySure Coalition Releases Statement on the FERC's Final Environmental Report for the Atlantic Coast Pipeline," Virginia Chamber of Commerce, accessed March 17, 2022, https://vachamber.com/2017/07/24/energysure-coalition-releases-statement-on-the-fercs-final-environmental-report-for-the-atlantic-coast-pipeline/.

70. For a detailed discussion of the barriers created by delayed and compressed tribal engagement timelines, see Emanuel and Wilkins, "Breaching Barriers."

71. Advisory Council on Historic Preservation, *Guide to Working with Non-Federally Recognized Tribes.*

72. For a more detailed explanation of these events, see Emanuel and Wilkins, "Breach-ing Barriers." For the exact policy referenced here, see page 37 of "Guidelines for Reporting on Cultural Resources Investigations for Natural Gas Projects," Federal Energy Regulatory Commission, December 15, 2020, https://www.ferc.gov/media/guidelines-reporting-cultural-resources-investigations-natural-gas-projects-1. For a general explanation of why tribal consultation should not be delegated to corporations or other third parties, see Routel and Holth, "Toward Genuine Tribal Consultation."

73. "Order on Rehearing re Atlantic Coast Pipeline, LLC et al under CP15–554 et al. Commissioner LaFleur Dissenting with a Separate Statement," Federal Energy Regulatory Commission, accessed April 10, 2023, https://elibrary.ferc.gov/eLibrary/docinfo?accession_number=20180810–3073.

74. Many scholarly reviews highlight the essential role of governments in . . . well . . . government-to-government consultation. See, for example, Routel and Holth, "Toward Genuine Tribal Consultation"; Miller, "Consultation or Consent"; and Warner, Lynn, and Whyte, "Changing Consultation."

75. Estes, *Our History Is the Future,* 49–50.

76. "UCAR Congressional Briefing Highlights Flood, Drought Prediction: Nation Poised to Make Major Advances in 'Water Intelligence,'" University Corporation for Atmo-spheric Research, accessed April 10, 2023, https://news.ucar.edu/122813/ucar-congressional-briefing-highlights-flood-drought-prediction.

77. I attended the meeting as an ad hoc member of the Commission of Indian Affairs' environmental justice committee. At two points during the meeting, I was called on to

speak about the ACP or to respond to corporate representatives. For that reason, I was unable to take my own notes during the meeting. Robie Goins made a video recording of the meeting and graciously loaned me videotapes so that I could review the meeting details.

78. Researchers often highlight Robeson County's status as the poorest county in North Carolina as a contributing factor to serious disparities in health and well-being among Lumbee people, especially youth. See, for example, Langdon et al., "Lessons Learned."

79. Industrialized livestock production is a clear example that applies to Robeson County. See the example of Sanderson Farms discussed in Emanuel, "Water in the Lumbee World" and chapter 5 of this book.

80. See news report by Jim Polson, "Duke CEO Sees Coal Entirely Disappearing from Its Power Mix," BloombergQuint, accessed March 20, 2022, https://www.bloombergquint .com/business/duke-energy-s-piedmont-gas-buy-to-aid-switch-from-coal-ceo-says.

81. To assist in their marketing efforts, energy companies behind the ACP commissioned two different reports that cast the project as an engine of economic development in the three-state region. Opponents of the project criticized both reports as unverifiable, subjective, and overly optimistic. In particular, the Southern Environmental Law Center concluded that the reports' claims were "overstated, lack[ed] sufficient supporting data, and fail[ed] to account for environmental and societal costs." See "Press Release: New Study Questions Economic Benefit Claims of ACP," Southern Environmental Law Center, accessed March 20, 2022, https://www.southernenvironment.org/press-release/new-study -questions-economic-benefit-claims-of-atlantic-coast-pipeline/.

82. The ACP's 2017 environmental impact statement clearly indicated that 80 percent of the pipeline's capacity had been reserved by the developers for electricity generation at company-owned power plants. For more information about ACP supporters in Robeson County (including interviews with prominent Robeson County supporters and opponents), see the essay by Adina Solomon and Asher Elbein, "A Pipeline in the Sand," *The Bitter Southerner*, accessed March 3, 2022, https://bittersoutherner.com/a-pipeline-in-the -sand-atlantic-coast-lumbee-tribe.

83. As early as 2014—the year the ACP was publicly announced—developers made ambiguous claims about economic development in communities impacted by the pipeline. For example, a 2014 report released by Duke Energy described the ACP as a "key infrastructure engine to drive economic development and create jobs, helping counties along its route attract new, energy-dependent businesses and industries." Duke Energy, *Connected: 2014 Sustainability Report*, 24.

84. This statement by Robeson County Manager Ricky Harris was one of the most succinct and clearly articulated arguments that I could identify in favor of building the pipeline. Some advocates expressed fears about losing out on opportunities if gas were not available, but commercial and industrial gas service was already available in many parts of Robeson County at this time. In the same interview with Solomon and Elbein for their *Bitter Southerner* essay, Harris also expressed concerns that existing gas pipelines could be shut off. See Solomon and Elbein, "A Pipeline in the Sand."

85. In the leaked recording published by Sarah Rankin (Associated Press), Dominion Energy Vice President Dan Weekley mistakenly identified the pipeline's southern terminus as Lumberton instead of Prospect during this conference. (Lumberton is the county seat of Robeson and nearly twenty miles away from Prospect.) In the same recording, Weekley

declared that South Carolinians could see as much as 1 billion cubic feet per day—two-thirds of the pipeline's proposed capacity of 1.5 billion cubic feet per day! It is possible that Weekley may have been referencing a provision in the environmental impact statement that would allow the pipeline capacity to expand from 1.5 to 2 billion cubic feet per day by constructing additional compressor stations and infrastructure in Virginia and North Carolina. Even if the pipeline's capacity had been expanded to the full 2 billion cubic feet per day, the amount of gas that Weekley suggested could be shipped to South Carolina appears to have been overstated by at least 50 percent (i.e., 500 million cubic feet per day) given that the developers had previously committed to shipping 1.5 billion cubic feet per day to customers in North Carolina and Virginia. See Sarah Rankin, "APNewsBreak: Disputed East Coast Pipeline Likely to Expand," AP NEWS, September 29, 2017, https://apnews.com/article/north-carolina-virginia-richmond-south-carolina-only-on-ap-d9e121 6747d642abb025dedb0043462f. See also Federal Energy Regulatory Commission, *Final Environmental Impact Statement*, ES-1.

86. The meeting with corporate representatives occurred in September 2018 at the quarterly meeting of the North Carolina Commission of Indian Affairs hosted by the Coharie Tribe in Clinton, North Carolina. At this meeting, I was again asked to raise questions on behalf of the commission's environmental justice committee.

87. Other examples suggest that the experiences of tribal nations in North Carolina are not unique. Instead, it seems these encounters are consistent with a general pattern of behavior in which corporate representatives seek to persuade tribes to support a company's predetermined plan rather than bring recommendations from tribes back to corporate leadership. One highly relevant example occurred in 2014 when representatives from the Dakota Access Pipeline learned from the Standing Rock Sioux Tribal Council that the tribe had current legislation opposing pipeline development on treaty lands, including lands where the Dakota Access Pipeline would be built. Tribal leaders recommended that representatives relay their opposition to corporate leadership and suggested that they pursue alternative plans. Years later, when the pipeline was embroiled in legal turmoil and construction work was stalled because of actions by Water Protectors at Standing Rock, Kelcy Warren, CEO of the company developing the Dakota Access Pipeline, claimed that he wished he had known about the tribe's opposition earlier, when the company still had time to do something about it. The Standing Rock Sioux Tribal Council responded by releasing, publicly, an audio recording of the 2014 meeting. See "Dakota Pipeline's Builder Says Obstacles Will Disappear under Donald Trump," *Wall Street Journal*, November 16, 2016; "Sept 30th DAPL Meeting with SRST," Standing Rock Sioux Tribe, accessed July 24, 2022, https://www.youtube.com/watch?v=ZlwdtnZXmtY. See also Estes, *Our History Is the Future*, 41–47.

88. Shifflett's documentary film is viewable online: "A Walk through American Indian Activism," LumbeeJoJo: Native Daughter Dialogues, accessed April 10, 2023, https://www.youtube.com/watch?v=3PIGZa7jMx8.

89. I think that most developers are sincere in their beliefs that pipelines can resuscitate flagging industries, provide stable jobs, and reduce our dependence on foreign energy sources. However, most operate under powerful financial incentives to ignore the unsustainability of pipeline-based solutions and the history of pipelines not providing the promised solutions—including assurances half a century earlier that pipelines would transform and revitalize eastern North Carolina's economy.

90. Oberg's translation of *Ossomocomuck* is not lost on me here. See Oberg, *Head in Edward Nugent's Hand*, 3.

91. Dial and Eliades, *The Only Land I Know*, 78.

92. Annie Ruth Locklear Revels, "Relates Saving 'Old Main' to 'Acting with the Heart,'" *The Robesonian*, January 19, 1972.

93. The US National Climate Assessment's chapter on tribes and Indigenous peoples reviews several examples of Indigenous peoples' land loss due to climate change and other factors. The chapter also discusses the physical, emotional, and cultural losses that accompany these losses. Jantarasami et al., "Tribes and Indigenous Peoples."

94. "Gas Leak Makes Noise in Prospect," *The Robesonian*, November 21, 2017.

95. Guidance provided in National Environmental Justice Advisory Council, *Guide on Consultation and Collaboration*.

96. In fact, the engineers who planned the ACP route highlighted the fact that they did not consider any information about tribes or other communities when they were initially drafting the route. The engineers framed their "colorblindness" as a positive aspect of route planning, but David Wilkins and I argued in 2020 that "colorblind planning" is a major oversight in environmental decision-making that can have negative impacts on tribes and marginalized communities. See Emanuel and Wilkins, "Breaching Barriers." More recently, when the White House announced in 2022 that a new environmental justice screening tool would not consider race, critics raised similar concerns about the weaknesses of colorblind remedies. Dorothy Brown, a law professor at Emory University, typified criticism when she told Lisa Friedman from the *New York Times*, "If you want to address environmental racism, there is no colorblind way to do that. The best defense would be to say this is remedial work based on past governmental discrimination. In 2022, if you want to help Black people, you're going to get sued. So either you're with the effort to help Black people or you're not. But you can't be timid about it." Brown's comment suggests to me that "colorblind" policies may reflect a feeling among governmental actors that it is preferable to be sued by communities than by corporations. See "White House Takes Aim at Environmental Racism, but Won't Mention Race," *New York Times*, February 15, 2022.

97. Routel and Holth, "Toward Genuine Tribal Consultation," 458–60.

98. Ex parte rules come into play at a certain point during the regulatory process, and we discuss how this timing disadvantages tribes in Emanuel and Wilkins, "Breaching Barriers." For examples of other tribes encountering similar difficulties, see "Infrastructure Projects Listening and Consultations Session Key Points: Updated October 28, 2016," National Congress of American Indians, accessed April 10, 2023, https://www.ncai.org/resources/In frastListeningSessionKeyPoints-Updated-102816.pdf; "Comment of Coalition for American Heritage under PL18–1," Federal Energy Regulatory Commission, accessed April 10, 2023, https://elibrary.ferc.gov/eLibrary/docinfo?accession_number=20180726–5021.

99. North Carolina formally established the Department of Environmental Quality Secretary's Environmental Justice and Equity advisory board in May 2018. The board was charged with "achieving and maintaining the fair and equal treatment and meaningful involvement of North Carolinians regardless of race, color, national origin, or income with respect to the development, implementation, and enforcement of environmental laws, regulations, and policies." The board's charter focuses primarily on forward-looking issues of equity and public participation, but it does not empower the body to advise the

department on systemic changes to eliminate existing disparities in pollution or environmental harm (and existing practices that give rise to these disparities). As such, it could be described more aptly as an environmental equity board rather than an environmental justice board. The group's charter and other materials can be found on its website, "Secretary's Environmental Justice and Equity Advisory Board," North Carolina Department of Environmental Quality, accessed April 10, 2023, https://deq.nc.gov/outreach-education /environmental-justice/secretarys-environmental-justice-and-equity-board.

100. Quote from UNDRIP Article 32. When the General Assembly of the United Nations adopted the Declaration on the Rights of Indigenous Peoples in September 2007, only the United States, Canada, Australia, and New Zealand refused to join. The United States eventually signed the declaration in 2010 but considered language around free, prior, and informed consent to be aspirational. See Champagne, "UNDRIP"; Gilio-Whitaker, "Idle No More."

101. In 2021, two advocacy groups, the Indigenous Environmental Network and Oil Change International, estimated that in recent years, Indigenous groups had mounted resistance to fossil fuel projects that represented the equivalent of 25 percent of US and Canadian greenhouse gas pollution, and that these groups had helped to stop projects that would have emitted approximately eight hundred million metric tons of carbon dioxide (equivalent) annually. This count included the Atlantic Coast Pipeline. Their report can be found at "Indigenous Resistance against Carbon," Indigenous Environmental Network, August 2021, https://www.ienearth.org/indigenous-resistance-against-carbon/.

Chapter Five

1. Consult the following studies for more detailed numbers on industrial livestock and industrial livestock waste: Mallin et al., "Industrial Swine and Poultry Production"; Calhoun and Cecala, "At the Expense of the Environment."

2. In Duplin County, which is located near the epicenter of North Carolina's swine industry, one recent study found that twenty-eight thousand acres of land were used to dispose of nearly two billion gallons, annually, of partially treated liquid waste from industrial hog operations. See Christenson and Serre, "Integrating Remote Sensing."

3. A series of federal lawsuits brought by neighbors against Murphy-Brown, LLC—a large vertical integrator in the swine industry—have found that the industry's waste management practices constitute a nuisance to people who live nearby. For the initial case in the series, see McKiver v. Murphy-Brown LLC, E.D.N.C., No. 7:14-CV-180-BR (2018).

4. The 1982 US Department of Agriculture's Census of Agriculture reported approximately six thousand small-scale hog farmers in North Carolina at that time. Small-scale hog farmers raised between one and twenty-four hogs per year with an average of seven or eight hogs per farm. By 2017, only about one thousand small-scale hog farmers remained in the state. See "North Carolina," US Department of Agriculture Historical Archive, accessed May 1, 2022, https://agcensus.library.cornell.edu/census_parts/1982-north-carolina/; "2017 Census Volume 1, Chapter 2: State Level Data," US Department of Agriculture, National Agricultural Statistics Service, accessed May 1, 2022, https://www.nass.usda.gov /Publications/AgCensus/2017/Full_Report/Volume_1,_Chapter_2_US_State_Level/.

5. See "Revisiting Elsie Herring and the Law of Propaganda," *Farmkeepers Blog*, accessed May 1, 2022, https://www.ncfarmfamilies.com/farmkeepersblog/tag/Right+to+Harm.

6. This is not a figurative statement; deed books from around the time of the Revolutionary War show that my Coharie ancestors once owned more than one hundred acres of property in the general vicinity of where this encounter took place. By the mid-nineteenth century, though, nearly all of those land holdings had been lost.

7. Deloria, *Custer Died for Your Sins*, 167.

8. The US Department of Agriculture's 2017 Agricultural Census includes demographic data for more than 2,100 swine producers (NAICS category 1122) in North Carolina. Of these producers, 1,967 (92 percent) are white. The Census also shows more than 5,100 poultry producers (NAICS category 1123, includes egg producers), of which 4,828 are white. "Table 75. Summary by North American Industry Classification System," 2017 Census of Agriculture, North Carolina State and County Data, accessed May 1, 2022, https://www.nass.usda.gov/Publications/AgCensus/2017/Full_Report/Volume_1,_Chapter_1_State_Level/North_Carolina/ncv1.pdf.

9. For decades, researchers have documented racial disparities in communities surrounding CAFOs in North Carolina. A recent review and discussion of these studies can be found in Son et al., "Distribution of Environmental Justice Metrics."

10. See Schlosberg, *Defining Environmental Justice*, 14.

11. Son et al., "Distribution of Environmental Justice Metrics."

12. Read more about other elements of colonialism built into industrial livestock production and related systems in Oliveira, "Soy, Domestication, and Colonialism," 335–45.

13. Arnstein, "Ladder of Citizen Participation."

14. See, for example, Scarry and Scarry, "Native American 'Garden Agriculture'"; Wood and Lowery, "As We Cooked."

15. See Carney, "Seeds of Memory," 13–33.

16. Notably, the system was designed to generate slightly less than 1.5 million gallons of waste per day—the threshold for an even higher level of scrutiny by environmental regulators.

17. I found this information after inspecting a hard copy of the modeling report at the Department of Environmental Quality Division of Water Resources Non-Discharge Branch offices (Raleigh) in November 2015. The report, *Groundwater Mounding Analysis - Supplement to the Hydrogeologic Report, Proposed Sanderson Farms, Inc. St. Paul's Wastewater Irrigation System: Technical Memorandum No. 15–002.01* was prepared for Sanderson Farms by Nutter and Associates (Athens, GA) and dated May 4, 2015.

18. See "Groundwater Mounding Analysis."

19. In recent years, antibiotic-resistant bacteria have appeared in groundwater samples near industrial livestock operations. See, for example, Lopatto et al., "Characterizing the Soil Microbiome."

20. My maternal grandparents were even married illegally due to segregation-era laws. My maternal grandfather was a white man who met my grandmother while they were both working in Washington, DC, near the end of World War II. Their marriage in Virginia violated the state's miscegenation law. My grandparents moved back to Robeson County before Virginia law enforcement officers caught on.

21. Native Americans and African Americans, whose statistics are combined in the agricultural records, tended to work dramatically smaller farms than whites. In 1950, the average white-operated farm in Robeson County was seventy-eight acres, whereas the average

was forty-one acres for Native Americans and African Americans. "Statistics for Counties— North Carolina," US Department of Agriculture Census of Agriculture Historical Archive, accessed May 1, 2022, https://agcensus.library.cornell.edu/wp-content/uploads/1950-North _and_South_Carolina-Table_of_Contents-1795-Table-03.pdf.

22. Pearmain, *Report of John Pearmain*, 37.

23. Bethel Hill Baptist Church sits across Saddletree Swamp from my father's homeplace on the Great Desert, and it is the home church for many Robeson County Emanuels. My great-grandfather—the farmer and brick mason—built a new brick sanctuary for Bethel Hill church some years after Pearmain's interview with Bell. Pearmain, 31–32.

24. Note that Pearmain also interviewed the local doctor in Pembroke, NC, who thought that Bell's estimate for family size was low based on observations of hundreds of Lumbee families that visited his medical practice each year. Pearmain, 52.

25. In 1950, the average size of a tenant or sharecropper farm in Robeson County operated by Native Americans and African Americans was thirty-six acres. "Statistics for Counties—North Carolina," US Department of Agriculture Census of Agriculture Historical Archive, accessed May 1, 2022, https://agcensus.library.cornell.edu/wp-content/uploads /1950-North_and_South_Carolina-Table_of_Contents-1795-Table-03.pdf.

26. See examples of this usage in Harrison, "Odor in the Court!"; and "Court Upholds Hog Verdict; Smithfield Announces Settlement," Associated Press, accessed May 1, 2022, https://apnews.com/article/north-carolina-courts-4b2f1db4c21e03653851e81b81996410.

27. Murphy-Brown was implicated in more than twenty nuisance lawsuits. With no legal mechanism to sue over allegations of environmental racism, neighbors used existing nuisance law to enumerate long-standing complaints. The company defended itself vigorously in court, but in 2018, a string of juries found Murphy-Brown liable for miserable living conditions near the lagoon and sprayfield systems attached to the specific swine facilities identified in each lawsuit. In each of the five cases that went to trial, juries awarded plaintiffs large compensatory and punitive damages, including one award that totaled nearly half a billion dollars. See Miller and Longest, "Reconciling Environmental Justice."

28. "The Fight for the Right to Farm in North Carolina," NC Pork Report, accessed October 13, 2021, https://www.ncporkreport-digital.com/ncpq/0318_fall_2018/MobilePaged Article.action?articleId=1428663.

29. "Neighbor Complaints and Response: The Basics of North Carolina's Right to Farm and Bona Fide Zoning," NC State Extension, accessed October 13, 2021, https://farmlaw .ces.ncsu.edu/land-use-and-zoning/land-ownership-and-liability/neighbor-complaints -and-response-the-basics-of-north-carolinas-right-to-farm-and-bona-fide-zoning/.

30. This quote comes from an amicus brief of American Farm Bureau Federation et al. in McKiver et al. v. Murphy-Brown, LLC, No. 19–1019, https://www.fb.org/files/McKiver_v _Murphy-Brown_(CA4)_-_Amicus_Brief_of_AFBF_et_al.pdf.

31. One interesting point raised in the amicus brief is the assumption that plaintiffs attacked industrial livestock operations "while promoting visions of small 75-hog, multi-crop farms as the ideal." The idea of small diversified farms as an alternative to massive industrial operations is noteworthy, and closely resembles the model of Lumbee farming practiced for centuries following colonization (apart from the number of hogs—seventy-five—which is actually quite large for a diversified Lumbee farm).

32. The Pork Council's magazine article is accessible online at "The Truth of the Matter: The Real Story behind a Complaint against the NC Pork Industry," NC Pork Report, Spring 2018, http://www.ncpork.org/wp-content/uploads/2018/05/The-Truth-of-the -Matter.pdf.

33. Steve Wing, the scientist who led the research that the Pork Council attempted to discredit, was a longtime advocate for environmental justice. Wing passed away in 2016. One of the groups that he worked for, the North Carolina Environmental Justice Network, created the Steve Wing International Environmental Justice Award in his memory as a way to recognize academic research on environmental justice. I was honored to receive that award in 2019, and it motivated me to learn more about Wing and his work. It also led me to the Pork Council magazine article attacking Wing's research.

34. Miller and Longest, "Reconciling Environmental Justice," 526.

35. Aman Azhar "Civil Rights Groups in North Carolina Say 'Biogas' from Hog Waste Will Harm Communities of Color," *Inside Climate News*, September 29, 2021, https:// insideclimatenews.org/news/29092021/north-carolina-biogas-environmental-justice/.

Chapter Six

1. Two other lakes in the Coastal Plain—Phelps and Mattamuskeet—are larger than Lake Waccamaw, but the two lakes do not have the same distinct shape and orientation as Carolina Bays, leading scientists to believe that they were likely created by large peat fires and not by the same process that created other Carolina Bays.

2. Lerch, *Waccamaw Legacy*, 31–47.

3. "High Water Level Terminology," National Weather Service, accessed November 28, 2021, https://www.weather.gov/aprfc/terminology.

4. "All of I-95 in NC Is Now Open after Flooding Closures from Hurricane Florence" *Citizen-Times*, September 24, 2018.

5. Photos and description of sewage infrastructure flooding can be found in a 2018 blog post by Riverkeeper, Forrest English, "Hurricane Florence Exposes Problems with Waste-water Infrastructure," Sound Rivers, accessed November 28, 2021, https://soundrivers.org /hurricane-florence-exposes-problems-with-wastewater-infrastructure/.

6. Dikes and levees both refer to earthen structures that protect low-lying areas from flooding. The terms are often used interchangeably in the United States. See the 2010 pamphlet, "So You Live behind a Levee," American Society of Civil Engineers, accessed November 28, 2021, https://www.lrh.usace.army.mil/Portals/38/docs/civil%20works /So%20You%20Live%20Behind%20a%20Levee.pdf.

7. In North Carolina, the clearest illustration of this phenomenon comes from the towns of Tarboro and Princeville, which face one another on opposing sides of the Tar River. Tarboro, a colonial town, sits on high ground northwest of the river. Princeville was founded after the Civil War by formerly enslaved African Americans on the low-lying side of the river opposite Tarboro. Princeville has struggled with repeated floods on the Tar River including floods after Hurricanes Matthew (2016) and Florence (2018). Nearly two decades before Hurricane Matthew, Hurricane Floyd (1999) also brought catastrophic flooding to Princeville and ele-vated the town's profile as well. As historian Victor Blue wrote soon after the 1999 flood, "Before Hurricane Floyd, the rest of the state and the nation knew little about Princeville and

its legacy. The drama of the flood changed that; everybody seems to be asking about the old black town now." See Blue, "Reclaiming Sacred Ground."

8. Toni Goodyear, "NCSCS To Utilize Computers in Jacob Swamp Dike Study," *The Robesonian*, July 20, 1973.

9. Construction began on the Jacob Swamp Dike project around 1974, but the project's specifications were likely finalized a few years beforehand. For the Lumbee River, the oldest scientific streamflow records (which are used to develop probabilities for floods of certain magnitudes) extend back to the 1920s. Planners likely would have developed specifications for the levee—specifically its maximum height—using only about forty years of streamflow data, which is the bare minimum that hydrologists recommend for these types of calculations.

10. Toni Goodyear, "NCSCS To Utilize Computers in Jacob Swamp Dike Study," *The Robesonian*, July 20, 1973.

11. "Armed with Boats and Air Mattresses, Cajun Navy Rescues 160 Trapped by Florence," ABC News, accessed December 6, 2021, https://abcnews.go.com/US/cajun-navy-mobilizes -volunteers-boats-carolinas-ahead-hurricane/story?id=57799162.

12. "Protect Yourself: Floodwaters Teem with Bacteria from Human and Animal Waste, Carcasses," *News & Observer*, September 20, 2018.

13. See September 19, 2018, press release by state officials, "NCDA&CS Moving into Communities to Assess Damage & Assist in Recovery," North Carolina Department of Agriculture & Consumer Services, accessed June 1, 2021, https://www.ncagr.gov/paffairs /release/2018/NCDACSmovingintocommunitiestoassessdamageassistinrecovery.htm.

14. "Florence's Floodwaters Breach Defenses at Duke Energy Plant, Sending Toxic Coal Ash into River," *New York Times*, September 21, 2018.

15. Details can be found in Niedermeyer et al., "Search for *Campylobacter* Spp."; Harris et al., "Microbial Contamination in Environmental Waters."

16. A popular chestnut, "the solution to pollution is dilution," expresses this idea in a way that simultaneously dismisses concerns about the dispersal of a contaminant and the total load (i.e., the mass or volume) of a contaminant that is flushed downstream. In practice, the expression often signals disinterest in critical engagement with issues related to water and air pollution.

17. Water scientists who work in this part of the world generally consider a "water year" to run from October 1 of one year to September 30 of the following year. The reason involves a combination of climatological and bureaucratic factors that are usually explained in introductory hydrology courses. Hurricane Matthew arrived in October 2016, which is the beginning of the 2017 water year, and Hurricane Florence arrived in September 2018, which was the end of the 2018 water year.

18. This is why, for example, hydrologists add one to the total number of years in their data record when they compute flood probabilities. Adding one year to the record is a way to acknowledge, mathematically, that the largest observed flood is never the largest possible flood.

19. Thie and Tart, "On the Front Lines."

20. Emanuel, "Climate Change in the Lumbee River Watershed."

21. Thie and Tart, "On the Front Lines."

22. Hsiang et al., "Estimating Economic Damage."

23. Specifically, Duke Energy's Charlotte headquarters is located in Mecklenburg County, and the state capital, Raleigh, is located in Wake County. These two counties were among North Carolina counties expected to see the least economic damages from climate change according to Hsiang et al., "Estimating Economic Damage."

24. Nixon, *Slow Violence*, 266.

25. One striking example was shared by Swinomish Nation's environmental director, Todd Mitchell, who gave an enlightening presentation at the Geological Society of America's 2017 annual meeting on the incorporation of culture into tribal wetland assessment efforts. In a talk entitled "Using Traditional Ecological Knowledge to Protect Wetlands, the Swinomish Tribe's Wetlands Cultural Assessment Project," Mitchell shared a powerful story about having to request permission from a major university to access information collected by academic researchers about his direct ancestors' cultural ties to certain plant species.

26. See the discussion in chapter 5 about the potential impacts of climate change on wastewater sprayfields.

27. Energy companies behind the Atlantic Coast Pipeline advertised heavily on the greenhouse gas advantages of natural gas over coal. There is compelling evidence, however, that natural gas from shale formations—which is the type of gas that energy companies in Virginia and North Carolina hope to exploit—is not as climate-friendly as companies advertise. In fact, once the full inventory of natural gas leaks is taken into account, this energy source has a very similar carbon footprint to coal over a twenty-year timespan. See Cooper, Stamford, and Azapagic, "Sustainability of UK Shale Gas."

28. Researchers and clean-energy advocates offer strong critiques against this method of emissions counting. One of the most interesting argument holds that the most climate-beneficial fate of swine-based methane is to burn it at the site of capture, because piping the methane into a regional network of pipelines and other infrastructure will result in fugitive emissions that would not occur if the gas were burned on-site. The same study also warned that the negative emissions scheme could also incentivize the creation of new methane sources (e.g., more swine lagoons) that could be captured for credit. See Grubert, "At Scale."

29. Miller and Longest, "Reconciling Environmental Justice."

30. Quote from Yeoman's article, "Poultry Waste Plant That Has Polluted in the Past Gets New Approval in Robeson County," *Border Belt Independent*, May 27, 2022.

31. There is some scholarly literature on carbon neutrality and environmental justice, and most of it warns about the kinds of unacknowledged consequences that I bring up in these examples. See, for example, Lejano, Kan, and Chau, "The Hidden Disequities of Carbon Trading."

Chapter Seven

1. "About the People," Coharie Tribe, accessed April 13, 2023, https://coharietribe.org/history/.

2. Historian Leo Schelbert gives a summary of archival evidence and scholarly analysis on cultural ties between Tuscarora and Neusiok peoples. Much of Schelbert's work focuses on the experiences of Swiss people in America, and his interest in the Coastal Plain stems from the Swiss. See Schelbert, "The Enmeshment of Five Worlds," 28.

3. If this image seems confusing, understand that North Carolinians call knitted winter hats *toboggans* and call winter sliding conveyances *sleds*.

4. Beginning in the 1880s, Lumbee ancestors received state funding to educate Native students in Robeson County. Lumbee teachers fanned out to work in Native schools in various parts of eastern North Carolina, but as a general rule, Lumbees did not allow students from outside Robeson County to attend their schools.

5. The Native community in Person County is now recognized as the Sappony Tribe. When the East Carolina Indian School operated, they were known by outsiders simply as *Person County Indians*. Even though they do not, technically, live in eastern North Carolina, Sappony people have social and family ties to Lumbee, Coharie, and other tribal communities in the east. For a personal account of the strong kinship ties between Sappony and eastern NC tribes (specifically Lumbee), see the memoir of Brooker, *Hot Dogs on the Road*.

6. Lawson, 213.

7. Greg's quote comes from a 2016 video created as a class project by environmental studies students, "A People and Their River: The Story of the Coharie Tribe and Their Connection to the Great Coharie River," UNC Chapel Hill, accessed July 2022, https://www.youtube.com/watch?v=ngpDvSyUgro

8. See Faircloth, "Ensuring American Indian Students," 28–29.

9. "History of SCC," Sampson Community College, accessed April 13, 2023, https://www.sampsoncc.edu/about/history/.

10. In any case, Coharie people claim all of this land as their ancestral territory from a time that predates colonial land claims.

11. Ironically, the governor's order included a nondiscrimination clause that required the tribe to comply with Title VI of the Civil Rights Act. Title VI prohibits racial and other forms of discrimination by institutions receiving government support. Of course, Coharie people complied, but the State of North Carolina's condition of nondiscrimination was ironic given the long (and recent) history of state-sanctioned discrimination against Coharies and other people of color.

12. Dugout canoes were stored underwater to prevent the wood from drying out and causing damage to the boat. See Stager, Fadden, and Wolf, "Dugout Canoes." And although I have not encountered any research on this topic, perhaps dugout canoes were also purposefully sunk at the end of their useful lives to improve fish habitat.

13. Minutes of the Provincial Council of Pennsylvania, 533.

14. This migration occurred at a time when Lumbee and Coharie people were collectively known as Croatans, and the place where they sojourned in Georgia is still called the *Croatan settlement*. The Croatans worked on the two-thousand-acre Wiregrass Plantation near the town of Claxton. Their settlement was abandoned around 1920, but the cemetery remains at the site. Lumbee and Coharie descendants have traveled to Georgia annually since the mid-1980s to maintain the cemetery and to do other work that preserves the memory of the Croatan settlement. Historian and Emory University PhD student Jessica Locklear is studying this topic and has shared about her experiences traveling with to the cemetery with her Lumbee kin. See https://twitter.com/JRMLocklear/status/1462894741666807820.

15. Stahle et al., "Longevity, Climate Sensitivity."

16. See Sampson County Register of Deeds, volume 1027, page 763.

17. Journalist John Murawski reported on this issue several years ago in "Lack of Mineral Rights Puts Some Homebuyers in Legal Limbo," *Winston-Salem Journal*, November 13, 2012.

18. The question of exactly which wetlands are regulated under the Clean Water Act has been open to debate for decades. In the 2000s, two US Supreme Court rulings, SWANCC v. US Army Corps of Engineers (2001) and Rapanos v. United States (2006), gave the US Army Corps of Engineers a much greater role than it previously held in determining which wetlands fell under the jurisdiction of the Clean Water Act. While *SWANCC* ruled that some wetlands were absolutely outside of federal jurisdiction under the Clean Water Act (specifically, wetlands that seemed to be geographically isolated from other jurisdictional waters but were still of interest to the federal government because they served as habitat for migratory birds), *Rapanos* created a situation in which Army Corps regulators made jurisdictional determinations on a case-by-case basis for many wetlands. No one actually knew whether more or fewer wetlands in the United States were protected after the *Rapanos* decision. The federal government spent several years attempting to clarify the nebulous jurisdictional standards created by *Rapanos* through a rule-making process. The process involved a thorough review of the scientific literature that culminated in the proposed Clean Water Rule, a 2015 regulation that was criticized as federal "overreach" by proponents of limited government. Ironically, the goal of the rule was to eliminate the need for federal involvement in every question of wetland jurisdiction. An extensive body of scholarship grew following *SWANCC* and *Rapanos*, mostly in the law and policy literature. For a perspective that incorporates hydrologic science and benefits from several years' distance from *Rapanos* and from the 2015 Clean Water Rule, see Jackson et al., "Redefining Waters of the US." For a more general look at the scientific basis for the Clean Water Rule, see the Executive Summary of the Environmental Protection Agency's 2015 review and synthesis report on 1,200 research articles covering this topic. Environmental Protection Agency, *Connectivity of Streams and Wetlands*.

19. For a general overview of the wetland credit and banking system in North Carolina and a discussion of the regulatory criteria and their changes through time, see Hill et al., "Compensatory Stream and Wetland Mitigation." For a broader overview of the mitigation banking market and its actors, see Doyle and BenDor, "Markets for Freshwater Ecosystem Services."

20. Often, restoration of former wetlands involves blocking or plugging old ditches and canals to prevent artificial drainage of the landscape, followed by replanting wetland-specific trees, shrubs, or grasses. Mitigation bank operators keep records of water levels and plant health to demonstrate that their restoration efforts are successful, and regulators allow the bank to sell credits once they are satisfied with the efforts. In North Carolina, credits had an initial value of about one dollar per square foot, or about $43,000 per acre. Buyers usually must find a mitigation bank in the same river basin where wetland impacts occur, so credit prices may vary by basin. Regulatory actions, development pressures, and natural landscape characteristics can all factor into the actual price of credits in any given basin. The general principles here also apply to restoration and mitigation banking for streams, except that credits are based on linear feet for streams instead of acres for wetlands. In my early years on faculty at North Carolina State University, the university operated mitigation banks for wetlands and streams on its massive (nearly 80,000 acre) forest in eastern North Carolina. See Andrews, "Hofmann Forest Wetland Mitigation Bank."

21. Regulators use a concept called *mitigation ratios* to place financial premiums on high-value wetlands. For example, a party that plans to drain or fill in a rare type of wetland may

have to purchase five or ten acres of mitigation credits per acre of wetland to be damaged or destroyed. The idea is that the high ratio will disincentivize the destruction and loss of rare or otherwise valuable wetlands. The underlying assumptions of this idea have received some scrutiny and criticism, with researchers questioning the effectiveness of mitigation ratios as a strategy to promote the national "no net loss" policy. See, in particular, BenDor, "A Dynamic."

22. The program is described in D'Ignazio et al., *North Carolina's Ecosystem Enhancement Program*.

23. For a review of "no net loss" policies globally, see zu Ermgassen et al., "The Ecological Outcomes."

24. D'Ignazio et al., *North Carolina's Ecosystem Enhancement Program*, 12.

25. Triangle J Council of Governments, *Great Coharie Creek Local Watershed Plan*.

26. Triangle J Council of Governments, 52.

27. Siurua, "Nature above People."

28. Some of these sensors can cost tens of thousands of dollars, consume large amounts of energy, and have high maintenance requirements.

29. In the mid-1990s, one of my early jobs involved maintaining hardware and software on an early version of the USGS real-time stream gaging network. The stations that I worked on communicated with the outside world via landline modems. The stations either connected to a server to upload their data, or—in the event of a flood or other threshold event—they transmitted a few basic pieces of information to a pager worn by USGS staff.

30. The full citation can be found in the Fall 2019 issue of the North Carolina Wildlife Federation Journal, "Water Conservationist of the Year," accessed on June 1, 2022, https://ncwf.org/wp-content/uploads/WEB-NCWF-Journal-FALL19.pdf.

31. "Preserving a Piece of Sampson," *Sampson Independent*, July 25, 2018.

32. "Preserving a Piece of Sampson."

Chapter Eight

1. For those who are curious, the North Carolina Language and Life Project at North Carolina State University has published educational resources on Lumbee English that include numerous recorded video and sound clips of Lumbee English as well as documentaries. See "Indian by Birth," North Carolina Language and Life Project, accessed June 1, 2022, https://languageandlife.org/documentaries/indian-by-birth/.

2. Dannenberg, "The Roots of Lumbee Language," 24.

3. I attended public schools in Charlotte between 1982 and 1995, a period that coincided with the height of Charlotte-Mecklenburg Schools' bus-based racial desegregation program. Personally, I view that period as a golden era for the school district, specifically because of its commitment to policies and programs aimed at unraveling the harms of Jim Crow segregation. As a student, I knew nothing other than one- to two-hour rides on school buses (each way) and considered it a normal part of the education experience. In return, my classrooms were microcosms of racial, ethnic, and cultural diversity that existed in few other places in the South. Many students and parents did not share my optimistic view of long bus rides, however, and busing-based integration in the county began to dissolve in the 1990s. In Charlotte and elsewhere, backlash against bus integration led to resegregation of schools

in ways that remapped preexisting structural inequities related to race and wealth. For a detailed discussion of desegregation and re-segregation of Charlotte-Mecklenburg Schools, see Ayscue et al., "School Segregation and Resegregation in Charlotte and Raleigh, 1989–2010."

4. During my early elementary school years, I often brought home official school forms for my parents to complete. Many of the forms requested demographic information, including whether students identified as "black," "white," or "other." As a young child I fixated on my own "othering" but later realized that the situation was not unique to Native American students. It turned out that Charlotte-Mecklenburg Schools had a practice of treating "other" students (including Asian, Latino, multiracial, and other racially minoritized students) as white for purposes of tracking the success of its desegregation plan. This administrative decision illustrates the widespread nature of binary thinking around race in the South during the 1980s. For additional details on this policy see Smith and Mickelson, "All That Glitters Is Not Gold."

5. The Indian Education Act followed on the heels of the Indian Civil Rights Act of 1968, and one of its key goals was to turn over control of federal Indian education programs and resources to Native peoples themselves. A key figure in the creation and implementation of the Act was Helen Maynor Scheirbeck, a Lumbee educator and policy expert who spent more than twenty years at the forefront of nearly every federal Indian education initiative. Scheirbeck directed the federal Office of Indian Education and helped launch a network of tribal colleges and universities. Decades earlier, Scheirbeck's father, Judge Lacy Maynor, tried the Ku Klux Klan leader whose instigations led up to the Battle of Hayes Pond in 1958. See Lowery, "In Memoriam: Helen Maynor Scheirbeck."

6. Author Tommy Orange writes about both the reluctancy and the authenticity of urban Native voices in the prologue to his novel *There There*. In particular, Orange highlights some of the charges leveled at urban Natives: "They used to call us sidewalk Indians. Called us citified, superficial, inauthentic, cultureless refugees, apples. An apple is red on the outside and white on the inside." Orange, *There There*, 20.

7. Malinda Maynor Lowery eloquently summarizes the Lumbee notion of returning home through a recounted conversation with a visitor who told her that Lumbees return home "because the blood of our ancestors is buried here." Maynor, *The Lumbee Indians*, 245.

8. Journalist Jane Palmer alluded to this concept in an article for the American Geophysical Union's monthly magazine that featured interviews with Indigenous water scientists. The scientists (myself included) shared different versions of this experience from their own research, teaching, and outreach programs. See "Water Wisdom: The Indigenous Scientists Walking in Two Worlds," *Eos*, November 22, 2021. "Two-eyed seeing" is a subtly different concept from "walking in two worlds" that begins to address the idea that Indigenous scholars inhabit two distinct identities. See Marshall, Marshall, and Bartlett, "Two-Eyed Seeing in Medicine."

9. I acknowledge that many tribal nations have, in fact, been violently separated from their homelands and have certainly persisted as distinct nations despite this separation. Other Indigenous peoples have lost their homelands to sea level rise, erosion, and other forms of degradation. These groups have important lessons to teach all of us about survival, adaptation, and flourishing in a changed world. As Kyle Whyte explains, the world is already post-apocalyptic and post-climate change for many Indigenous peoples. See Whyte, "Indigenous Climate Change Studies."

10. For example, Duke Energy, which continues to site natural gas transmission and storage infrastructure in Lumbee territory without free, prior, and informed consent of Lumbee people, has formal policies on both environmental justice and human rights. Both policies have been featured prominently on the company's website in recent years. Duke Energy has also published a table of corporate Human Rights Indicators based on metrics recommended by the Global Reporting Initiative, an international effort to standardize corporate sustainability reports. Between 2010 and 2022, Duke Energy reported "none known" under the "Indigenous Rights Violations" section of the table—despite multiple official statements in recent years from the Lumbee tribal government citing specific concerns about the company's practice of disregarding the core Indigenous Rights principle of free, prior, and informed consent in decisions about natural gas projects. Given media coverage of these issues as well as the presence of high-ranking corporate officials at some of the tribal council meetings where these issues have been discussed, it is unlikely that Duke Energy is unaware of the tribal government's concerns. Perhaps the company decided internally that the concerns did not qualify as Indigenous Rights issues or that the issues did not rise to the level of violations. Whatever the case, the disconnect between the company's "none known" response and the Lumbee government's opposite perception illustrates a common criticism around transparency and corporate self-reporting on Indigenous rights violations. Corporate sustainability and human rights expert Damiano de Felice summarizes this criticism as, "What appears as a good score ... would not derive from few adverse human rights impacts but from lack of transparency." de Felice, "Business and Human Rights Indicators," 541. For corporate policy statements and metrics, see "Engaging Communities through the Clean Energy Transition," Duke Energy, accessed June 1, 2022, https://news.duke-energy.com/our-perspective/engaging-communities-through-the-clean-energy-transition; "Duke Energy Human Rights Policy," Duke Energy, accessed April 14, 2023, https://p-cd.duke-energy.com/esg/-/media/pdfs/our-company/190797-human-rights-policy.pdf; and "Human Rights Indicators," Duke Energy, accessed July 27, 2021, https://www.duke-energy.com/our-company/sustainability/global-reporting-initiative-index/human-rights-indicators and April 14, 2023, https://web.archive.org/web/20160901000000*/http://www.duke-energy.com/sustainability/human-rights-indicators.asp.

11. This is not a novel statement, as Navajo scholar and nurse Timian Godfrey points out in a 2020 piece on health justice during the COVID-19 pandemic. Godfrey opens by reciting a litany of familiar phrases about health disparities in tribal communities in the United States and later asserts, "Only when we as a society *acknowledge* the injustice that has been inflicted upon Indigenous Peoples in this country, and strive to rectify centuries of wrongdoing, then will we start to progress towards health justice." Italics in the original. See "Health Justice Begins with ACKNOWLEDGMENT," *Johns Hopkins Nursing Magazine*, November 10, 2020.

12. See reporting by Rob Capriccioso, "The Obama Administration Now Supports UNDRIP—But That's Not Enough," *Indian Country Today*, June 30, 2011.

13. This quote is taken from a formal statement issued by the Lumbee Tribal Council, soon after the Council's health committee received a report on the destruction of archaeological sites during clear-cutting of a six-hundred-acre tract by Duke Energy's wholly owned subsidiary, Piedmont Natural Gas. Piedmont clear-cut the tract to build a liquified natural gas processing and storage facility in the Lumbee community of Wakulla. See

"CLLO-2020-0917-01: Tribal Consultation Mandate (September 17, 2020)," Lumbee Tribe of North Carolina, accessed April 13, 2023, https://www.lumbeetribe.com/_files/ugd /6ca8af_d3cdc22f37544948859cc206f2368e67.pdf.

14. See "Comments on Section 401 Certification Application for Construction of the Atlantic Coast Pipeline: August 18, 2017," Haliwa Saponi Tribe, accessed April 14, 2023, https://www.scribd.com/document/421499167/2017-Haliwa-Saponi-Comment-to-NC -DEQ-August-2017.

15. See articles 29 and 32 of UNDRIP, which cover the concept of free, prior, and informed consent as it pertains to development in present-day or traditional tribal territories. United Nations Declaration on the Rights of Indigenous Peoples (UNDRIP), Resolution 61/295, United Nations General Assembly, October 2, 2007, https://www.un.org/development /desa/indigenouspeoples/wp-content/uploads/sites/19/2018/11/UNDRIP_E_web.pdf.

16. Some of these perspectives are covered in Barry Yeoman's 2022 reporting on state permitting of a poultry waste incinerator in Lumberton, and Lisa Sorg has also covered some of these issues in reporting about the NC General Assembly's investigation of the Atlantic Coast Pipeline. In particular, a 2019 piece by Sorg mentions the General Assembly's use of a private investigation firm, Eagle Intel, which interviewed several state environmental officials and revealed a relative lack of knowledge and concern about environmental justice as a factor in decisions about environmental permitting in North Carolina. See Yeoman's reporting in "Poultry Waste Plant That Has Polluted in the Past Gets New Approval in Robeson County," *Border Belt Independent*, May 27, 2022. See also Sorg's reporting in "The Atlantic Coast Pipeline Investigation: Much Ado about . . . Something?," NC Policy Watch, accessed April 14, 2023, https://ncnewsline.com/briefs/the-atlantic-coast -pipeline-investigation-much-ado-about-something/.

17. Elsewhere, colleagues and I have raised the possibility that racial and socioeconomic disparities are emergent properties of complex systems of environmental governance. Maybe this statement is just a fancy rephrasing of the aphorism "Evil triumphs when good men do nothing," but at any rate, the assertion is ripe for further investigation. See Emanuel et al., "Natural Gas Gathering." See also "Fact Check - Edmund Burke Did Not Say Evil Triumphs When Good Men Do Nothing," Reuters, accessed April 13, 2023, https://www .reuters.com/article/factcheck-edmund-burke-quote-idUSL1N2PG1EY.

18. For example, when community groups asked state regulators in 2019 to examine the cumulative impacts of several natural gas transmission projects traversing Lumbee communities in Robeson County, a Duke Energy spokesperson dismissed the concerns about cumulative impacts of gas infrastructure as a "conspiracy theory that the Indigenous population in that area is specifically targeted." Lisa Sorg documented the corporate statement in "Several Members of Lumbee Tribe, Climate Coalition Ask DEQ to Revoke Atlantic Coast Pipeline Permit; EPA Proposes to Clamp down on States' Authority," NC Policy Watch, accessed April 14, 2023, https://ncnewsline.com/briefs/lumbee-indians-climate-coalition -ask-deq-to-revoke-atlantic-coast-pipeline-permit-epa-proposes-to-clamp-down-on-states -authority/.

19. In addition to the North Carolina Pork Council special report discussed in chapter 5, another prominent example comes from a case before the Fourth Circuit Court of Appeals that examined Virginia's state-issued air permit for a compressor station along the proposed Atlantic Coast Pipeline route in the predominantly African American community of Union

Hill, Virginia. During oral arguments, an attorney representing the pipeline developers told judges, "If you draw your circle small enough, there's always going to be a disproportionate impact." In this case, the attorney attempted to argue that the alleged racial disparity introduced by the proposed compressor station was an artifact of the method used to delineate the impacted population (i.e., the chosen radius of a circle drawn around the facility determined the size of the disparity). Mathematically speaking, the attorney's statement could only be true if the facility were sited in the center of a racially marginalized population. Even though this situation described Union Hill and the compressor station with reasonable accuracy, I am not convinced that the attorney realized he was proposing a mathematical argument against his client's interests. Michael Martz reported on the hearing in "Under Questioning by 4th Circuit at Pipeline Hearing, State Concedes Union Hill's Racial Status," *Richmond Times-Dispatch*, October 29, 2019.

20. As one example, Duke Energy claimed that the Atlantic Coast Pipeline would "help restore social justice" to impacted communities in response to a 2018 civil rights complaint filed with the EPA on behalf of some of those communities. See "Atlantic Coast Pipeline Opponents Say State Ignored Minorities' Civil Rights," *News & Observer*, May 15, 2018.

21. The 1987 study on race and toxic waste conducted by the United Church of Christ's Commission for Racial Justice—a foundational report in the development of environmental justice policies in the United States—warns specifically against offering economic incentives to mitigate opposition to polluting facilities. The report warns that these incentives "raise disturbing social policy questions." See Commission for Racial Justice, *Toxic Wastes and Race in the United States*, xii. Environmental justice activist and policy advisor Charles Lee fleshes out this idea in less ambiguous terms when he notes that economic incentives, wielded as policy solutions to mitigate harm inflicted on overburdened communities, leave "considerable room for potential discrimination and racist exploitation." See Lee, "Beyond Toxic Wastes and Race," 44. Lastly, David Wilkins and I discuss how economic incentives (e.g., promises of job creation) bolster power imbalances that limit tribal nations' participation in environmental governance. See Emanuel and Wilkins, "Breaching Barriers."

22. David Wilkins and I discuss these power dynamics in greater detail as they relate to barriers to tribal participation in environmental governance. Emanuel and Wilkins, "Breaching Barriers."

23. In the case of tribal nations, UNDRIP also speaks into this space by affirming that decisions by Indigenous communities should be made without coercion, subterfuge, or other pressures. This is central tenet of the principle of free, prior, and informed consent.

24. In the Coastal Plain, these harms include pursuing development actions that damage or destroy cultural landscapes, attempting to buy or acquiescence from tribal governments, and bolstering colonial myths that Indigenous peoples were "driven out" of their homelands centuries ago. In addition to chapter 4 of this book, you can find a detailed analysis of these actions and a graphical timeline in Emanuel and Wilkins, "Breaching Barriers."

25. An attorney for a large energy company once told me that corporate stances on environmental justice were weak because environmental justice was only an executive order—with emphasis on the word *only*. A conclusion one could draw from this conversation is that companies—or at least this company—will not take environmental justice seriously until it is required by law to do so. However, there are existing legal strategies that currently

aim to uphold environmental justice through Title VI of the Civil Rights Act, through the Administrative Procedures Act, or through state laws.

26. Presently, there is little indication that efforts to recruit Indigenous people into the corporate workforce actually trickle up to the level of executives and key decision-makers. As a result, the senior leadership and boards of directors for major livestock companies, energy utilities, and other polluters in the Coastal Plain do not share the perspectives and life experiences of Indigenous peoples and others who shoulder the environmental burdens created by these companies.

27. The Dakota Access Pipeline may be the most widely known example of this practice. See, for example, Whyte, "The Dakota Access Pipeline."

28. Elsewhere, I discuss some of the ways that federal recognition supports environmental governance. See Emanuel, "Climate Change in the Lumbee River Watershed."

29. See "CLLO-2020-0917-01: Tribal Consultation Mandate (September 17, 2020)," Lumbee Tribe of North Carolina, accessed April 13, 2023, https://www.lumbeetribe.com/_files/ugd/6ca8af_d3cdc22f37544948859cc206f2368e67.pdf.

30. Jeffries, "Whole Indian," 105.

31. By *ambiguity that hinders effort*, I mean confusion (or ignorance) over protocols and expectations to the extent that it prevents meaningful interaction. Some examples that I have witnessed in North Carolina alone include confusion over different definitions of consultation held by state agencies and tribal governments, attempts to engage with the wrong official or branch of government, and even clerical errors such as addressing critical paperwork to nonexistent individuals.

32. See "What Is a National Heritage Area?," National Park Service, accessed June 20, 2022, https://www.nps.gov/articles/what-is-a-national-heritage-area.htm. Note also that fifty-five National Heritage Areas already exist throughout the United States, including two in North Carolina.

33. Some of the opportunities and challenges that come with designating a new National Heritage Area are described in a report by the Congressional Research Service. See DeSantis, *Heritage Areas*, 11–13.

34. The quote in the main text comes from a pre-election commentary by Domenico Montanaro of National Public Radio that captured the general feeling among US voters and political observers that the 2020 election would be the "most consequential" of a lifetime. See "The Most Consequential Election in A Lifetime (And This Time They Mean It)," National Public Radio, accessed June 30, 2022, https://www.npr.org/2020/11/02/930077437/the-most-consequential-election-in-a-lifetime-and-this-time-they-mean-it. However, in light of North Carolina's exceptional turnout (75 percent of registered voters), the severity of Robeson County's underperformance (62 percent turnout of registered voters) is astonishing, and so is the sub-60 percent turnout Native American voters in Robeson County. (Note that tribal affiliation is not recorded in voter registration or turnout data, so I use race here as a proxy for Lumbee identity with the understanding that most but not all non-Hispanic Native Americans in Robeson County identify as Lumbee.) In particular, of more than 26,500 Native Americans registered to vote in Robeson County, fewer than 16,000 actually turned out to vote in the 2020 election. These numbers look even bleaker when viewed alongside figures from the US Census, which indicate that 33,487 voting-age Native Americans lived in Robeson County at the time—meaning that only 47 percent of

Native American adults in Robeson County voted in the 2020 election. More than 20,000 of Donald Trump's 27,806 votes in Robeson County (nearly 75 percent) came from precincts with only a small fraction of Native American voters. County-wide, it is likely that many more non-Native voters than Native American voters supported Trump during the 2020 election. And the overall Presidential vote count in Robeson County—nearly 49,000 votes cast (27,806 votes for Trump and 19,020 votes for Biden)—makes it clear that non-Lumbee voters outnumbered Lumbee voters by a margin of about two to one. Nevertheless, political commentators seized the opportunity to frame Trump's 9,000-vote margin as a story of Lumbees buoying Trump in Robeson County, if not North Carolina as whole. Some pundits linked Trump's Robeson County performance to enthusiastic support among Lumbees after a fall campaign rally in Robeson County and a nominal statement of support for amending the 1956 Lumbee Act to grant the Lumbee Tribe full federal recognition. For example, right after the election, Eric Garcia—journalist, author, and political observer—tweeted from his personal account (@EricMGarcia), "One reason why Trump does so well with the Lumbee tribe? He's pledged to federally recognize the tribe and sign legislation to do so." See https://twitter.com/EricMGarcia/status/1324389675612688385. A few weeks later, journalist Michael Kruse published an in-depth analysis on Lumbee voters and concluded that Lumbees were the "linchpin" in Trump's Robeson County victory. See "How Trump Won One of America's Most Diverse Counties—By a Lot," Politico, accessed January 10, 2021, https://www.politico.com/news/magazine/2020/12/10/robeson-county-rural-rainbow-coalition-north-carolina-trump-republicans-443978. Garcia and Kruse, like many other commentators, overlooked two key points: First, Donald Trump enjoyed a base of support among Lumbees that predated the 2020 presidential campaign by years—support for Trump among Lumbees emerged early during the 2016 presidential campaign (four years earlier) and was evident in the November 2016 election results for Robeson County. Some political commentators and analysts acknowledge Trump's strong performance in Robeson County during 2016, but most treat Trump's 2020 campaign promise and visit as pivotal to winning large numbers of Lumbee votes. Second, commentators overlooked Lumbee tendencies not to register or vote at especially high rates, instead treating Lumbees as a 60,000-person voting bloc when—political diversity within the community aside—only a small fraction of that number votes with any regularity in Robeson County. Because of low voter registration and turnout among Native Americans, the math does not support efforts by commentators to center Trump's victory in Robeson County on Lumbee voting behavior. All partisan arguments aside, attempts to peg Lumbee voting behavior on Trump's 2020 campaign promises or Robeson County rally are demeaning, because they paint Lumbee people as gullible to political pandering around federal recognition, when in reality Lumbees—for the most part—have expressed cynicism for decades on politicians' promises concerning federal recognition. Note that voter statistics were taken from the following sources: "N.C. Voter Statistics 2020 General Election: Updated Version April 16, 2021," North Carolina State Board of Elections, accessed June 1, 2022, https://www.ncsbe.gov/results-data/voter-turnout/2020-general-election-turnout; "Turnout in 2020 Election Spiked among Both Democratic and Republican Voting Groups, New Census Data Shows," Brookings Institution, accessed June 1, 2022, https://www.brookings.edu/research/turnout-in-2020-spiked-among-both-democratic-and-republican-voting-groups-new-census-data-shows/; and "US Census Bureau 2020 Redistricting Data

PL 94–171, Table P3, 'Race for the Population 18 Years and Over' in Robeson County, NC," US Census Bureau, accessed June 1, 2022, https://data.census.gov/cedsci/table?g =0500000US37155&y=2020&d=DEC%20Redistricting%20Data%20%28PL%2094–171%29&tid=DECENNIALPL2020.P3.

35. "Rosa Revels Winfree Obituary (1938–2017)," *Charlotte Observer*, June 14, 2017.

Conclusion

1. Statistically rigorous support for this statement comes from Emanuel et al., "Natural Gas Gathering and Transmission Pipelines and Social Vulnerability in the United States."

2. "Wuskitahkamik Miyai: Intersection of Worlds," University of North Carolina at Pembroke, accessed April 30, 2022, https://www.uncp.edu/resources/museum-southeast -american-indian/museum-exhibits/wuskitahkamik-miyai-intersection-worlds.

Bibliography

Primary Sources

ARCHIVES AND RECORDS

Albemarle County Papers, 1678–1714. State Archives of North Carolina. https://digital
.ncdcr.gov/digital/collection/p15012coll11/id/2045/rec/1.
Costo Papers (Rupert and Jeannette Costo). Special Collections and Archives. University
of California, Riverside.
Executive Journals of the Council of Colonial Virginia. Virginia State Library. https://
archive.org/details/executivejournal_co3virg/.
Lumbee Oral History Collection. Samuel Proctor Oral History Program. Department of
History, University of Florida. https://ufdc.ufl.edu/UF00006995/00001.
Minutes of the Provincial Council of Pennsylvania, from the Organization to the
Termination of the Proprietary Government. Pennsylvania State University. https://
catalog.hathitrust.org/Record/008003060.
Vine Deloria Papers. Yale Collection of Western Americana, Beinecke Rare Book and
Manuscript Library. Yale University.

PERIODICALS

Border Belt Independent (Whiteville, NC)
Carolina Indian Voice (Pembroke, NC)
Charlotte Observer
Cherokee One Feather (Cherokee, NC)
Citizen-Times (Asheville, NC)
Daily Times-News (Burlington, NC)
Eos (Washington, DC)
Evening Chronicle (Charlotte, NC)
Globe-Times (Amarillo, TX)
High Country News (Paonia, CO)
Indian Country Today (Phoenix, AZ)
Inside Climate News (Brooklyn, NY)
Johns Hopkins Nursing Magazine
(Baltimore, MD)
Nelson County Times (Lovingston, VA)
New Republic (New York)
New Yorker
New York Times
News & Observer (Raleigh, NC)

News Leader (Staunton, VA)
North-Carolina Star (Raleigh, NC)
Orlando Sentinel
Pittsburgh Post-Gazette (Pittsburgh, PA)
Richmond Times-Dispatch
The Robesonian (Lumberton, NC)
Rocky Mount Telegram (Rocky Mount, NC)
Sampson Independent (Clinton, NC)
Scientific American (New York)
Times-Picayune (New Orleans, LA)
Virginian-Pilot (Norfolk, VA)
Wall Street Journal
Washington Post
Weekly Observer (Fayetteville, NC)
Weekly Raleigh Register
Weekly Standard (Raleigh, NC)
Wilmington Morning Star (Wilmington, NC)
Winston-Salem Journal

BOOKS, MANUSCRIPTS, AND DIARIES

Barnwell, John. "Journal of John Barnwell." Reprint. *The Virginia Magazine of History and Biography* 5 no. 4 (1898), 391–402.

Brooker, Lena Epps. *Hot Dogs on the Road: An American Indian Girl's Reflections on Growing Up Brown in a Black and White World.* Columbia, SC: Lena Epps Brooker, 2017.

Green, Paul. *The Lost Colony: A Symphonic Drama of American History.* Reprint, Chapel Hill: University of North Carolina Press, 2014.

Hariot, Thomas. *A Brief and True Report of the New Found Land of Virginia.* Reprint, New York: Dover Publications, Inc., 1972.

Kaczorowski, Raymond T. *The Carolina Bays: A Comparison with Modern Lakes.* Coastal Research Division, Department of Geology, University of South Carolina, 1977.

Lawson, John, *A New Voyage to Carolina; Containing the Exact Description and Natural History of That Country: Together with the Present State Thereof. And a Journal of a Thousand Miles, Travel'd Thro' Several Nations of Indians. Giving a Particular Account of Their Customs, Manners, &c.* London, 1709. https://docsouth.unc.edu/nc/lawson/lawson.html.

McMillan, Hamilton. *Sir Walter Raleigh's Lost Colony. An Historical Sketch of the Attempts of Sir Walter Raleigh to Establish a Colony in Virginia, with the Traditions of an Indian Tribe in North Carolina. Indicating the Fate of the Colony of Englishmen Left on Roanoke Island in 1587.* Wilson, North Carolina: Advance Presses, 1888.

Orange, Tommy. *There There: A Novel.* Vintage: New York, 2014.

REPORTS

Advisory Council on Historic Preservation. *Guide to Working with Non-Federally Recognized Tribes in the Section 106 Process.* Washington: Advisory Council on Historic Preservation, 2017.

Commission for Racial Justice. *Toxic Wastes and Race in the United States: A National Report on the Racial and Socio-Economic Characteristics of Communities with Hazardous Waste Sites.* New York: United Church of Christ, 1987.

DeSantis, Mark K. *Heritage Areas: Background, Proposals, and Current Issues—Report RL33462.* Congressional Research Service: Washington, 2021.

D'Ignacio, Janet, Kathryn McDermott, Bill Gilmore, and Chris Russo. *North Carolina's Ecosystem Enhancement Program: Mitigation for the Future.* Transportation Research Board, Task Force on Ecology and Transportation, 2005 Transportation Research Board Annual Meeting, 2004.

Dominion Energy. *2018 Sustainability & Corporate Responsibility Report.* 2018. https://www.responsibilityreports.com/HostedData/ResponsibilityReportArchive/d/NYSE_D_2018.pdf.

Duke Energy. *Connected: 2014 Sustainability Report.* April 17, 2015. https://p-cd.duke-energy.com/esg/-/media/pdfs/our-company/esg-archive/2014-duke-energy-sustainability-report-complete.pdf.

———. *Bringing the Future to Light: 2016 Sustainability Report.* April 7, 2017. https://www.responsibilityreports.com/HostedData/ResponsibilityReportArchive/d/NYSE_DUK_2016.pdf.

Environmental Protection Agency. *Connectivity of Streams and Wetlands to Downstream Waters: A Review and Synthesis of the Scientific Evidence (Final Report).* EPA/600/R-14/475F. Washington: Office of Research and Development, 2015.

Federal Energy Regulatory Commission *Draft Environmental Impact Statement - Atlantic Coast Pipeline and Supply Header Project.* Washington: Office of Energy Projects, 2016.

———. *Final Environmental Impact Statement—Atlantic Coast Pipeline and Supply Header Project.* Washington: Office of Energy Projects, 2017.

National Environmental Justice Advisory Council. *Guide on Consultation and Collaboration with Indian Tribal Governments and the Public Participation of Indigenous Groups and Tribal Members in Environmental Decision Making.* Washington: Environmental Protection Agency, 2000.

Pearmain, John. *Report of John Pearmain, Assistant Regional Specialist—Indian Rehabilitation Division Resettlement Administrations—on Conditions of the Indians of Robeson County, North Carolina.* File 64190-1935-066-General Services. Washington: National Archives and Records Administration, 1935.

Triangle J Council of Governments. *Great Coharie Creek Local Watershed Plan.* Raleigh: North Carolina Ecosystem Enhancement Program, 2014.

Secondary Sources

BOOKS

Boughman, Arvis Locklear, and Loretta O. Oxendine. *Herbal Remedies of the Lumbee Indians.* Jefferson, North Carolina: McFarland, 2003.

Deloria, Vine. *Custer Died for Your Sins: An Indian Manifesto.* Norman: University of Oklahoma Press, 1969.

———. *Spirit and Reason: The Vine Deloria, Jr. Reader.* Denver: Fulcrum Books, 1999.

———. *We Talk, You Listen: New Tribes, New Turf.* Lincoln: University of Nebraska Press, 2007.

Dial, Adolph L., and David K. Eliades. *The Only Land I Know: A History of the Lumbee Indians.* San Francisco: The Indian Historian Press, 1975.

Dowie, Mark. *The Haida Gwaii Lesson: A Strategic Playbook for Indigenous Sovereignty.* Oakland, California: Inkshares, 2017.

Dunbar-Ortiz, Roxanne. *An Indigenous Peoples' History of the United States.* Boston: Beacon Press, 2014.

Estes, Nick. *Our History Is the Future: Standing Rock Versus the Dakota Access Pipeline, and the Long Tradition of Indigenous Resistance.* New York: Verso Books, 2019.

Evans, William M. *To Die Game: The Story of the Lowry Band, Indian Guerillas of Reconstruction.* Baton Rouge: Louisiana State University Press, 1971.

Gallay, Alan. *The Indian Slave Trade: The Rise of the English Empire in the American South, 1670–1717.* New Haven: Yale University Press, 2002.

Garrow, Patrick. *The Mattamuskeet Documents: A Study in Social History.* Raleigh: North Carolina Department of Cultural Resources, 1975.

Gilio-Whitaker, Dina. *As Long as Grass Grows: The Indigenous Fight for Environmental Justice, from Colonization to Standing Rock.* Boston: Beacon Press, 2019.

Goreham, Steve. *The Mad, Mad, Mad World of Climatism: Mankind and Climate Change Mania*. New Lenox, IL: New Lenox Books, 2012.

La Vere, David. *The Tuscarora War: Indians, Settlers, and the Fight for the Carolina Colonies*. Chapel Hill: University of North Carolina Press, 2013.

Lerch, Patricia Barker. *Waccamaw Legacy: Contemporary Indians Fight for Survival*. Tuscaloosa: University of Alabama Press, 2004.

Lowery, Malinda Maynor. *The Lumbee Indians: An American Struggle*. Chapel Hill: University of North Carolina Press, 2018.

———. *Lumbee Indians in the Jim Crow South: Race, Identity, and the Making of a Nation*. Chapel Hill: University of North Carolina Press, 2010.

Merrell, James. *The Indians' New World: Catawbas and Their Neighbors from European Contact through the Era of Removal*. Chapel Hill: University of North Carolina Press, 2010.

Morgan, Edmund S. *American Slavery, American Freedom*. New York: W. W. Norton & Company, 2003.

Nixon, Rob. *Slow Violence and the Environmentalism of the Poor*. Cambridge, MA: Harvard University Press, 2011.

Oberg, Michael Leroy. *The Head in Edward Nugent's Hand: Roanoke's Forgotten Indians*. Philadelphia: University of Pennsylvania Press, 2008.

Perdue, Theda. *Native Carolinians: The Indians of North Carolina*. Raleigh: North Carolina Department of Cultural Resources, Division of Archives and History, 1985.

Ridgely, J. V. *Nineteenth-Century Southern Literature*. Lexington: University Press of Kentucky, 1980.

Schlosberg, David. *Defining Environmental Justice*. Oxford: Oxford University Press, 2007.

Sloane, Kim. *A New World: England's First View of America*. Chapel Hill: University of North Carolina Press, 2007.

Smith, Joseph Michael, and Lula Jane Smith. *The Lumbee Methodists: Getting to Know Them, a Folk History*. Raleigh: Commission of Archives and History, North Carolina Methodist Conference, 1990.

Wallace, Anthony F. C. *Tuscarora: A History*. Albany, SUNY Press, 2012.

Ward, H. Trawick, and R. P. Stephen Davis. *Time before History: The Archaeology of North Carolina*. Chapel Hill: University of North Carolina Press, 1999.

JOURNAL ARTICLES AND DISSERTATIONS

Allen, Barbara L. "Cradle of a Revolution?: The Industrial Transformation of Louisiana's Lower Mississippi River." *Technology and Culture* 47, no. 1 (2006): 112–19.

Alvarez, Ramón A., Daniel Zavala-Araiza, David R. Lyon, David T. Allen, Zachary R. Barkley, Adam R. Brandt, Kenneth J. Davis, Scott C. Herndon, Daniel J. Jacob, and Anna Karion. "Assessment of Methane Emissions from the US Oil and Gas Supply Chain." *Science* 361, no. 6398 (2018): 186–88.

Andrews, Richard. "Hofmann Forest Wetland Mitigation Bank Restoration Plans Versions 1, 2 and 3." Master of Natural Resources Professional Papers, North Carolina State University, 2009.

Arnstein, Sherry R. "A Ladder of Citizen Participation." *Journal of the American Planning Association* 35, no. 4 (1969): 216–24.

Ayscue J. B., G. Siegel-Hawley, J. Kucsera, and B. Woodward. "School Segregation and Resegregation in Charlotte and Raleigh, 1989–2010." *Educational Policy* 32, no. 1 (2018): 3–54.

Bell, Jessica R., and Hampden Macbeth. "Putting the Public Back into Public Convenience and Necessity in Natural Gas Pipeline Certificates." *Natural Resources & Environment* 36, no. 4 (2022), 1–4.

BenDor, Todd. "A Dynamic Analysis of the Wetland Mitigation Process and Its Effects on No Net Loss Policy." *Landscape and Urban Planning* 89, no. 1 (2009): 17–27.

Bennett, K. D., and J. Provan. "What Do We Mean by 'Refugia'?" *Quaternary Science Reviews, Ice Age Refugia and Quaternary Extinctions: An Issue of Quaternary Evolutionary Palaeoecology* 27, no. 27 (2008): 2449–55.

Blue, Victor E. "Reclaiming Sacred Ground: How Princeville Is Recovering from the Flood of 1999." *NC Crossroads* 4, no. 3 (2000).

Brayboy, Bryan McKinley Jones. "Toward a Tribal Critical Race Theory in Education." *The Urban Review* 37, no. 5 (2006): 425–46.

Bowen, Sarah, Sinikka Elliott, and Annie Hardison-Moody. "The Structural Roots of Food Insecurity: How Racism Is a Fundamental Cause of Food Insecurity." *Sociology Compass* 15, no. 7 (2021): e12846.

Brown, Jovana J. "Treaty Rights: Twenty Years after the Boldt Decision." *Wicazo Sa Review* 10, no. 2 (1994): 1–16.

Bullard, Robert D. "Dismantling Environmental Racism in the USA." *Local Environment* 4, no. 1 (1999): 5–19.

———. "Environmental Justice for All: It's the Right Thing to Do." *Journal of Environmental Law and Litigation* 9 (1994): 281–308.

———. "Environmental Justice in the 21st Century: Race Still Matters." *Phylon* 49, no. 3/4 (2001): 151–71.

Bullard, Robert D., Paul Mohai, Robin Saha, and Beverly Wright. "Toxic Wastes and Race at Twenty: Why Race Still Matters after All of These Years." *Environmental Law* 38 no. 2 (2008): 371–411.

Calhoun, W. Reid, and Kristen K. Cecala. "At the Expense of the Environment: Economic and Regulatory Factors Impacting the Location and Management of Concentrated Animal Feeding Operations (CAFOs) in North Carolina." *Case Studies in the Environment* 5, no. 1 (2021): 1428433.

Champagne, Duane. "UNDRIP (United Nations Declaration on the Rights of Indigenous Peoples): Human, Civil, and Indigenous Rights." *Wicazo Sa Review* 28, no. 1 (2013): 9–22.

Christenson, Elizabeth C., and Marc L. Serre. "Integrating Remote Sensing with Nutrient Management Plans to Calculate Nitrogen Parameters for Swine CAFOs at the Sprayfield and Sub-Watershed Scales." *Science of the Total Environment* 580 (2017): 865–72.

Cooper, Jasmin, Laurence Stamford, and Adisa Azapagic. "Sustainability of UK Shale Gas in Comparison with Other Electricity Options: Current Situation and Future Scenarios." *Science of The Total Environment* 619 (2018): 804–14.

Cronon, William. "The Trouble with Wilderness: Or, Getting Back to the Wrong Nature." *Environmental History* 1, no. 1 (1996): 7–28.

Currie, Jefferson II. "Laying the Foundation: American Indian Education in North Carolina." *Tar Heel Junior Historian* Fall Issue (2005): 9.

Dannenberg, Clare J. "The Roots of Lumbee Language." *The Publication of the American Dialect Society* 87, no. 1 (2002): 9–35.

De Felice, Damiano. "Business and Human Rights Indicators to Measure the Corporate Responsibility to Respect: Challenges and Opportunities." *Human Rights Quarterly* 37, no. 2 (2015): 511–55.

Delborne, Jason A., Dresden Hasala, Aubrey Wigner, and Abby Kinchy. "Dueling Metaphors, Fueling Futures: 'Bridge Fuel' Visions of Coal and Natural Gas in the United States." *Energy Research & Social Science* 61 no. 101350 (2020): 1–10.

Emanuel, Ryan E. "Climate Change in the Lumbee River Watershed and Potential Impacts on the Lumbee Tribe of North Carolina." *Journal of Contemporary Water Research & Education* 163, no. 1 (2018): 79–93.

———. "Flawed Environmental Justice Analyses." *Science* 357, no. 6348 (2017): 260.

———. "Water in the Lumbee World: A River and Its People in a Time of Change." *Environmental History* 24, no. 1 (2019): 25–51.

Emanuel, Ryan E., Martina A. Caretta, Louie Rivers III, and Pavithra Vasudevan. "Natural Gas Gathering and Transmission Pipelines and Social Vulnerability in the United States." *GeoHealth* 5, no. 6 (2021): 1–12.

Emanuel, Ryan E., and David E. Wilkins. "Breaching Barriers: The Fight for Indigenous Participation in Water Governance." *Water* 12, no. 8 (2020): 1–37.

Emanuel, Ryan E., and Karen Dial Bird. "Stories We Tell: Unpacking Extractive Research and Its Legacy of Harm to Lumbee People." *Southern Cultures* 28, no. 3 (2022): 48–69.

Evans-Campbell, Teresa. "Historical Trauma in American Indian/Native Alaska Communities: A Multilevel Framework for Exploring Impacts on Individuals, Families, and Communities." *Journal of Interpersonal Violence* 23, no. 3 (2008): 316–38.

Ewing, Rebecca. "Pipeline Companies Target Small Farmers and Use Eminent Domain for Private Gain." *North Carolina Central Law Review* 38 (2016): 125–41.

Faircloth, Susan C. "Ensuring American Indian Students Receive an Equitable, Just, and Appropriate Education: A Matter of Personal and Professional Concern." *American Educator* 44, no. 4 (2021): 28–40.

Feeley, Stephen. "Tuscarora Trails: Indian Migrations, War, and Constructions of Colonial Frontiers." PhD diss., College of William & Mary, 2007.

Fibiger, Thomas. "Heritage Erasure and Heritage Transformation: How Heritage Is Created by Destruction in Bahrain." *International Journal of Heritage Studies* 21, no. 4 (2015): 390–404.

Finley-Brook, Mary, Travis L. Williams, Judi Anne Caron-Sheppard, and Mary Kathleen Jaromin. "Critical Energy Justice in US Natural Gas Infrastructuring." *Energy Research & Social Science* 41 (2018): 176–90.

Gilio-Whitaker, Dina. "Idle No More and Fourth World Social Movements in the New Millennium." *South Atlantic Quarterly* 114, no. 4 (2015): 866–77.

Grubert, Emily. "At Scale, Renewable Natural Gas Systems Could Be Climate Intensive: The Influence of Methane Feedstock and Leakage Rates." *Environmental Research Letters* 15, no. 8 (2020): 084041.

Hailu, Meseret, and Amanda Tachine. "Black and Indigenous Theoretical Considerations for Higher Education Sustainability." *Journal of Comparative & International Higher Education* 13 (2021): 20–42.

Harris, Angela R., Emine N. Fidan, Natalie G. Nelson, Ryan E. Emanuel, Theo Jass, Sophia Kathariou, Jeffrey Niedermeyer, et al. "Microbial Contamination in Environmental Waters of Rural and Agriculturally-Dominated Landscapes Following Hurricane Florence." *Environmental Science & Technology, Water* 1, no. 9 (2021): 2012–19.

Harrison, Emily E. "Odor in the Court! And It Smells like Environmental Racism: How Big Pork Is Legally Abusing Poor Communities of Color in Eastern North Carolina." *Wake Forest Journal of Law & Policy* 11 (2021): 433–50.

Hill, Richard W., and Daniel Coleman. "The Two Row Wampum-Covenant Chain Tradition as a Guide for Indigenous-University Research Partnerships." *Cultural Studies* ↔ *Critical Methodologies* 19, no. 5 (2019): 339–59.

Hill, Tammy, Eric Kulz, Breda Munoz, and John R. Dorney. "Compensatory Stream and Wetland Mitigation in North Carolina: An Evaluation of Regulatory Success." *Environmental Management* 51 (2013): 1077–91.

Hirschberger, Gilad. "Collective Trauma and the Social Construction of Meaning." *Frontiers in Psychology* 9, 1441 (2018): 1–14.

Hite, Timothy Blake. "'Whoz Ya People?': Defining Lumbee Citizenship and Belonging in the 21st Century." Master's thesis, University of South Carolina, 2022.

Hsiang, Solomon, Robert Kopp, Amir Jina, James Rising, Michael Delgado, Shashank Mohan, D. J. Rasmussen, et al. "Estimating Economic Damage from Climate Change in the United States." *Science* 356, no. 6345 (2017): 1362–69.

Jackson, C. Rhett, Caleb Sytsma, Lori A. Sutter, and Darold P. Batzer. "Redefining Waters of the US: A Case Study from the Edge of the Okefenokee Swamp." *Wetlands* 41, no. 8 (2021): 1–10.

Jeffries, Marshall. "Whole Indian: Racism, Resistance, and (Re)Membering Turtle Island." PhD diss., Georgia State University, 2018.

Jennings, Francis. "The Indian Trade of the Susquehanna Valley." *Proceedings of the American Philosophical Society* 110, no. 6 (1966): 406–24.

Johnson, Veronica E., Kevin L. Nadal, D. R. Gina Sissoko, and Rukiya King. "'It's Not in Your Head': Gaslighting, 'Splaining, Victim Blaming, and Other Harmful Reactions to Microaggressions." *Perspectives on Psychological Science* 16, no. 5 (2021): 1024–36.

Kimmerer, Robin Wall, and Frank Kanawha Lake. "The Role of Indigenous Burning in Land Management." *Journal of Forestry* 99, no. 11 (2001): 36–41.

King, Joyce Tekahnawiiaks. "The Value of Water and the Meaning of Water Law for the Native Americans Known as the Haudenosaunee." *Cornell Journal of Law and Public Policy* 16, no. 3 (2007): 449–72.

Knick, Stanley. "Because It Is Right." *Native South* 1, no. 1 (2008): 80–89.

Langdon, Sarah E., Shannon L. Golden, Elizabeth Mayfield Arnold, Rhonda F. Maynor, Alfred Bryant, V. Kay Freeman, and Ronny A. Bell. "Lessons Learned from a Community-Based Participatory Research Mental Health Promotion Program for American Indian Youth." *Health Promotion Practice* 17, no. 3 (2016): 457–63.

Lejano, Raul P., Wing Shan Kan, and Ching Chit Chau. "The Hidden Disequities of Carbon Trading: Carbon Emissions, Air Toxics, and Environmental Justice." *Frontiers in Environmental Science* 8 (2020): 1–6.

Lemly, Dennis A. "Damage Cost of the Dan River Coal Ash Spill." *Environmental Pollution* 197 (2015): 55–61.

Link, Bruce G., and Jo Phelan. "Social Conditions as Fundamental Causes of Disease." *Journal of Health and Social Behavior*. Extra Issue (1995): 80–94.

Lopez, Julisa J., Arianne E. Eason, and Stephanie A. Fryberg. "The Same, Yet Different: Understanding the Perceived Acceptability of Redface and Blackface." *Social Psychological and Personality Science* 13, no. 3 (2021): 698–709.

Lomawaima, K. Tsianina, and Jeffrey Ostler. "Reconsidering Richard Henry Pratt: Cultural Genocide and Native Liberation in an Era of Racial Oppression." *Journal of American Indian Education* 57, no. 1 (2018): 79–100.

Lopatto, Edward, Jinlyung Choi, Alfredo Colina, Lanying Ma, Adina Howe, and Shannon Hinsa-Leasure. "Characterizing the Soil Microbiome and Quantifying Antibiotic Resistance Gene Dynamics in Agricultural Soil Following Swine CAFO Manure Application." *PLOS ONE* 14, no. 8 (2019): 1–20.

Lowery, Malinda M. "Telling Our Own Stories: Lumbee History and the Federal Acknowledgment Process." *The American Indian Quarterly* 33, no. 4 (2009): 499–522.

———. "In Memoriam: Helen Maynor Scheirbeck August 21, 1935–December 19, 2010." *Journal of American Indian Education* 50, no. 2 (2011): 12.

MacCord, Howard. "The McLean Mound, Cumberland County, North Carolina." *Southern Indian Studies* 18 (1966): 3–66.

MacKenzie, Jr., Clyde L., Allan Morrison, David L. Taylor, Jr., Victor G. Burrell, William S. Arnold, and Armando T. Wakida-Kusunoki. "Quahogs in Eastern North America: Part II, History by Province and State." *Marine Fisheries Review* 64, no. 3 (2002): 1–64.

MacMillan, Donald L., and Daniel J. Reschly. "Overrepresentation of Minority Students: The Case for Greater Specificity or Reconsideration of the Variables Examined." *The Journal of Special Education* 32, no. 1 (1998): 15–24.

Mallin, Michael A., Matthew R. McIver, Anna R. Robuck, and Amanda Kahn Dickens. "Industrial Swine and Poultry Production Causes Chronic Nutrient and Fecal Microbial Stream Pollution." *Water, Air, & Soil Pollution* 226, no. 12 (2015): 1–13.

Maxwell, William. "The Back Swamp Drainage Project, Robeson County, North Carolina: Biopolitical Intervention in the Lives of Indian Farmers." *Water History* 9, no. 1 (2017): 9–28.

McCulloch, Emily. "Free, Prior, and Informed Consent: A Struggling International Principle." *Public Land & Resources Law Review* 44, no. 1 (2021): 241–64.

Michanowicz, Drew R., Archana Dayalu, Curtis L. Nordgaard, Jonathan J. Buonocore, Molly W. Fairchild, Robert Ackley, Jessica E. Schiff, et al. "Home Is Where the Pipeline Ends: Characterization of Volatile Organic Compounds Present in Natural Gas at the Point of the Residential End User." *Environmental Science & Technology* 56 (2022): 10258–68.

Mickler, Robert A., David P. Welch, and Andrew D. Bailey. "Carbon Emissions during Wildland Fire on a North American Temperate Peatland." *Fire Ecology* 13, no. 1 (2017): 34–57.

Midtrød, Tom Arne. "'Calling for More Than Human Vengeance': Desecrating Native Graves in Early America." *Early American Studies: An Interdisciplinary Journal* 17, no. 3 (2019): 281–314.

Miller, D. Lee, and Ryke Longest. "Reconciling Environmental Justice with Climate Change Mitigation: A Case Study of NC Swine CAFOs." *Vermont Journal of Environmental Law* 21 (2020): 523–43.

Miller, Robert J. "Consultation or Consent: The United States' Duty to Confer with American Indian Governments." *North Dakota Law Review* 91, no. 1 (2015): 37–98.

Noss, Reed F., William J. Platt, Bruce A. Sorrie, Alan S. Weakley, D. Bruce Means, Jennifer Costanza, and Robert K. Peet. "How Global Biodiversity Hotspots May Go Unrecognized: Lessons from the North American Coastal Plain." *Diversity and Distributions* 21, no. 2 (2015): 236–44.

Niedermeyer, Jeffrey A., William G. Miller, Emma Yee, Angela Harris, Ryan E. Emanuel, Theo Jass, Natalie Nelson, and Sophia Kathariou. "Search for *Campylobacter* Spp. Reveals High Prevalence and Pronounced Genetic Diversity of *Arcobacter butzleri* in Floodwater Samples Associated with Hurricane Florence in North Carolina, USA." *Applied and Environmental Microbiology* 86, no. 20 (2020): 1–14.

Oberg, Michael Leroy. "Tribes and Towns: What Historians Still Get Wrong about the Roanoke Ventures." *Ethnohistory* 67, no. 4 (2020): 579–602.

Panich, Lee M., and Tsim D. Schneider. "Categorical Denial: Evaluating Post-1492 Indigenous Erasure in the Paper Trail of American Archaeology." *American Antiquity* 84, no. 4 (October 2019): 651–68.

Pieratos, Nikki A, Sarah S Manning, and Nick Tilsen. "Land Back: A Meta Narrative to Help Indigenous People Show up as Movement Leaders." *Leadership* 17, no. 1 (2021): 47–61.

Platt, Steven G., and Christopher G. Brantley. "Canebrakes: An Ecological and Historical Perspective." *Castanea* 62, no. 1 (1997): 8–21.

Red Shirt-Shaw, Megan. "Beyond the Land Acknowledgement: College 'LAND BACK' or Free Tuition for Native Students." Policy and Practice Brief, *Hack the Gates*, 2020.

Rodriguez, Antonio B., Matthew N. Waters, and Michael F. Piehler. "Burning Peat and Reworking Loess Contribute to the Formation and Evolution of a Large Carolina-Bay Basin." *Quaternary Research* 77, no. 1 (2012): 171–81.

Rostlund, Erhard. "The Geographic Range of the Historic Bison in the Southeast." *Annals of the Association of American Geographers* 50, no. 4 (1960): 395–407.

Routel, Colette, and Jeffrey Holth. "Toward Genuine Tribal Consultation in the 21st Century." *University of Michigan Journal of Law Reform* 46 no. 2 (2013): 417–75.

Scarry, C Margaret, and John F Scarry. "Native American 'Garden Agriculture' in Southeastern North America." *World Archaeology* 37, no. 2 (2005): 259–74.

Schelbert, Leo. "The Enmeshment of Five Worlds, 1710–1713: The Making of New Bern in Southern Iroquoia." *Swiss American Historical Society Review* 45, no. 3 (2009), 8–56.

Skiba, Russell J., Robert S. Michael, Abra Carroll Nardo, and Reece L. Peterson. "The Color of Discipline: Sources of Racial and Gender Disproportionality in School Punishment." *The Urban Review* 34, no. 4 (2002): 317–42.

Siurua, Hanna. "Nature above People: Rolston and 'Fortress' Conservation in the South." *Ethics and the Environment* 11, no. 1 (2006): 71–96.

Smith, Stephen Samuel, and Roslyn Arlin Mickelson. "All That Glitters Is Not Gold: School Reform in Charlotte-Mecklenburg," *Educational Evaluation and Policy Analysis* 22, no. 2 (2000): 101–27.

Son, Ji-Young, Rebecca L. Muenich, Danica Schaffer-Smith, Marie Lynn Miranda, and Michelle L. Bell. "Distribution of Environmental Justice Metrics for Exposure to CAFOs in North Carolina, USA." *Environmental Research* 195 no. 110862 (2021): 1–9.

Stager, Jay, David Fadden, and Christopher Wolff. "Dugout Canoes from Lakes of the Adirondack Uplands." *Adirondack Journal of Environmental Studies* 25, no. 1 (2022): 21–32.

Stahle, D. W., J. R. Edmondson, I. M. Howard, C. R. Robbins, R. D. Griffin, A. Carl, C. B. Hall, D. K. Stahle, and M. C. A. Torbenson. "Longevity, Climate Sensitivity, and Conservation Status of Wetland Trees at Black River, North Carolina." *Environmental Research Communications* 1, no. 4 (2019): 1–8.

Stein, Sharon. "'Truth before Reconciliation': The Difficulties of Transforming Higher Education in Settler Colonial Contexts." *Higher Education Research & Development* 39, no. 1 (2020): 156–70.

Stein, Wayne. "Founding of the American Indian Higher Education Consortium." *Tribal College Journal of American Indian Higher Education* 2, no. 1 (1990). https://tribalcollegejournal.org/founding-american-indian-higher-education-consortium/.

Stewart, T. D. "Notes on the Human Bones Recovered from Burial in the McLean Mound, North Carolina." *Southern Indian Studies* 18 (1966): 67–82.

Stewart-Ambo, Theresa, and K. Wayne Yang. "Beyond Land Acknowledgment in Settler Institutions." *Social Text* 39, no. 1 (146) (2021): 21–46.

Stutz, Matthew L., and Orrin H. Pilkey. "Open-Ocean Barrier Islands: Global Influence of Climatic, Oceanographic, and Depositional Settings." *Journal of Coastal Research* 27, no. 2 (2011): 207–22.

Subica, Andrew M., and Bruce G. Link. "Cultural Trauma as a Fundamental Cause of Health Disparities." *Social Science & Medicine* 292, no. 114574 (2022): 1–19.

Thie, Lauren, and Kimberly Thigpen Tart. "On the Front Lines of Climate Health Effects in North Carolina." *North Carolina Medical Journal* 79, no. 5 (2018): 318–23.

Tooker, William Wallace. "The Adopted Algonquian Term 'Poquosin.'" *American Anthropologist* 1, no. 1 (1899): 162–70.

Tuck, Eve, and K. Wayne Yang. "Decolonization Is Not a Metaphor." *Decolonization: Indigeneity, Education & Society* 1, no. 1 (2012): 1–40.

Vasudevan, Pavithra. "Performance and Proximity: Revisiting Environmental Justice in Warren County, North Carolina." *Performance Research* 17, no. 4 (2012): 18–26.

Warner, Elizabeth Kronk, Kathy Lynn, and Kyle Powys Whyte. "Changing Consultation." *UC Davis Law Review* 54, no. 2 (2021): 1127–84.

Wheeler Ryan J., James J. Miller, Ray M. McGee, Donna Ruhl, Brenda Swann, and Melissa Memory. "Archaic Period Canoes from Newnans Lake, Florida." *American Antiquity* 68, no. 3 (2003): 533–51.

Whyte, Kyle Powys. "The Dakota Access Pipeline, Environmental Injustice, and US Colonialism." *Red Ink* 19, no. 1 (2017): 154–69.

———. "Indigenous Climate Change Studies: Indigenizing Futures, Decolonizing the Anthropocene." *English Language Notes* 55, no. 1 (2017): 153–62.

———. "Justice Forward: Tribes, Climate Adaptation and Responsibility." *Climatic Change* 120, no. 3 (2013): 517–30.

Wilson, Sacoby M. "Environmental Justice Movement: A Review of History, Research, and Public Health Issues." *Journal of Public Management & Social Policy* 16, no. 1 (2010): 19–50.

Wood, Sara, and Malinda Maynor Lowery. "As We Cooked, As We Lived: Lumbee Foodways." *Southern Cultures* 21, no. 1 (2015): 84–91.

Wright, Tiffany, Ciarra Carr, and Jade Gasek. "Truth and Reconciliation: The Ku Klux Klan Hearings of 1871 and the Genesis of Section 1983." *Dickinson Law Review* 126, no. 3 (2022): 685–717.

zu Ermgassen, Sophus O. S. E., Julia Baker, Richard A. Griffiths, Niels Strange, Matthew J. Struebig, and Joseph W. Bull. "The Ecological Outcomes of Biodiversity Offsets under 'No Net Loss' Policies: A Global Review." *Conservation Letters* 12, no. 6 (2019): 1–17.

CHAPTERS IN EDITED VOLUMES

Calcaterra, Angela. "Bad Timing: Indigenous Reception and American Literary Style." In *A Question of Time: American Literature from Colonial Encounter to Contemporary Fiction*, edited by Cindy Weinstein, 93–110. New York: Cambridge University Press, 2019.

Carney, Judith. "Seeds of Memory: Botanical Legacies of the African Diaspora." In *African Ethnobotany in the Americas*, edited by Robert Voeks and John Rashford, 13–33. New York: Springer, 2013.

Doyle Martin W., and Todd BenDor. "Markets for Freshwater Ecosystem Services." In *Aquanomics*, edited by B. D. Gardner and R. T. Simmons, 17–42. New York: Routledge, 2017.

Emanuel, Ryan E. "Sovereignty's Cycle: Revisiting Vine Deloria's Support for Unrecognized Tribes in a Time of Environmental Crises." In *Of Living Stone: Perspectives on the Work of Vine Deloria, Jr.*, edited by David Wilkins, Shelly Wilkins. Denver: Fulcrum Books, forthcoming.

Feeley, Stephen. "Before Long to Be Good Friends." In *Creating and Contesting Carolina: Proprietary Era Histories*, edited by Michelle Lemaster, 140–63. Columbia: University of South Carolina Press, 2013.

Jantarasami, Lesley. C., Rachael Novak, Roberto Delgado, Elizabeth Marino, Shannon McNeeley, Chris Narducci, Julie Raymond-Yakoubian, Loretta Singletary, and Kyle P. Whyte. "Tribes and Indigenous Peoples." In *Impacts, Risks, and Adaptation in the United States: Fourth National Climate Assessment, Volume II*, edited by D. R. Reidmiller, C. W. Avery, D. R. Easterling, K. E. Kunkel, K. L. M. Lewis, T. K. Maycock, and B. C. Stewart, 572–603. Washington: US Global Change Research Program, 2018.

Lee, Charles. "Beyond Toxic Wastes and Race." In *Confronting Environmental Racism: Voices from the Grassroots*, edited by Robert Bullard, 41–52. Boston: South End Press, 1993.

Mallinson, David, Stephen Culver, Eduardo Leorri, Siddhartha Mitra, Ryan Mulligan, and Stanley Riggs. "Barrier Island and Estuary Co-Evolution in Response to Holocene Climate and Sea-Level Change: Pamlico Sound and the Outer Banks Barrier Islands, North Carolina, USA." In *Barrier Dynamics and Response to Changing Climate*, edited by Laura J. Moore and A. Brad Murray, 91–120. Cham: Springer International Publishing, 2018.

Marshall, Murdena, Albert Marshall, and Cheryl Bartlett. "Two-Eyed Seeing in Medicine." In *Determinants of Indigenous Peoples' Health: Beyond the Social, Second Edition*, edited by Margo Greenwood, Sarah de Leeuw, and Nicole Marie Lindsay, 44–53. Toronto: CSP Books, 2018.

Mt. Pleasant, Jane. "The Science behind the Three Sisters Mound System: An Agronomic Assessment of an Indigenous Agricultural System in the Northeast." In *Histories of*

Maize: Multidisciplinary Approaches to the Prehistory, Linguistics, Biogeography, Domestication, and Evolution of Maize, edited by John Staller, Robert Tykot, and Bruce Benz, 529–35. Walnut Creek, California: Left Coast Press, 2009.

Oliveira, Gustavo. "Soy, Domestication, and Colonialism." In *The Routledge Handbook of Critical Resource Geography*, edited by Matthew Himley, Elizabeth Havice, and Gabriela Valdivia, 335–45. New York: Routledge, 2022.

Ward, Lauck W., Richard H. Bailey, and Joseph G. Carter. "Pliocene and Early Pleistocene Stratigraphy, Depositional History, and Molluscan Paleobiogeography of the Coastal Plain." In *The Geology of the Carolinas: Carolina Geological Society Fiftieth Anniversary Volume*, edited by. J. Wright Horton Jr and Victor A. Zullo, 274–79. Knoxville: University of Tennessee Press, 1991.

Whyte, Kyle Powys. "Indigeneity and US Settler Colonialism." In *The Oxford Handbook of Philosophy and Race*, edited by Naomi Zack, 91–101. New York: Oxford University Press, 2017.

———. "Way Beyond the Lifeboat: An Indigenous Allegory of Climate Justice." In *Climate Futures: Reimagining Global Climate Justice*, edited by Kum-Kum Bhavnani, John Foran, Priya Kurian, and Debashish Munshi, 11–20. London: Zed Books, 2019.

Index

Please note that page numbers with *t* indicate tables; page numbers with *f* indicate figures; page numbers with n indicate endnotes.